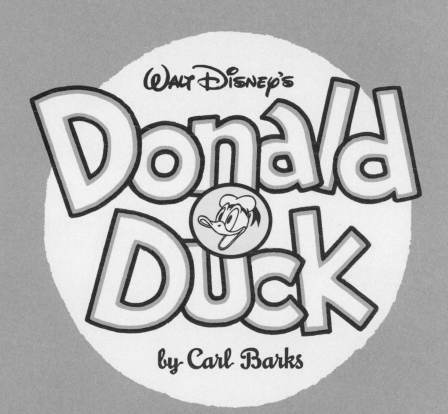

Walt Disney's

Donald Duck

by Carl Barks

Publisher and Executive Editor: GARY GROTH
Senior Editor: J. MICHAEL CATRON
Color Editor: MIKE BAEHR
Colorist: RICH TOMMASO
Series Design: JACOB COVEY
Volume Design: KEELI McCARTHY
Production: PAUL BARESH
Editorial Consultant: DAVID GERSTEIN
Associate Publisher: ERIC REYNOLDS

- -

Fantagraphics Books, Inc.
7563 Lake City Way NE
Seattle WA 98115

To receive a free catalog of more books like this, as well as an amazing variety of
cutting-edge graphic novels, classic comic book and newspaper strip collections, eclectic prose novels, uniquely
insightful cultural criticism, and other fine works of artistry, call (800) 657-1100 or visit fantagraphics.com.
Follow us on Twitter at @fantagraphics and on Facebook at facebook.com/fantagraphics.

Special thanks to: Thomas Jensen and Kim Weston

First printing, October 2015
ISBN 978-1-60699-874-8
Printed in Singapore
Library of Congress Control Number: 2015941748

Now available in this series:

- -

Boxed sets of some titles are available at select locations.

Walt Disney's

Donald Duck

"Trick or Treat"

----

by Carl Barks

FANTAGRAPHICS BOOKS

Contents

All comics stories written and drawn by Carl Barks

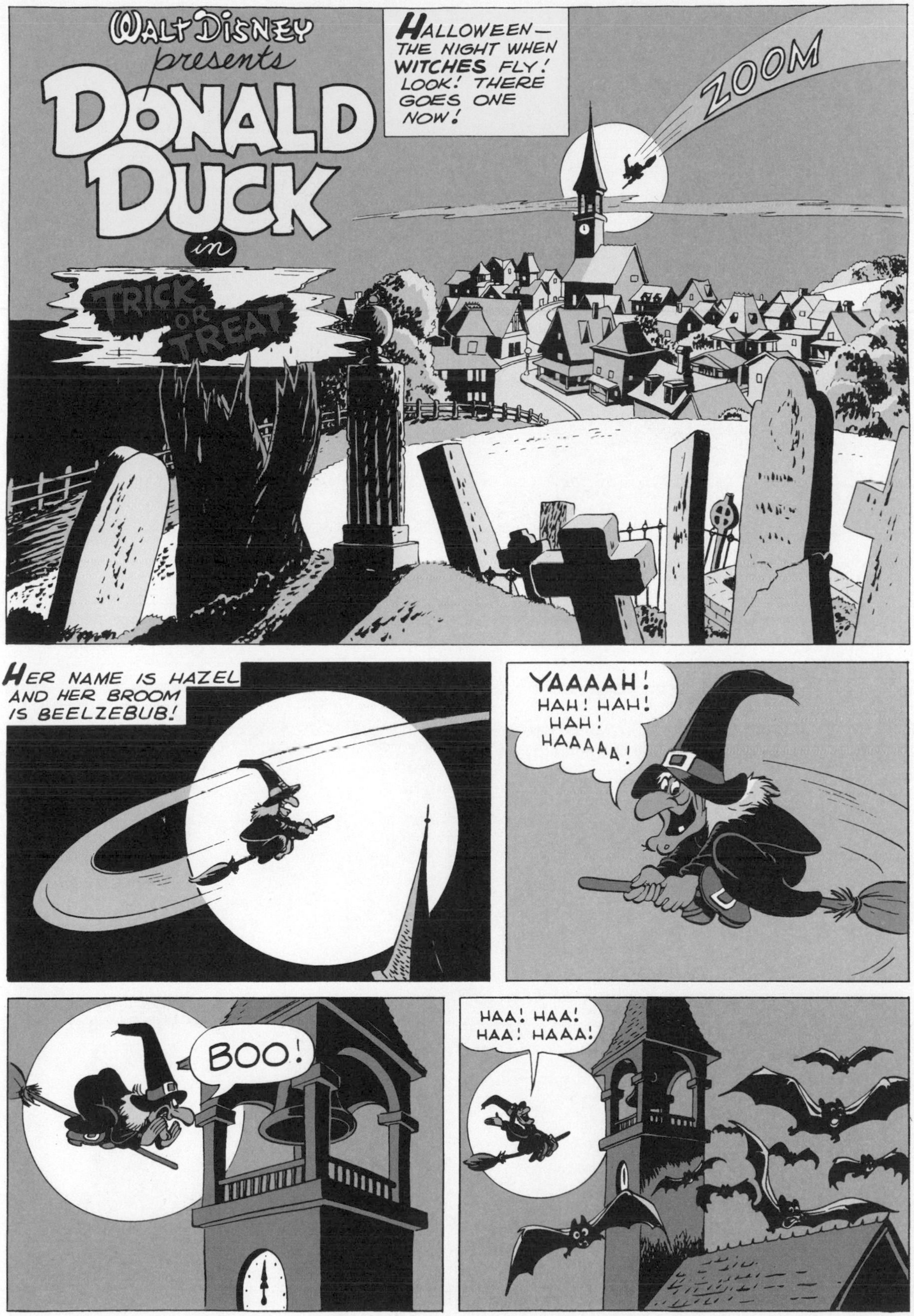
WALT DISNEY
presents
DONALD DUCK
in
TRICK OR TREAT
HALLOWEEN— THE NIGHT WHEN WITCHES FLY! LOOK! THERE GOES ONE NOW!
ZOOM
HER NAME IS HAZEL AND HER BROOM IS BEELZEBUB!
YAAAAH! HAH! HAH! HAH! HAAAAA!
BOO!
HAA! HAA! HAA! HAAA!

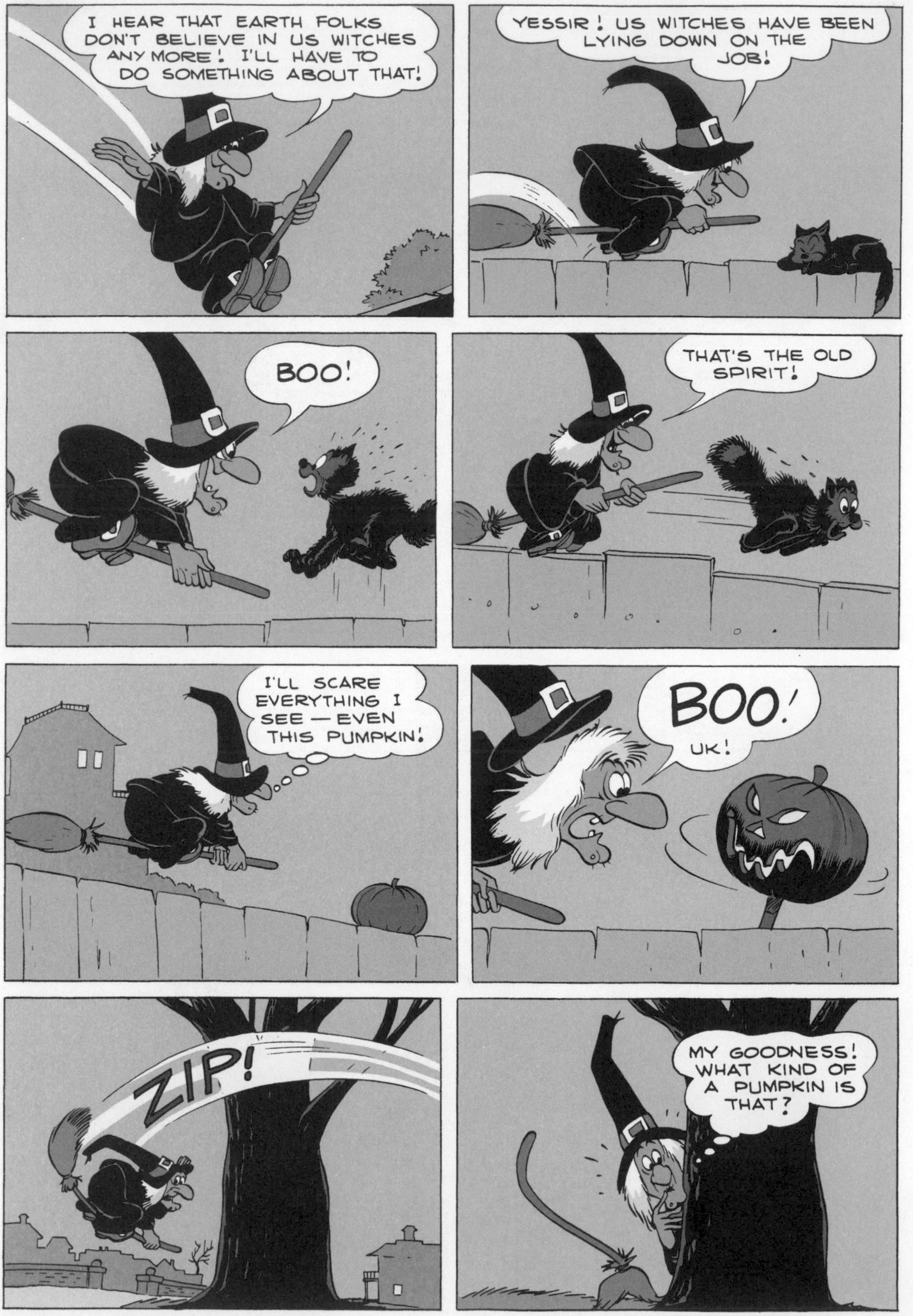
I HEAR THAT EARTH FOLKS DON'T BELIEVE IN US WITCHES ANY MORE! I'LL HAVE TO DO SOMETHING ABOUT THAT!
YESSIR! US WITCHES HAVE BEEN LYING DOWN ON THE JOB!
BOO!
THAT'S THE OLD SPIRIT!
I'LL SCARE EVERYTHING I SEE — EVEN THIS PUMPKIN!
BOO!
UK!
ZIP!
MY GOODNESS! WHAT KIND OF A PUMPKIN IS THAT?

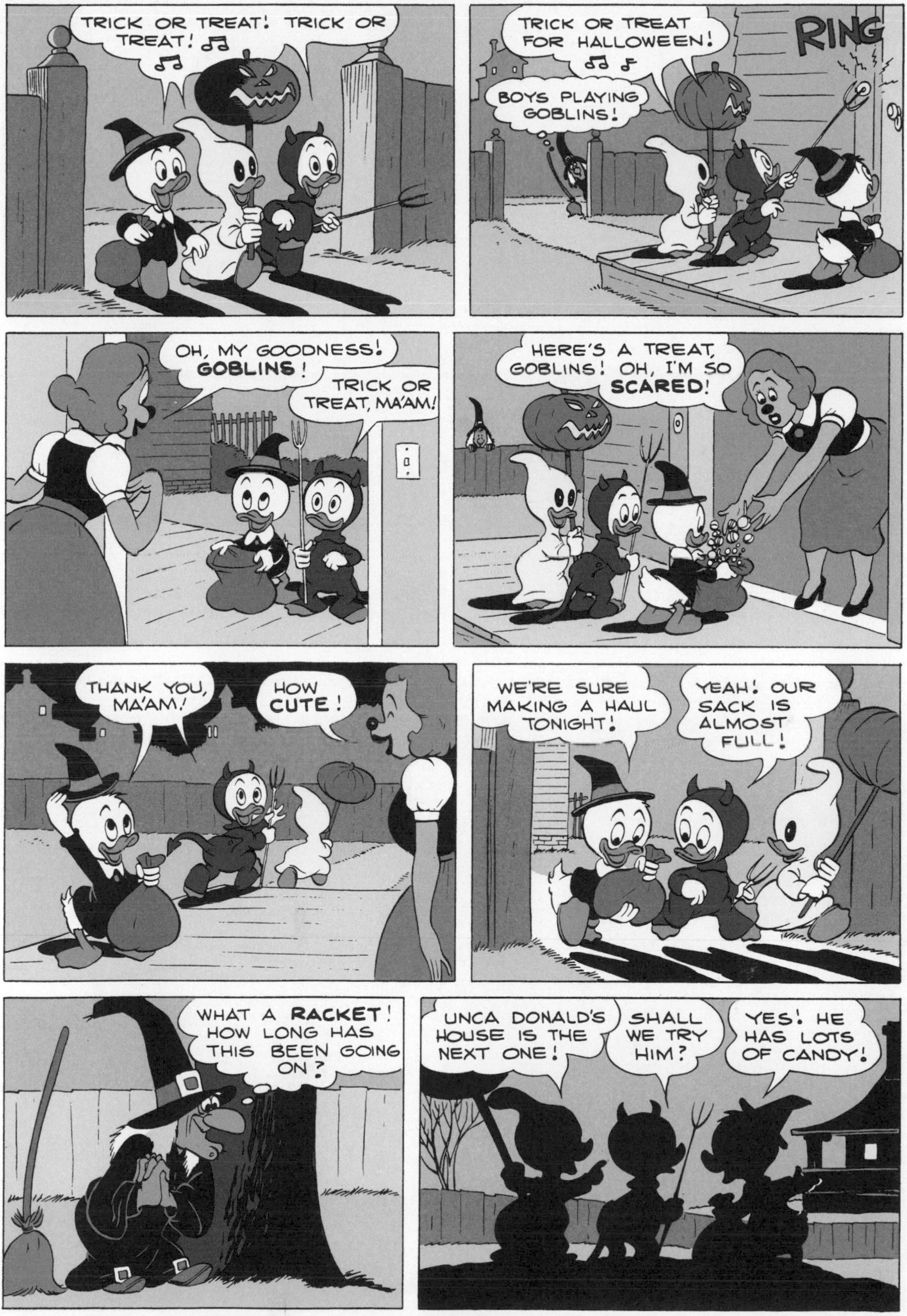
TRICK OR TREAT! TRICK OR TREAT!
TRICK OR TREAT FOR HALLOWEEN!
RING
BOYS PLAYING GOBLINS!
OH, MY GOODNESS! GOBLINS!
TRICK OR TREAT, MA'AM!
HERE'S A TREAT, GOBLINS! OH, I'M SO SCARED!
THANK YOU, MA'AM!
HOW CUTE!
WE'RE SURE MAKING A HAUL TONIGHT!
YEAH! OUR SACK IS ALMOST FULL!
WHAT A RACKET! HOW LONG HAS THIS BEEN GOING ON?
UNCA DONALD'S HOUSE IS THE NEXT ONE!
SHALL WE TRY HIM?
YES! HE HAS LOTS OF CANDY!

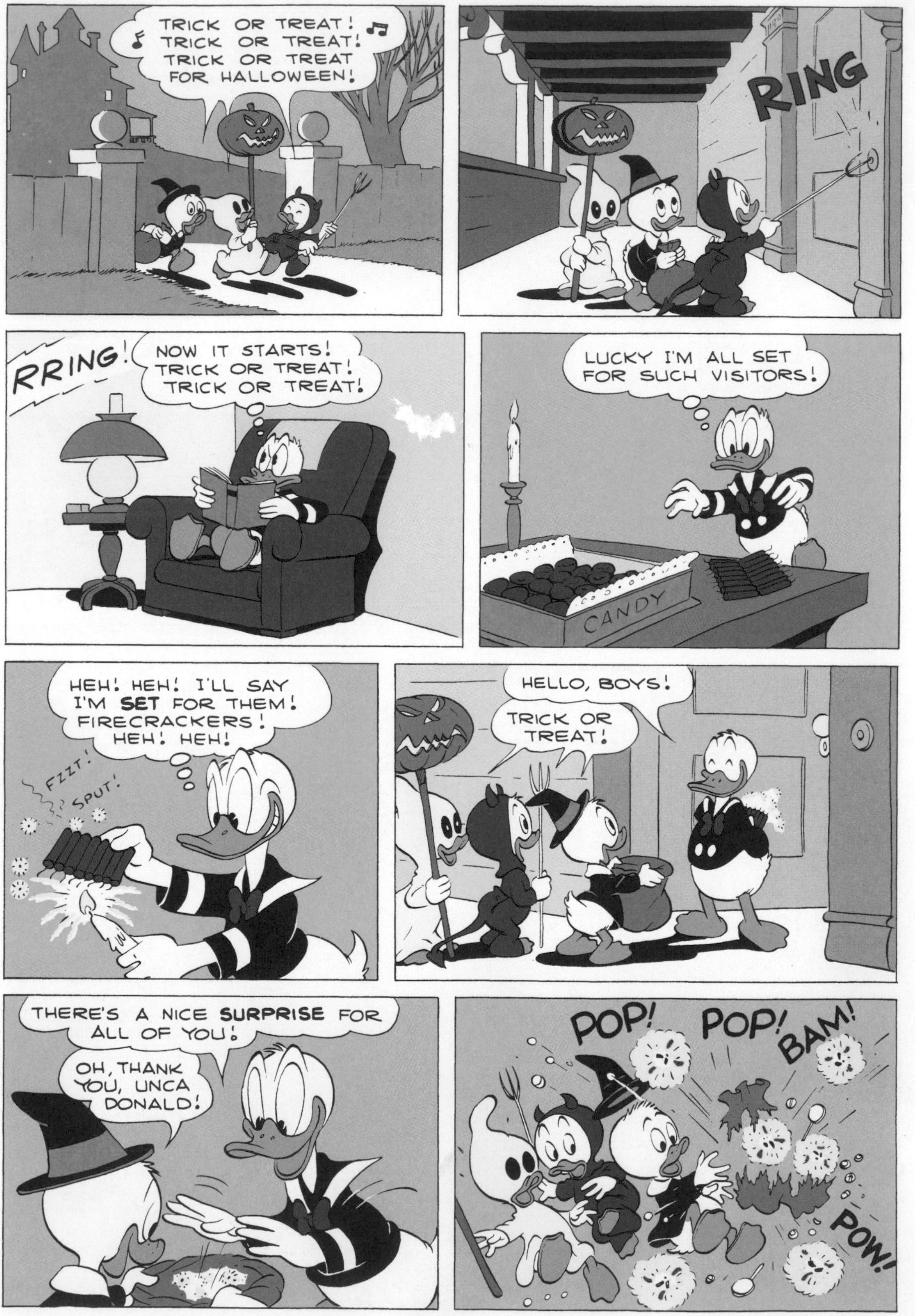
TRICK OR TREAT! TRICK OR TREAT! TRICK OR TREAT FOR HALLOWEEN!
RING
RRING!
NOW IT STARTS! TRICK OR TREAT! TRICK OR TREAT!
LUCKY I'M ALL SET FOR SUCH VISITORS!
CANDY
HEH! HEH! I'LL SAY I'M **SET** FOR THEM! FIRECRACKERS! HEH! HEH!
FZZT!
SPUT!
HELLO, BOYS!
TRICK OR TREAT!
THERE'S A NICE **SURPRISE** FOR ALL OF YOU!
OH, THANK YOU, UNCA DONALD!
POP!
POP!
BAM!
POW!

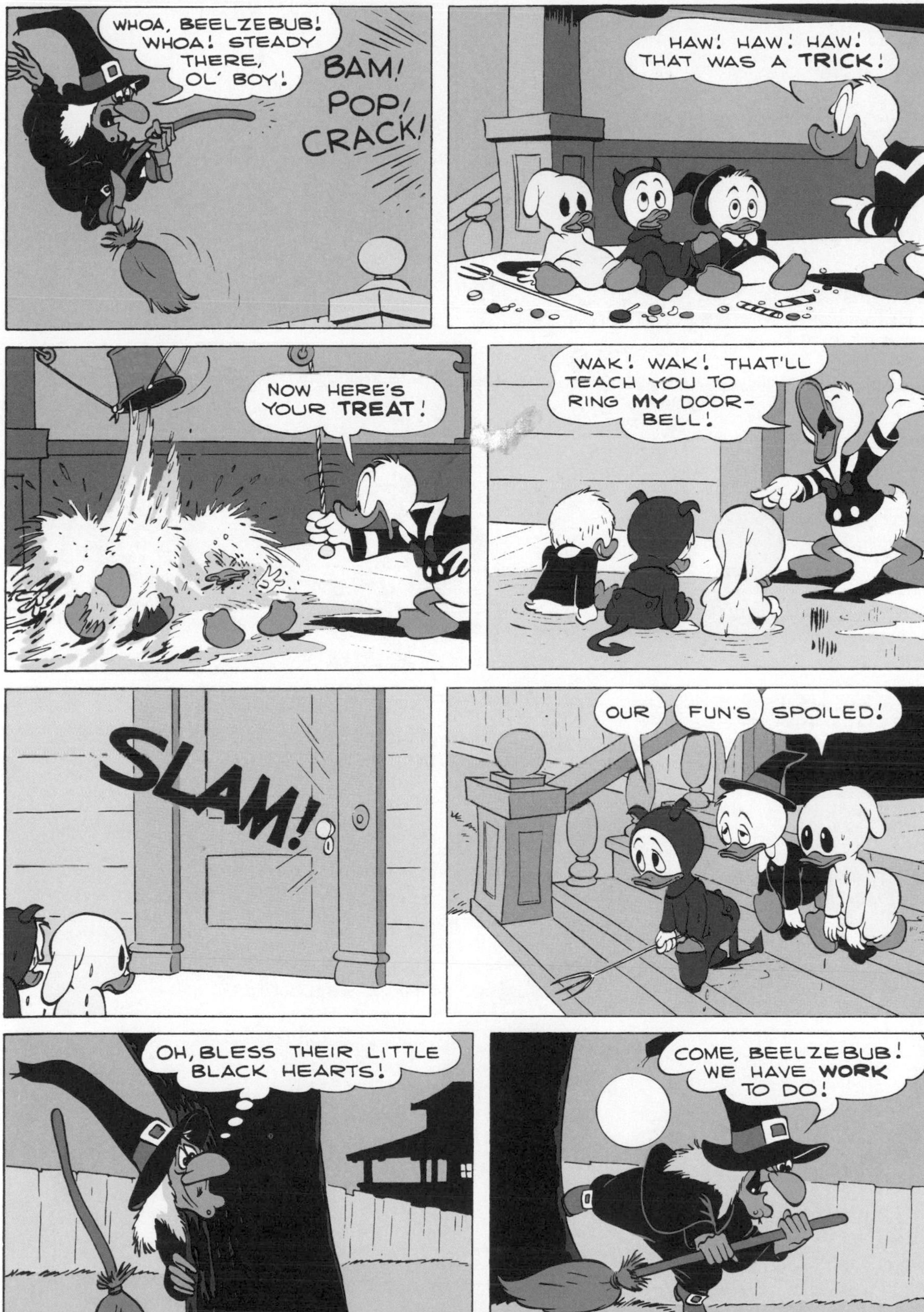
WHOA, BEELZEBUB! WHOA! STEADY THERE, OL' BOY!
BAM! POP! CRACK!
HAW! HAW! HAW! THAT WAS A TRICK!
NOW HERE'S YOUR TREAT!
WAK! WAK! THAT'LL TEACH YOU TO RING MY DOOR-BELL!
SLAM!
OUR
FUN'S
SPOILED!
OH, BLESS THEIR LITTLE BLACK HEARTS!
COME, BEELZEBUB! WE HAVE WORK TO DO!

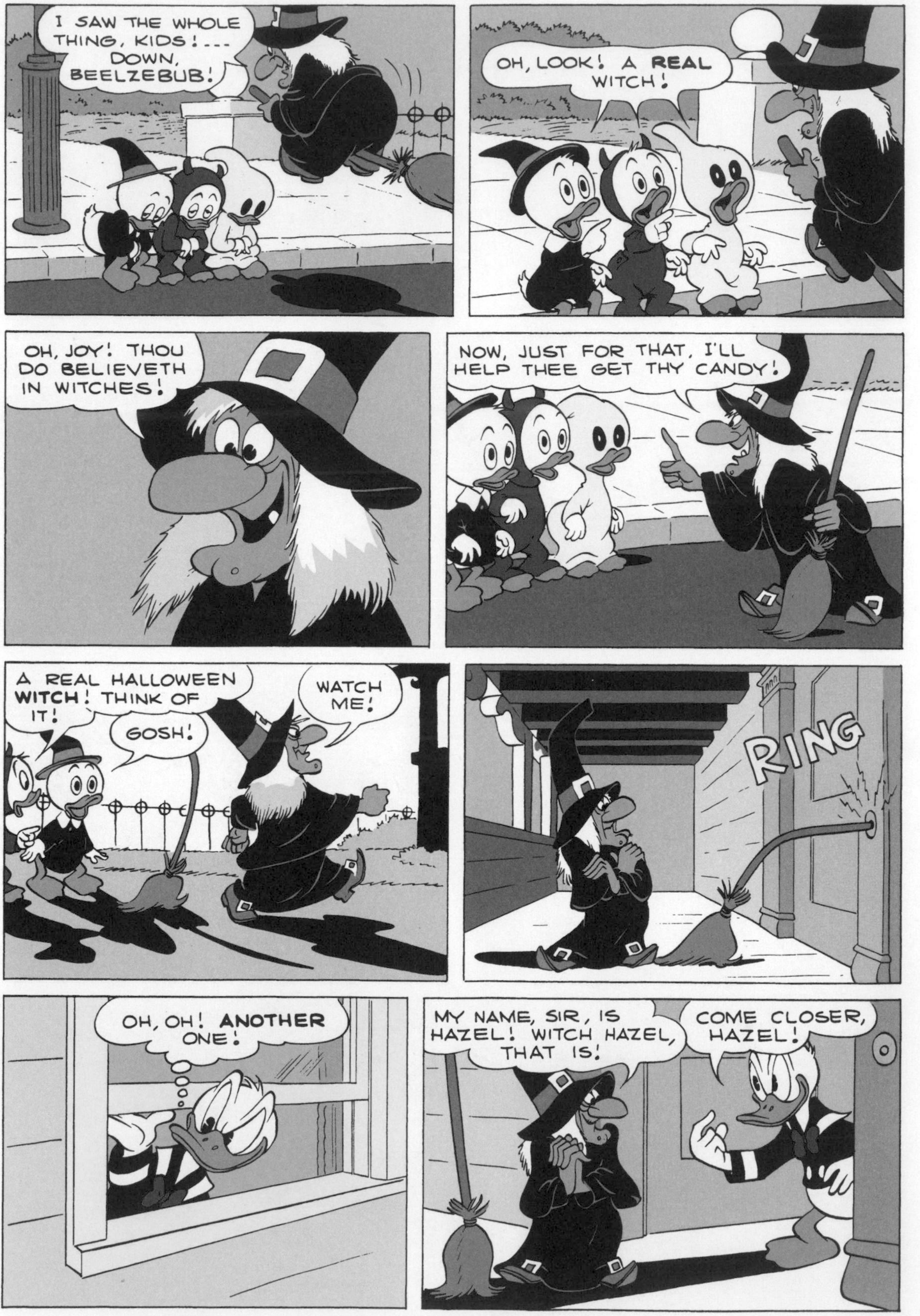
I SAW THE WHOLE THING, KIDS! --- DOWN, BEELZEBUB!
OH, LOOK! A **REAL** WITCH!
OH, JOY! THOU DO BELIEVETH IN WITCHES!
NOW, JUST FOR THAT, I'LL HELP THEE GET THY CANDY!
A REAL HALLOWEEN **WITCH**! THINK OF IT!
GOSH!
WATCH ME!
RING
OH, OH! **ANOTHER** ONE!
MY NAME, SIR, IS HAZEL! WITCH HAZEL, THAT IS!
COME CLOSER, HAZEL!

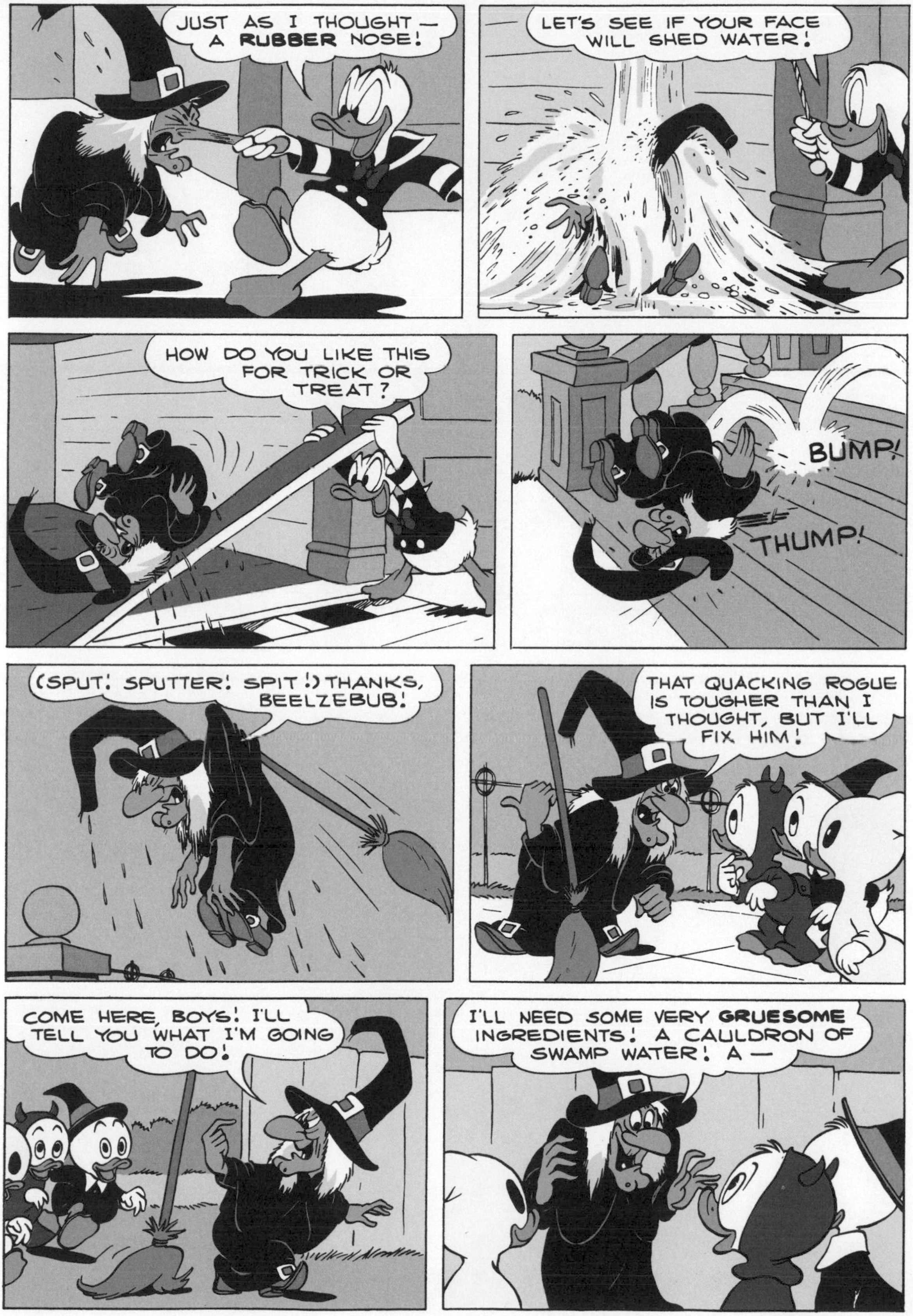
JUST AS I THOUGHT — A RUBBER NOSE!
LET'S SEE IF YOUR FACE WILL SHED WATER!
HOW DO YOU LIKE THIS FOR TRICK OR TREAT?
BUMP!
THUMP!
(SPUT! SPUTTER! SPIT!) THANKS, BEELZEBUB!
THAT QUACKING ROGUE IS TOUGHER THAN I THOUGHT, BUT I'LL FIX HIM!
COME HERE, BOYS! I'LL TELL YOU WHAT I'M GOING TO DO!
I'LL NEED SOME VERY GRUESOME INGREDIENTS! A CAULDRON OF SWAMP WATER! A —

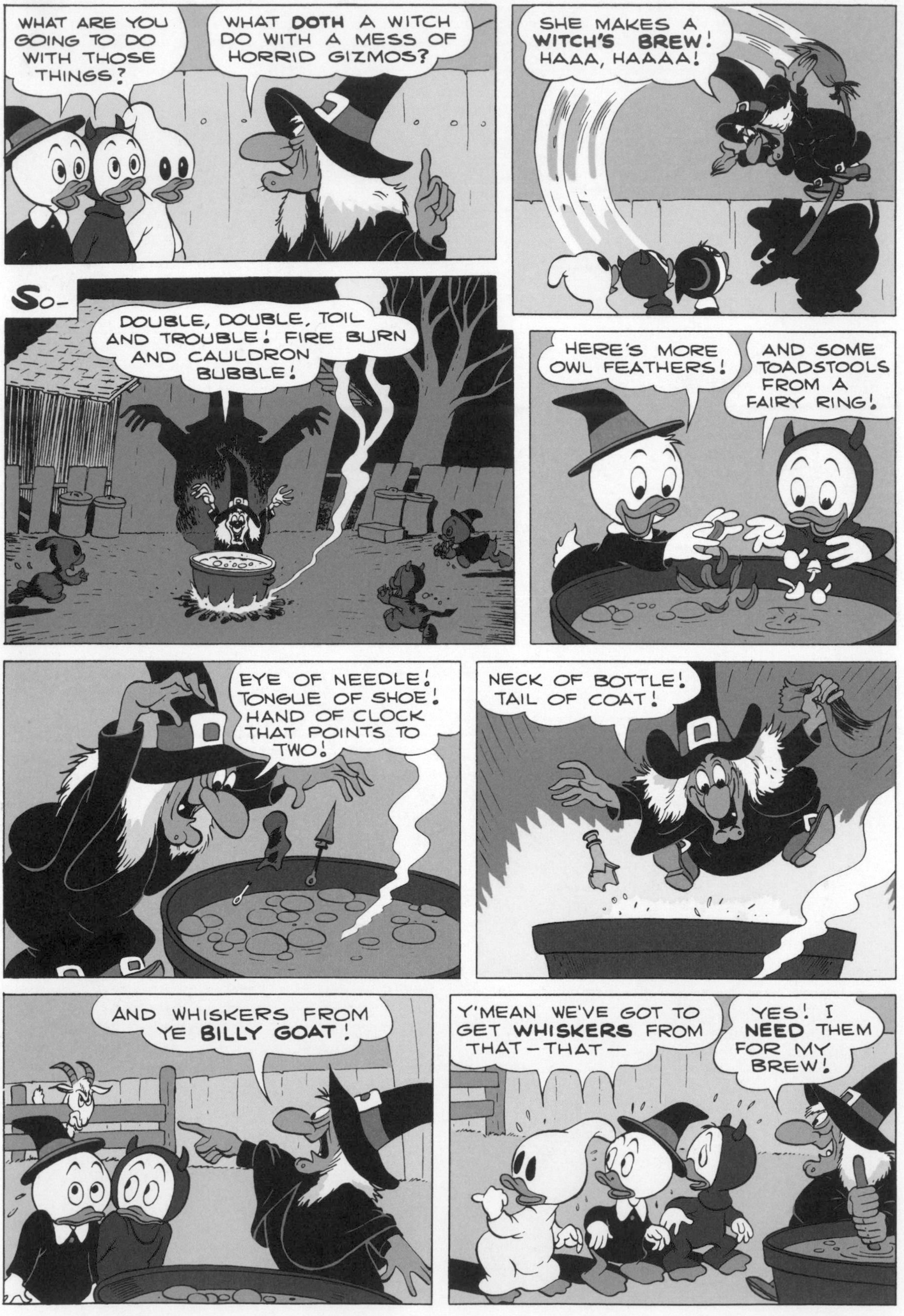
WHAT ARE YOU GOING TO DO WITH THOSE THINGS?
WHAT DOTH A WITCH DO WITH A MESS OF HORRID GIZMOS?
SHE MAKES A WITCH'S BREW! HAAA, HAAAA!
SO-
DOUBLE, DOUBLE, TOIL AND TROUBLE! FIRE BURN AND CAULDRON BUBBLE!
HERE'S MORE OWL FEATHERS!
AND SOME TOADSTOOLS FROM A FAIRY RING!
EYE OF NEEDLE! TONGUE OF SHOE! HAND OF CLOCK THAT POINTS TO TWO!
NECK OF BOTTLE! TAIL OF COAT!
AND WHISKERS FROM YE BILLY GOAT!
Y'MEAN WE'VE GOT TO GET WHISKERS FROM THAT—THAT—
YES! I NEED THEM FOR MY BREW!

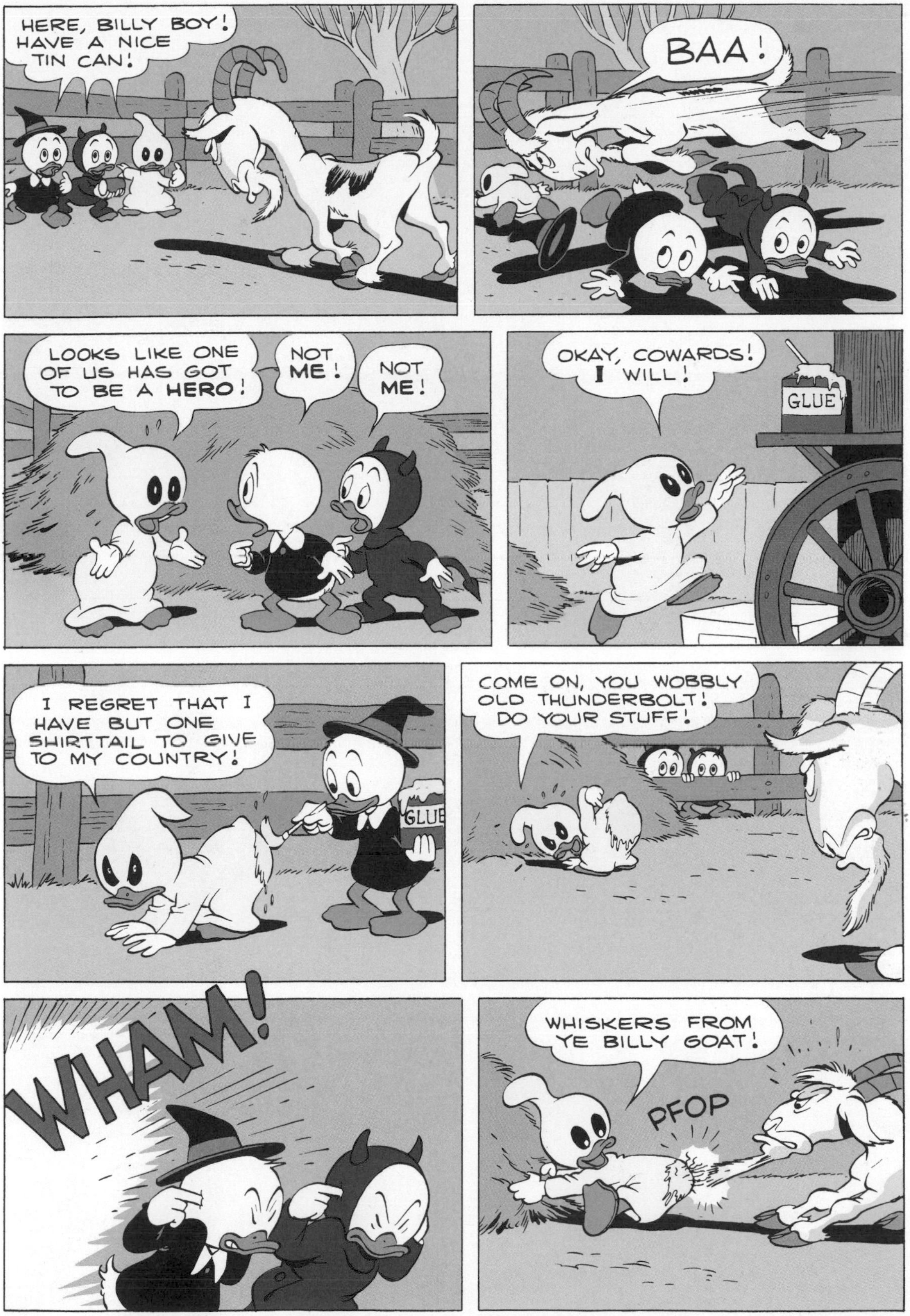
HERE, BILLY BOY! HAVE A NICE TIN CAN!
BAA!
LOOKS LIKE ONE OF US HAS GOT TO BE A **HERO**!
NOT **ME**!
NOT **ME**!
OKAY, COWARDS! **I** WILL!
GLUE
I REGRET THAT I HAVE BUT ONE SHIRTTAIL TO GIVE TO MY COUNTRY!
GLUE
COME ON, YOU WOBBLY OLD THUNDERBOLT! DO YOUR STUFF!
WHAM!
WHISKERS FROM YE BILLY GOAT!
PFOP

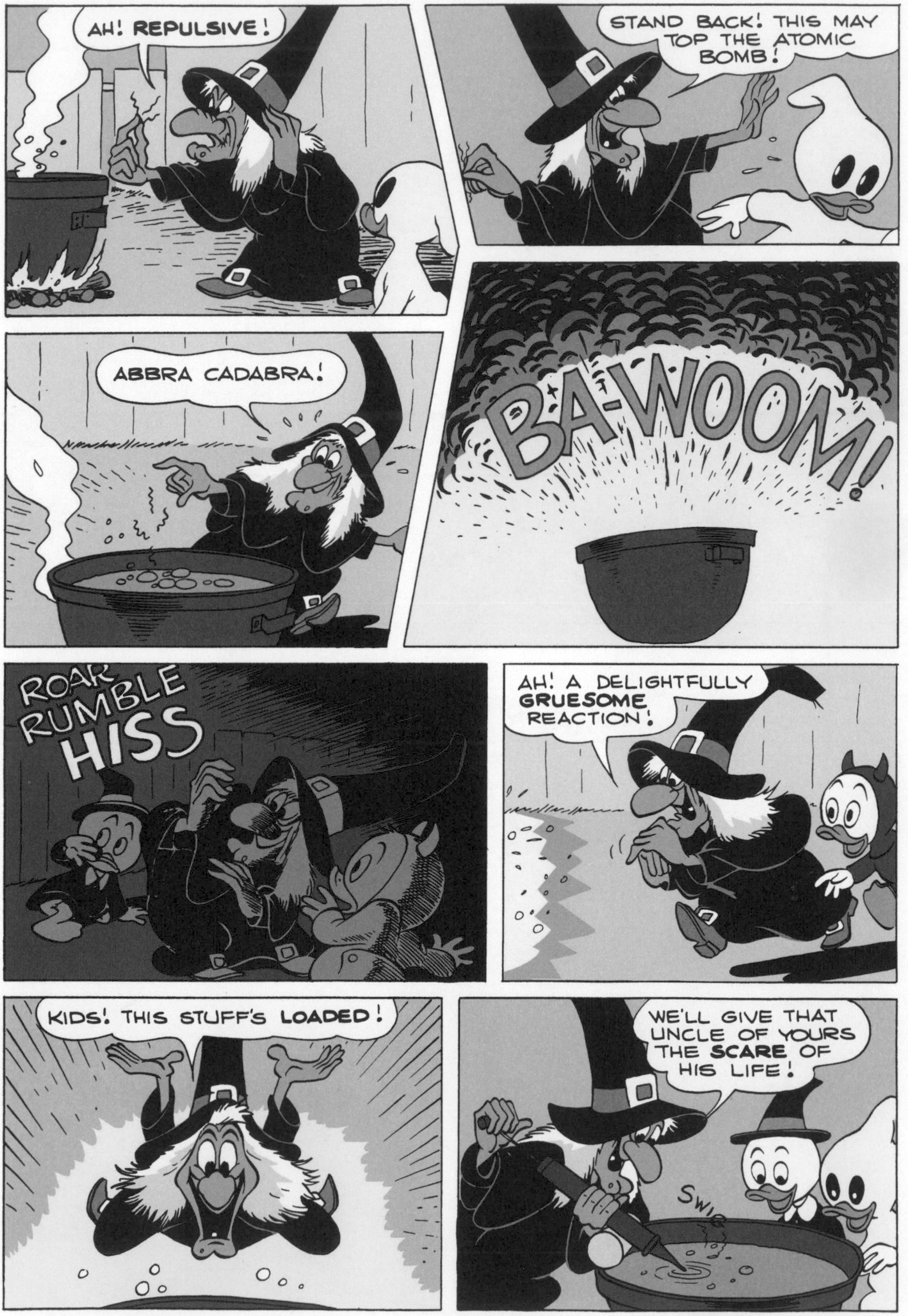

AH! REPULSIVE!
STAND BACK! THIS MAY TOP THE ATOMIC BOMB!
ABBRA CADABRA!
BA-WOOM!
ROAR RUMBLE HISS
AH! A DELIGHTFULLY GRUESOME REACTION!
KIDS! THIS STUFF'S LOADED!
WE'LL GIVE THAT UNCLE OF YOURS THE SCARE OF HIS LIFE!
SWI

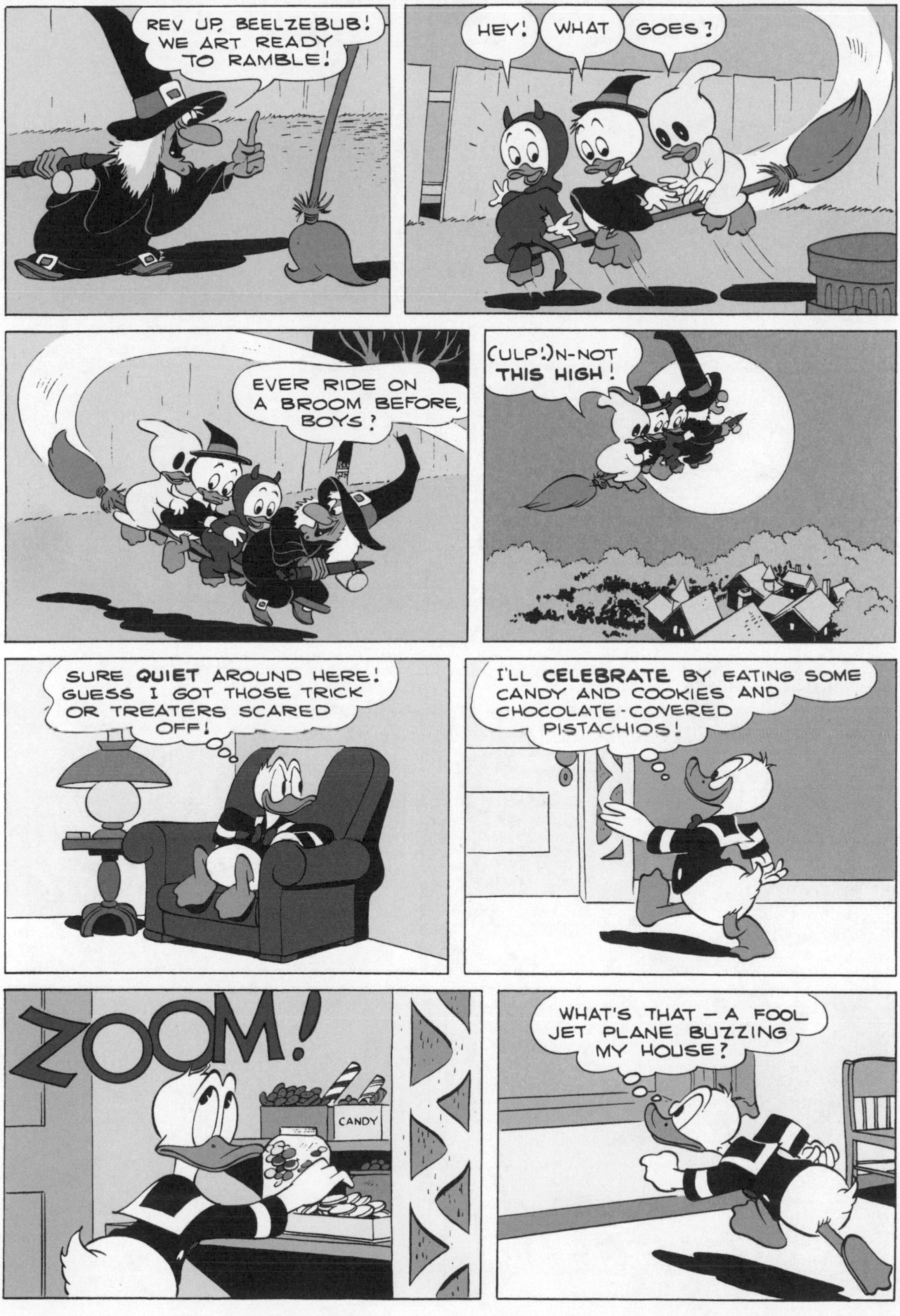
REV UP, BEELZEBUB! WE ART READY TO RAMBLE!
HEY!
WHAT
GOES?
EVER RIDE ON A BROOM BEFORE, BOYS?
(ULP!) N-NOT THIS HIGH!
SURE QUIET AROUND HERE! GUESS I GOT THOSE TRICK OR TREATERS SCARED OFF!
I'LL CELEBRATE BY EATING SOME CANDY AND COOKIES AND CHOCOLATE-COVERED PISTACHIOS!
ZOOM!
CANDY
WHAT'S THAT — A FOOL JET PLANE BUZZING MY HOUSE?

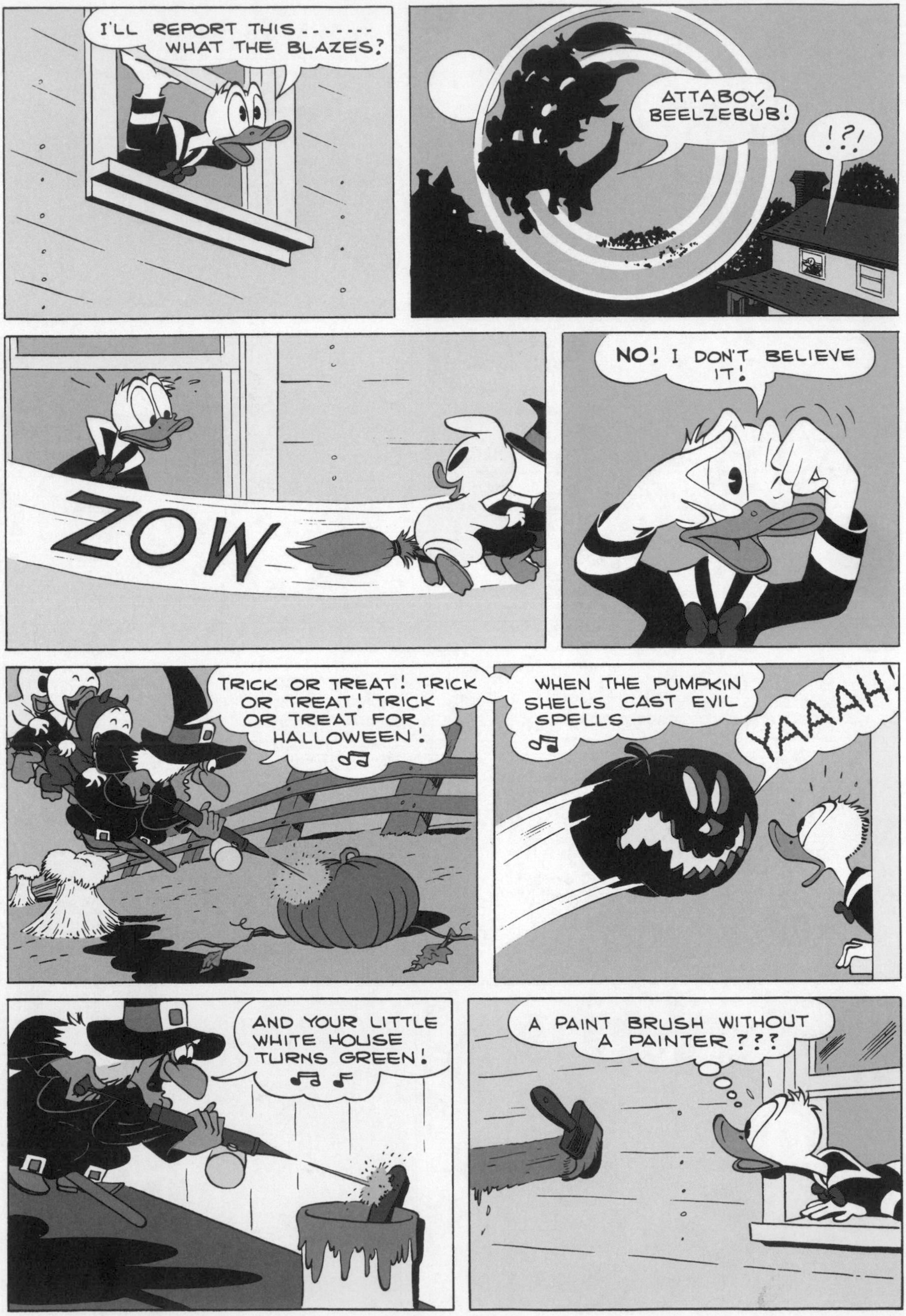
I'LL REPORT THIS....... WHAT THE BLAZES?
ATTABOY, BEELZEBUB!
!?!
ZOW
NO! I DON'T BELIEVE IT!
TRICK OR TREAT! TRICK OR TREAT! TRICK OR TREAT FOR HALLOWEEN!
WHEN THE PUMPKIN SHELLS CAST EVIL SPELLS —
YAAAH!
AND YOUR LITTLE WHITE HOUSE TURNS GREEN!
A PAINT BRUSH WITHOUT A PAINTER???

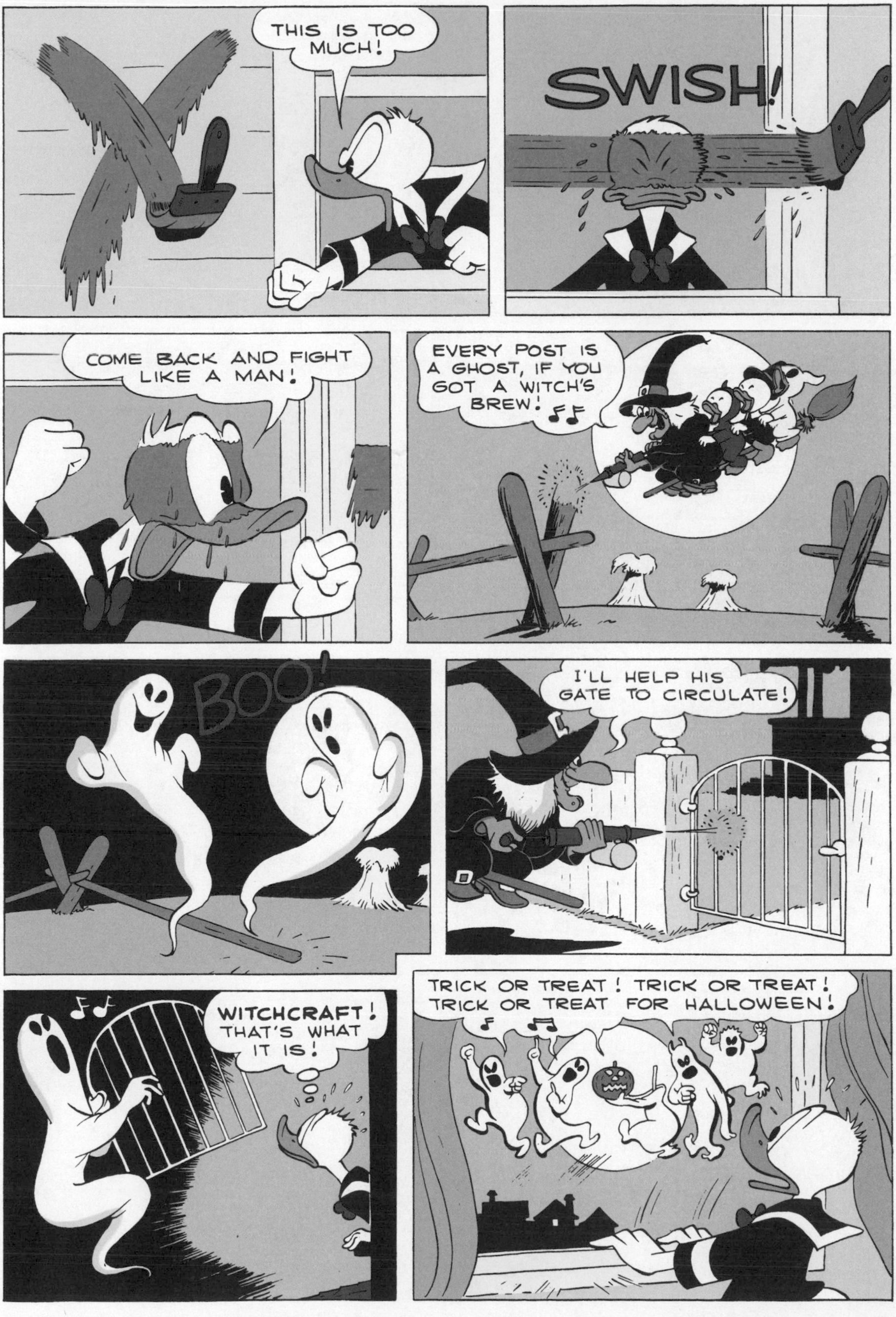
THIS IS TOO MUCH!
SWISH!
COME BACK AND FIGHT LIKE A MAN!
EVERY POST IS A GHOST, IF YOU GOT A WITCH'S BREW!
BOO!
I'LL HELP HIS GATE TO CIRCULATE!
WITCHCRAFT! THAT'S WHAT IT IS!
TRICK OR TREAT! TRICK OR TREAT! TRICK OR TREAT FOR HALLOWEEN!

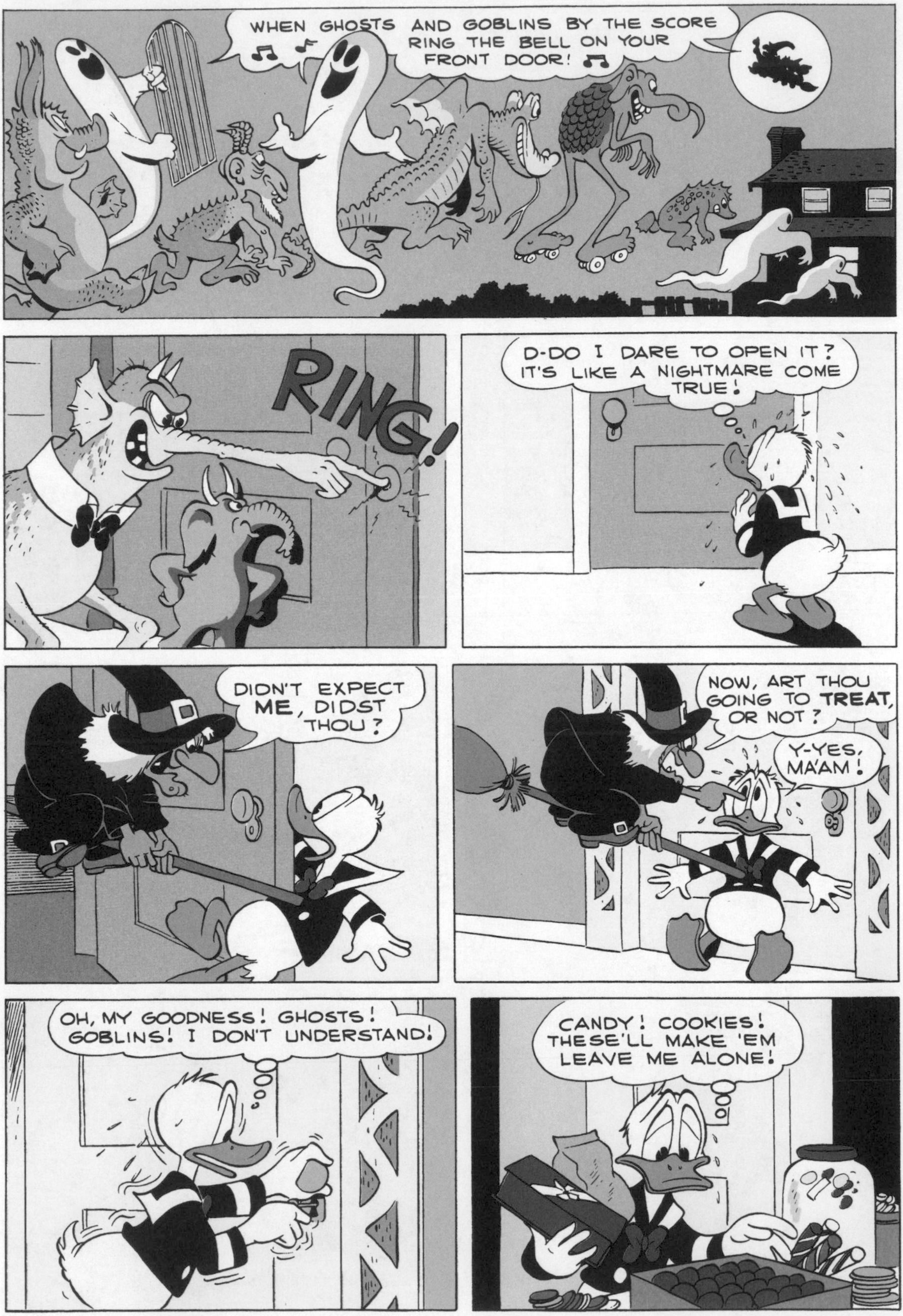
WHEN GHOSTS AND GOBLINS BY THE SCORE RING THE BELL ON YOUR FRONT DOOR!
RING!
D-DO I DARE TO OPEN IT? IT'S LIKE A NIGHTMARE COME TRUE!
DIDN'T EXPECT ME, DIDST THOU?
NOW, ART THOU GOING TO TREAT, OR NOT?
Y-YES, MA'AM!
OH, MY GOODNESS! GHOSTS! GOBLINS! I DON'T UNDERSTAND!
CANDY! COOKIES! THESE'LL MAKE 'EM LEAVE ME ALONE!

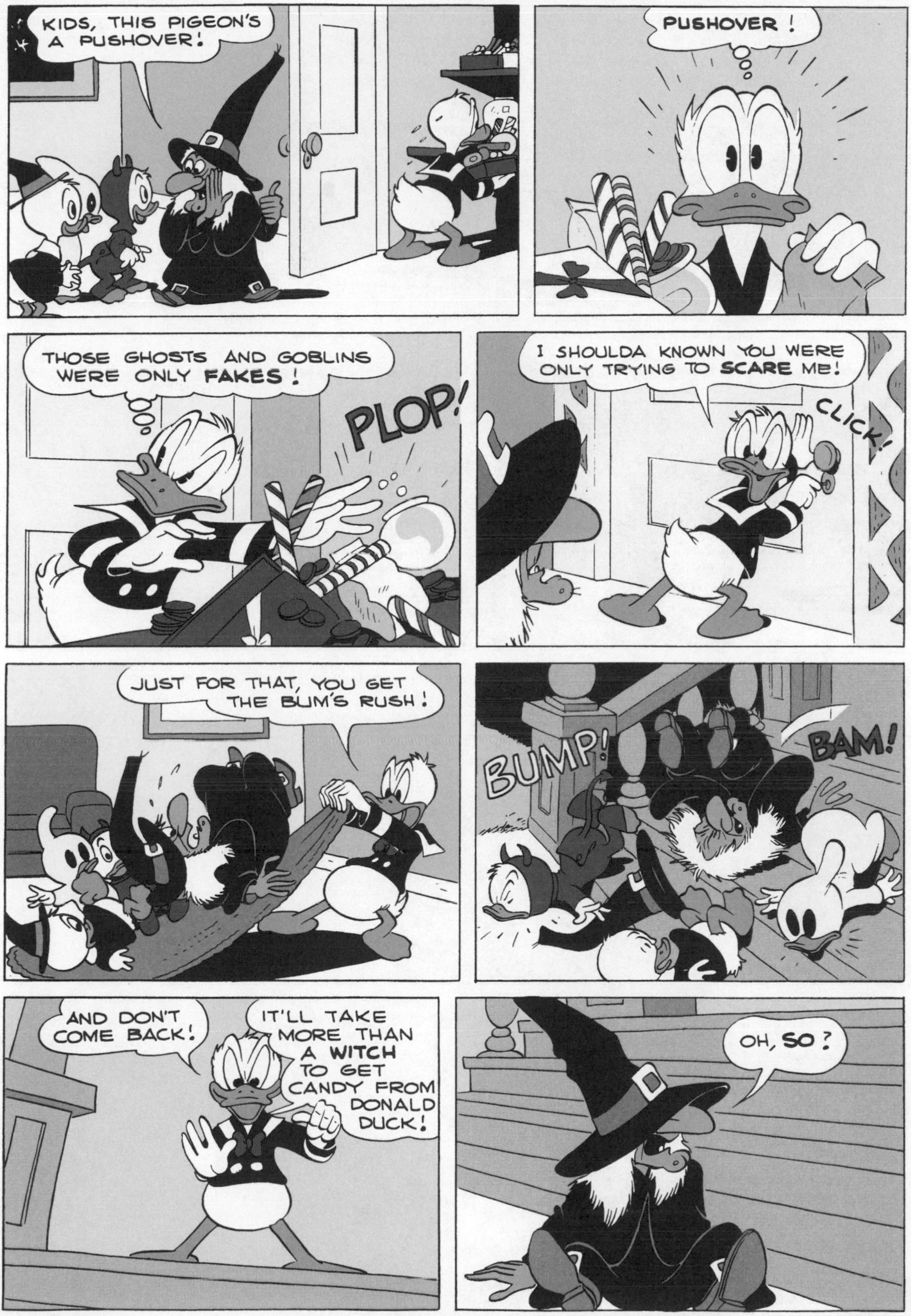
KIDS, THIS PIGEON'S A PUSHOVER!
PUSHOVER!
THOSE GHOSTS AND GOBLINS WERE ONLY FAKES!
PLOP!
I SHOULDA KNOWN YOU WERE ONLY TRYING TO SCARE ME!
CLICK!
JUST FOR THAT, YOU GET THE BUM'S RUSH!
BUMP!
BAM!
AND DON'T COME BACK!
IT'LL TAKE MORE THAN A WITCH TO GET CANDY FROM DONALD DUCK!
OH, SO?

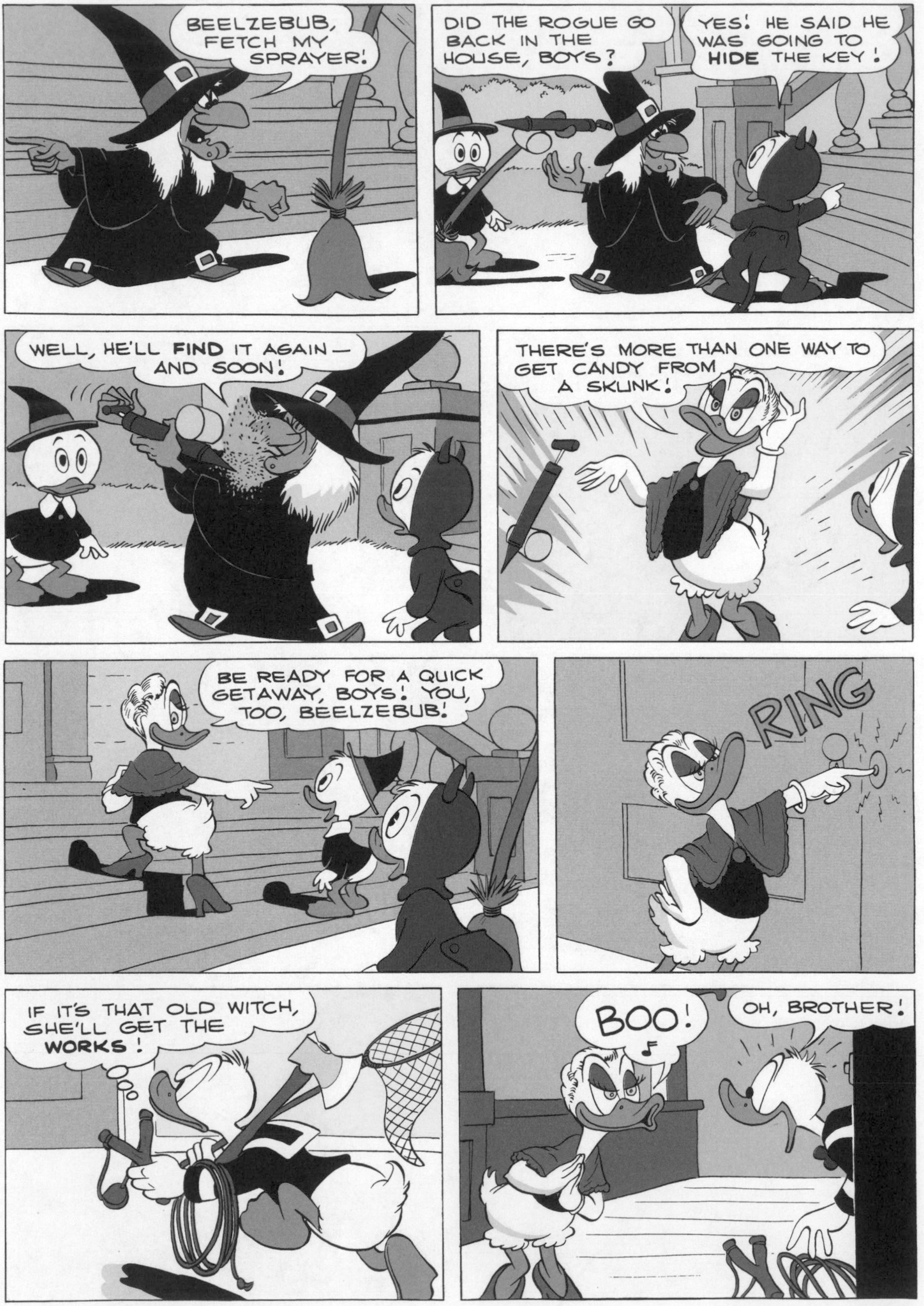
BEELZEBUB, FETCH MY SPRAYER!
DID THE ROGUE GO BACK IN THE HOUSE, BOYS?
YES! HE SAID HE WAS GOING TO HIDE THE KEY!
WELL, HE'LL FIND IT AGAIN— AND SOON!
THERE'S MORE THAN ONE WAY TO GET CANDY FROM A SKUNK!
BE READY FOR A QUICK GETAWAY, BOYS! YOU, TOO, BEELZEBUB!
RING
IF IT'S THAT OLD WITCH, SHE'LL GET THE WORKS!
BOO!
OH, BROTHER!

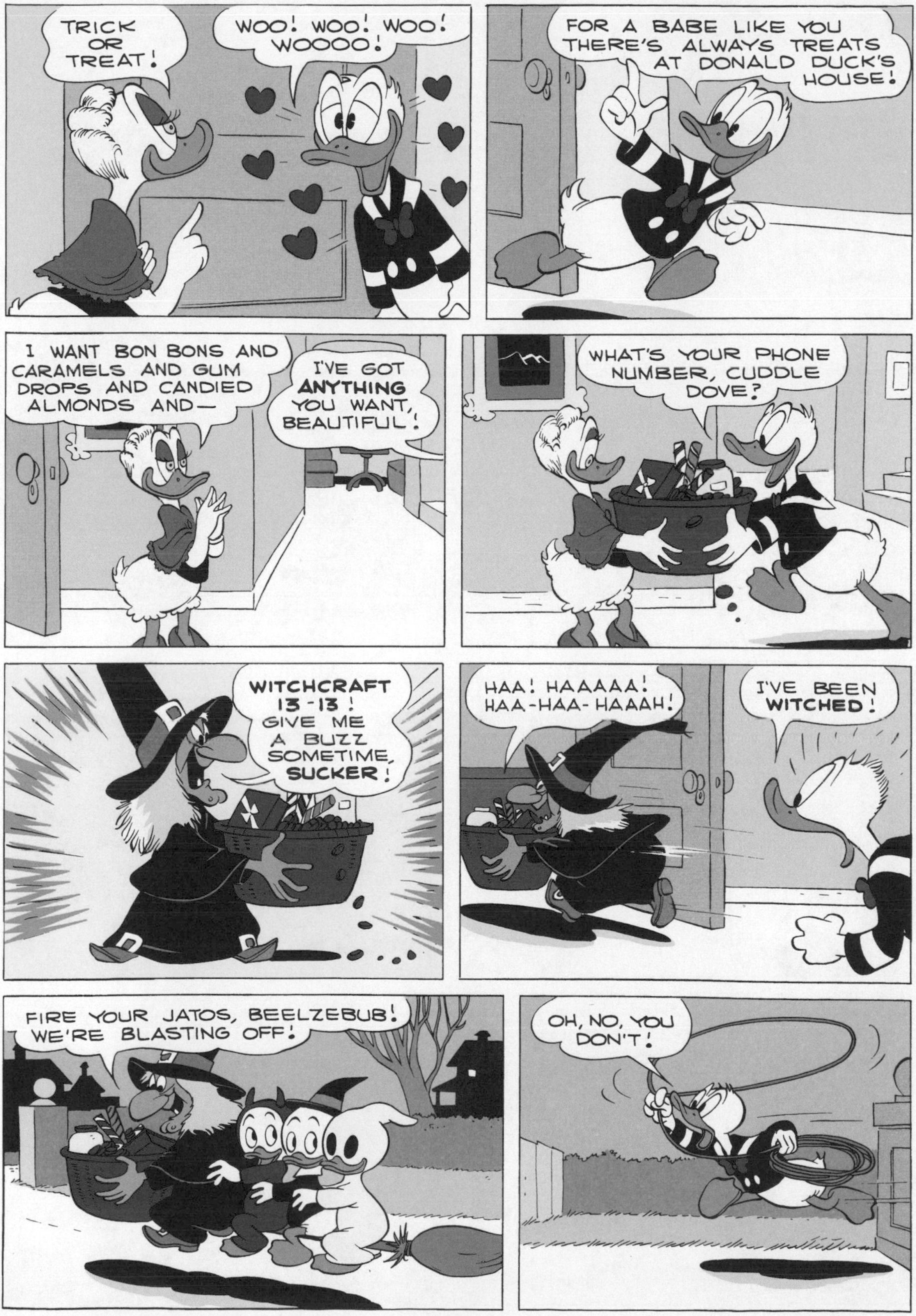
TRICK OR TREAT!
WOO! WOO! WOO! WOOOO!
FOR A BABE LIKE YOU THERE'S ALWAYS TREATS AT DONALD DUCK'S HOUSE!
I WANT BON BONS AND CARAMELS AND GUM DROPS AND CANDIED ALMONDS AND—
I'VE GOT ANYTHING YOU WANT, BEAUTIFUL!
WHAT'S YOUR PHONE NUMBER, CUDDLE DOVE?
WITCHCRAFT 13-13! GIVE ME A BUZZ SOMETIME, SUCKER!
HAA! HAAAAA! HAA-HAA-HAAAH!
I'VE BEEN WITCHED!
FIRE YOUR JATOS, BEELZEBUB! WE'RE BLASTING OFF!
OH, NO, YOU DON'T!

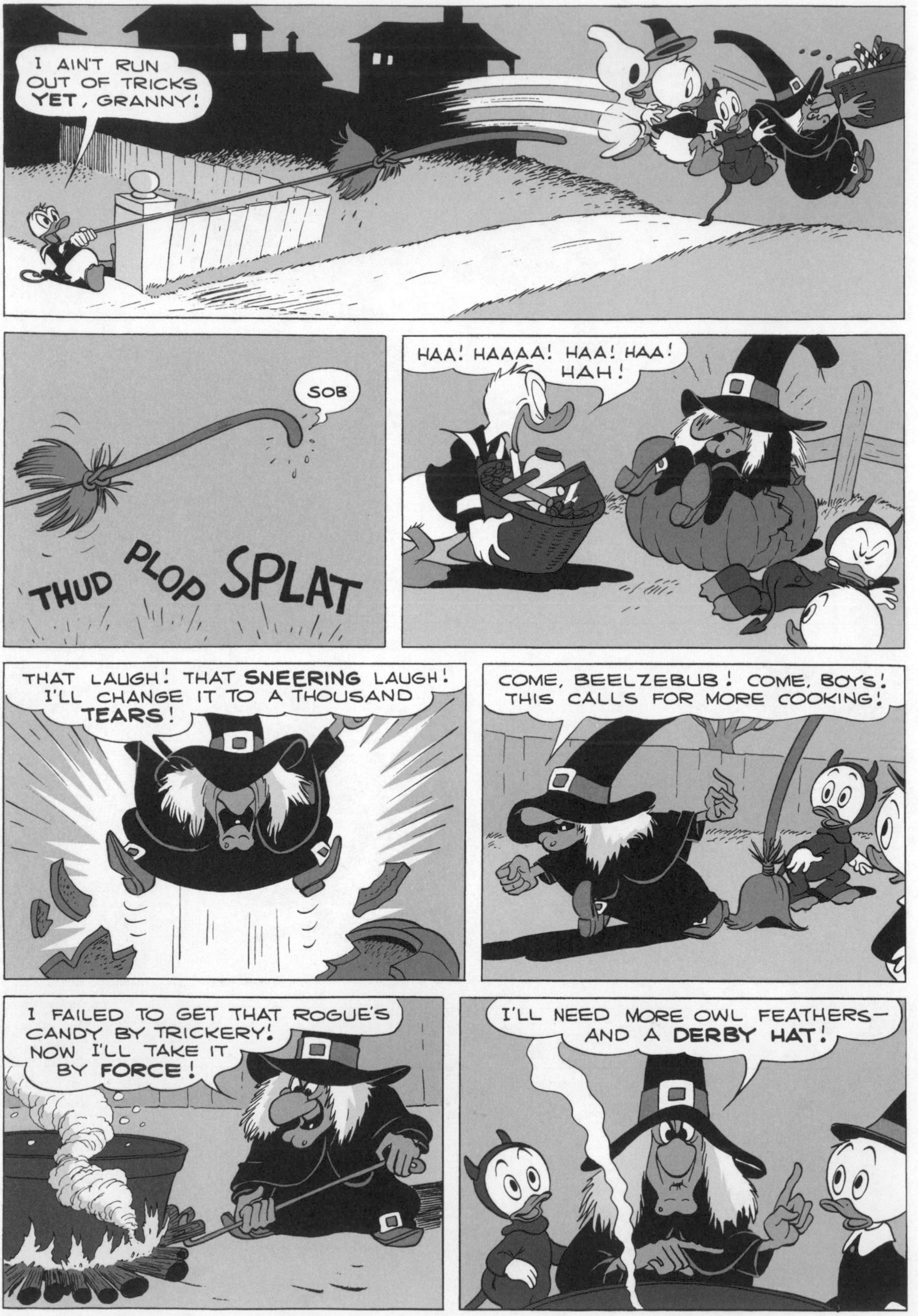

I AIN'T RUN OUT OF TRICKS YET, GRANNY!
SOB
THUD PLOP SPLAT
HAA! HAAAA! HAA! HAA! HAH!
THAT LAUGH! THAT SNEERING LAUGH! I'LL CHANGE IT TO A THOUSAND TEARS!
COME, BEELZEBUB! COME, BOYS! THIS CALLS FOR MORE COOKING!
I FAILED TO GET THAT ROGUE'S CANDY BY TRICKERY! NOW I'LL TAKE IT BY FORCE!
I'LL NEED MORE OWL FEATHERS— AND A DERBY HAT!

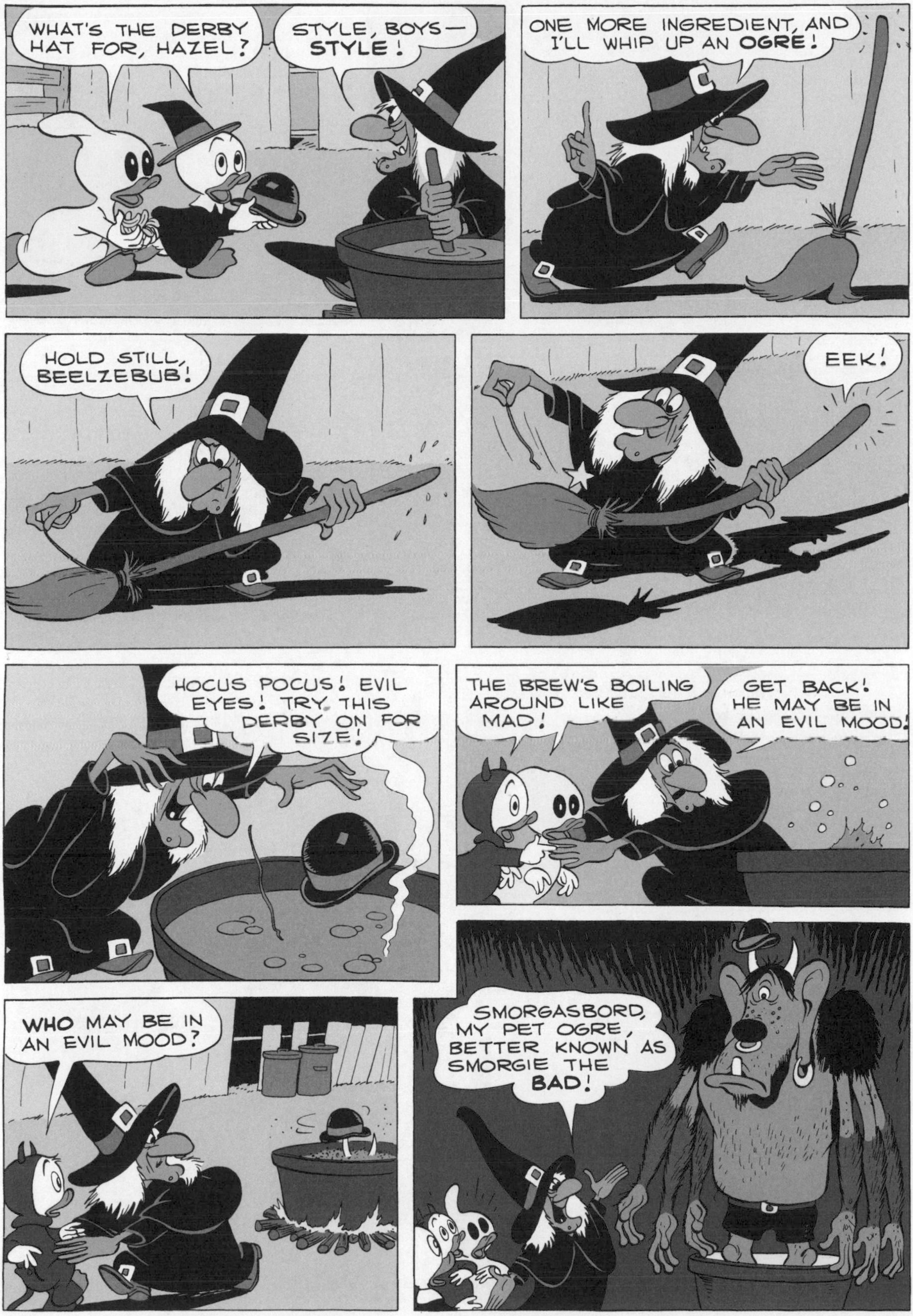

WHAT'S THE DERBY HAT FOR, HAZEL?
STYLE, BOYS— STYLE!
ONE MORE INGREDIENT, AND I'LL WHIP UP AN OGRE!
HOLD STILL, BEELZEBUB!
EEK!
HOCUS POCUS! EVIL EYES! TRY THIS DERBY ON FOR SIZE!
THE BREW'S BOILING AROUND LIKE MAD!
GET BACK! HE MAY BE IN AN EVIL MOOD!
WHO MAY BE IN AN EVIL MOOD?
SMORGASBORD, MY PET OGRE, BETTER KNOWN AS SMORGIE THE BAD!

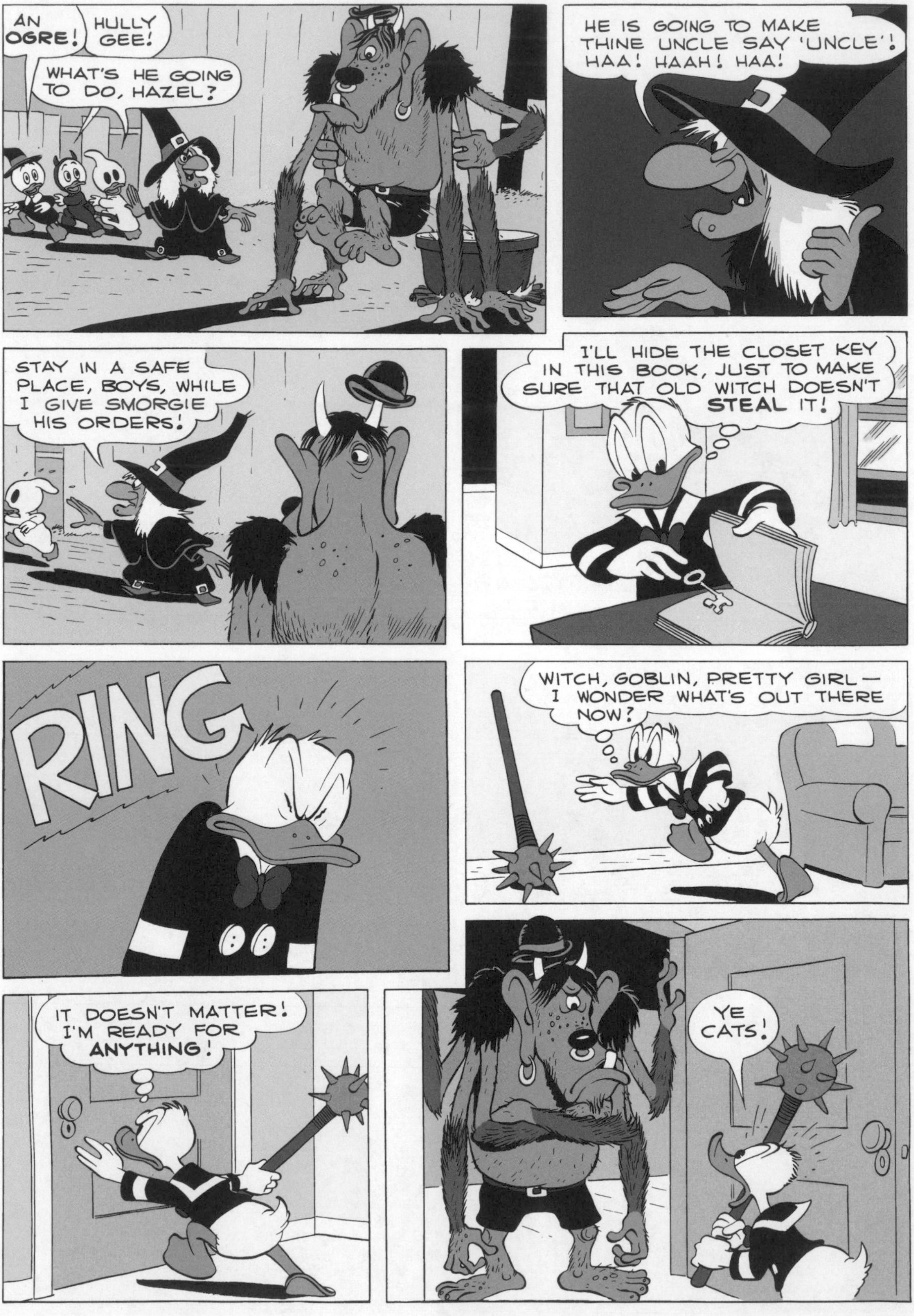
AN OGRE!
HULLY GEE!
WHAT'S HE GOING TO DO, HAZEL?
HE IS GOING TO MAKE THINE UNCLE SAY 'UNCLE'! HAA! HAAH! HAA!
STAY IN A SAFE PLACE, BOYS, WHILE I GIVE SMORGIE HIS ORDERS!
I'LL HIDE THE CLOSET KEY IN THIS BOOK, JUST TO MAKE SURE THAT OLD WITCH DOESN'T STEAL IT!
RING
WITCH, GOBLIN, PRETTY GIRL— I WONDER WHAT'S OUT THERE NOW?
IT DOESN'T MATTER! I'M READY FOR ANYTHING!
YE CATS!

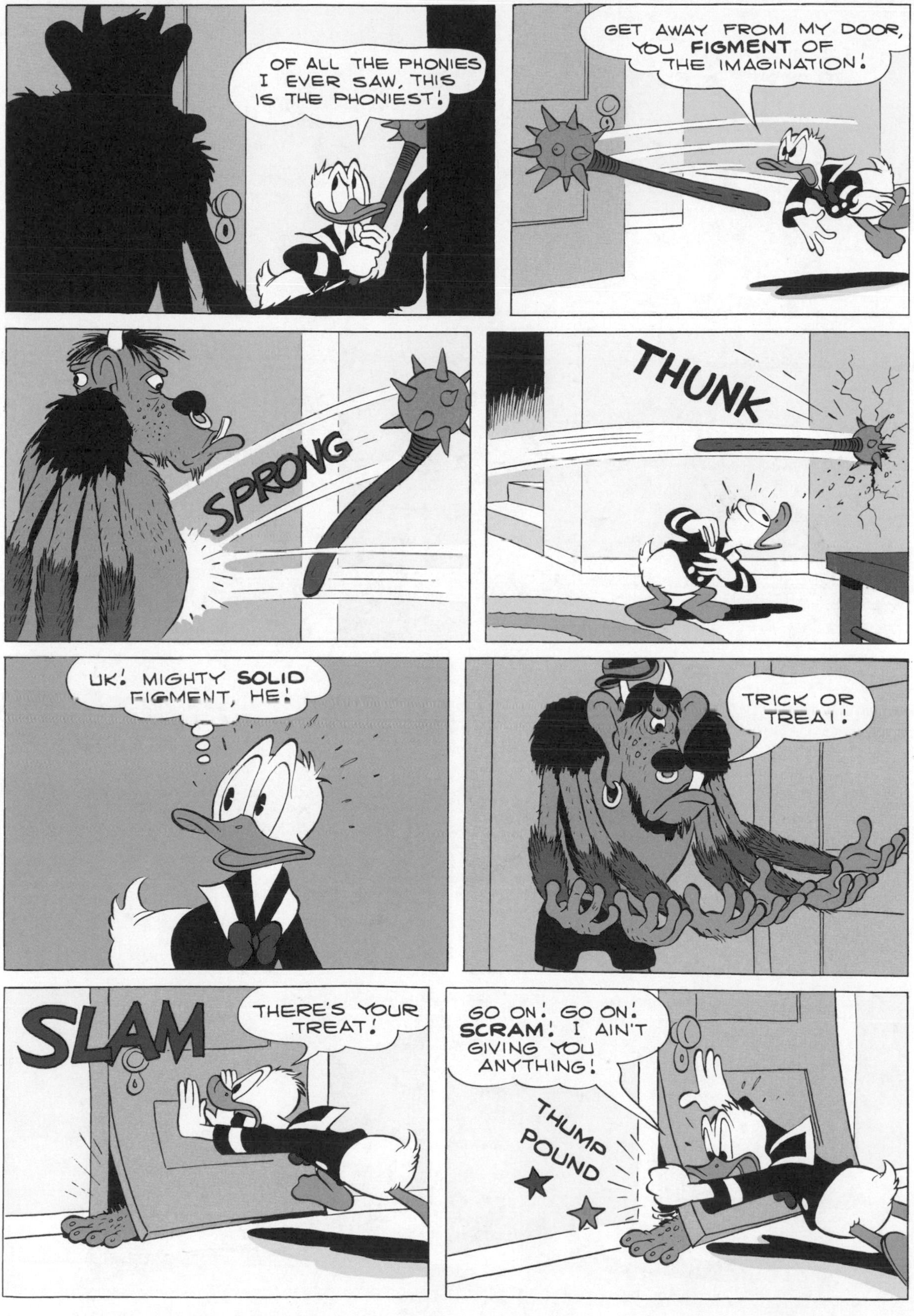
OF ALL THE PHONIES I EVER SAW, THIS IS THE PHONIEST!
GET AWAY FROM MY DOOR, YOU FIGMENT OF THE IMAGINATION!
SPRONG
THUNK
UK! MIGHTY SOLID FIGMENT, HE!
TRICK OR TREAT!
SLAM
THERE'S YOUR TREAT!
GO ON! GO ON! SCRAM! I AIN'T GIVING YOU ANYTHING!
THUMP
POUND

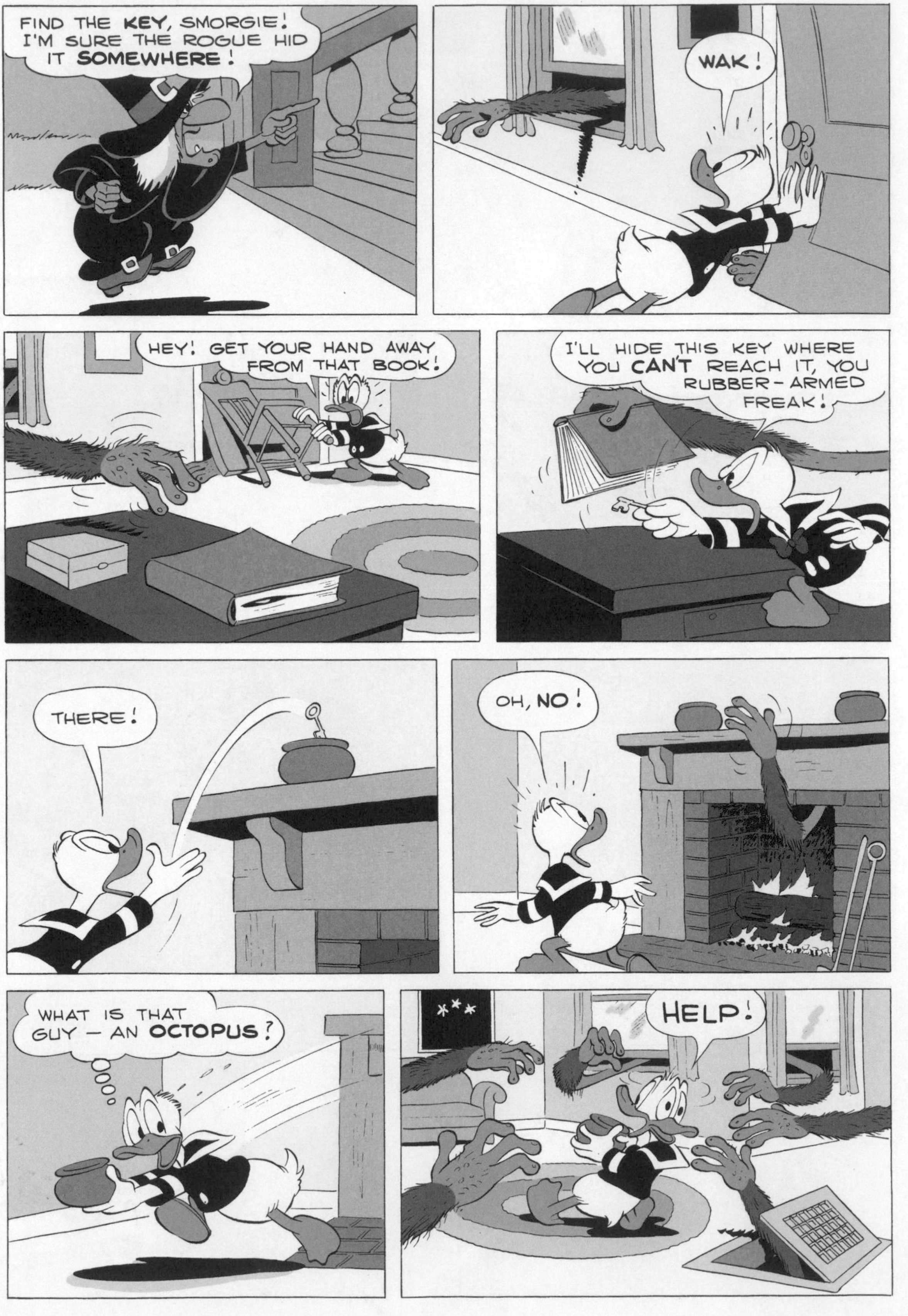
FIND THE KEY, SMORGIE! I'M SURE THE ROGUE HID IT SOMEWHERE!
WAK!
HEY! GET YOUR HAND AWAY FROM THAT BOOK!
I'LL HIDE THIS KEY WHERE YOU CAN'T REACH IT, YOU RUBBER-ARMED FREAK!
THERE!
OH, NO!
WHAT IS THAT GUY — AN OCTOPUS?
HELP!

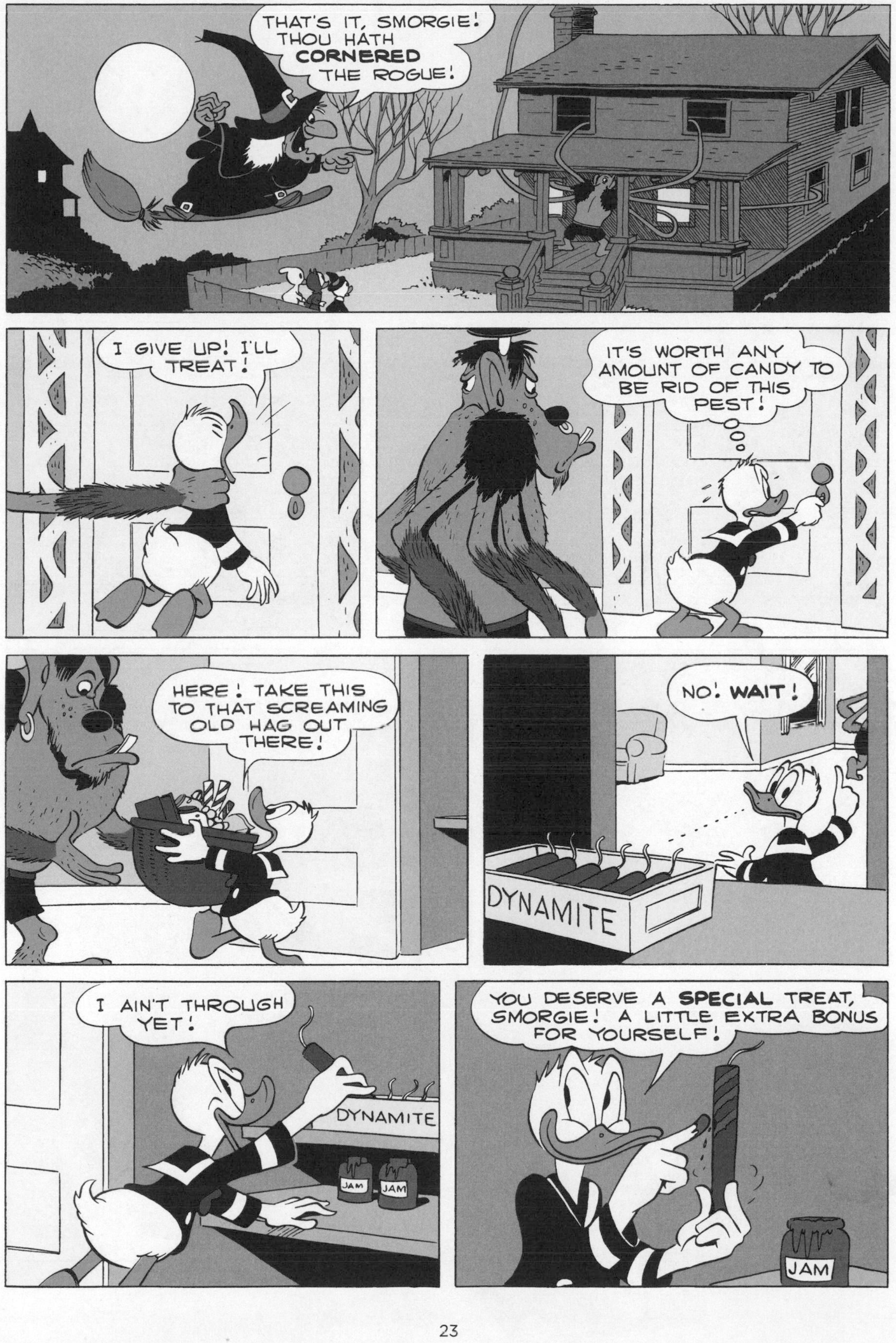
THAT'S IT, SMORGIE! THOU HATH CORNERED THE ROGUE!
I GIVE UP! I'LL TREAT!
IT'S WORTH ANY AMOUNT OF CANDY TO BE RID OF THIS PEST!
HERE! TAKE THIS TO THAT SCREAMING OLD HAG OUT THERE!
NO! WAIT!
DYNAMITE
I AIN'T THROUGH YET!
DYNAMITE
JAM
JAM
YOU DESERVE A SPECIAL TREAT, SMORGIE! A LITTLE EXTRA BONUS FOR YOURSELF!
JAM

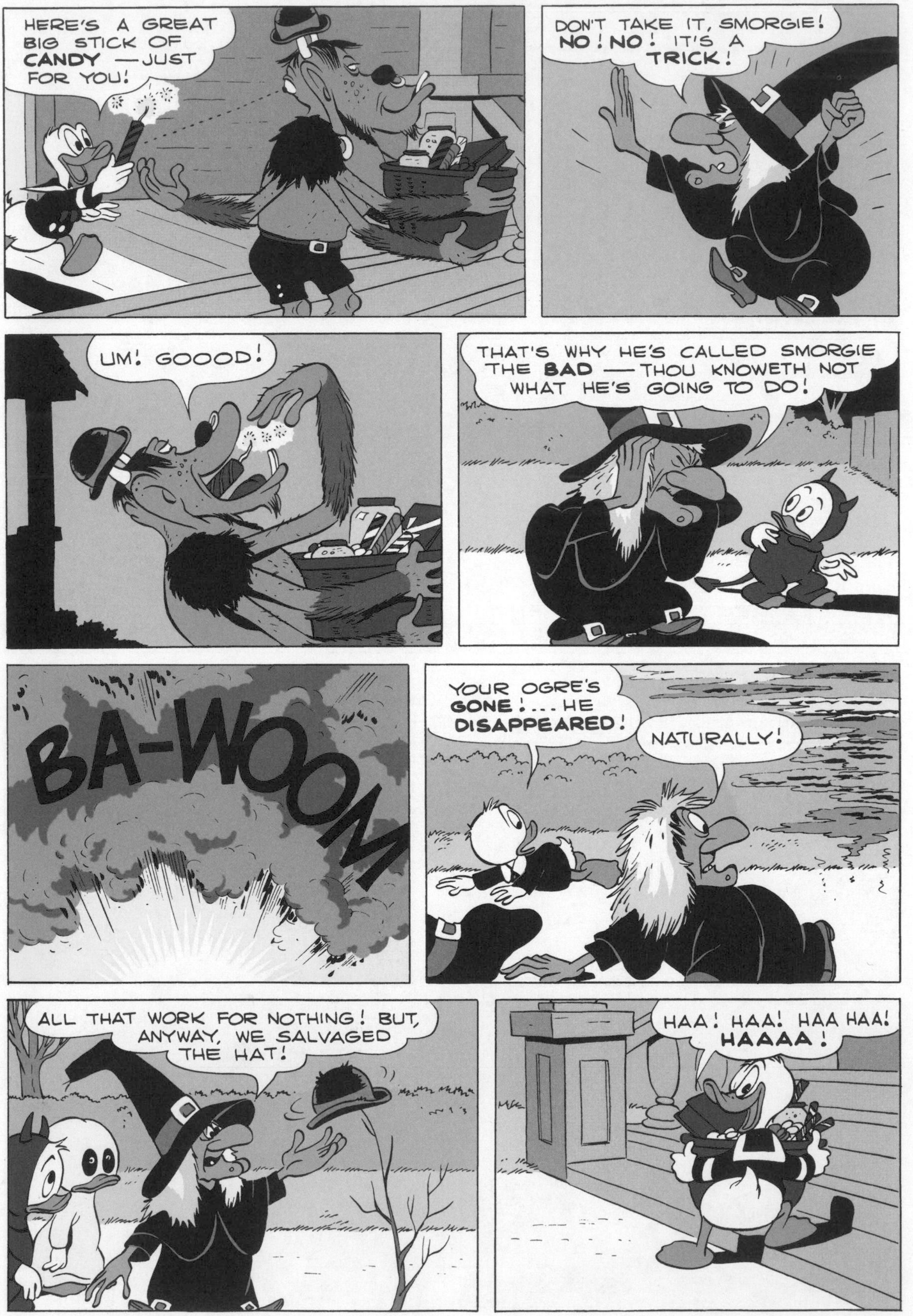
HERE'S A GREAT BIG STICK OF CANDY —JUST FOR YOU!
DON'T TAKE IT, SMORGIE! NO! NO! IT'S A TRICK!
UM! GOOOD!
THAT'S WHY HE'S CALLED SMORGIE THE BAD — THOU KNOWETH NOT WHAT HE'S GOING TO DO!
BA-WOOM
YOUR OGRE'S GONE!... HE DISAPPEARED!
NATURALLY!
ALL THAT WORK FOR NOTHING! BUT, ANYWAY, WE SALVAGED THE HAT!
HAA! HAA! HAA HAA! HAAAA!

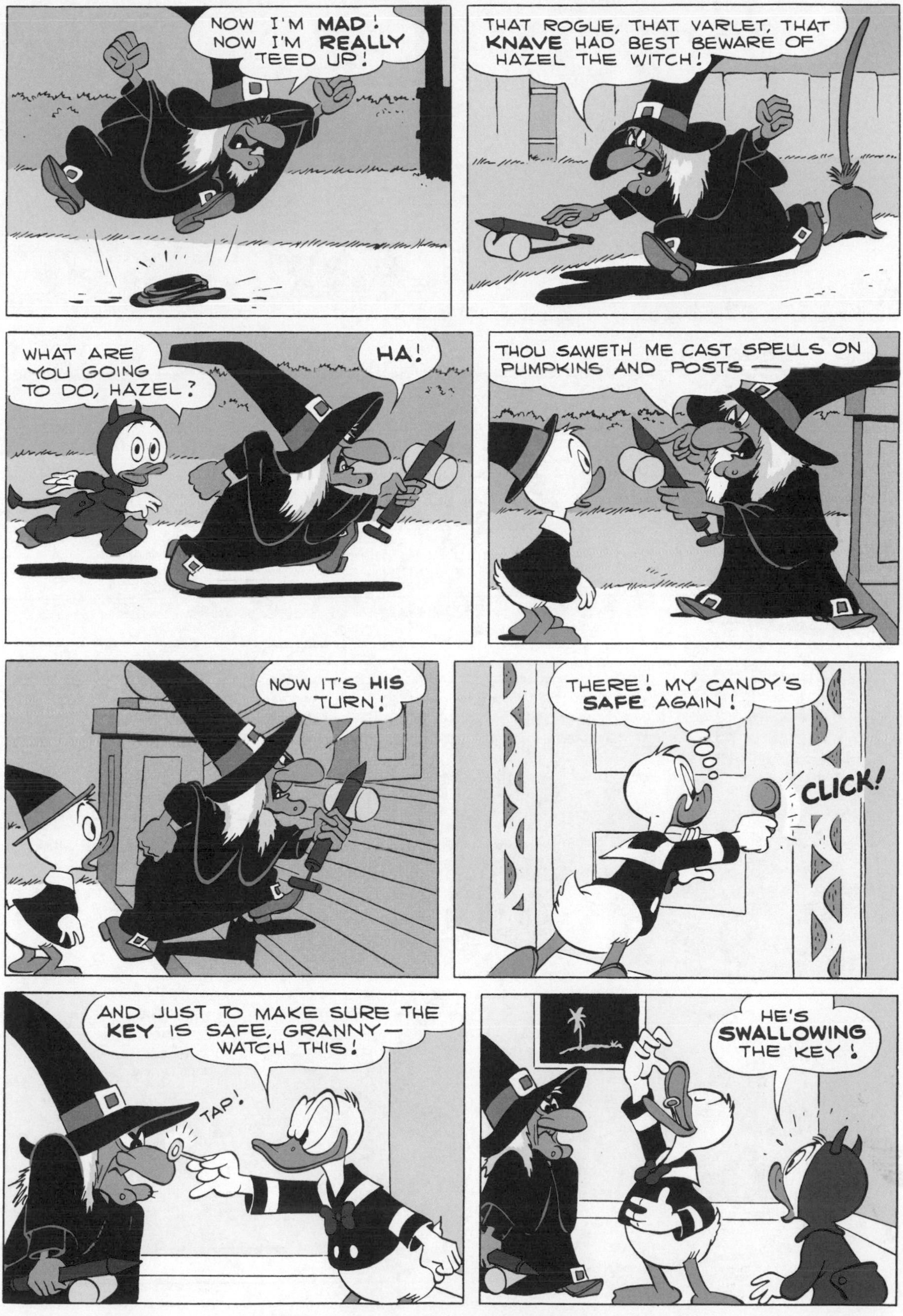
NOW I'M MAD! NOW I'M REALLY TEED UP!
THAT ROGUE, THAT VARLET, THAT KNAVE HAD BEST BEWARE OF HAZEL THE WITCH!
WHAT ARE YOU GOING TO DO, HAZEL?
HA!
THOU SAWETH ME CAST SPELLS ON PUMPKINS AND POSTS —
NOW IT'S HIS TURN!
THERE! MY CANDY'S SAFE AGAIN!
CLICK!
AND JUST TO MAKE SURE THE KEY IS SAFE, GRANNY— WATCH THIS!
TAP!
HE'S SWALLOWING THE KEY!

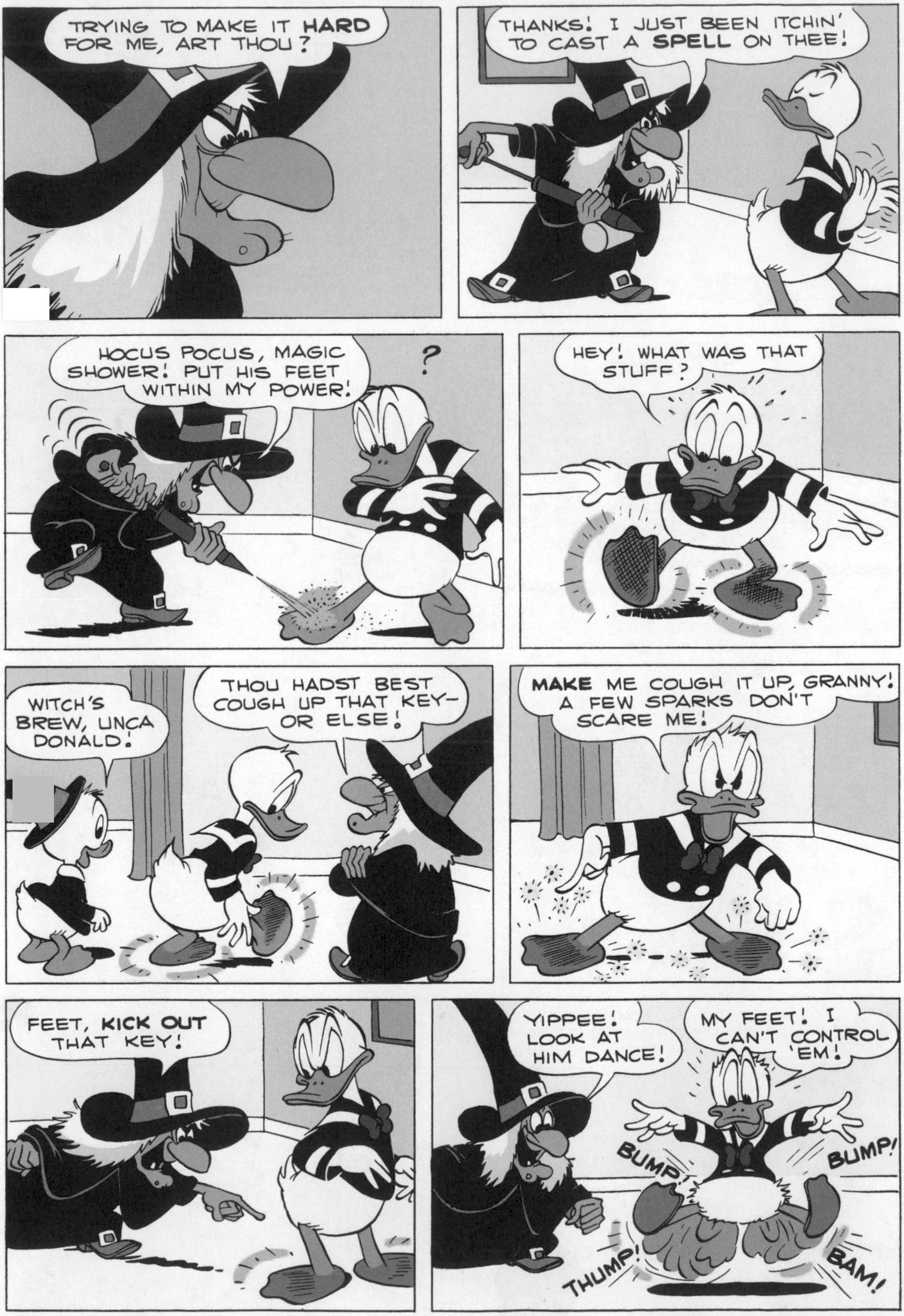
TRYING TO MAKE IT **HARD** FOR ME, ART THOU?
THANKS! I JUST BEEN ITCHIN' TO CAST A **SPELL** ON THEE!
HOCUS POCUS, MAGIC SHOWER! PUT HIS FEET WITHIN MY POWER!
?
HEY! WHAT WAS THAT STUFF?
WITCH'S BREW, UNCA DONALD!
THOU HADST BEST COUGH UP THAT KEY— OR ELSE!
MAKE ME COUGH IT UP, GRANNY! A FEW SPARKS DON'T SCARE ME!
FEET, **KICK OUT** THAT KEY!
YIPPEE! LOOK AT HIM DANCE!
MY FEET! I CAN'T CONTROL 'EM!
BUMP!
BUMP!
THUMP!
BAM!

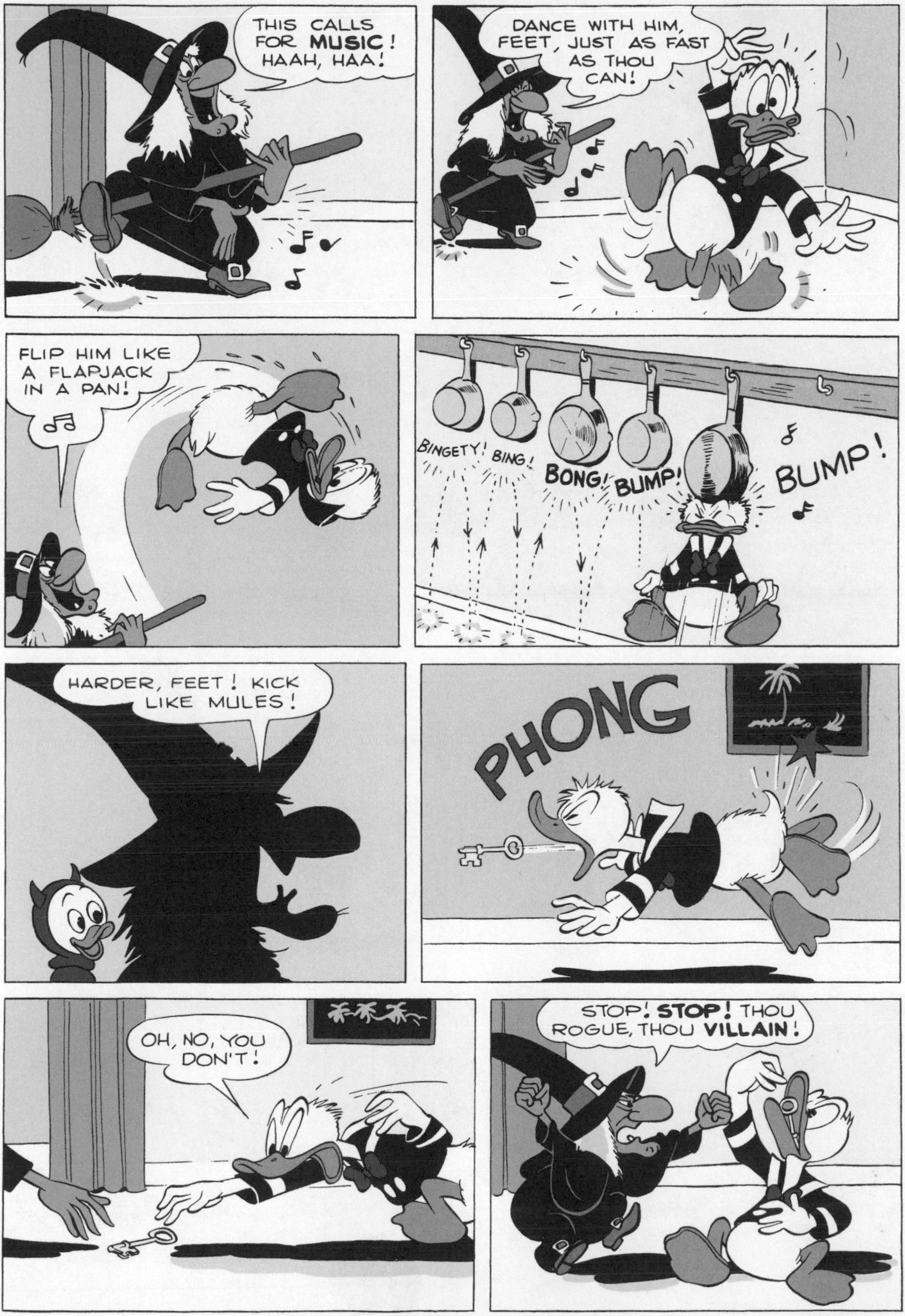
THIS CALLS FOR MUSIC! HAAH, HAA!
DANCE WITH HIM, FEET, JUST AS FAST AS THOU CAN!
FLIP HIM LIKE A FLAPJACK IN A PAN!
BINGETY! BING! BONG! BUMP! BUMP!
HARDER, FEET! KICK LIKE MULES!
PHONG
OH, NO, YOU DON'T!
STOP! STOP! THOU ROGUE, THOU VILLAIN!

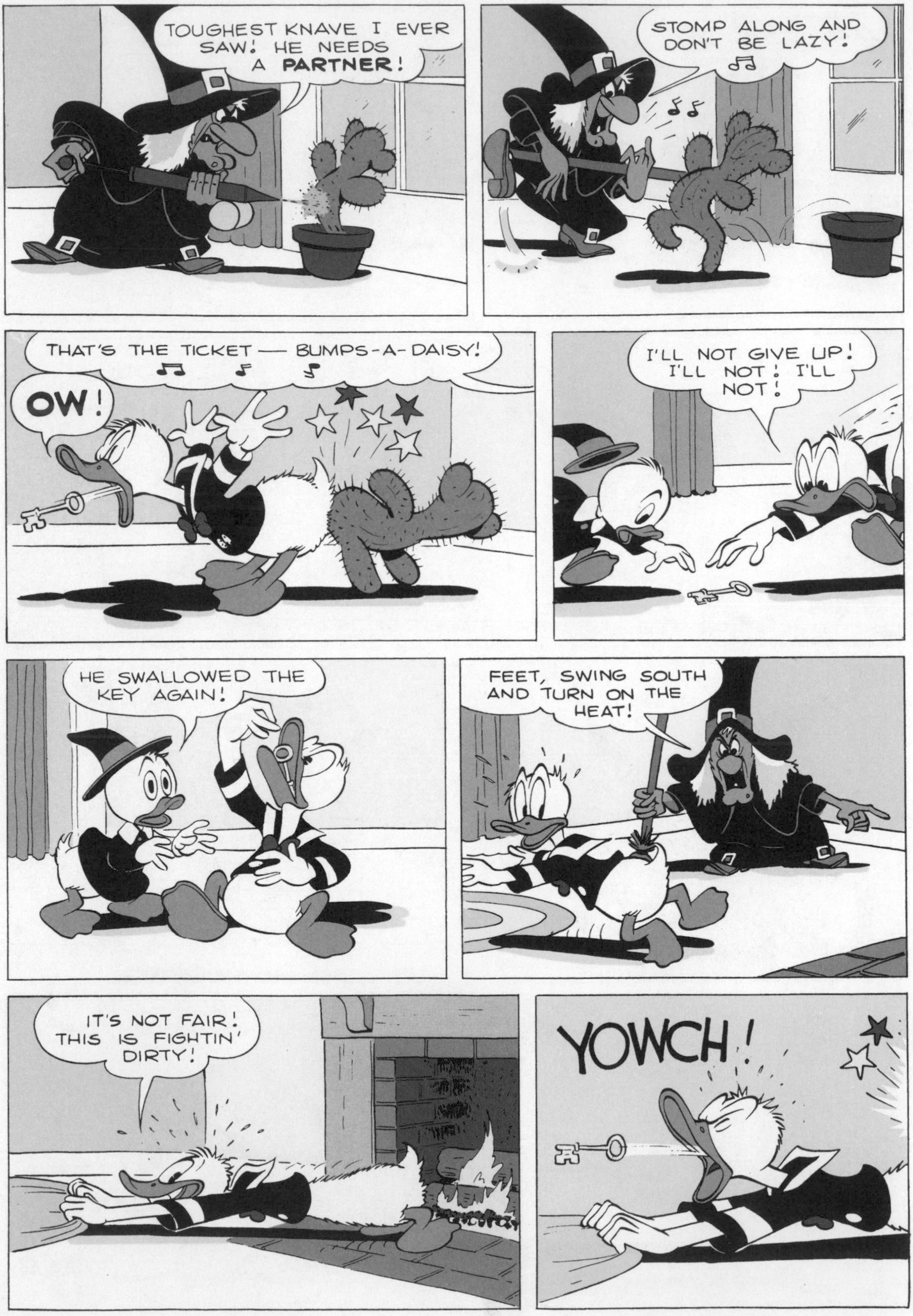
TOUGHEST KNAVE I EVER SAW! HE NEEDS A PARTNER!
STOMP ALONG AND DON'T BE LAZY!
THAT'S THE TICKET — BUMPS-A-DAISY!
OW!
I'LL NOT GIVE UP! I'LL NOT! I'LL NOT!
HE SWALLOWED THE KEY AGAIN!
FEET, SWING SOUTH AND TURN ON THE HEAT!
IT'S NOT FAIR! THIS IS FIGHTIN' DIRTY!
YOWCH!

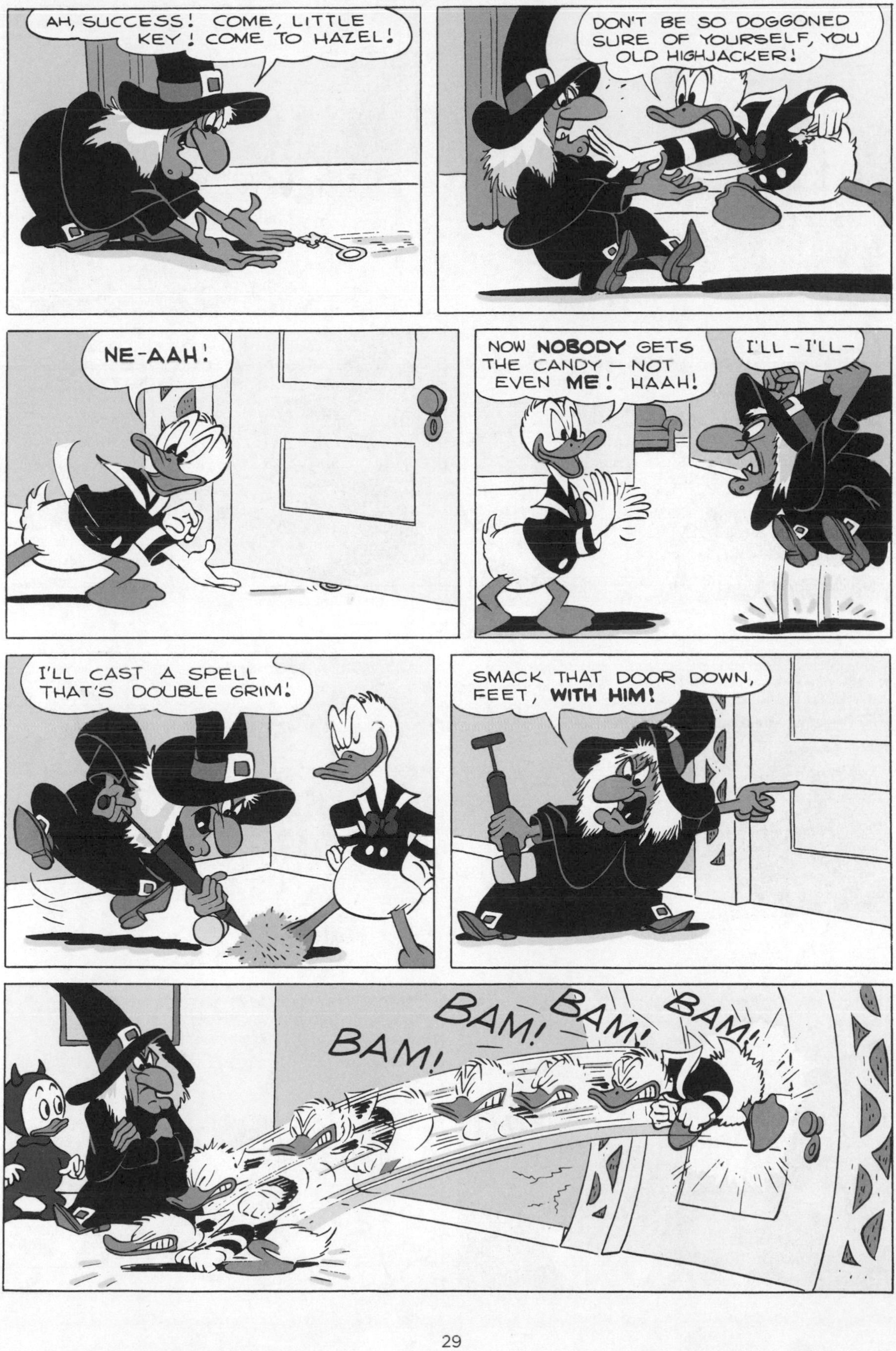

AH, SUCCESS! COME, LITTLE KEY! COME TO HAZEL!
DON'T BE SO DOGGONED SURE OF YOURSELF, YOU OLD HIGHJACKER!
NE-AAH!
NOW **NOBODY** GETS THE CANDY — NOT EVEN **ME**! HAAH!
I'LL - I'LL-
I'LL CAST A SPELL THAT'S DOUBLE GRIM!
SMACK THAT DOOR DOWN, FEET, **WITH HIM!**
BAM! BAM! BAM! BAM!

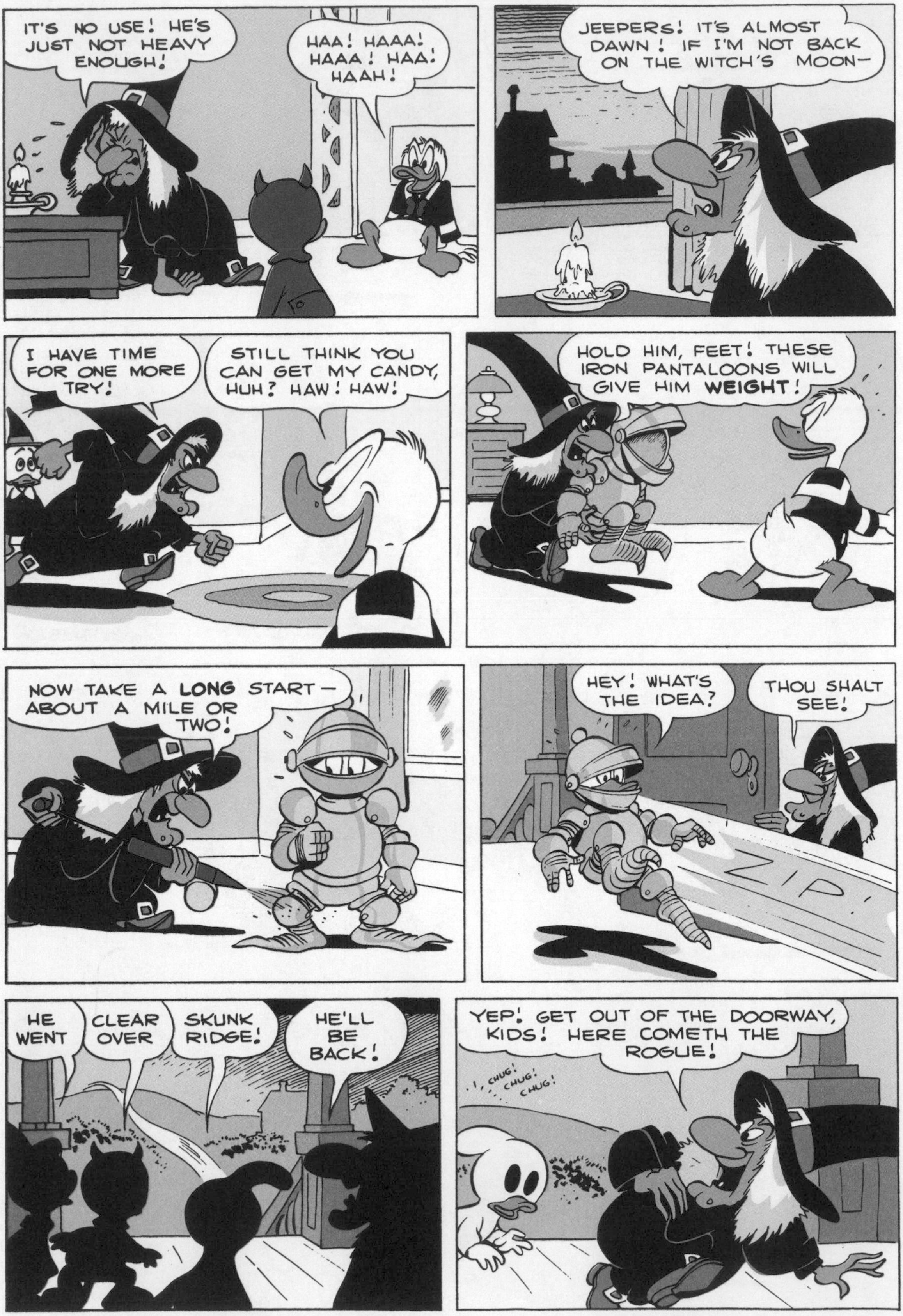

IT'S NO USE! HE'S JUST NOT HEAVY ENOUGH!
HAA! HAAA! HAAA! HAA! HAAH!
JEEPERS! IT'S ALMOST DAWN! IF I'M NOT BACK ON THE WITCH'S MOON—
I HAVE TIME FOR ONE MORE TRY!
STILL THINK YOU CAN GET MY CANDY, HUH? HAW! HAW!
HOLD HIM, FEET! THESE IRON PANTALOONS WILL GIVE HIM WEIGHT!
NOW TAKE A LONG START— ABOUT A MILE OR TWO!
HEY! WHAT'S THE IDEA?
THOU SHALT SEE!
ZIP
HE WENT
CLEAR OVER
SKUNK RIDGE!
HE'LL BE BACK!
YEP! GET OUT OF THE DOORWAY, KIDS! HERE COMETH THE ROGUE!
CHUG! CHUG! CHUG!

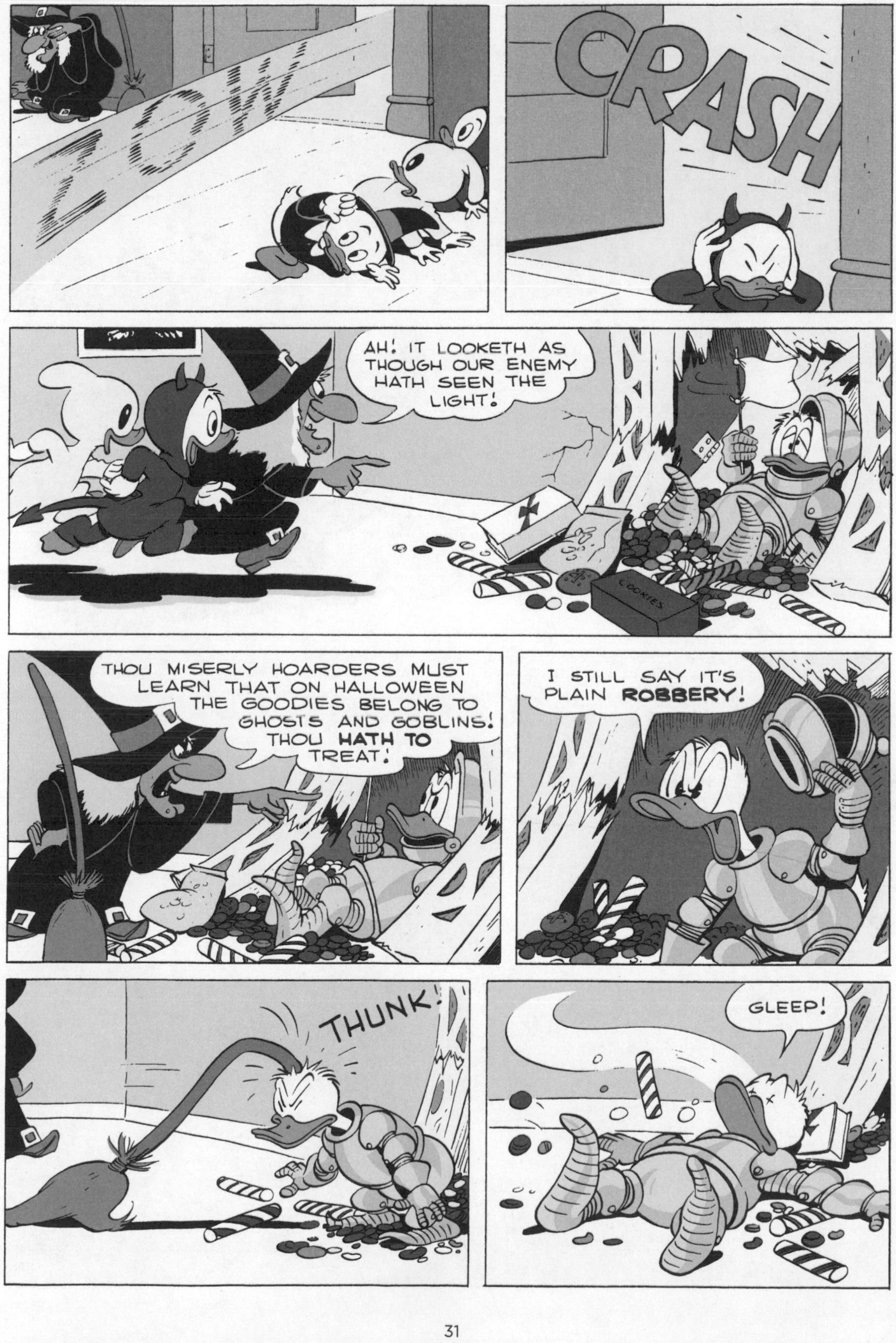
ZOW
CRASH
AH! IT LOOKETH AS THOUGH OUR ENEMY HATH SEEN THE LIGHT!
COOKIES
THOU MISERLY HOARDERS MUST LEARN THAT ON HALLOWEEN THE GOODIES BELONG TO GHOSTS AND GOBLINS! THOU **HATH TO** TREAT!
I STILL SAY IT'S PLAIN **ROBBERY**!
THUNK!
GLEEP!

As a result of this walloping victory, Huey, Louie, and Dewey have a perfect Halloween, after all!

OUR LOOT SACK

IS FILLED

WITH CANDY!

AND IT'LL BE FILLED **EVERY** HALLOWEEN FROM NOW ON! YON ROGUE, I'M SURE, HATH LEARNED HIS LESSON!

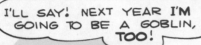

I'LL SAY! NEXT YEAR I'M GOING TO BE A GOBLIN, TOO!

GRACIOUS! IT'S CRACKING DAY! BLAST OFF, BEELZEBUB!

So into the fading harvest moon goes Hazel the Witch, and all the ghosts and goblins become boys and girls again, and posts become posts, and gates gates, and pumpkins are just pumpkins on a sunny hill!

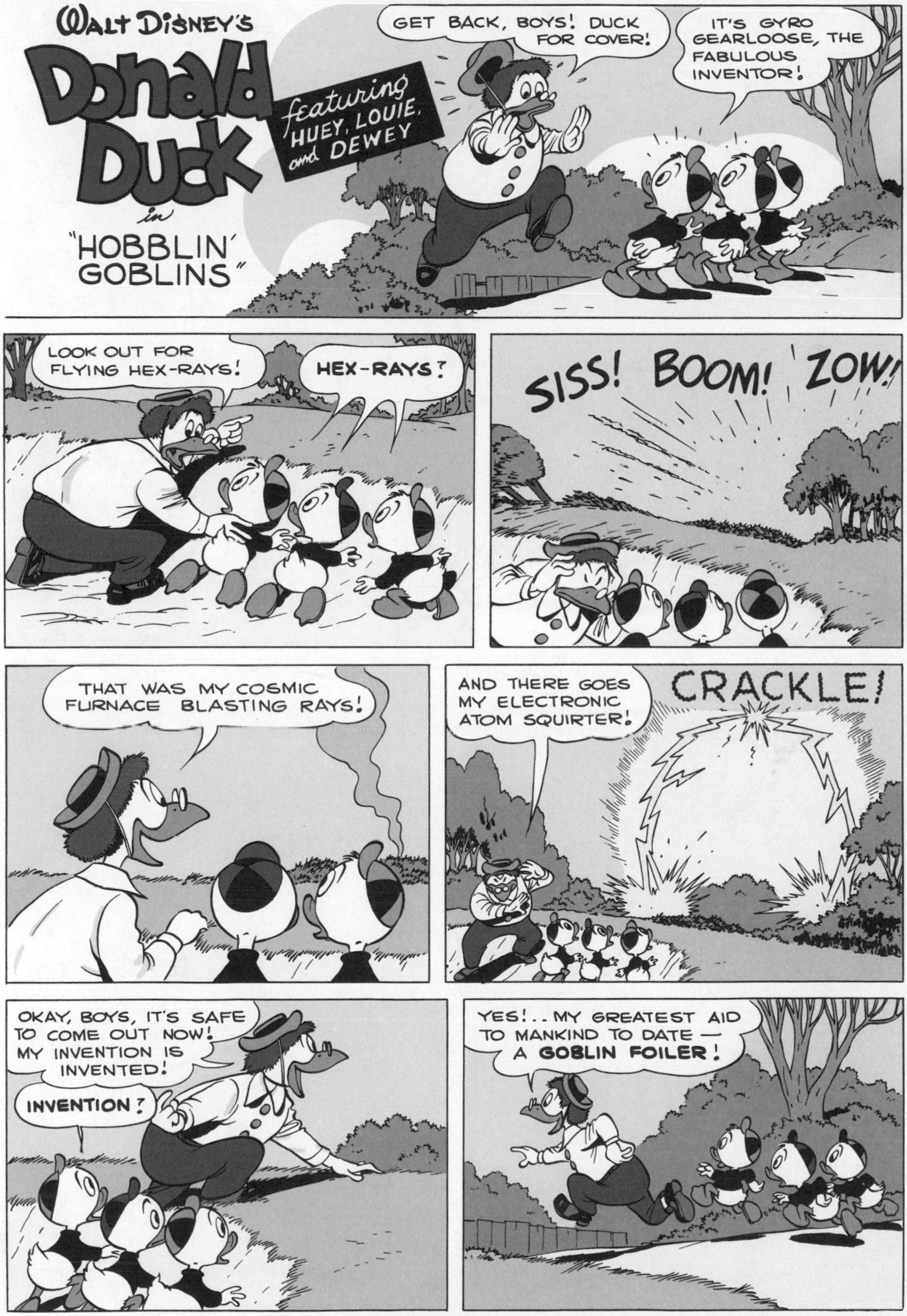
WALT DISNEY'S
Donald Duck
featuring HUEY, LOUIE, and DEWEY
in
"HOBBLIN' GOBLINS"
GET BACK, BOYS! DUCK FOR COVER!
IT'S GYRO GEARLOOSE, THE FABULOUS INVENTOR!
LOOK OUT FOR FLYING HEX-RAYS!
HEX-RAYS?
SISS! BOOM! ZOW!
THAT WAS MY COSMIC FURNACE BLASTING RAYS!
AND THERE GOES MY ELECTRONIC ATOM SQUIRTER!
CRACKLE!
OKAY, BOYS, IT'S SAFE TO COME OUT NOW! MY INVENTION IS INVENTED!
INVENTION?
YES!.. MY GREATEST AID TO MANKIND TO DATE — A GOBLIN FOILER!

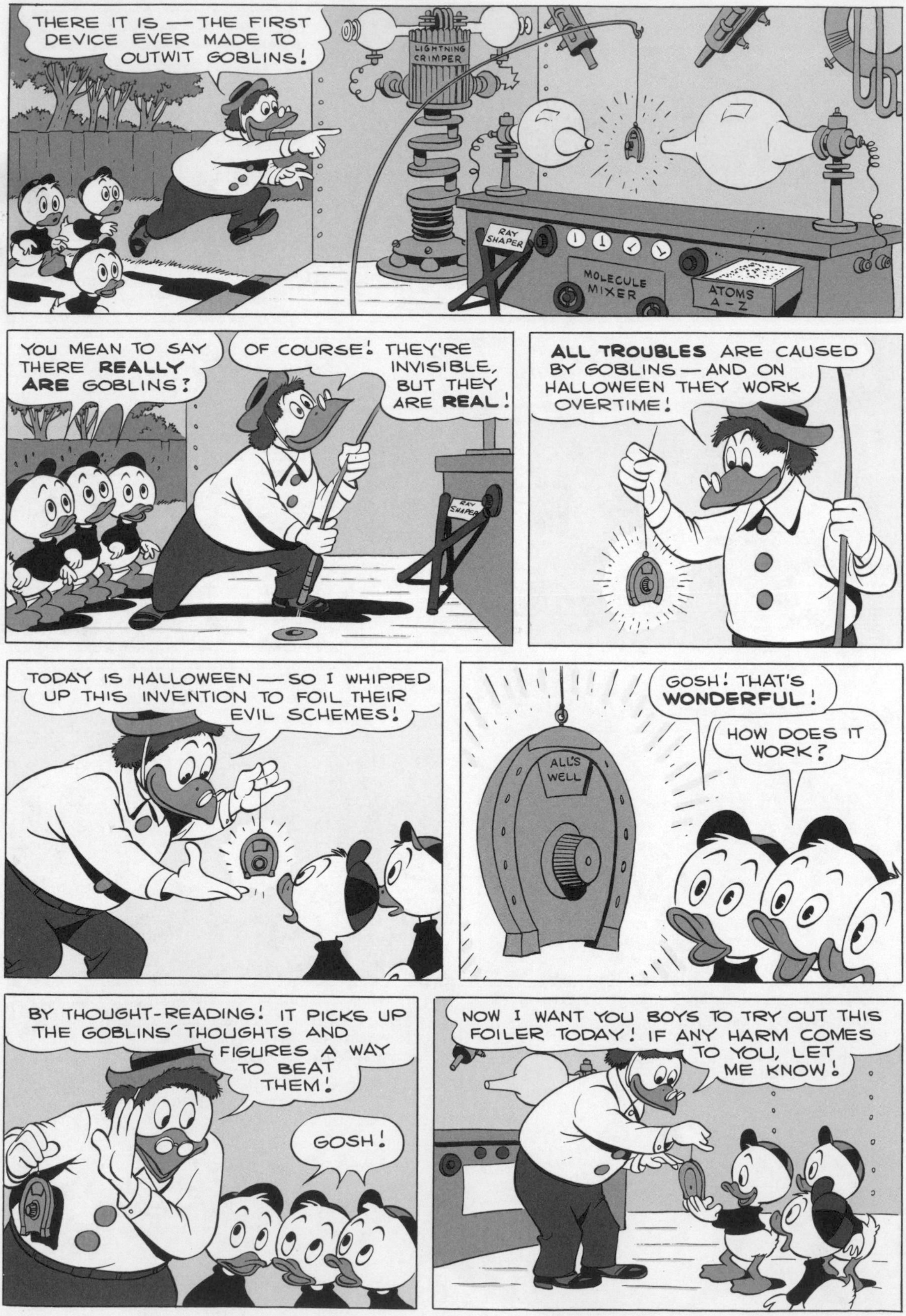
THERE IT IS — THE FIRST DEVICE EVER MADE TO OUTWIT GOBLINS!
LIGHTNING CRIMPER
RAY SHAPER
MOLECULE MIXER
ATOMS A – Z
YOU MEAN TO SAY THERE **REALLY ARE** GOBLINS?
OF COURSE! THEY'RE INVISIBLE, BUT THEY ARE **REAL**!
RAY SHAPER
ALL TROUBLES ARE CAUSED BY GOBLINS — AND ON HALLOWEEN THEY WORK OVERTIME!
TODAY IS HALLOWEEN — SO I WHIPPED UP THIS INVENTION TO FOIL THEIR EVIL SCHEMES!
ALL'S WELL
GOSH! THAT'S **WONDERFUL**!
HOW DOES IT WORK?
BY THOUGHT-READING! IT PICKS UP THE GOBLINS' THOUGHTS AND FIGURES A WAY TO BEAT THEM!
GOSH!
NOW I WANT YOU BOYS TO TRY OUT THIS FOILER TODAY! IF ANY HARM COMES TO YOU, LET ME KNOW!

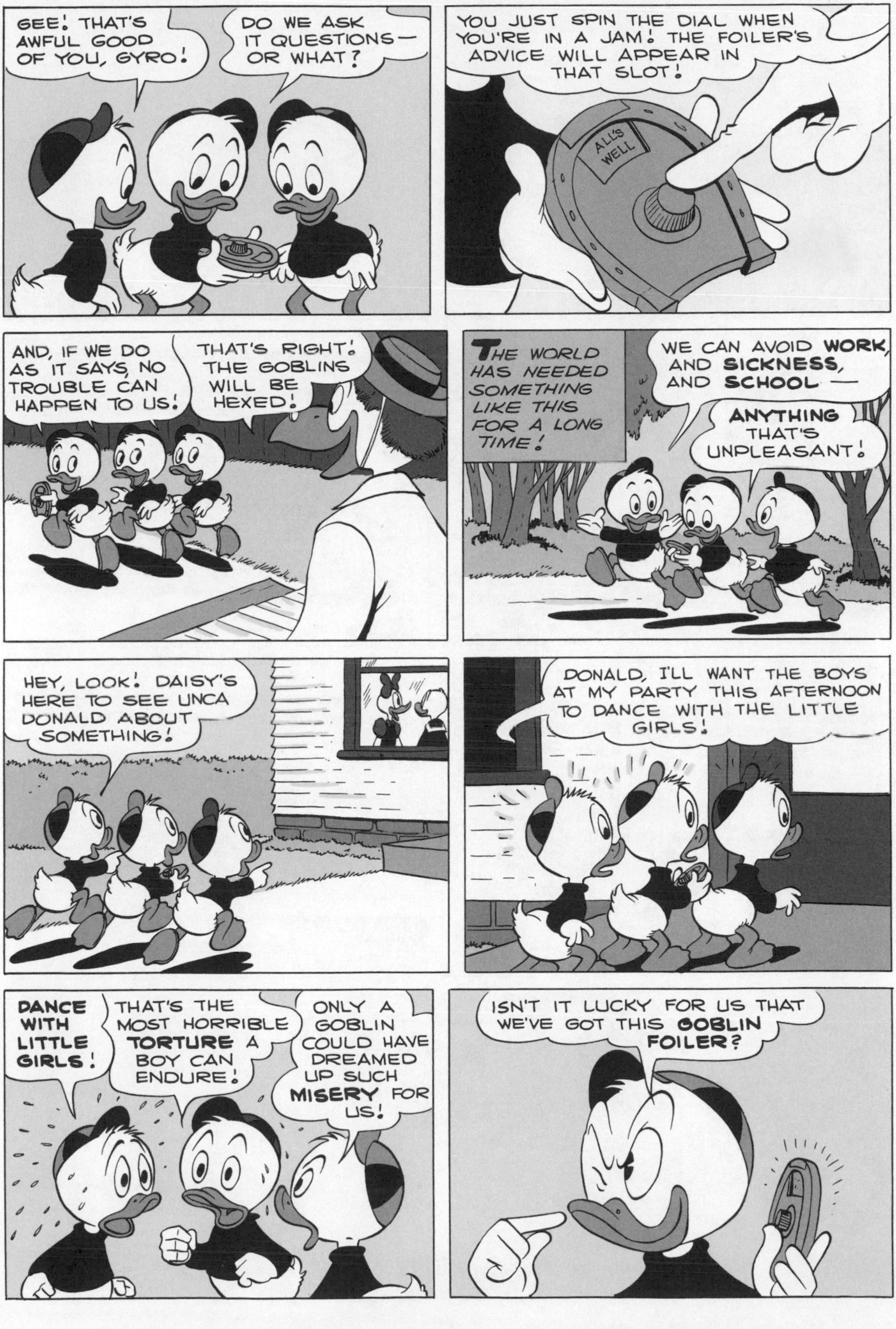
GEE! THAT'S AWFUL GOOD OF YOU, GYRO!
DO WE ASK IT QUESTIONS— OR WHAT?
YOU JUST SPIN THE DIAL WHEN YOU'RE IN A JAM! THE FOILER'S ADVICE WILL APPEAR IN THAT SLOT!
ALL'S WELL
AND, IF WE DO AS IT SAYS, NO TROUBLE CAN HAPPEN TO US!
THAT'S RIGHT! THE GOBLINS WILL BE HEXED!
THE WORLD HAS NEEDED SOMETHING LIKE THIS FOR A LONG TIME!
WE CAN AVOID WORK, AND SICKNESS, AND SCHOOL —
ANYTHING THAT'S UNPLEASANT!
HEY, LOOK! DAISY'S HERE TO SEE UNCA DONALD ABOUT SOMETHING!
DONALD, I'LL WANT THE BOYS AT MY PARTY THIS AFTERNOON TO DANCE WITH THE LITTLE GIRLS!
DANCE WITH LITTLE GIRLS!
THAT'S THE MOST HORRIBLE TORTURE A BOY CAN ENDURE!
ONLY A GOBLIN COULD HAVE DREAMED UP SUCH MISERY FOR US!
ISN'T IT LUCKY FOR US THAT WE'VE GOT THIS GOBLIN FOILER?

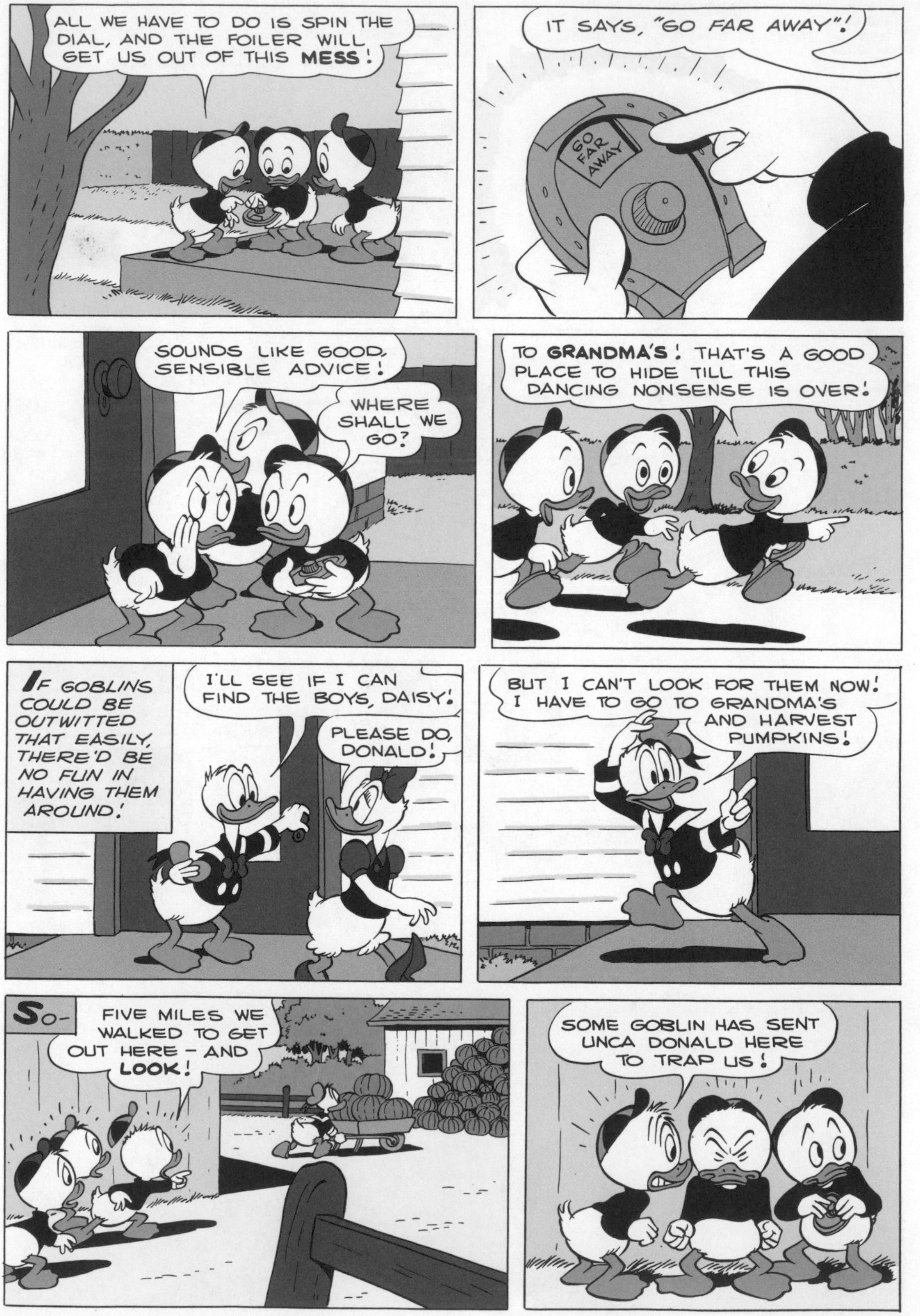
ALL WE HAVE TO DO IS SPIN THE DIAL, AND THE FOILER WILL GET US OUT OF THIS **MESS**!
IT SAYS, "GO *FAR AWAY*"!
GO FAR AWAY
SOUNDS LIKE GOOD, SENSIBLE ADVICE!
WHERE SHALL WE GO?
TO **GRANDMA'S**! THAT'S A GOOD PLACE TO HIDE TILL THIS DANCING NONSENSE IS OVER!
IF GOBLINS COULD BE OUTWITTED THAT EASILY, THERE'D BE NO FUN IN HAVING THEM AROUND!
I'LL SEE IF I CAN FIND THE BOYS, DAISY!
PLEASE DO, DONALD!
BUT I CAN'T LOOK FOR THEM NOW! I HAVE TO GO TO GRANDMA'S AND HARVEST PUMPKINS!
SO-
FIVE MILES WE WALKED TO GET OUT HERE — AND **LOOK**!
SOME GOBLIN HAS SENT UNCA DONALD HERE TO TRAP US!

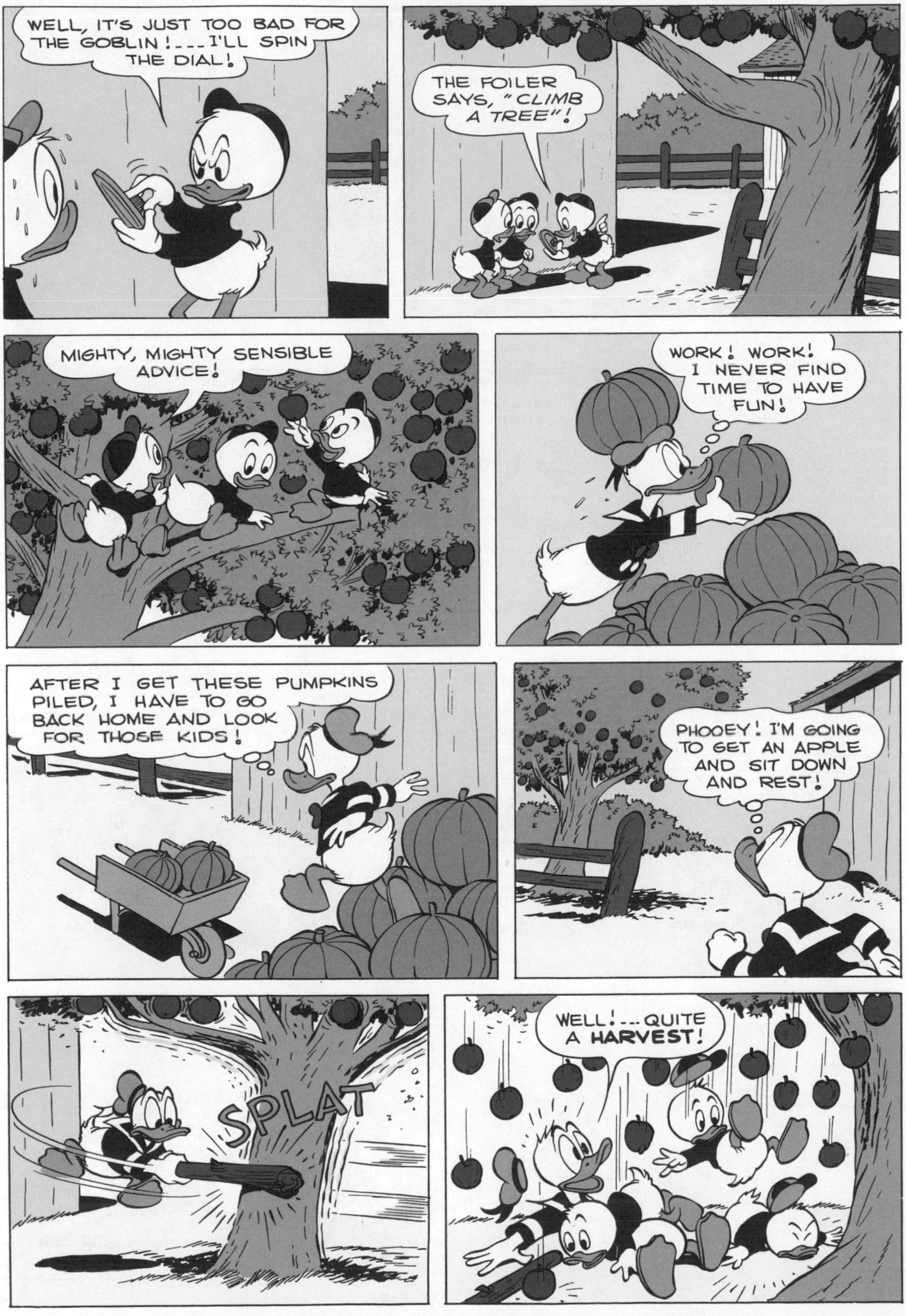
WELL, IT'S JUST TOO BAD FOR THE GOBLIN!---I'LL SPIN THE DIAL!
THE FOILER SAYS, "CLIMB A TREE"!
MIGHTY, MIGHTY SENSIBLE ADVICE!
WORK! WORK! I NEVER FIND TIME TO HAVE FUN!
AFTER I GET THESE PUMPKINS PILED, I HAVE TO GO BACK HOME AND LOOK FOR THOSE KIDS!
PHOOEY! I'M GOING TO GET AN APPLE AND SIT DOWN AND REST!
SPLAT
WELL!---QUITE A HARVEST!

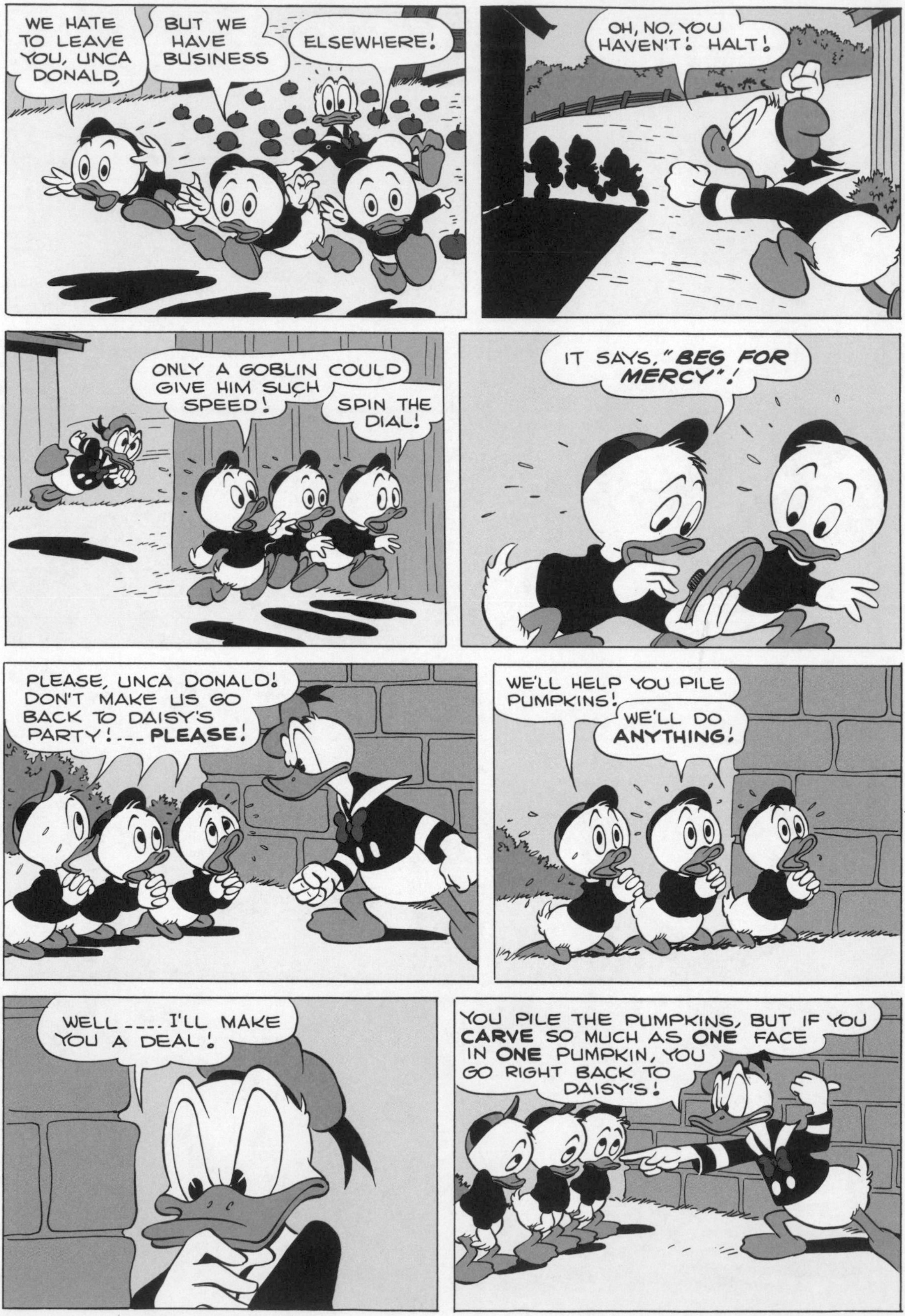
WE HATE TO LEAVE YOU, UNCA DONALD,
BUT WE HAVE BUSINESS
ELSEWHERE!
OH, NO, YOU HAVEN'T! HALT!
ONLY A GOBLIN COULD GIVE HIM SUCH SPEED!
SPIN THE DIAL!
IT SAYS, "BEG FOR MERCY"!
PLEASE, UNCA DONALD! DON'T MAKE US GO BACK TO DAISY'S PARTY!--- PLEASE!
WE'LL HELP YOU PILE PUMPKINS!
WE'LL DO ANYTHING!
WELL ---- I'LL MAKE YOU A DEAL!
YOU PILE THE PUMPKINS, BUT IF YOU CARVE SO MUCH AS ONE FACE IN ONE PUMPKIN, YOU GO RIGHT BACK TO DAISY'S!

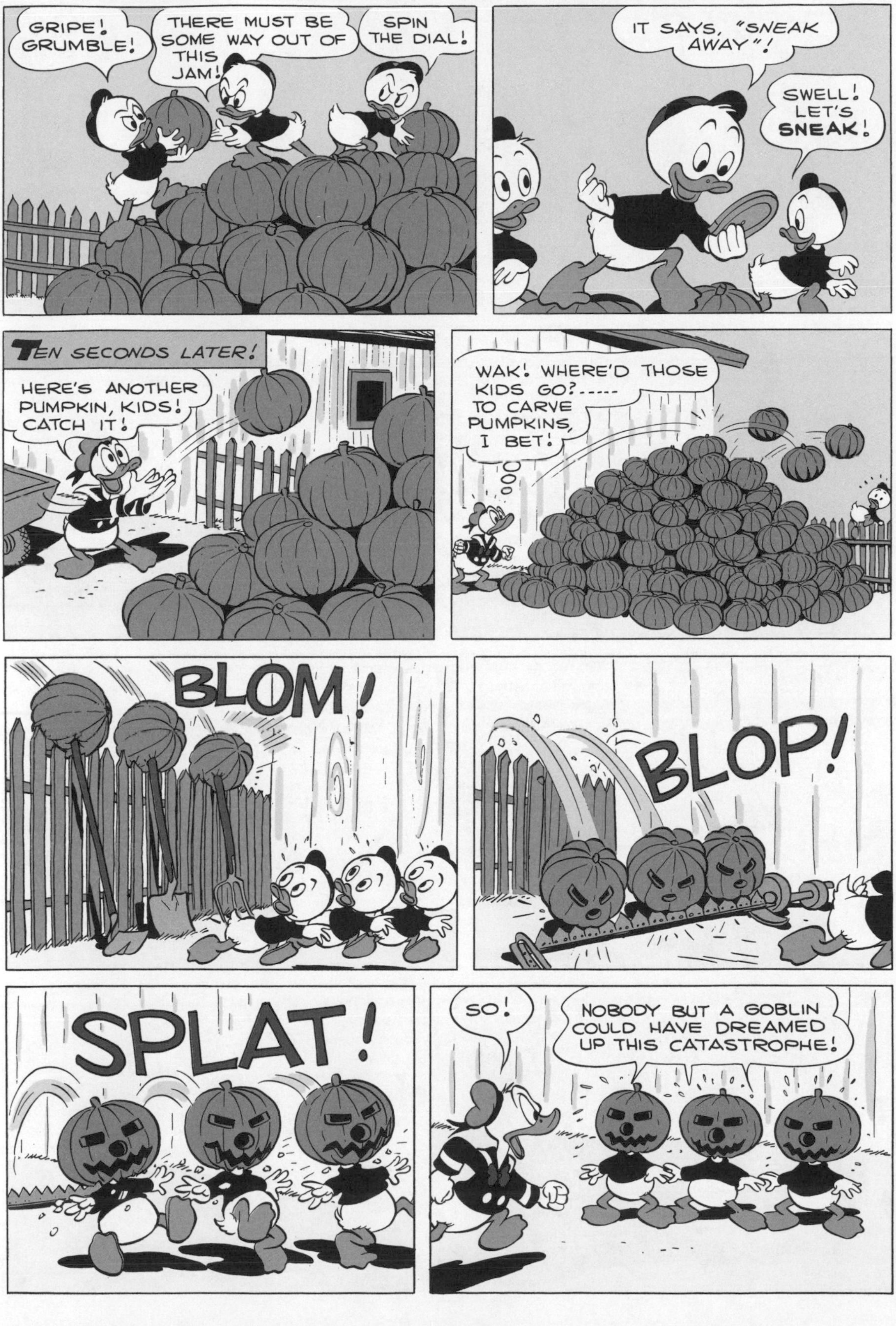
GRIPE! GRUMBLE!
THERE MUST BE SOME WAY OUT OF THIS JAM!
SPIN THE DIAL!
IT SAYS, "SNEAK AWAY"!
SWELL! LET'S SNEAK!
TEN SECONDS LATER!
HERE'S ANOTHER PUMPKIN, KIDS! CATCH IT!
WAK! WHERE'D THOSE KIDS GO?----- TO CARVE PUMPKINS, I BET!
BLOM!
BLOP!
SPLAT!
SO!
NOBODY BUT A GOBLIN COULD HAVE DREAMED UP THIS CATASTROPHE!

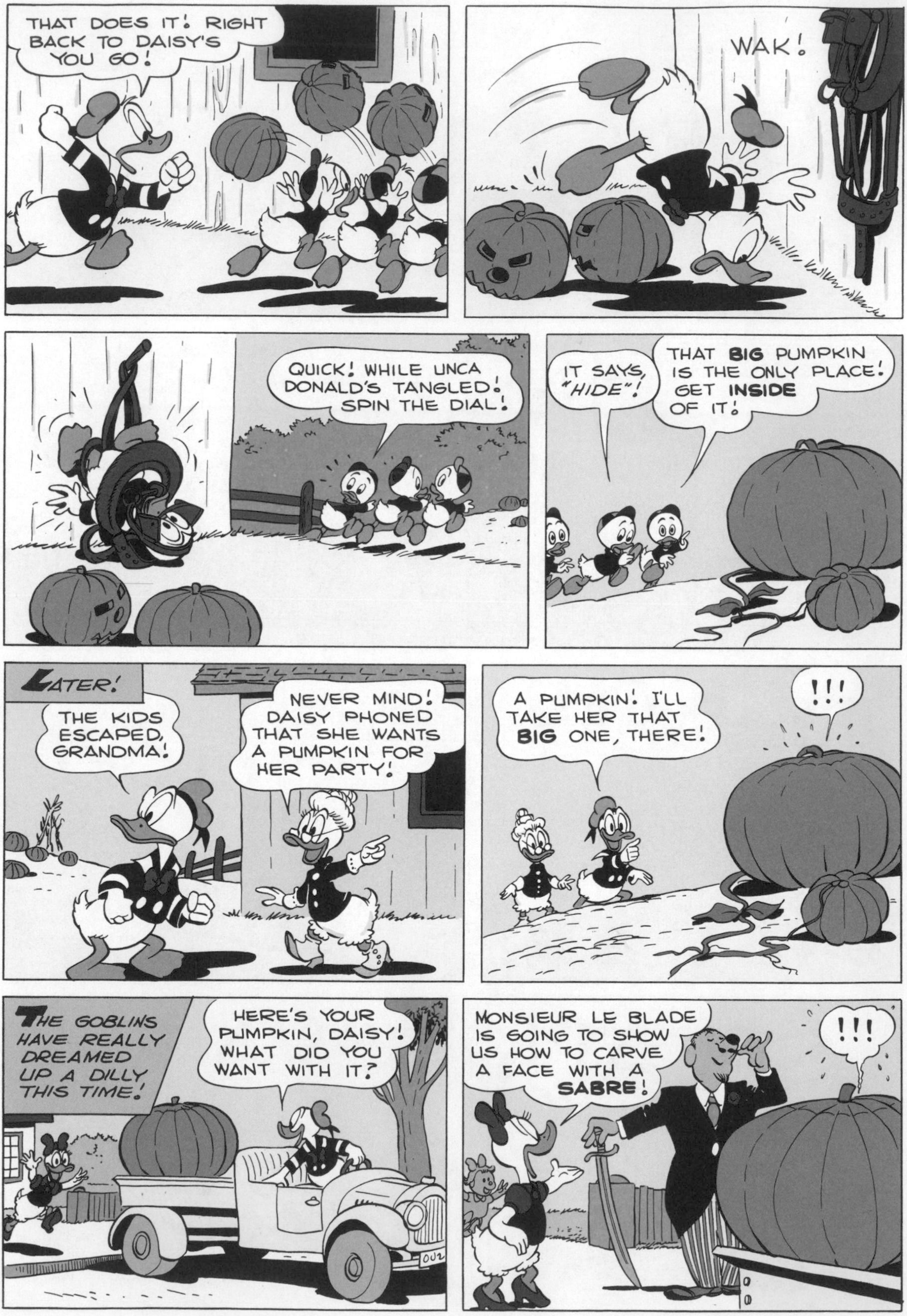
THAT DOES IT! RIGHT BACK TO DAISY'S YOU GO!
WAK!
QUICK! WHILE UNCA DONALD'S TANGLED! SPIN THE DIAL!
IT SAYS, "HIDE"!
THAT BIG PUMPKIN IS THE ONLY PLACE! GET INSIDE OF IT!
LATER!
THE KIDS ESCAPED, GRANDMA!
NEVER MIND! DAISY PHONED THAT SHE WANTS A PUMPKIN FOR HER PARTY!
A PUMPKIN! I'LL TAKE HER THAT BIG ONE, THERE!
!!!
THE GOBLINS HAVE REALLY DREAMED UP A DILLY THIS TIME!
HERE'S YOUR PUMPKIN, DAISY! WHAT DID YOU WANT WITH IT?
MONSIEUR LE BLADE IS GOING TO SHOW US HOW TO CARVE A FACE WITH A SABRE!
!!!

So—

VOILA! WIZ ZE CAVALRY THRUST, I CARVE ZE EYE! TOUCHÉ!

JIMINY CHRISTMAS!

NOW ZE TWO-HAND SLASH FOR ZE OZZER EYE! EN GARDE!

SACRÉ BLEU! ZE PUMPKIN WAS POPULATED!

OH, GOODIE! GOODIE! LITTLE BOYS TO DANCE WITH US!

As EVENING SHADOWS FALL!

WELL, WELL, WELL! WHAT A GALA AFTERNOON!

HEY! YOU KIDS SHOULD BE TIRED AFTER TWO HOURS OF DANCING! AREN'T YOU GOING HOME?

NOT YET, UNCA DONALD!

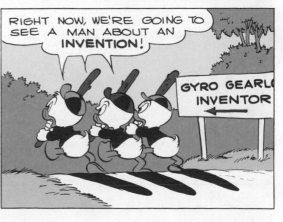

RIGHT NOW, WE'RE GOING TO SEE A MAN ABOUT AN INVENTION!

GYRO GEARLO INVENTOR

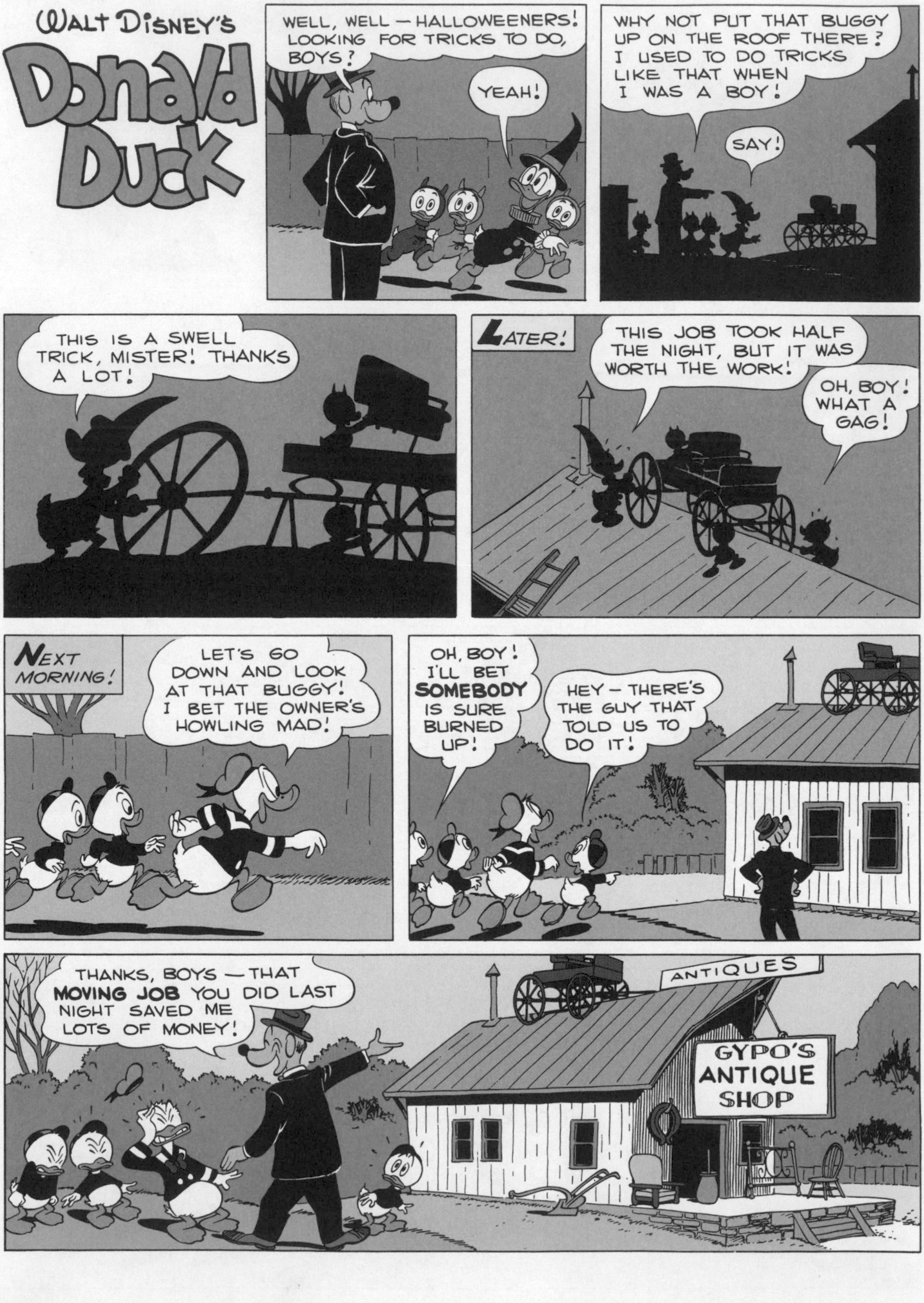
WALT DISNEY'S
Donald Duck
WELL, WELL — HALLOWEENERS! LOOKING FOR TRICKS TO DO, BOYS?
YEAH!
WHY NOT PUT THAT BUGGY UP ON THE ROOF THERE? I USED TO DO TRICKS LIKE THAT WHEN I WAS A BOY!
SAY!
THIS IS A SWELL TRICK, MISTER! THANKS A LOT!
LATER!
THIS JOB TOOK HALF THE NIGHT, BUT IT WAS WORTH THE WORK!
OH, BOY! WHAT A GAG!
NEXT MORNING!
LET'S GO DOWN AND LOOK AT THAT BUGGY! I BET THE OWNER'S HOWLING MAD!
OH, BOY! I'LL BET SOMEBODY IS SURE BURNED UP!
HEY — THERE'S THE GUY THAT TOLD US TO DO IT!
THANKS, BOYS — THAT MOVING JOB YOU DID LAST NIGHT SAVED ME LOTS OF MONEY!
ANTIQUES
GYPO'S ANTIQUE SHOP

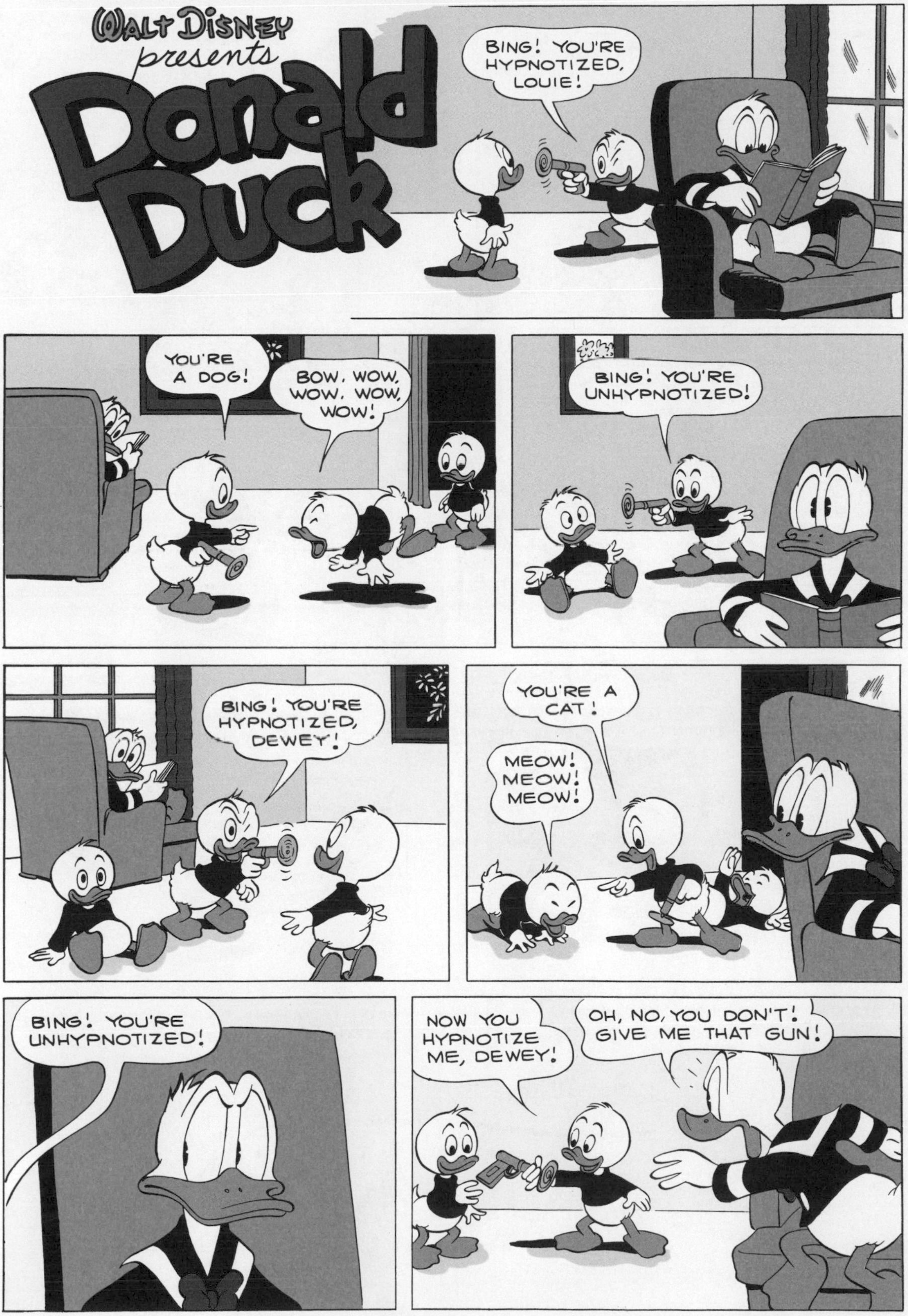
WALT DISNEY
presents
Donald Duck
BING! YOU'RE HYPNOTIZED, LOUIE!
YOU'RE A DOG!
BOW, WOW, WOW, WOW, WOW!
BING! YOU'RE UNHYPNOTIZED!
BING! YOU'RE HYPNOTIZED, DEWEY!
YOU'RE A CAT!
MEOW! MEOW! MEOW!
BING! YOU'RE UNHYPNOTIZED!
NOW YOU HYPNOTIZE ME, DEWEY!
OH, NO, YOU DON'T! GIVE ME THAT GUN!

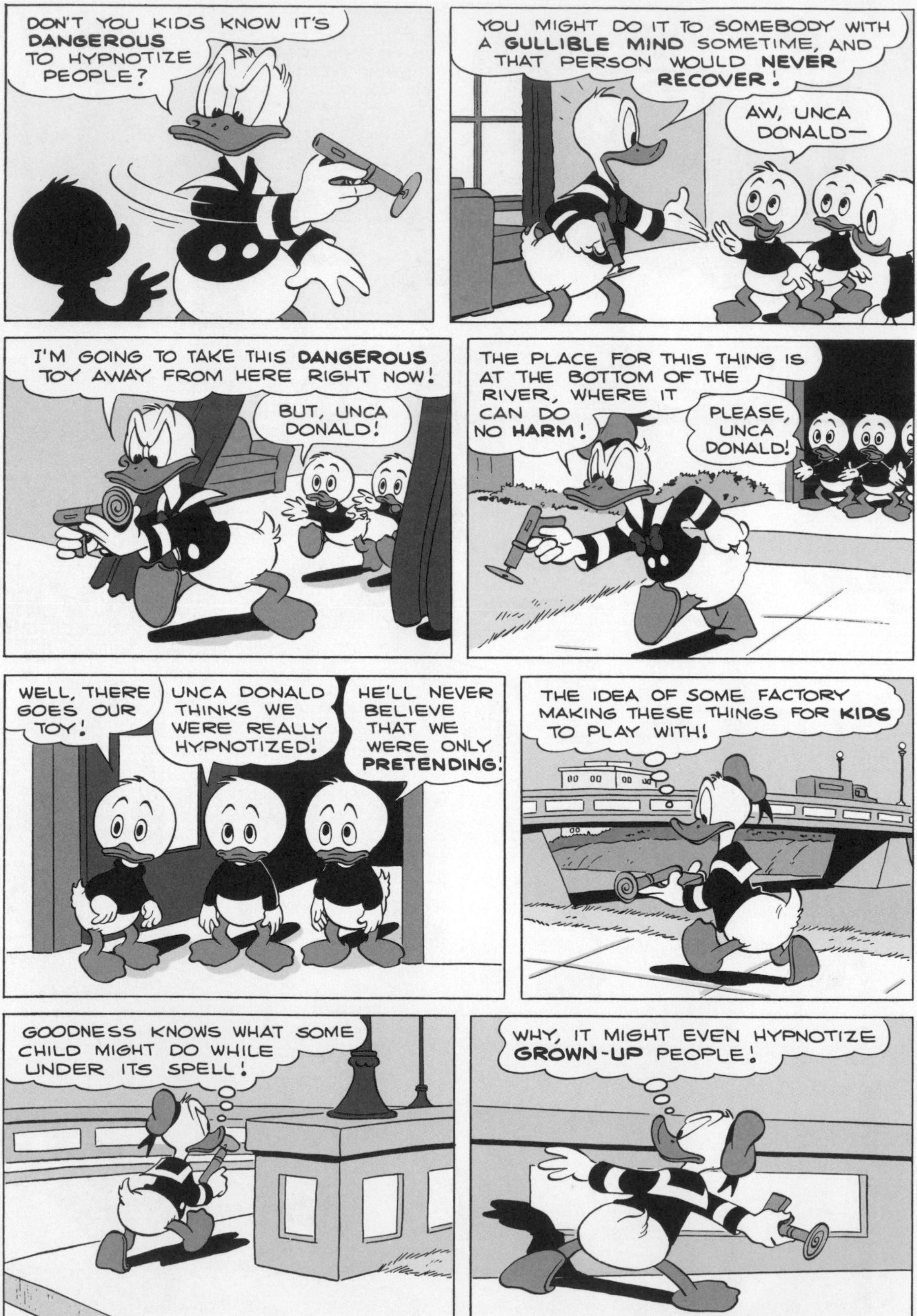
DON'T YOU KIDS KNOW IT'S **DANGEROUS** TO HYPNOTIZE PEOPLE?
YOU MIGHT DO IT TO SOMEBODY WITH A **GULLIBLE MIND** SOMETIME, AND THAT PERSON WOULD **NEVER RECOVER**!
AW, UNCA DONALD—
I'M GOING TO TAKE THIS **DANGEROUS** TOY AWAY FROM HERE RIGHT NOW!
BUT, UNCA DONALD!
THE PLACE FOR THIS THING IS AT THE BOTTOM OF THE RIVER, WHERE IT CAN DO NO **HARM**!
PLEASE, UNCA DONALD!
WELL, THERE GOES OUR TOY!
UNCA DONALD THINKS WE WERE REALLY HYPNOTIZED!
HE'LL NEVER BELIEVE THAT WE WERE ONLY **PRETENDING**!
THE IDEA OF SOME FACTORY MAKING THESE THINGS FOR **KIDS** TO PLAY WITH!
GOODNESS KNOWS WHAT SOME CHILD MIGHT DO WHILE UNDER ITS SPELL!
WHY, IT MIGHT EVEN HYPNOTIZE **GROWN-UP** PEOPLE!

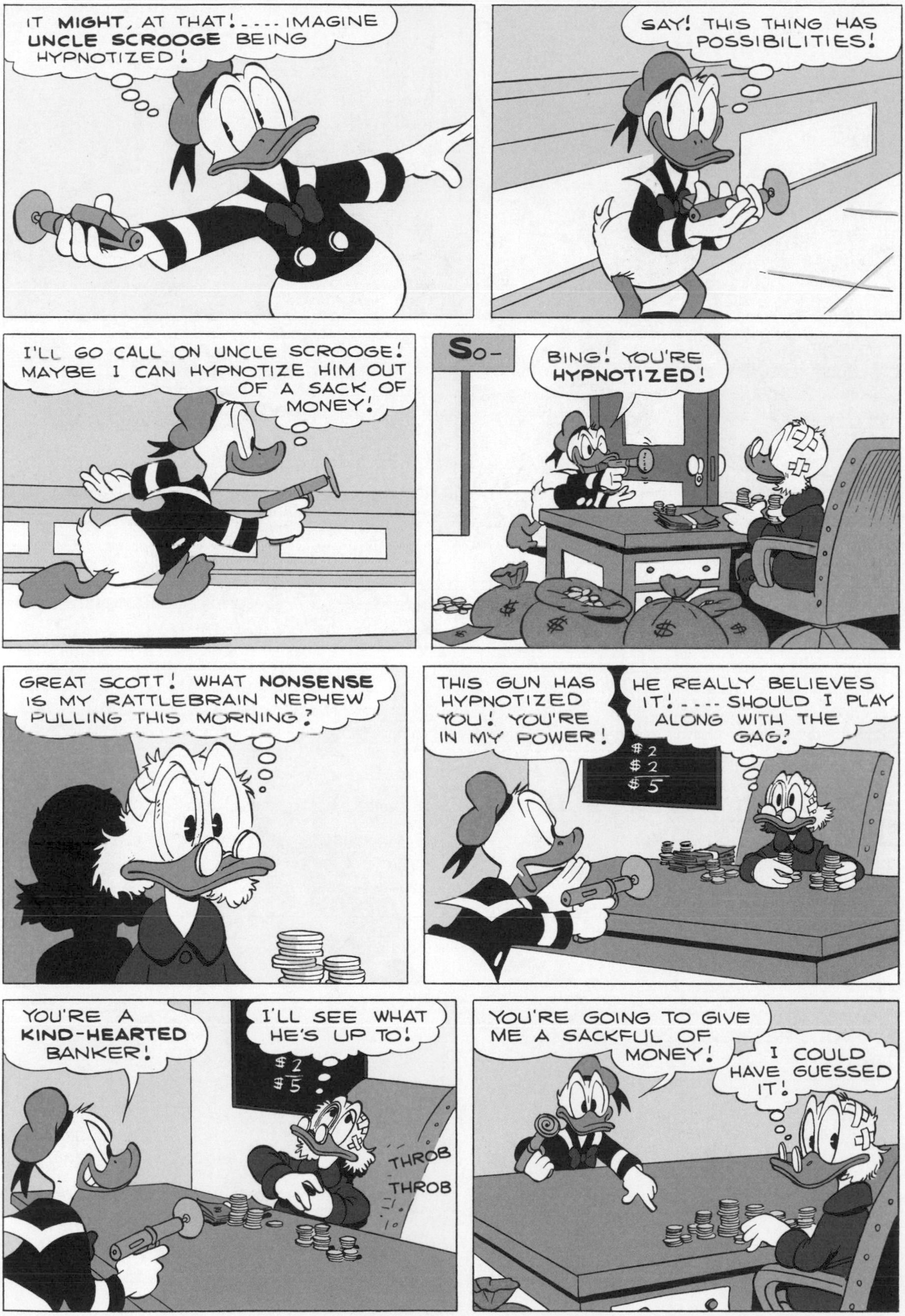
IT MIGHT, AT THAT! ---- IMAGINE UNCLE SCROOGE BEING HYPNOTIZED!
SAY! THIS THING HAS POSSIBILITIES!
I'LL GO CALL ON UNCLE SCROOGE! MAYBE I CAN HYPNOTIZE HIM OUT OF A SACK OF MONEY!
SO-
BING! YOU'RE HYPNOTIZED!
GREAT SCOTT! WHAT NONSENSE IS MY RATTLEBRAIN NEPHEW PULLING THIS MORNING?
THIS GUN HAS HYPNOTIZED YOU! YOU'RE IN MY POWER!
HE REALLY BELIEVES IT! ---- SHOULD I PLAY ALONG WITH THE GAG?
YOU'RE A KIND-HEARTED BANKER!
I'LL SEE WHAT HE'S UP TO!
THROB
THROB
YOU'RE GOING TO GIVE ME A SACKFUL OF MONEY!
I COULD HAVE GUESSED IT!

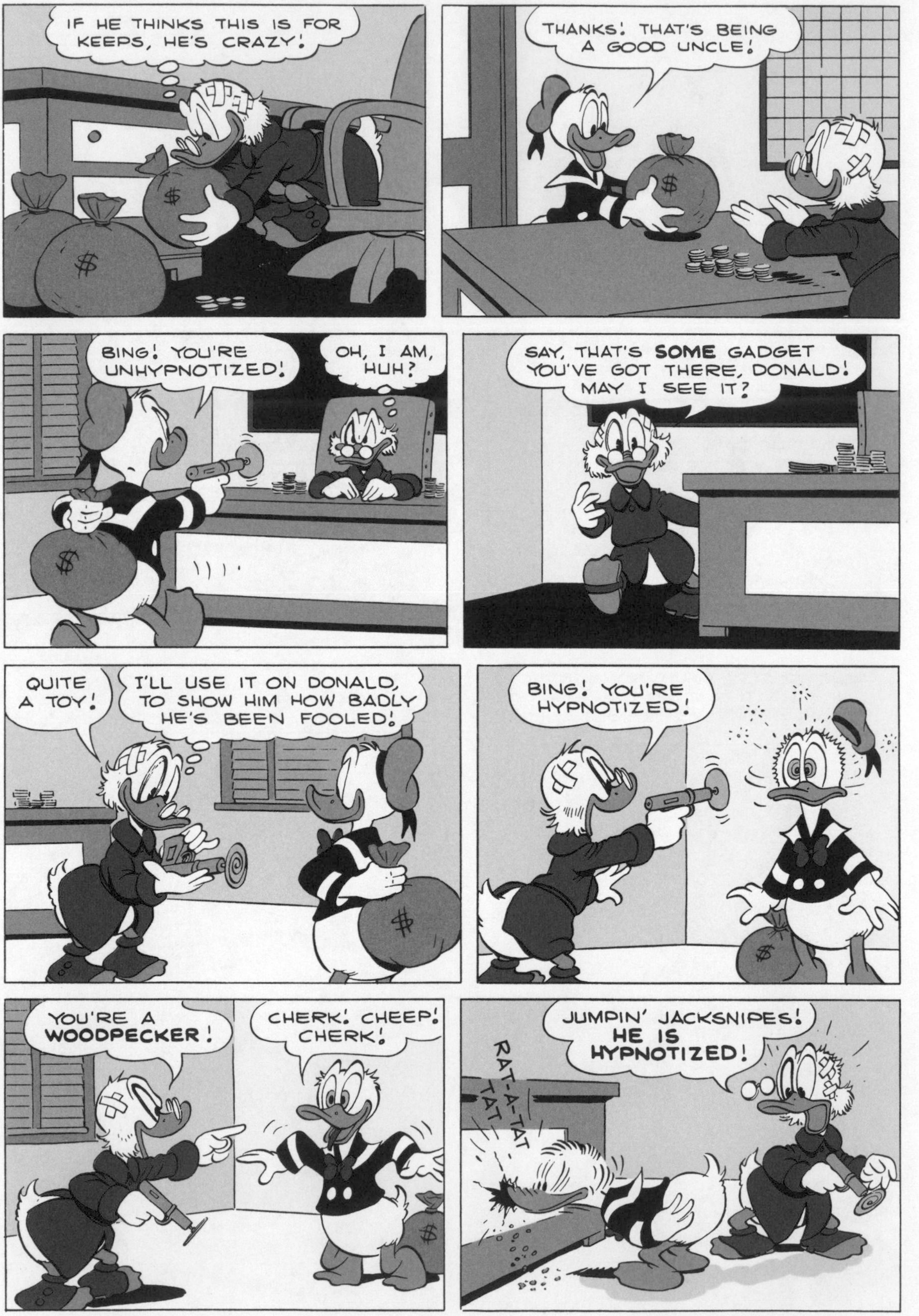
IF HE THINKS THIS IS FOR KEEPS, HE'S CRAZY!
THANKS! THAT'S BEING A GOOD UNCLE!
BING! YOU'RE UNHYPNOTIZED!
OH, I AM, HUH?
SAY, THAT'S SOME GADGET YOU'VE GOT THERE, DONALD! MAY I SEE IT?
QUITE A TOY!
I'LL USE IT ON DONALD, TO SHOW HIM HOW BADLY HE'S BEEN FOOLED!
BING! YOU'RE HYPNOTIZED!
YOU'RE A WOODPECKER!
CHERK! CHEEP! CHERK!
JUMPIN' JACKSNIPES! HE IS HYPNOTIZED!
RAT-A-TAT TAT-A-TAT

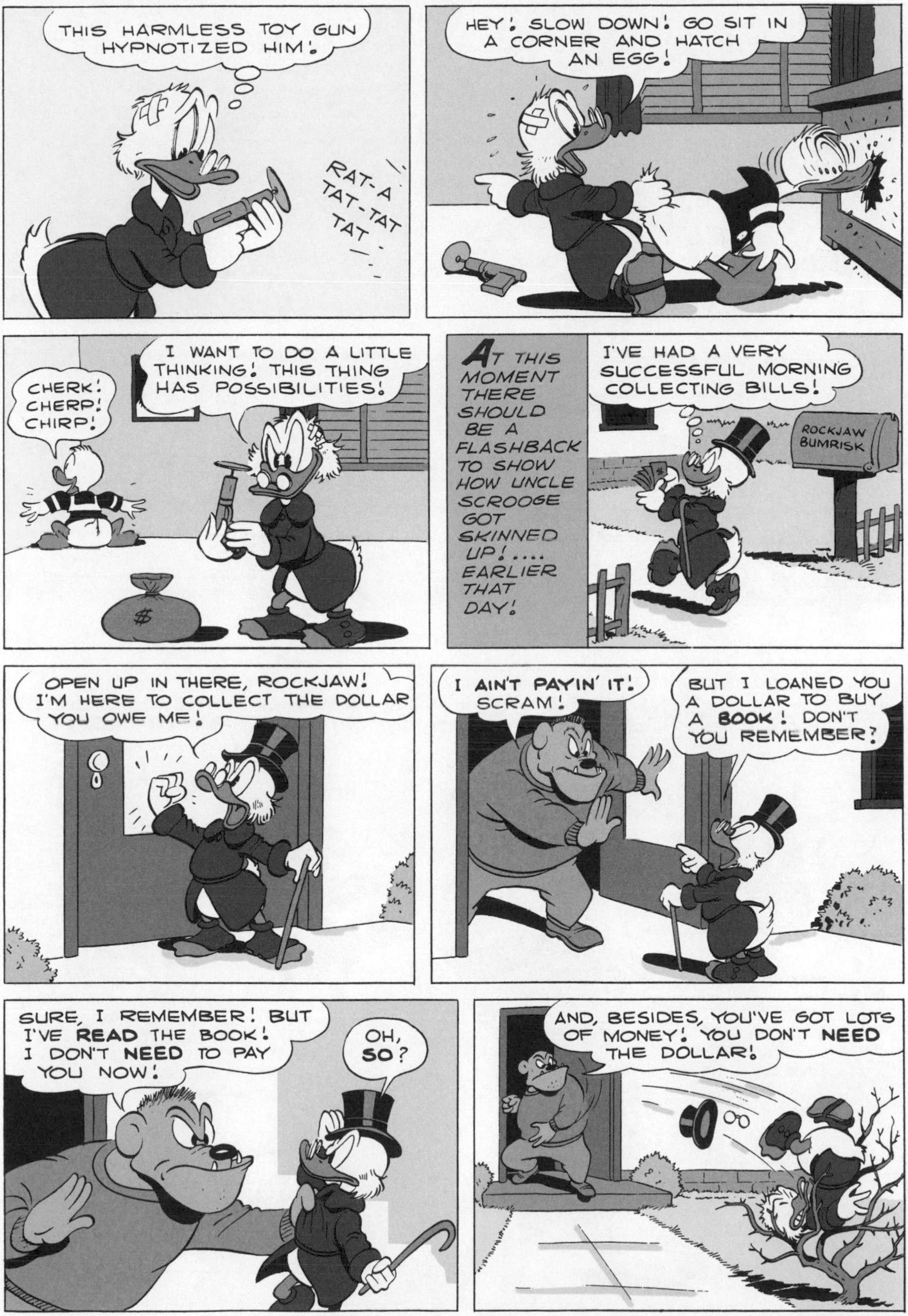
THIS HARMLESS TOY GUN HYPNOTIZED HIM!
RAT-A TAT-TAT TAT
HEY! SLOW DOWN! GO SIT IN A CORNER AND HATCH AN EGG!
CHERK! CHERP! CHIRP!
I WANT TO DO A LITTLE THINKING! THIS THING HAS POSSIBILITIES!
AT THIS MOMENT THERE SHOULD BE A FLASHBACK TO SHOW HOW UNCLE SCROOGE GOT SKINNED UP!.... EARLIER THAT DAY!
I'VE HAD A VERY SUCCESSFUL MORNING COLLECTING BILLS!
ROCKJAW BUMRISK
OPEN UP IN THERE, ROCKJAW! I'M HERE TO COLLECT THE DOLLAR YOU OWE ME!
I AIN'T PAYIN' IT! SCRAM!
BUT I LOANED YOU A DOLLAR TO BUY A BOOK! DON'T YOU REMEMBER?
SURE, I REMEMBER! BUT I'VE READ THE BOOK! I DON'T NEED TO PAY YOU NOW!
OH, SO?
AND, BESIDES, YOU'VE GOT LOTS OF MONEY! YOU DON'T NEED THE DOLLAR!

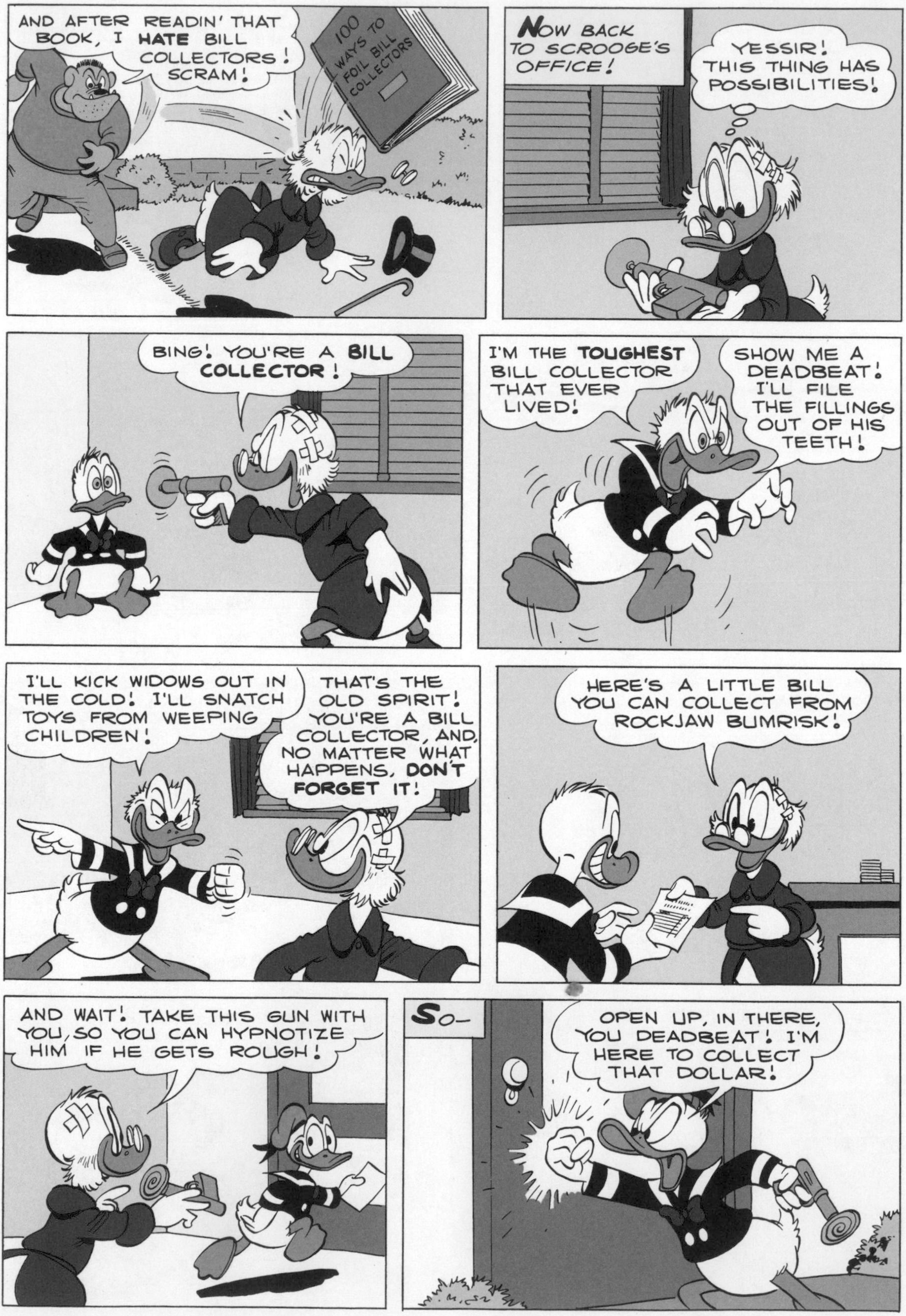
AND AFTER READIN' THAT BOOK, I HATE BILL COLLECTORS! SCRAM!
100 WAYS TO FOIL BILL COLLECTORS
NOW BACK TO SCROOGE'S OFFICE!
YESSIR! THIS THING HAS POSSIBILITIES!
BING! YOU'RE A BILL COLLECTOR!
I'M THE TOUGHEST BILL COLLECTOR THAT EVER LIVED!
SHOW ME A DEADBEAT! I'LL FILE THE FILLINGS OUT OF HIS TEETH!
I'LL KICK WIDOWS OUT IN THE COLD! I'LL SNATCH TOYS FROM WEEPING CHILDREN!
THAT'S THE OLD SPIRIT! YOU'RE A BILL COLLECTOR, AND, NO MATTER WHAT HAPPENS, DON'T FORGET IT!
HERE'S A LITTLE BILL YOU CAN COLLECT FROM ROCKJAW BUMRISK!
AND WAIT! TAKE THIS GUN WITH YOU, SO YOU CAN HYPNOTIZE HIM IF HE GETS ROUGH!
SO—
OPEN UP, IN THERE, YOU DEADBEAT! I'M HERE TO COLLECT THAT DOLLAR!

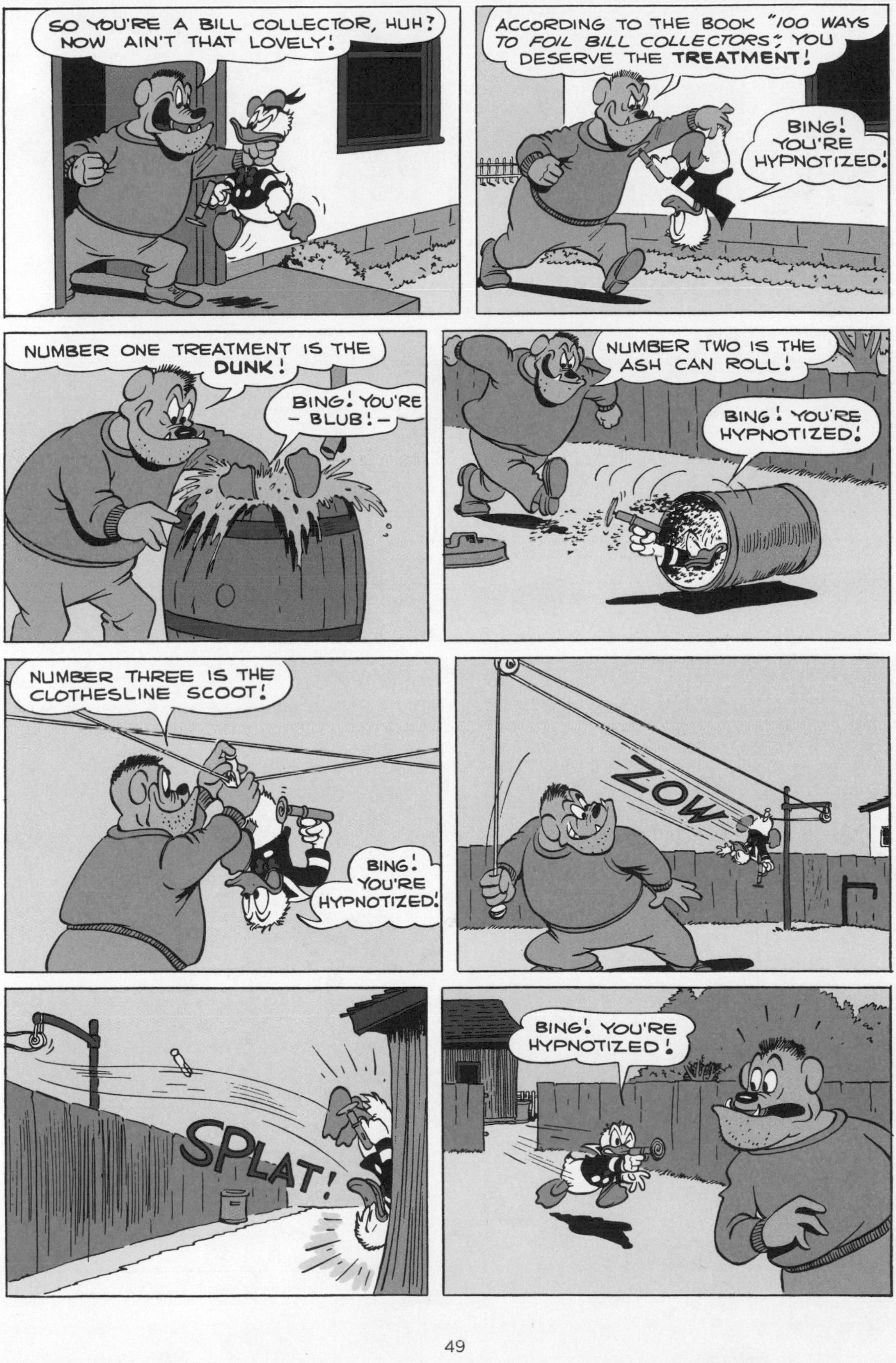
SO YOU'RE A BILL COLLECTOR, HUH? NOW AIN'T THAT LOVELY!
ACCORDING TO THE BOOK "100 WAYS TO FOIL BILL COLLECTORS," YOU DESERVE THE TREATMENT!
BING! YOU'RE HYPNOTIZED!
NUMBER ONE TREATMENT IS THE DUNK!
BING! YOU'RE - BLUB! -
NUMBER TWO IS THE ASH CAN ROLL!
BING! YOU'RE HYPNOTIZED!
NUMBER THREE IS THE CLOTHESLINE SCOOT!
BING! YOU'RE HYPNOTIZED!
ZOW
SPLAT!
BING! YOU'RE HYPNOTIZED!

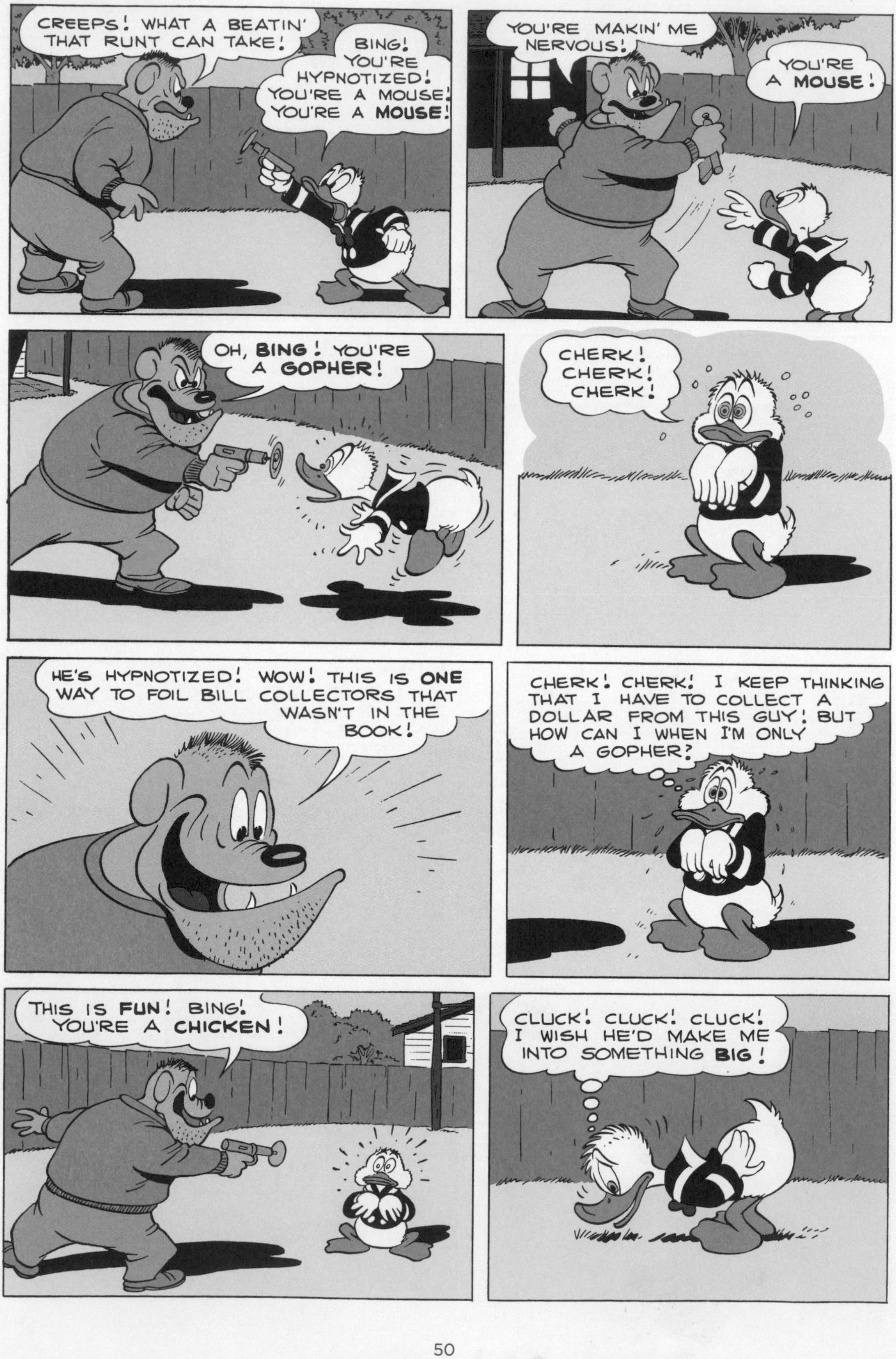

CREEPS! WHAT A BEATIN' THAT RUNT CAN TAKE!
BING! YOU'RE HYPNOTIZED! YOU'RE A MOUSE! YOU'RE A **MOUSE**!
YOU'RE MAKIN' ME NERVOUS!
YOU'RE A **MOUSE**!
OH, **BING**! YOU'RE A **GOPHER**!
CHERK! CHERK! CHERK!
HE'S HYPNOTIZED! WOW! THIS IS **ONE** WAY TO FOIL BILL COLLECTORS THAT WASN'T IN THE BOOK!
CHERK! CHERK! I KEEP THINKING THAT I HAVE TO COLLECT A DOLLAR FROM THIS GUY! BUT HOW CAN I WHEN I'M ONLY A GOPHER?
THIS IS **FUN**! BING! YOU'RE A **CHICKEN**!
CLUCK! CLUCK! CLUCK! I WISH HE'D MAKE ME INTO SOMETHING **BIG**!

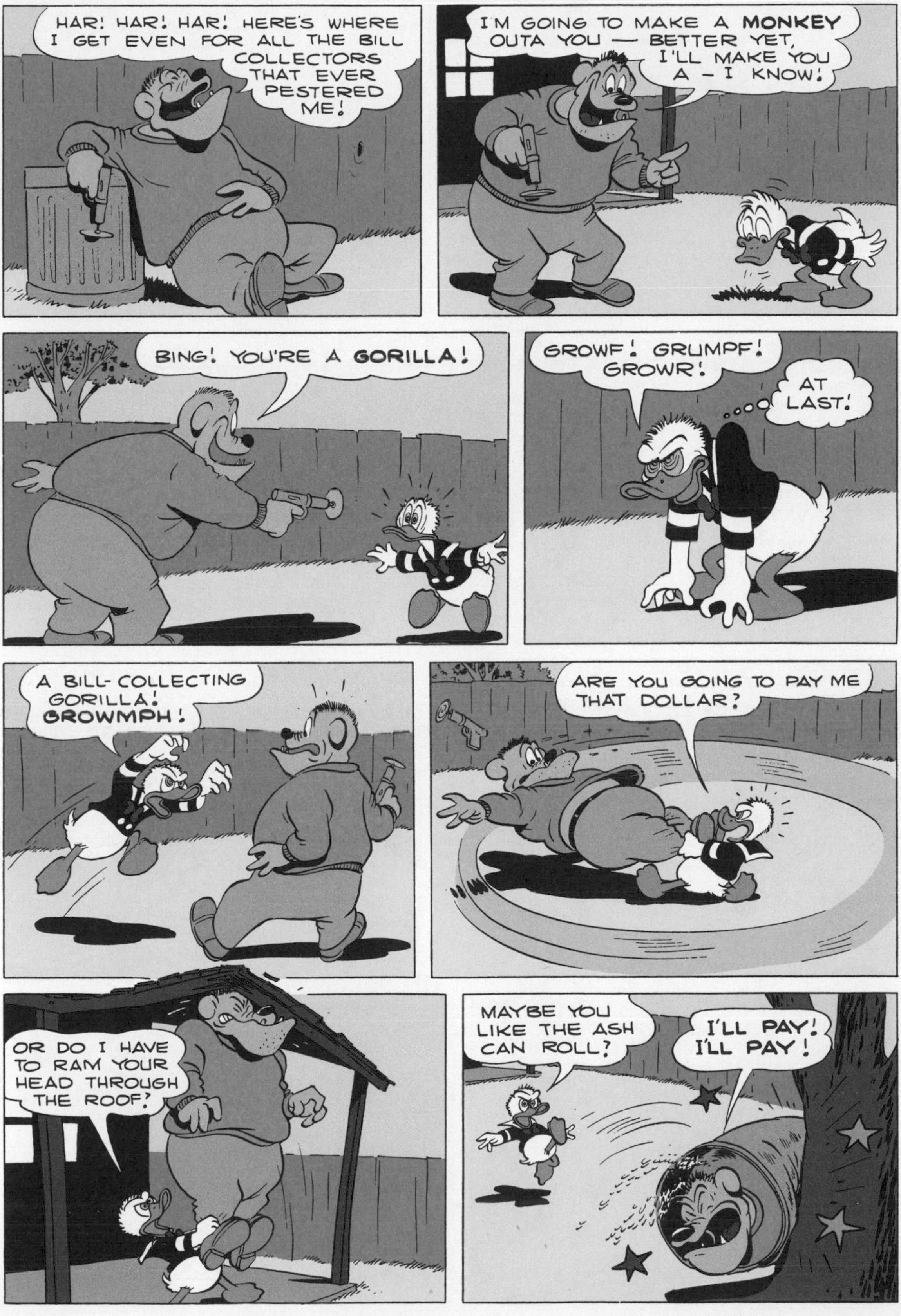
HAR! HAR! HAR! HERE'S WHERE I GET EVEN FOR ALL THE BILL COLLECTORS THAT EVER PESTERED ME!
I'M GOING TO MAKE A MONKEY OUTA YOU — BETTER YET, I'LL MAKE YOU A – I KNOW!
BING! YOU'RE A GORILLA!
GROWF! GRUMPF! GROWR!
AT LAST!
A BILL-COLLECTING GORILLA! GROWMPH!
ARE YOU GOING TO PAY ME THAT DOLLAR?
OR DO I HAVE TO RAM YOUR HEAD THROUGH THE ROOF?
MAYBE YOU LIKE THE ASH CAN ROLL?
I'LL PAY! I'LL PAY!

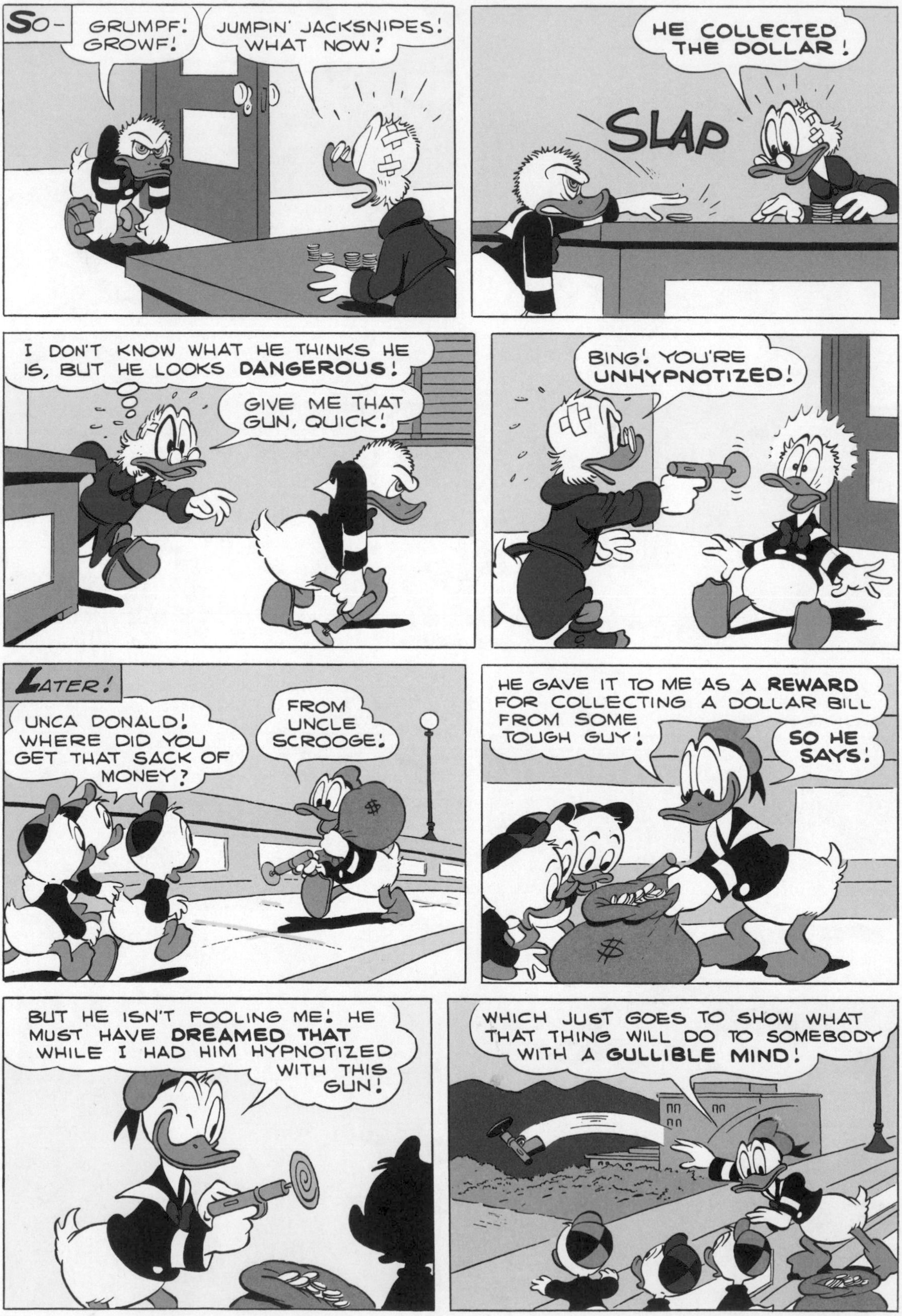
SO-
GRUMPF! GROWF!
JUMPIN' JACKSNIPES! WHAT NOW?
HE COLLECTED THE DOLLAR!
SLAP
I DON'T KNOW WHAT HE THINKS HE IS, BUT HE LOOKS DANGEROUS!
GIVE ME THAT GUN, QUICK!
BING! YOU'RE UNHYPNOTIZED!
LATER!
UNCA DONALD! WHERE DID YOU GET THAT SACK OF MONEY?
FROM UNCLE SCROOGE!
HE GAVE IT TO ME AS A REWARD FOR COLLECTING A DOLLAR BILL FROM SOME TOUGH GUY!
SO HE SAYS!
BUT HE ISN'T FOOLING ME! HE MUST HAVE DREAMED THAT WHILE I HAD HIM HYPNOTIZED WITH THIS GUN!
WHICH JUST GOES TO SHOW WHAT THAT THING WILL DO TO SOMEBODY WITH A GULLIBLE MIND!

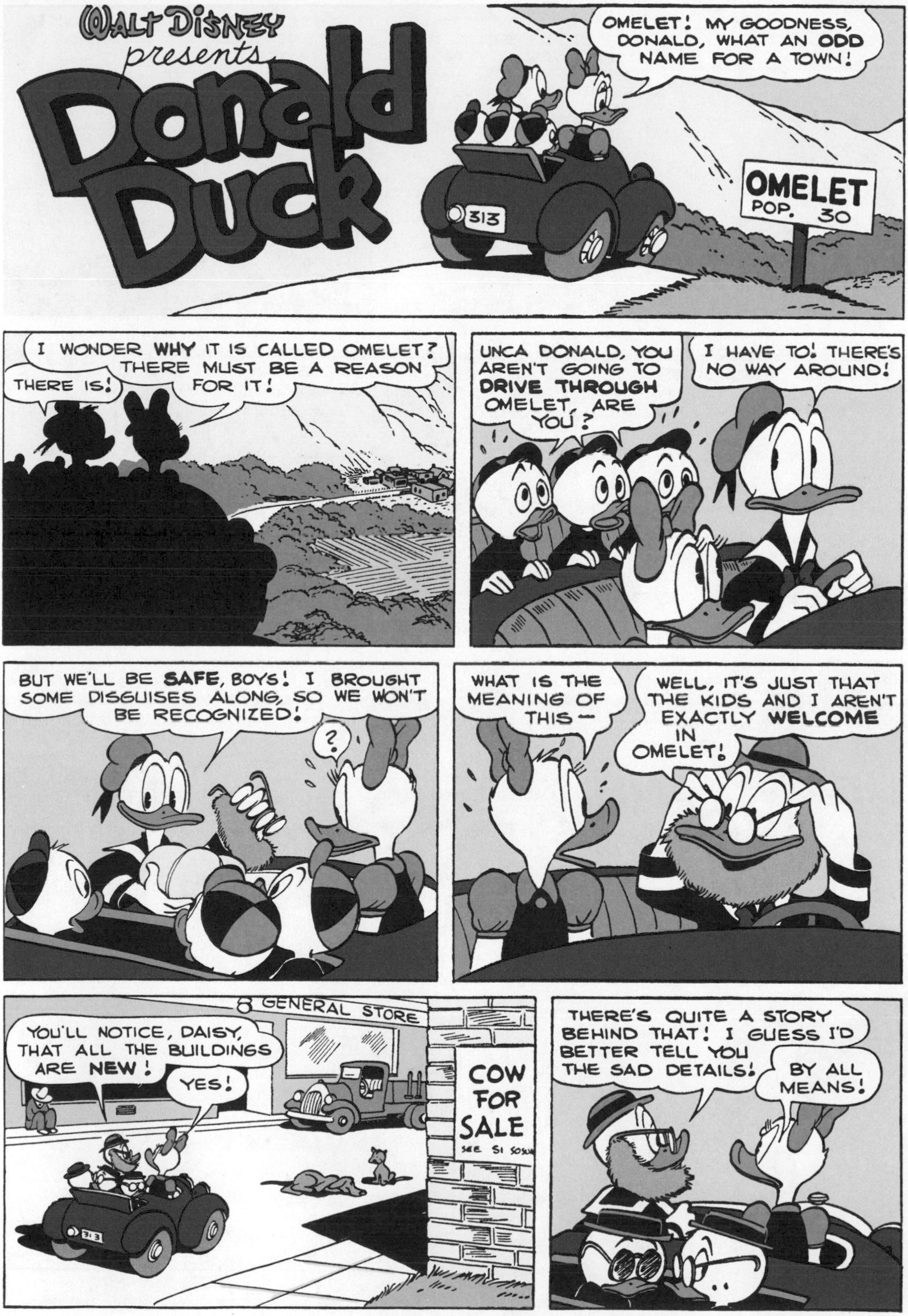

WALT DISNEY presents
Donald Duck
OMELET! MY GOODNESS, DONALD, WHAT AN ODD NAME FOR A TOWN!
OMELET POP. 30
313
I WONDER WHY IT IS CALLED OMELET? THERE MUST BE A REASON FOR IT!
THERE IS!
UNCA DONALD, YOU AREN'T GOING TO DRIVE THROUGH OMELET, ARE YOU?
I HAVE TO! THERE'S NO WAY AROUND!
BUT WE'LL BE SAFE, BOYS! I BROUGHT SOME DISGUISES ALONG, SO WE WON'T BE RECOGNIZED!
?
WHAT IS THE MEANING OF THIS—
WELL, IT'S JUST THAT THE KIDS AND I AREN'T EXACTLY WELCOME IN OMELET!
GENERAL STORE
YOU'LL NOTICE, DAISY, THAT ALL THE BUILDINGS ARE NEW!
YES!
COW FOR SALE
SEE SI SOSUA
313
THERE'S QUITE A STORY BEHIND THAT! I GUESS I'D BETTER TELL YOU THE SAD DETAILS!
BY ALL MEANS!

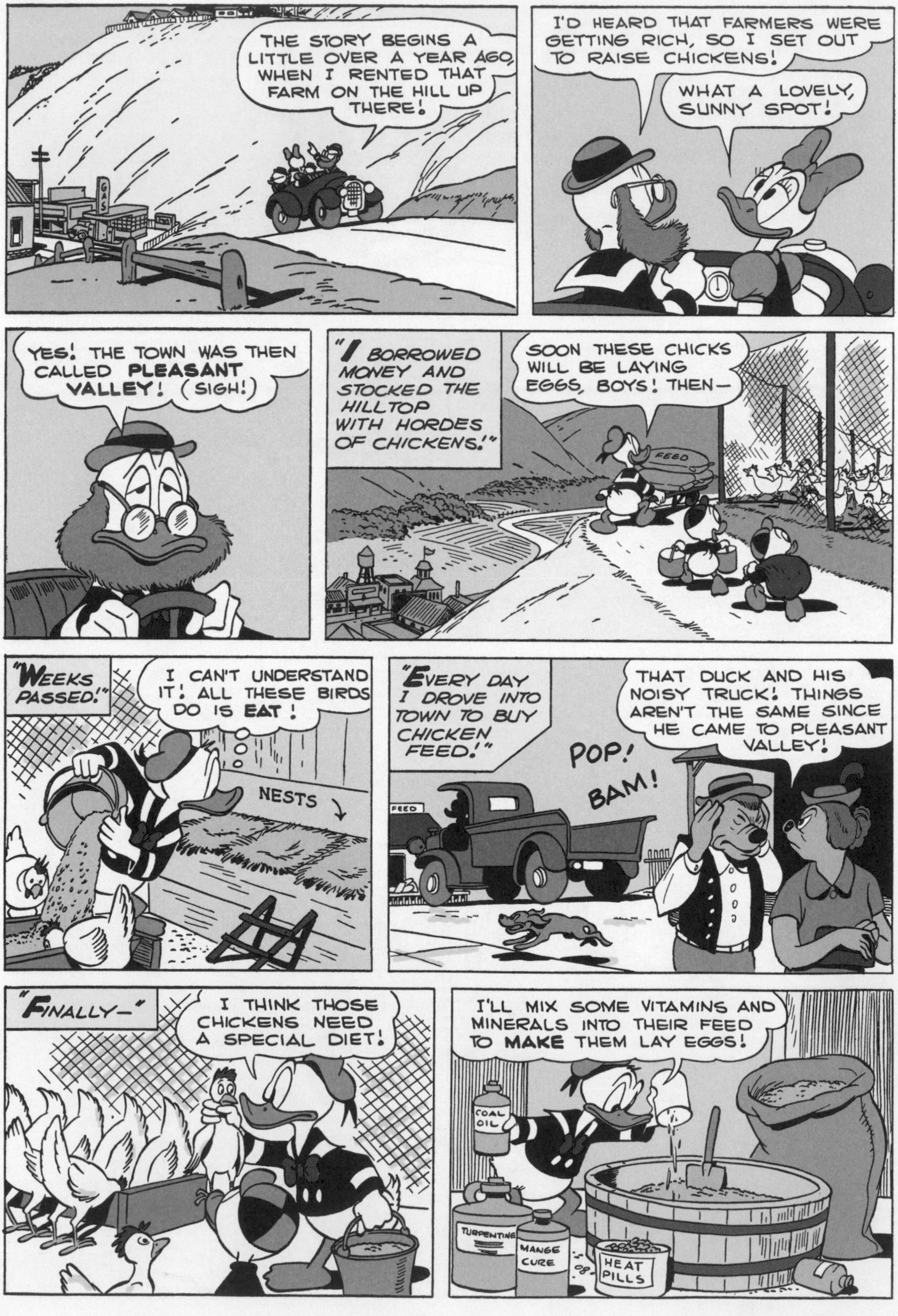
THE STORY BEGINS A LITTLE OVER A YEAR AGO, WHEN I RENTED THAT FARM ON THE HILL UP THERE!
GAS
I'D HEARD THAT FARMERS WERE GETTING RICH, SO I SET OUT TO RAISE CHICKENS!
WHAT A LOVELY, SUNNY SPOT!
YES! THE TOWN WAS THEN CALLED PLEASANT VALLEY! (SIGH!)
"I BORROWED MONEY AND STOCKED THE HILLTOP WITH HORDES OF CHICKENS!"
SOON THESE CHICKS WILL BE LAYING EGGS, BOYS! THEN—
FEED
"WEEKS PASSED!"
I CAN'T UNDERSTAND IT! ALL THESE BIRDS DO IS EAT!
NESTS
"EVERY DAY I DROVE INTO TOWN TO BUY CHICKEN FEED!"
THAT DUCK AND HIS NOISY TRUCK! THINGS AREN'T THE SAME SINCE HE CAME TO PLEASANT VALLEY!
POP!
BAM!
FEED
"FINALLY—"
I THINK THOSE CHICKENS NEED A SPECIAL DIET!
I'LL MIX SOME VITAMINS AND MINERALS INTO THEIR FEED TO MAKE THEM LAY EGGS!
COAL OIL
TURPENTINE
MANGE CURE
HEAT PILLS

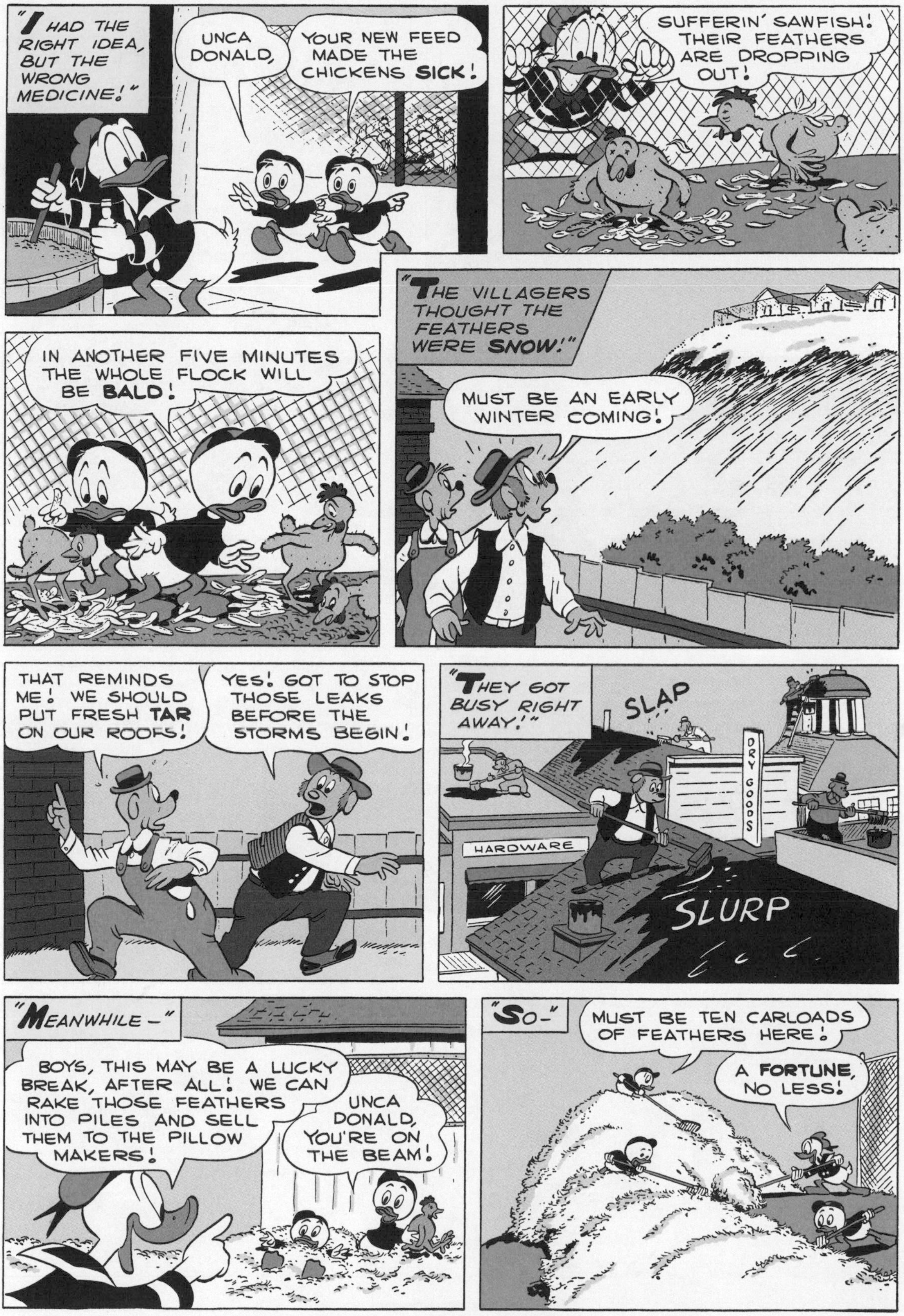
"I HAD THE RIGHT IDEA, BUT THE WRONG MEDICINE!"
UNCA DONALD,
YOUR NEW FEED MADE THE CHICKENS SICK!
SUFFERIN' SAWFISH! THEIR FEATHERS ARE DROPPING OUT!
IN ANOTHER FIVE MINUTES THE WHOLE FLOCK WILL BE BALD!
"THE VILLAGERS THOUGHT THE FEATHERS WERE SNOW!"
MUST BE AN EARLY WINTER COMING!
THAT REMINDS ME! WE SHOULD PUT FRESH TAR ON OUR ROOFS!
YES! GOT TO STOP THOSE LEAKS BEFORE THE STORMS BEGIN!
"THEY GOT BUSY RIGHT AWAY!"
SLAP
DRY GOODS
HARDWARE
SLURP
"MEANWHILE-"
BOYS, THIS MAY BE A LUCKY BREAK, AFTER ALL! WE CAN RAKE THOSE FEATHERS INTO PILES AND SELL THEM TO THE PILLOW MAKERS!
UNCA DONALD, YOU'RE ON THE BEAM!
"SO-"
MUST BE TEN CARLOADS OF FEATHERS HERE!
A FORTUNE, NO LESS!

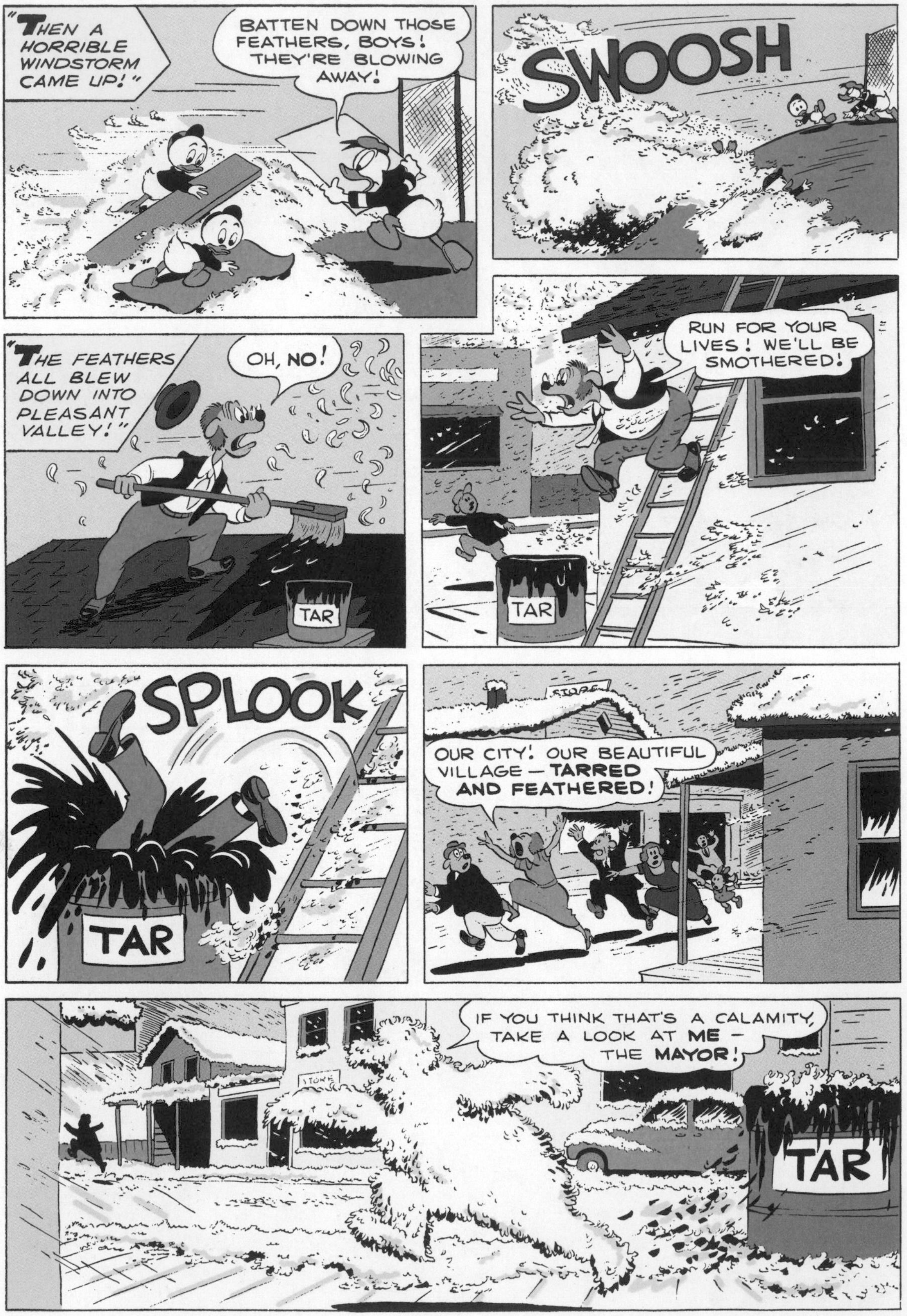
"THEN A HORRIBLE WINDSTORM CAME UP!"
BATTEN DOWN THOSE FEATHERS, BOYS! THEY'RE BLOWING AWAY!
SWOOSH
"THE FEATHERS ALL BLEW DOWN INTO PLEASANT VALLEY!"
OH, NO!
TAR
RUN FOR YOUR LIVES! WE'LL BE SMOTHERED!
TAR
SPLOOK
TAR
OUR CITY! OUR BEAUTIFUL VILLAGE — TARRED AND FEATHERED!
IF YOU THINK THAT'S A CALAMITY, TAKE A LOOK AT ME — THE MAYOR!
STORE
TAR

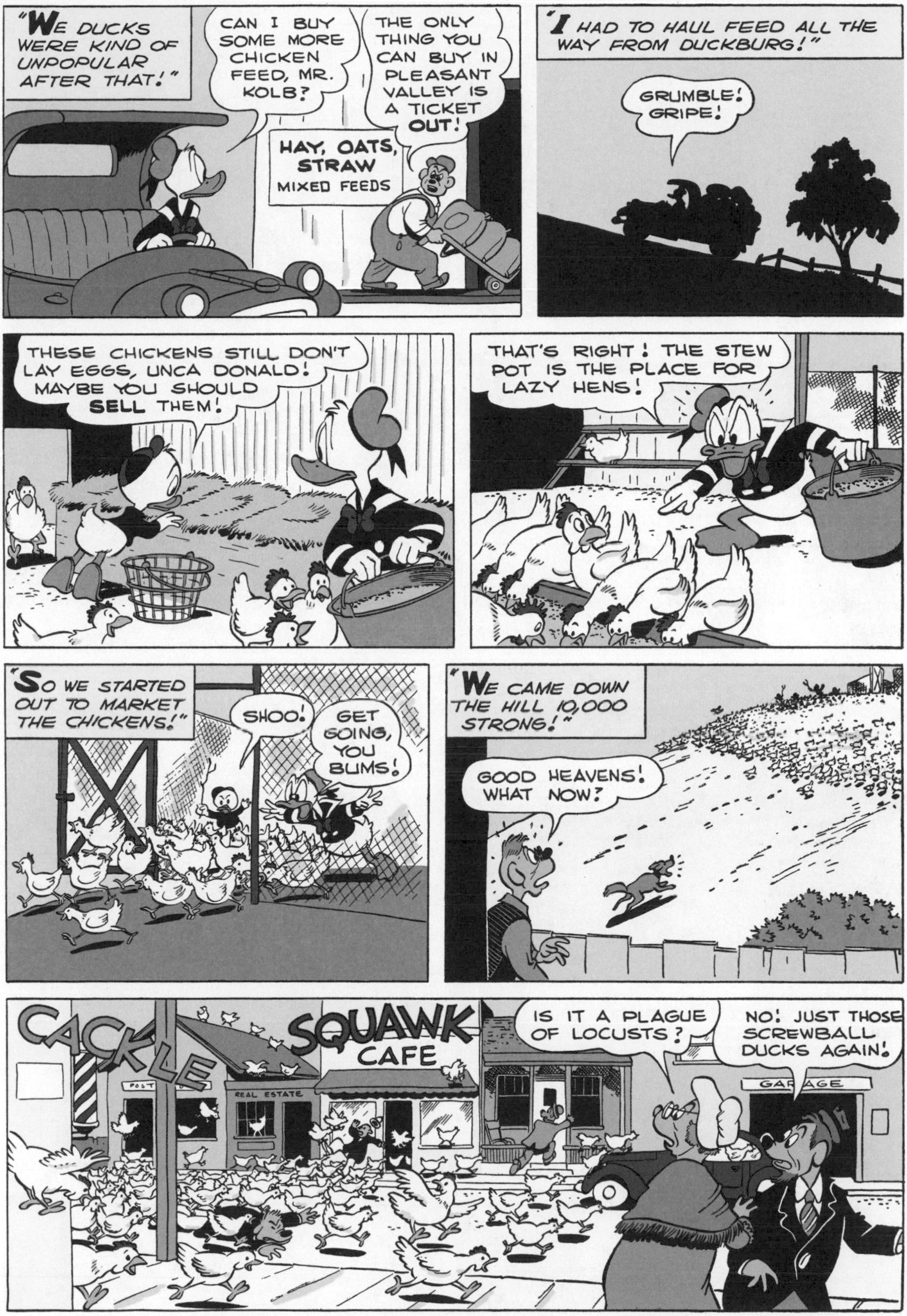
"WE DUCKS WERE KIND OF UNPOPULAR AFTER THAT!"
CAN I BUY SOME MORE CHICKEN FEED, MR. KOLB?
THE ONLY THING YOU CAN BUY IN PLEASANT VALLEY IS A TICKET OUT!
HAY, OATS, STRAW MIXED FEEDS
"I HAD TO HAUL FEED ALL THE WAY FROM DUCKBURG!"
GRUMBLE! GRIPE!
THESE CHICKENS STILL DON'T LAY EGGS, UNCA DONALD! MAYBE YOU SHOULD SELL THEM!
THAT'S RIGHT! THE STEW POT IS THE PLACE FOR LAZY HENS!
"SO WE STARTED OUT TO MARKET THE CHICKENS!"
SHOO!
GET GOING, YOU BUMS!
"WE CAME DOWN THE HILL 10,000 STRONG!"
GOOD HEAVENS! WHAT NOW?
CACKLE
SQUAWK CAFE
POST
REAL ESTATE
GARAGE
IS IT A PLAGUE OF LOCUSTS?
NO! JUST THOSE SCREWBALL DUCKS AGAIN!

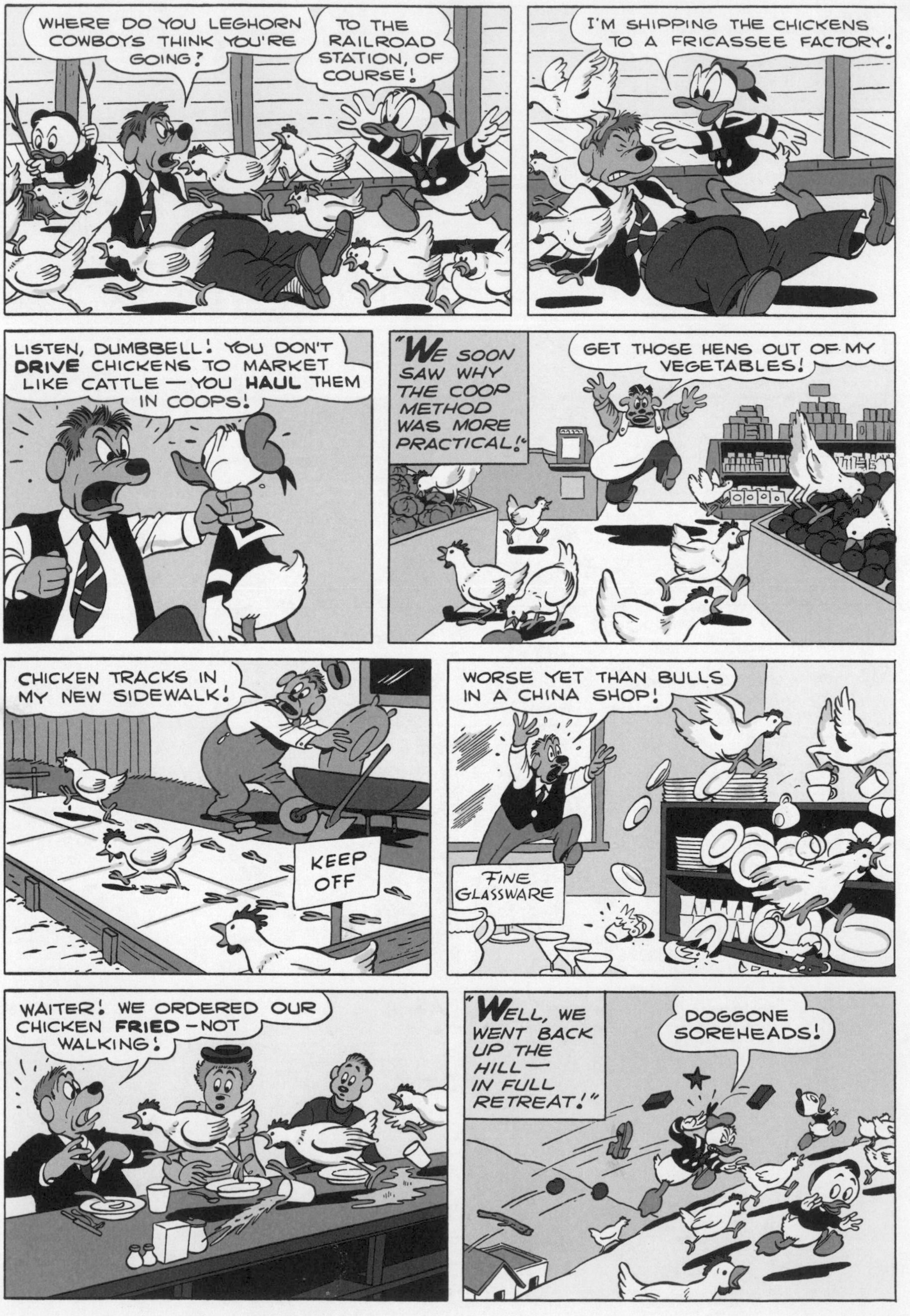
WHERE DO YOU LEGHORN COWBOYS THINK YOU'RE GOING?
TO THE RAILROAD STATION, OF COURSE!
I'M SHIPPING THE CHICKENS TO A FRICASSEE FACTORY!
LISTEN, DUMBBELL! YOU DON'T DRIVE CHICKENS TO MARKET LIKE CATTLE — YOU HAUL THEM IN COOPS!
"WE SOON SAW WHY THE COOP METHOD WAS MORE PRACTICAL!"
GET THOSE HENS OUT OF MY VEGETABLES!
CHICKEN TRACKS IN MY NEW SIDEWALK!
KEEP OFF
WORSE YET THAN BULLS IN A CHINA SHOP!
FINE GLASSWARE
WAITER! WE ORDERED OUR CHICKEN FRIED — NOT WALKING!
"WELL, WE WENT BACK UP THE HILL — IN FULL RETREAT!"
DOGGONE SOREHEADS!

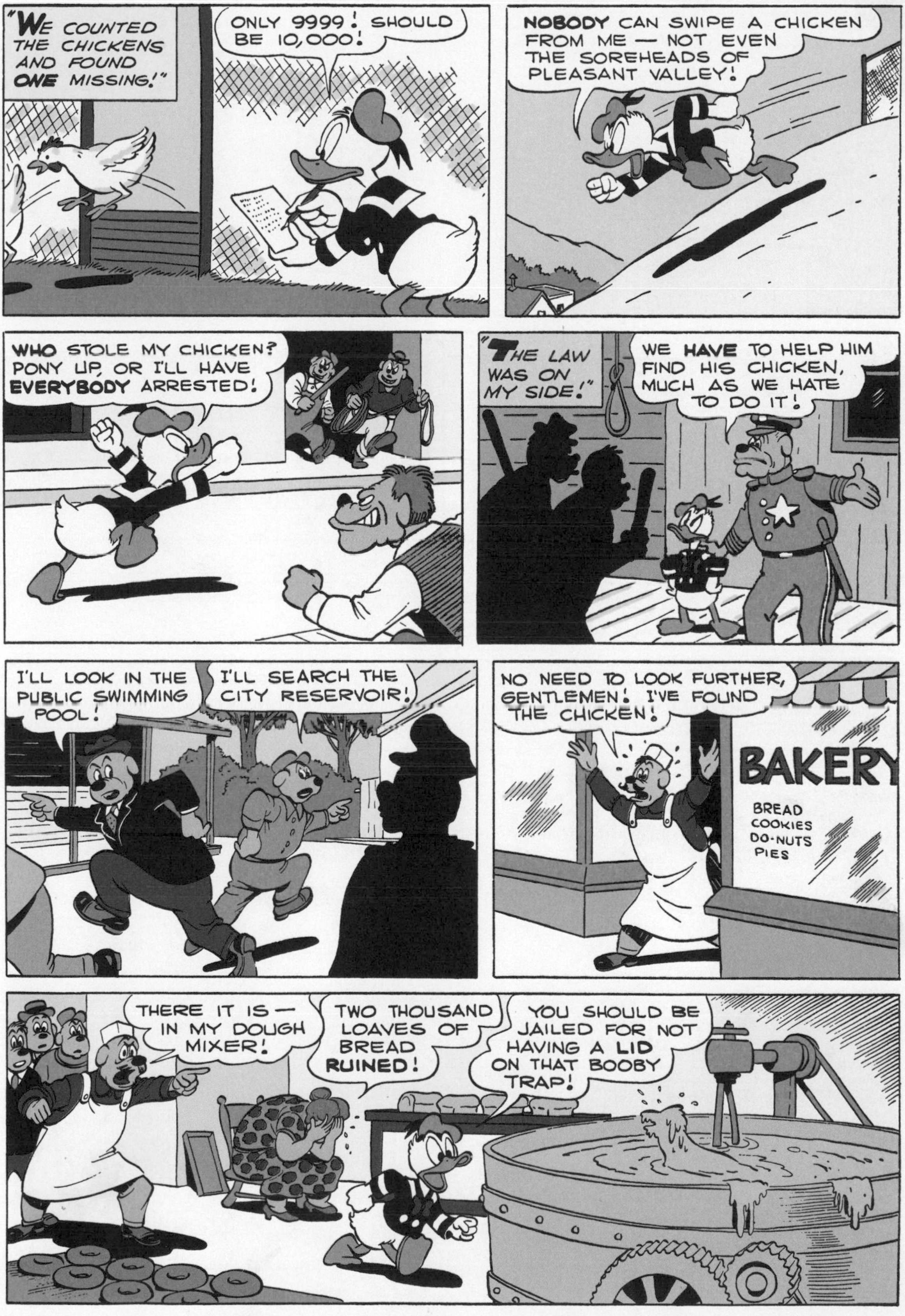
"WE COUNTED THE CHICKENS AND FOUND ONE MISSING!"
ONLY 9999! SHOULD BE 10,000!
NOBODY CAN SWIPE A CHICKEN FROM ME — NOT EVEN THE SOREHEADS OF PLEASANT VALLEY!
WHO STOLE MY CHICKEN? PONY UP, OR I'LL HAVE EVERYBODY ARRESTED!
"THE LAW WAS ON MY SIDE!"
WE HAVE TO HELP HIM FIND HIS CHICKEN, MUCH AS WE HATE TO DO IT!
I'LL LOOK IN THE PUBLIC SWIMMING POOL!
I'LL SEARCH THE CITY RESERVOIR!
NO NEED TO LOOK FURTHER, GENTLEMEN! I'VE FOUND THE CHICKEN!
BAKERY
BREAD
COOKIES
DO-NUTS
PIES
THERE IT IS — IN MY DOUGH MIXER!
TWO THOUSAND LOAVES OF BREAD RUINED!
YOU SHOULD BE JAILED FOR NOT HAVING A LID ON THAT BOOBY TRAP!

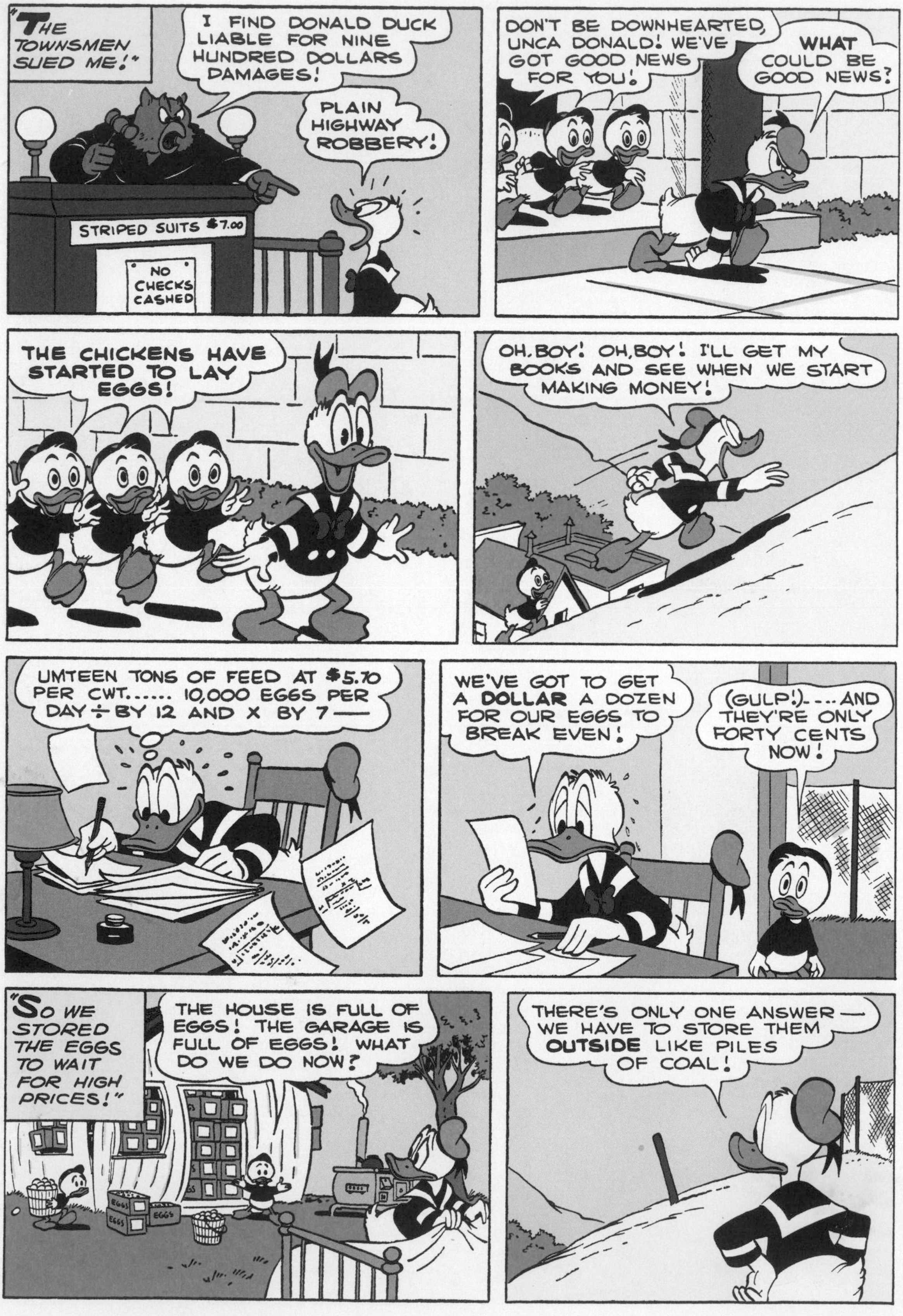
"THE TOWNSMEN SUED ME!"
I FIND DONALD DUCK LIABLE FOR NINE HUNDRED DOLLARS DAMAGES!
PLAIN HIGHWAY ROBBERY!
STRIPED SUITS $7.00
NO CHECKS CASHED
DON'T BE DOWNHEARTED, UNCA DONALD! WE'VE GOT GOOD NEWS FOR YOU!
WHAT COULD BE GOOD NEWS?
THE CHICKENS HAVE STARTED TO LAY EGGS!
OH, BOY! OH, BOY! I'LL GET MY BOOKS AND SEE WHEN WE START MAKING MONEY!
UMTEEN TONS OF FEED AT $5.70 PER CWT...... 10,000 EGGS PER DAY ÷ BY 12 AND X BY 7 —
WE'VE GOT TO GET A DOLLAR A DOZEN FOR OUR EGGS TO BREAK EVEN!
(GULP!)----AND THEY'RE ONLY FORTY CENTS NOW!
"SO WE STORED THE EGGS TO WAIT FOR HIGH PRICES!"
THE HOUSE IS FULL OF EGGS! THE GARAGE IS FULL OF EGGS! WHAT DO WE DO NOW?
EGGS
EGGS
EGGS
THERE'S ONLY ONE ANSWER — WE HAVE TO STORE THEM OUTSIDE LIKE PILES OF COAL!

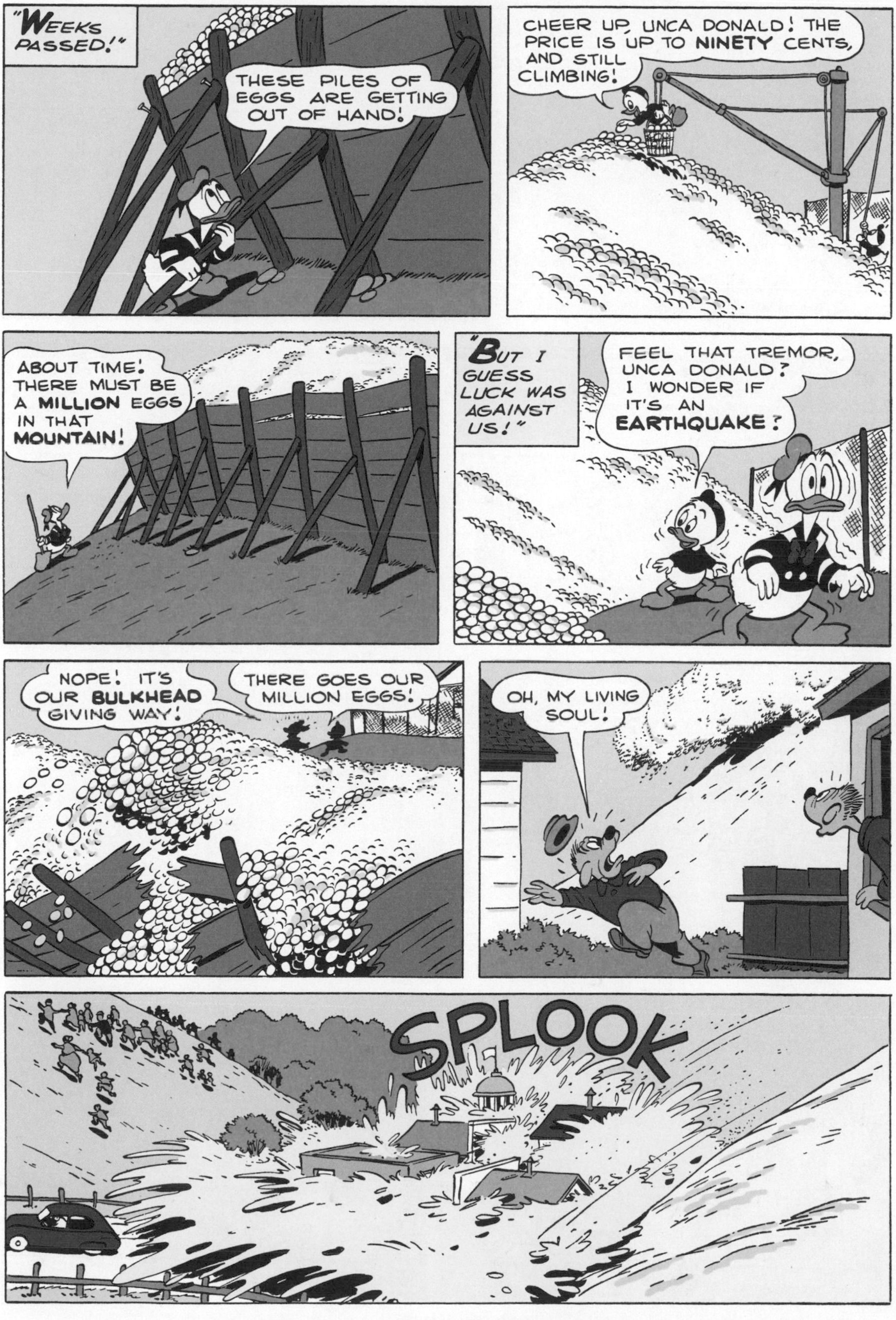
"WEEKS PASSED!"
THESE PILES OF EGGS ARE GETTING OUT OF HAND!
CHEER UP, UNCA DONALD! THE PRICE IS UP TO NINETY CENTS, AND STILL CLIMBING!
ABOUT TIME! THERE MUST BE A MILLION EGGS IN THAT MOUNTAIN!
"BUT I GUESS LUCK WAS AGAINST US!"
FEEL THAT TREMOR, UNCA DONALD? I WONDER IF IT'S AN EARTHQUAKE?
NOPE! IT'S OUR BULKHEAD GIVING WAY!
THERE GOES OUR MILLION EGGS!
OH, MY LIVING SOUL!
SPLOOK

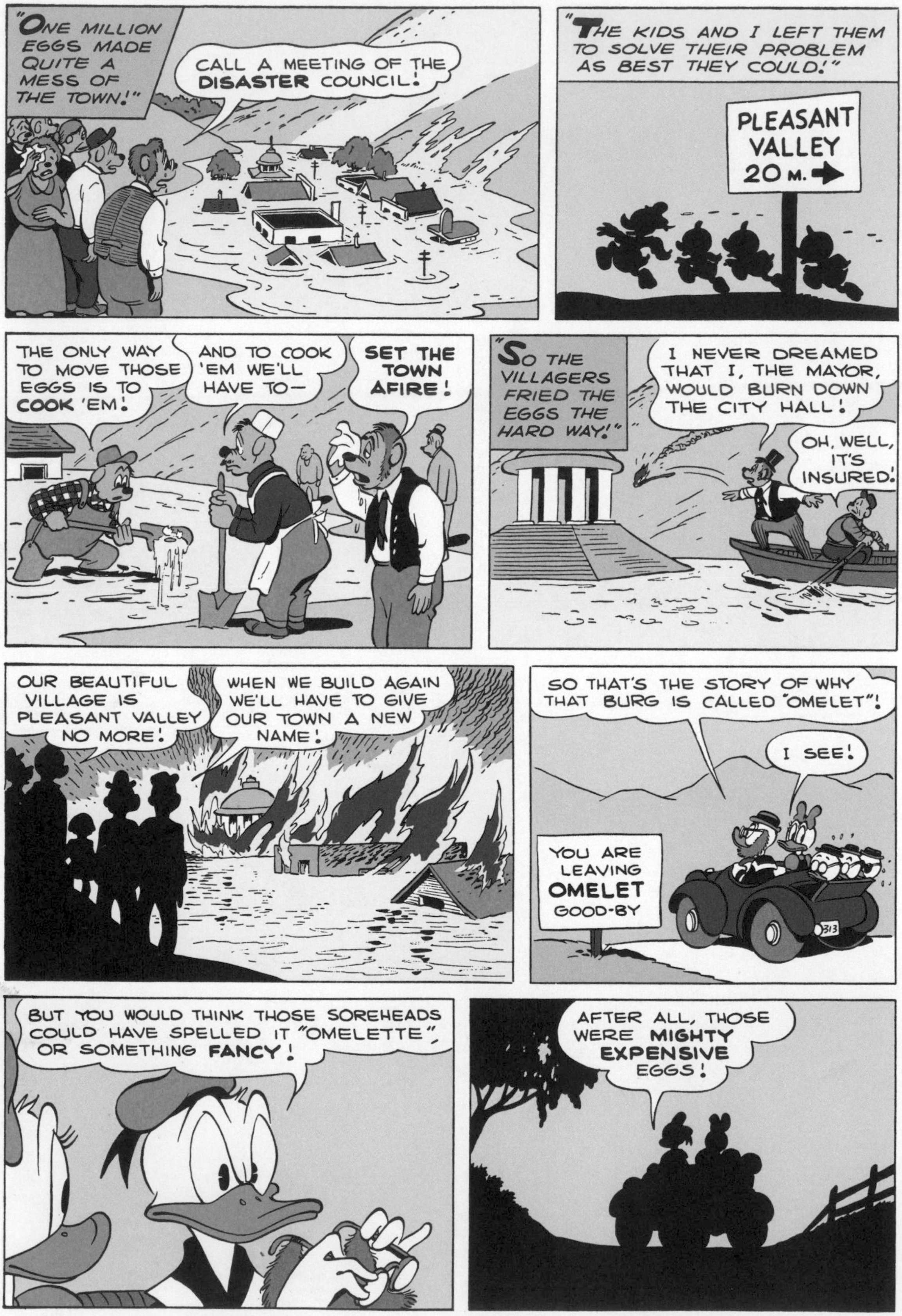
"ONE MILLION EGGS MADE QUITE A MESS OF THE TOWN!"
CALL A MEETING OF THE DISASTER COUNCIL!
"THE KIDS AND I LEFT THEM TO SOLVE THEIR PROBLEM AS BEST THEY COULD!"
PLEASANT VALLEY 20 M.
THE ONLY WAY TO MOVE THOSE EGGS IS TO COOK 'EM!
AND TO COOK 'EM WE'LL HAVE TO—
SET THE TOWN AFIRE!
"SO THE VILLAGERS FRIED THE EGGS THE HARD WAY!"
I NEVER DREAMED THAT I, THE MAYOR, WOULD BURN DOWN THE CITY HALL!
OH, WELL, IT'S INSURED!
OUR BEAUTIFUL VILLAGE IS PLEASANT VALLEY NO MORE!
WHEN WE BUILD AGAIN WE'LL HAVE TO GIVE OUR TOWN A NEW NAME!
SO THAT'S THE STORY OF WHY THAT BURG IS CALLED "OMELET"!
I SEE!
YOU ARE LEAVING OMELET GOOD-BY
313
BUT YOU WOULD THINK THOSE SOREHEADS COULD HAVE SPELLED IT "OMELETTE", OR SOMETHING FANCY!
AFTER ALL, THOSE WERE MIGHTY EXPENSIVE EGGS!

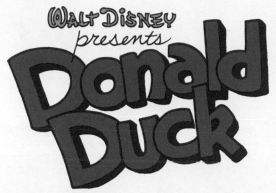

Walt Disney presents Donald Duck

JOIN DAISY DUCK'S **GOOD NEIGHBOR CLUB**!

Give some poor, hungry, deserving person a THANKSGIVING dinner in your home!

SIGN UP INSIDE →

NOW, ISN'T THAT A **NOBLE** IDEA!

HI, DAISY! I HAVE A LITTLE EXTRA MONEY THIS THANKSGIVING! I'LL FEED ONE OF YOUR POOR FOLKS!

OH, GOOD!

CHAIRMAN

WE HAVE THE NAMES OF THE POOR IN THIS BOX! YOU DRAW A NAME, AND THAT PERSON WILL BE YOUR GUEST!

TAKE HOME A HUNGRY SOUL!

I'LL DRAW A NAME RIGHT NOW! I'M **FOR** THIS KIND OF DEAL!

HERE! SEND WORD TO THIS PERSON THAT THERE'LL BE TURKEY AND TRIMMINGS AT DONALD DUCK'S HOUSE!

OH, SWELL!

TAKE HIM

GIVE THE CARD TO THE SECRETARY! SHE'LL COMPLETE THE ARRANGEMENTS! I MUST HURRY HOME!

'BYE!

Charity, sweet Charity!

SECRETARY

YOUR NAME, PLEASE! AND YOUR ADDRESS!

SECRET

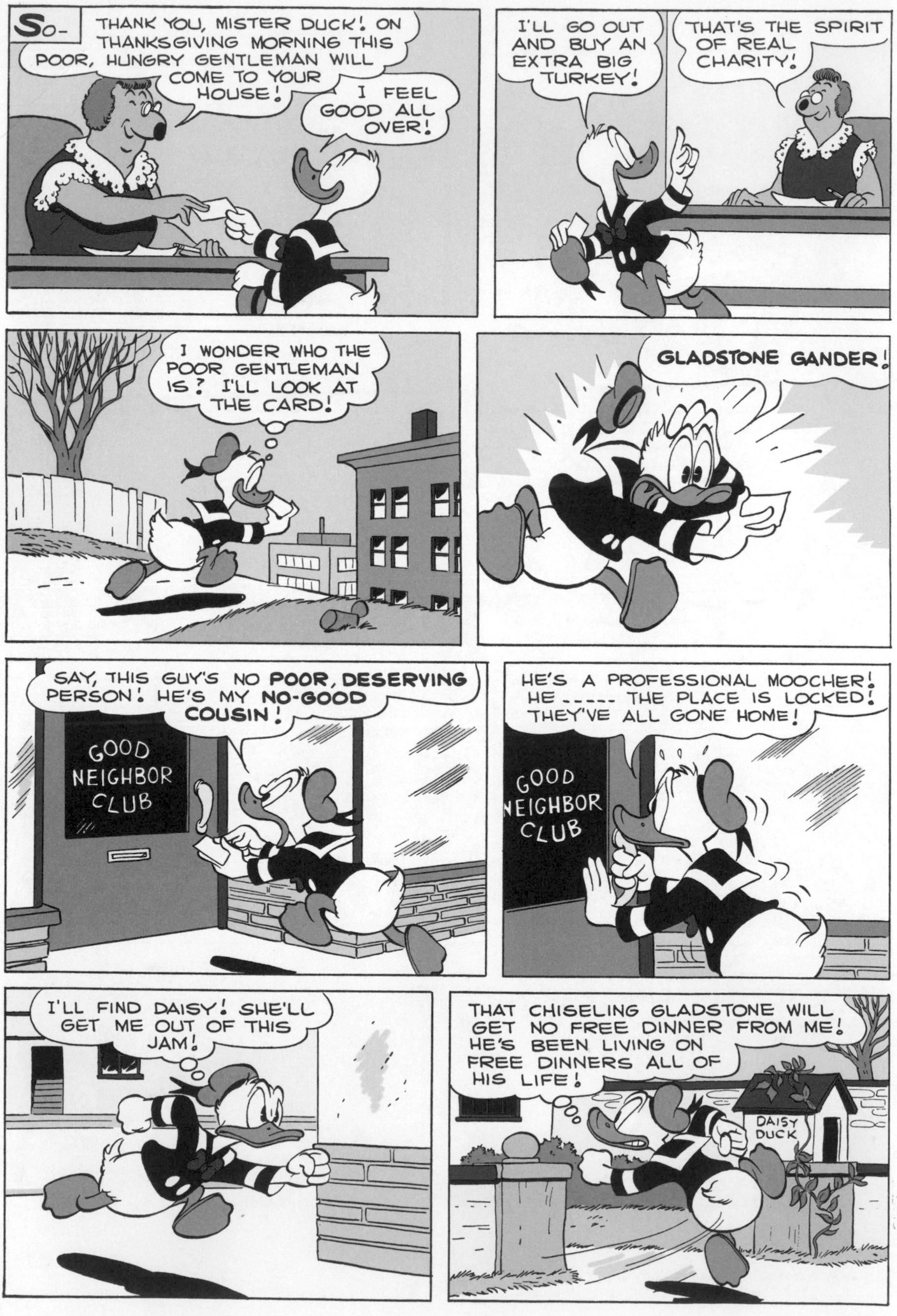
So-
THANK YOU, MISTER DUCK! ON THANKSGIVING MORNING THIS POOR, HUNGRY GENTLEMAN WILL COME TO YOUR HOUSE!
I FEEL GOOD ALL OVER!
I'LL GO OUT AND BUY AN EXTRA BIG TURKEY!
THAT'S THE SPIRIT OF REAL CHARITY!
I WONDER WHO THE POOR GENTLEMAN IS? I'LL LOOK AT THE CARD!
GLADSTONE GANDER!
SAY, THIS GUY'S NO POOR, DESERVING PERSON! HE'S MY NO-GOOD COUSIN!
GOOD NEIGHBOR CLUB
HE'S A PROFESSIONAL MOOCHER! HE ----- THE PLACE IS LOCKED! THEY'VE ALL GONE HOME!
GOOD NEIGHBOR CLUB
I'LL FIND DAISY! SHE'LL GET ME OUT OF THIS JAM!
THAT CHISELING GLADSTONE WILL GET NO FREE DINNER FROM ME! HE'S BEEN LIVING ON FREE DINNERS ALL OF HIS LIFE!
DAISY DUCK

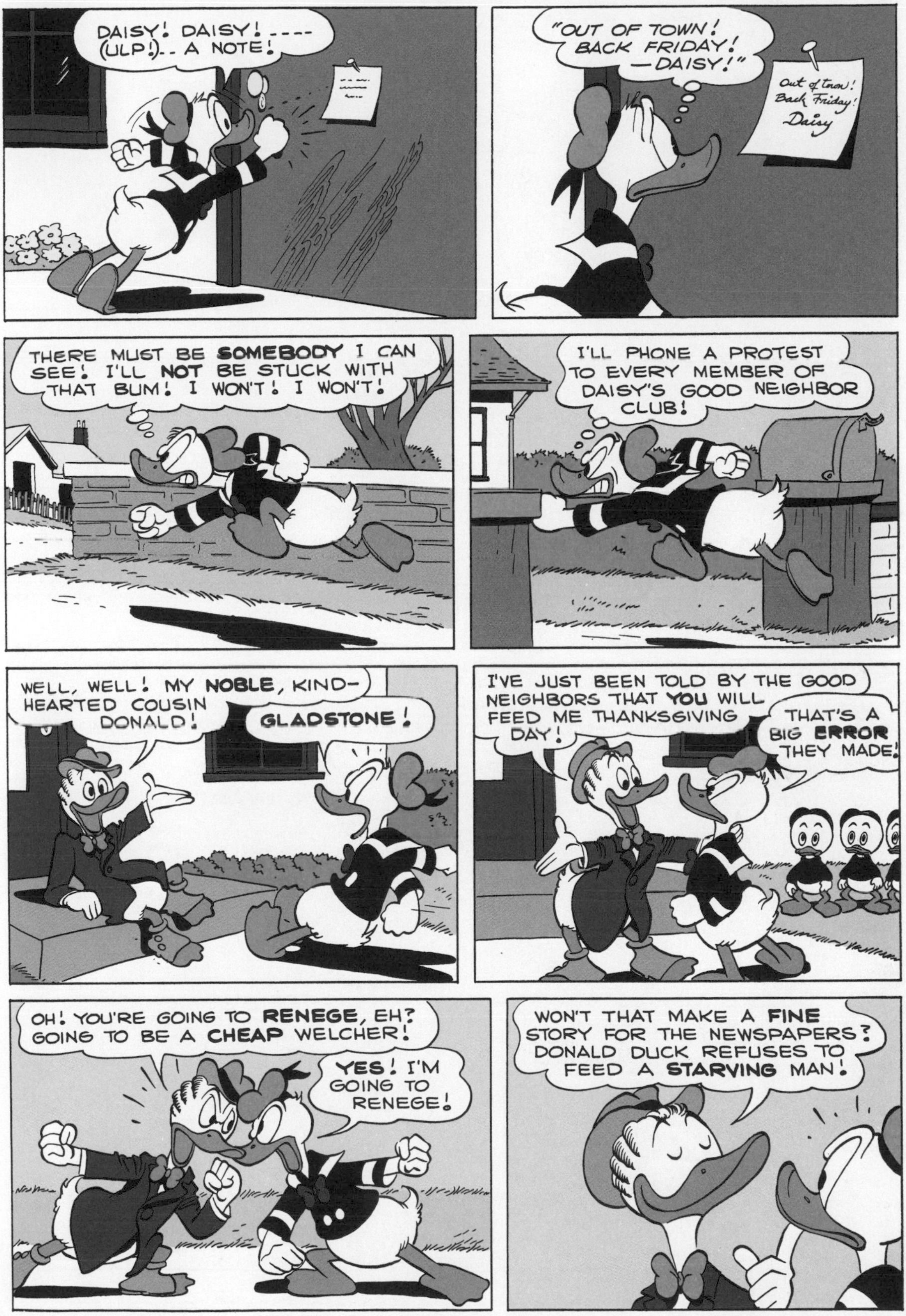
DAISY! DAISY! ---- (ULP!)-- A NOTE!
"OUT OF TOWN! BACK FRIDAY! —DAISY!"
Out of town! Back Friday! Daisy
THERE MUST BE SOMEBODY I CAN SEE! I'LL NOT BE STUCK WITH THAT BUM! I WON'T! I WON'T!
I'LL PHONE A PROTEST TO EVERY MEMBER OF DAISY'S GOOD NEIGHBOR CLUB!
WELL, WELL! MY NOBLE, KIND-HEARTED COUSIN DONALD!
GLADSTONE!
I'VE JUST BEEN TOLD BY THE GOOD NEIGHBORS THAT YOU WILL FEED ME THANKSGIVING DAY!
THAT'S A BIG ERROR THEY MADE!
OH! YOU'RE GOING TO RENEGE, EH? GOING TO BE A CHEAP WELCHER!
YES! I'M GOING TO RENEGE!
WON'T THAT MAKE A FINE STORY FOR THE NEWSPAPERS? DONALD DUCK REFUSES TO FEED A STARVING MAN!

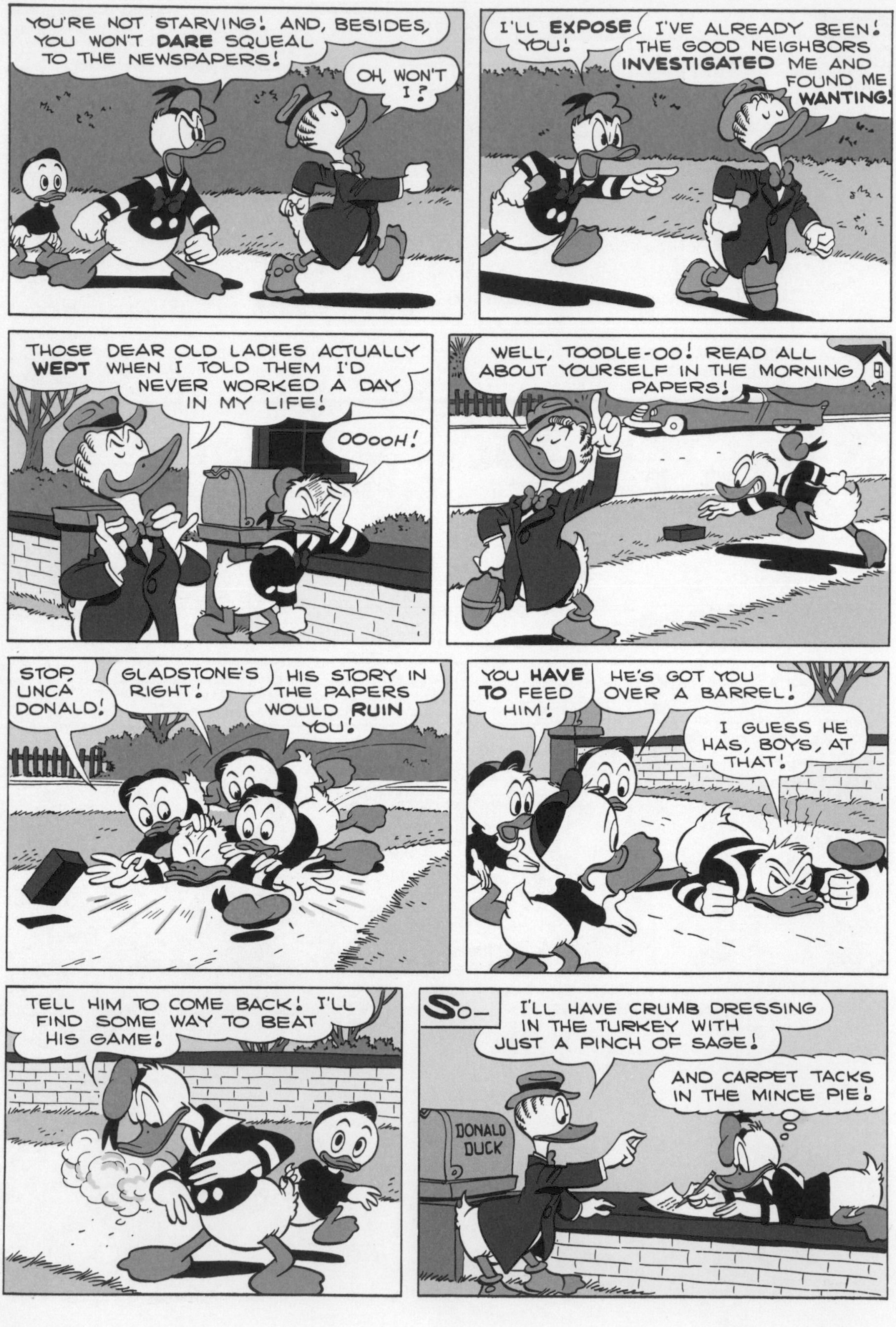

YOU'RE NOT STARVING! AND, BESIDES, YOU WON'T DARE SQUEAL TO THE NEWSPAPERS!
OH, WON'T I?
I'LL EXPOSE YOU!
I'VE ALREADY BEEN! THE GOOD NEIGHBORS INVESTIGATED ME AND FOUND ME WANTING!
THOSE DEAR OLD LADIES ACTUALLY WEPT WHEN I TOLD THEM I'D NEVER WORKED A DAY IN MY LIFE!
OOOOH!
WELL, TOODLE-OO! READ ALL ABOUT YOURSELF IN THE MORNING PAPERS!
STOP, UNCA DONALD!
GLADSTONE'S RIGHT!
HIS STORY IN THE PAPERS WOULD RUIN YOU!
YOU HAVE TO FEED HIM!
HE'S GOT YOU OVER A BARREL!
I GUESS HE HAS, BOYS, AT THAT!
TELL HIM TO COME BACK! I'LL FIND SOME WAY TO BEAT HIS GAME!
SO—
I'LL HAVE CRUMB DRESSING IN THE TURKEY WITH JUST A PINCH OF SAGE!
AND CARPET TACKS IN THE MINCE PIE!
DONALD DUCK

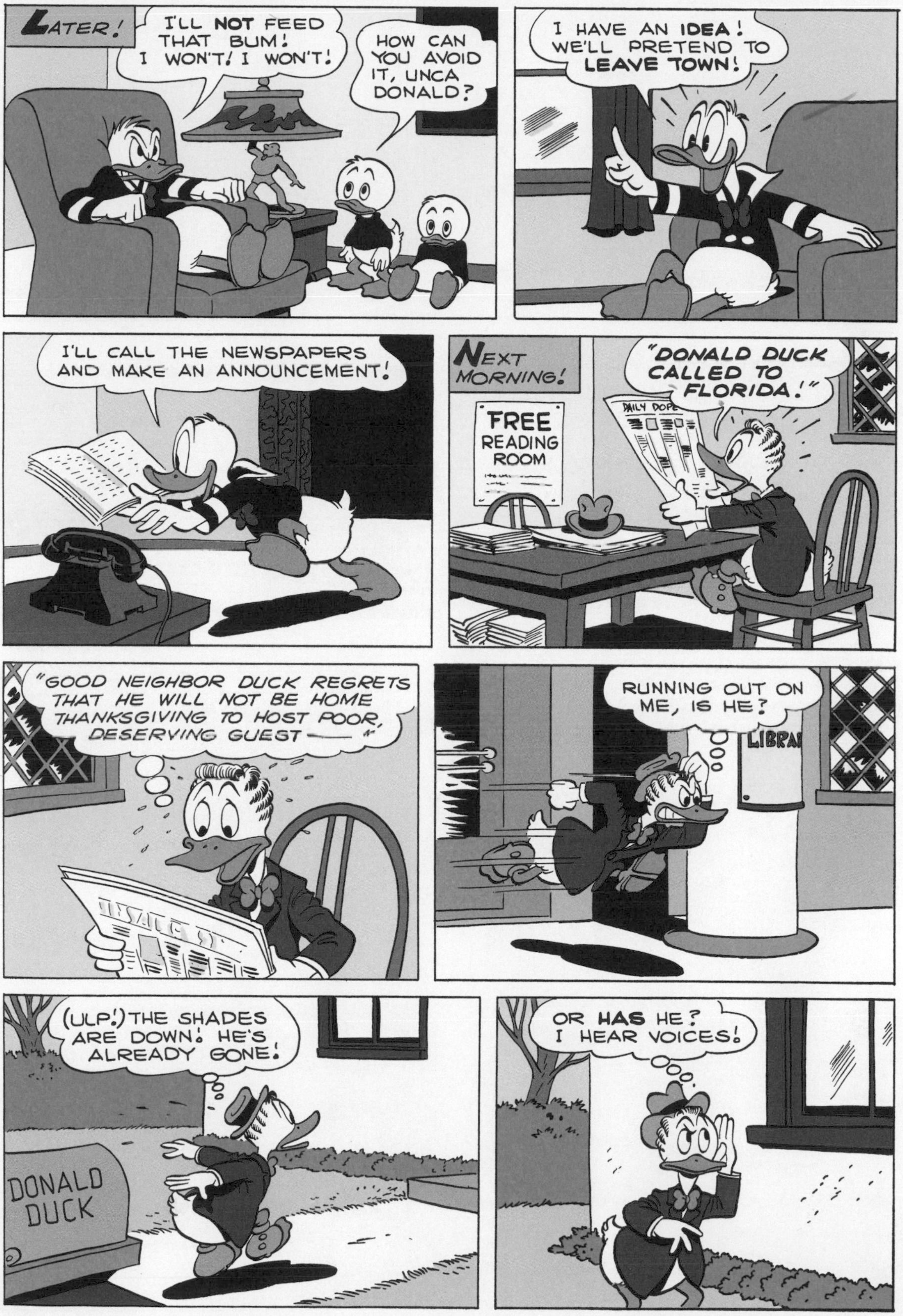
LATER!
I'LL NOT FEED THAT BUM! I WON'T! I WON'T!
HOW CAN YOU AVOID IT, UNCA DONALD?
I HAVE AN IDEA! WE'LL PRETEND TO LEAVE TOWN!
I'LL CALL THE NEWSPAPERS AND MAKE AN ANNOUNCEMENT!
NEXT MORNING!
FREE READING ROOM
"DONALD DUCK CALLED TO FLORIDA!"
"GOOD NEIGHBOR DUCK REGRETS THAT HE WILL NOT BE HOME THANKSGIVING TO HOST POOR, DESERVING GUEST—— "
RUNNING OUT ON ME, IS HE?
(ULP!) THE SHADES ARE DOWN! HE'S ALREADY GONE!
DONALD DUCK
OR HAS HE? I HEAR VOICES!

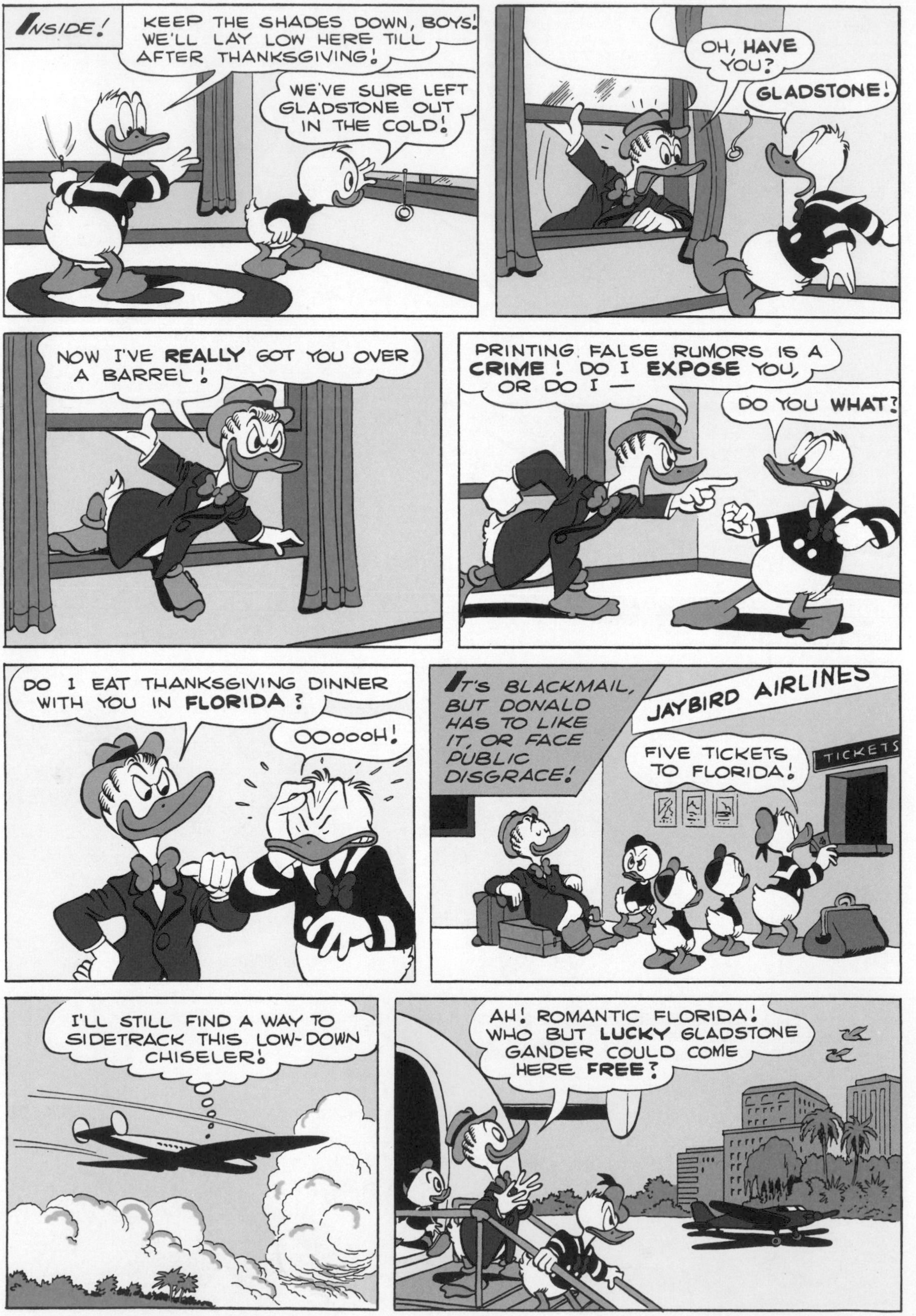
INSIDE!
KEEP THE SHADES DOWN, BOYS! WE'LL LAY LOW HERE TILL AFTER THANKSGIVING!
WE'VE SURE LEFT GLADSTONE OUT IN THE COLD!
OH, HAVE YOU?
GLADSTONE!
NOW I'VE REALLY GOT YOU OVER A BARREL!
PRINTING FALSE RUMORS IS A CRIME! DO I EXPOSE YOU, OR DO I —
DO YOU WHAT?
DO I EAT THANKSGIVING DINNER WITH YOU IN FLORIDA?
OOooOH!
IT'S BLACKMAIL, BUT DONALD HAS TO LIKE IT, OR FACE PUBLIC DISGRACE!
JAYBIRD AIRLINES
TICKETS
FIVE TICKETS TO FLORIDA!
I'LL STILL FIND A WAY TO SIDETRACK THIS LOW-DOWN CHISELER!
AH! ROMANTIC FLORIDA! WHO BUT LUCKY GLADSTONE GANDER COULD COME HERE FREE?

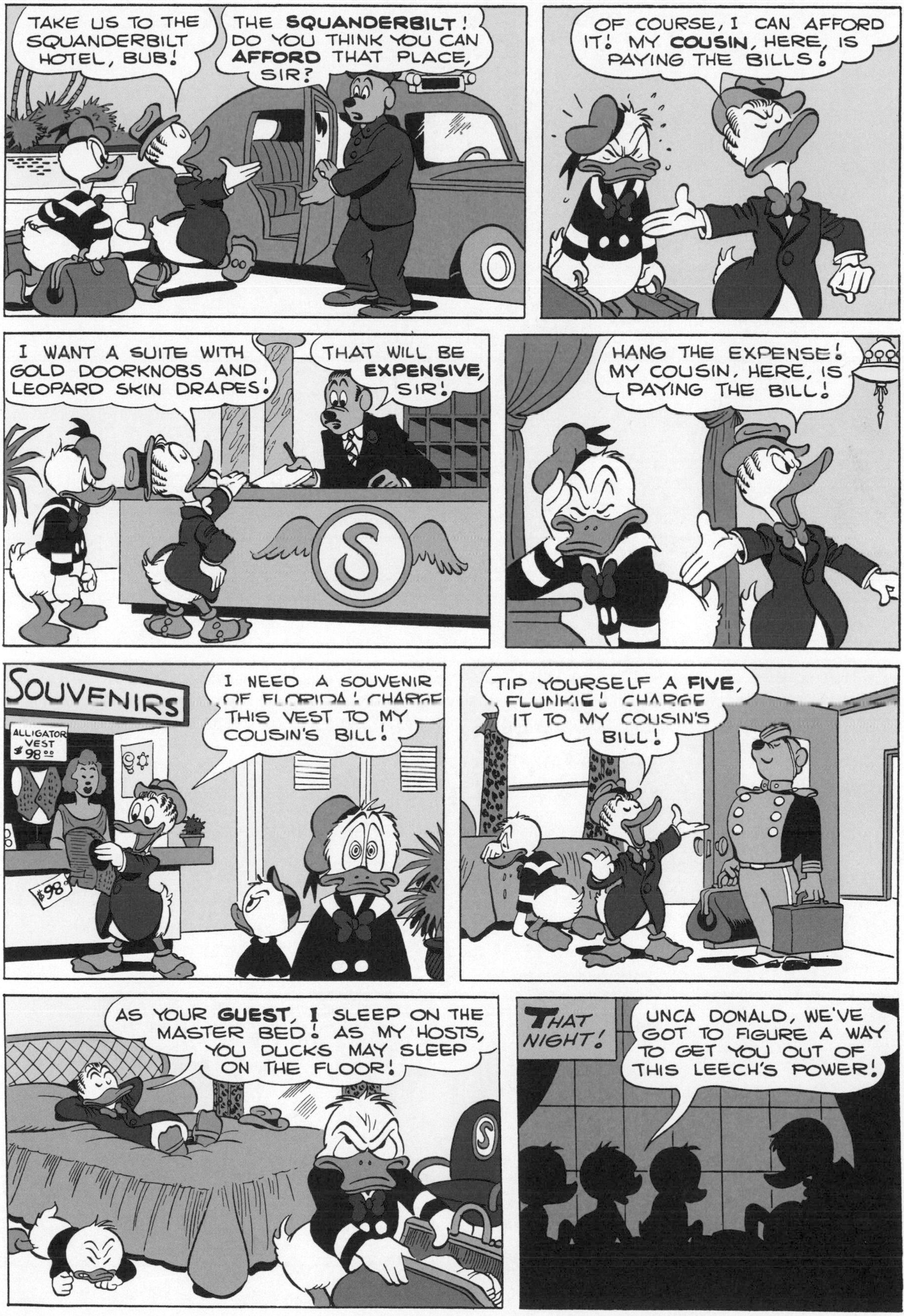
TAKE US TO THE SQUANDERBILT HOTEL, BUB!
THE SQUANDERBILT! DO YOU THINK YOU CAN AFFORD THAT PLACE, SIR?
OF COURSE, I CAN AFFORD IT! MY COUSIN, HERE, IS PAYING THE BILLS!
I WANT A SUITE WITH GOLD DOORKNOBS AND LEOPARD SKIN DRAPES!
THAT WILL BE EXPENSIVE, SIR!
HANG THE EXPENSE! MY COUSIN, HERE, IS PAYING THE BILL!
SOUVENIRS
ALLIGATOR VEST $98.00
I NEED A SOUVENIR OF FLORIDA! CHARGE THIS VEST TO MY COUSIN'S BILL!
$98
TIP YOURSELF A FIVE, FLUNKIE! CHARGE IT TO MY COUSIN'S BILL!
AS YOUR GUEST, I SLEEP ON THE MASTER BED! AS MY HOSTS, YOU DUCKS MAY SLEEP ON THE FLOOR!
THAT NIGHT!
UNCA DONALD, WE'VE GOT TO FIGURE A WAY TO GET YOU OUT OF THIS LEECH'S POWER!

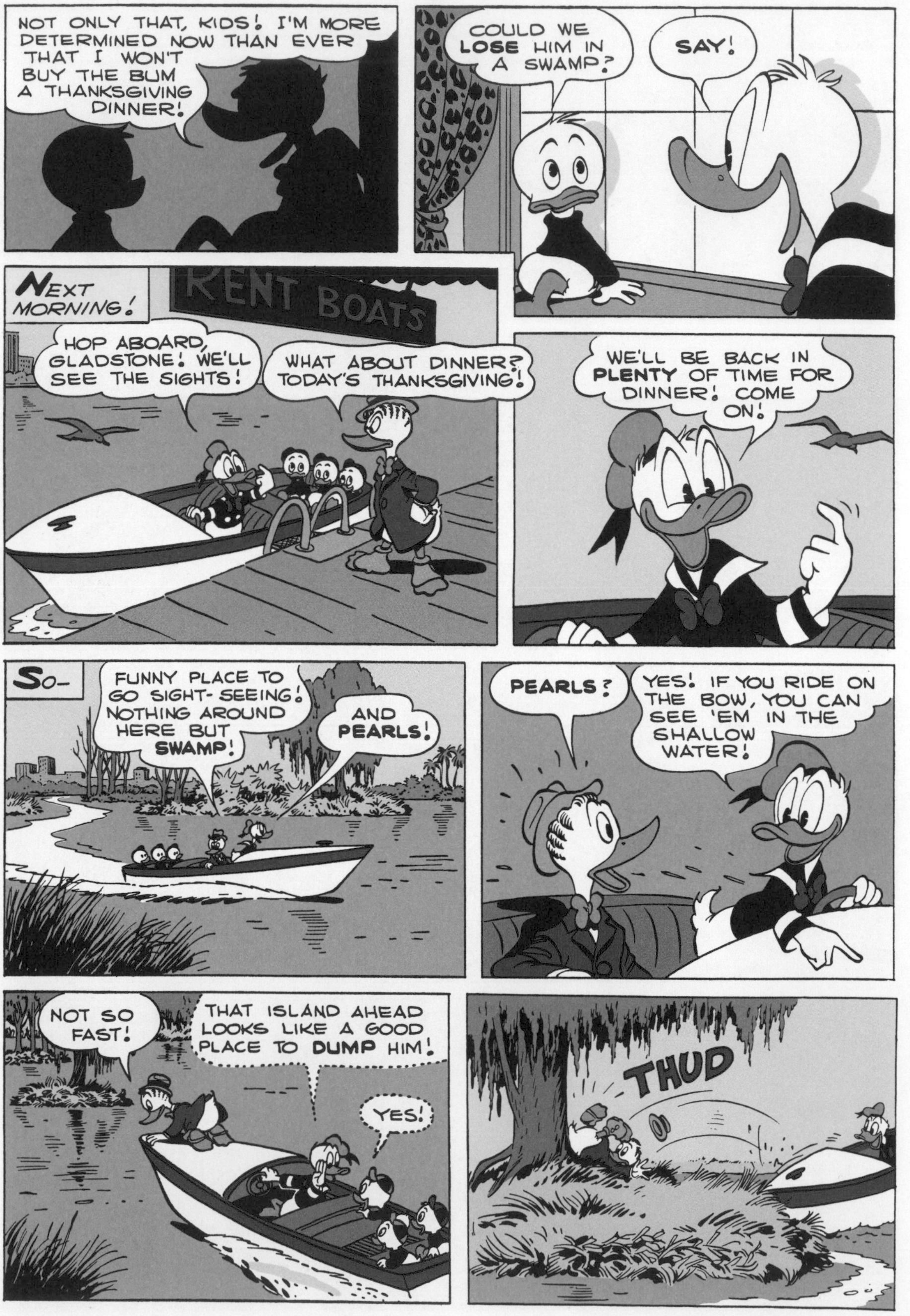
NOT ONLY THAT, KIDS! I'M MORE DETERMINED NOW THAN EVER THAT I WON'T BUY THE BUM A THANKSGIVING DINNER!
COULD WE LOSE HIM IN A SWAMP?
SAY!
NEXT MORNING!
RENT BOATS
HOP ABOARD, GLADSTONE! WE'LL SEE THE SIGHTS!
WHAT ABOUT DINNER? TODAY'S THANKSGIVING!
WE'LL BE BACK IN PLENTY OF TIME FOR DINNER! COME ON!
SO-
FUNNY PLACE TO GO SIGHT-SEEING! NOTHING AROUND HERE BUT SWAMP!
AND PEARLS!
PEARLS?
YES! IF YOU RIDE ON THE BOW, YOU CAN SEE 'EM IN THE SHALLOW WATER!
NOT SO FAST!
THAT ISLAND AHEAD LOOKS LIKE A GOOD PLACE TO DUMP HIM!
YES!
THUD

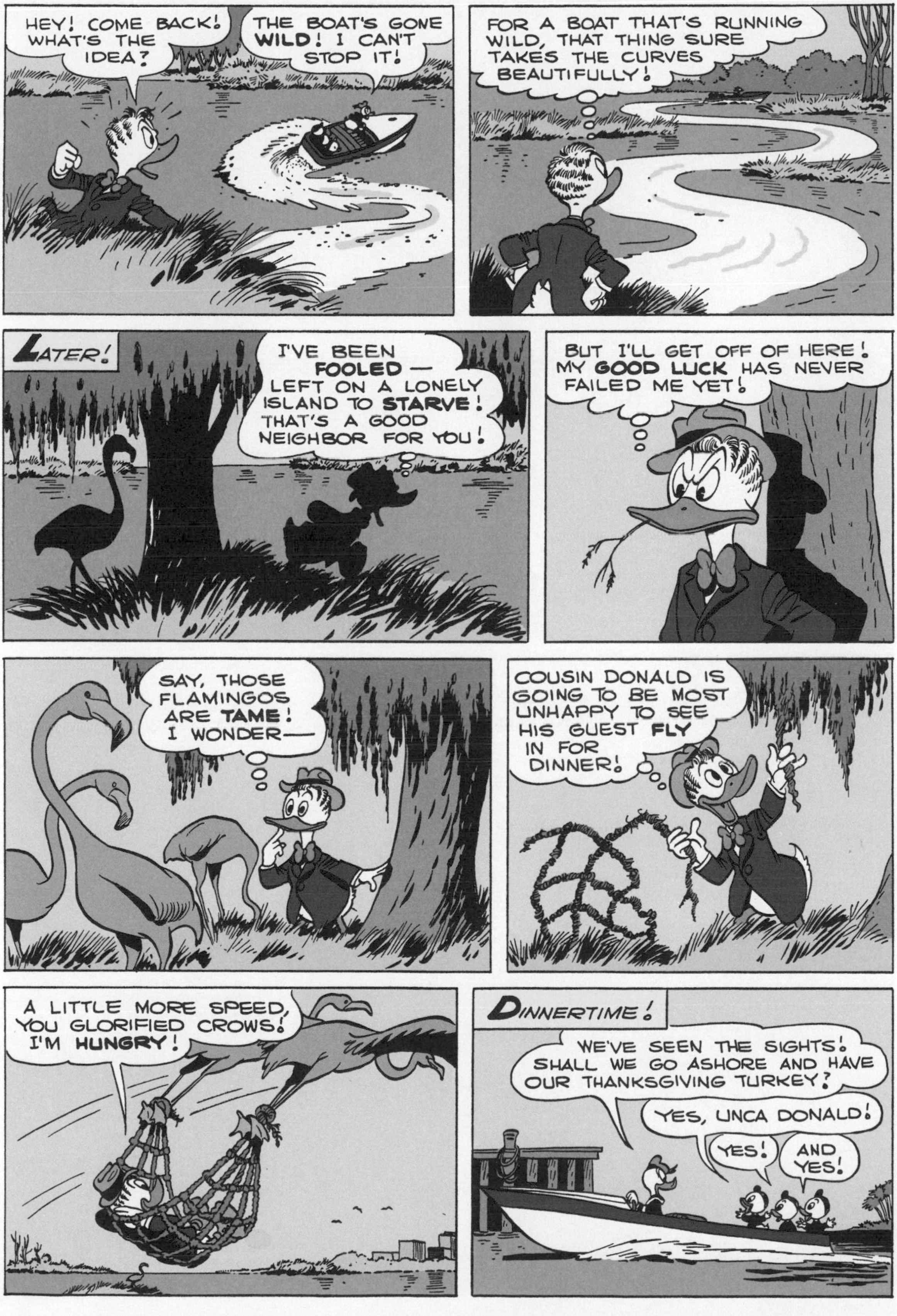
HEY! COME BACK! WHAT'S THE IDEA?
THE BOAT'S GONE WILD! I CAN'T STOP IT!
FOR A BOAT THAT'S RUNNING WILD, THAT THING SURE TAKES THE CURVES BEAUTIFULLY!
LATER!
I'VE BEEN FOOLED — LEFT ON A LONELY ISLAND TO STARVE! THAT'S A GOOD NEIGHBOR FOR YOU!
BUT I'LL GET OFF OF HERE! MY GOOD LUCK HAS NEVER FAILED ME YET!
SAY, THOSE FLAMINGOS ARE TAME! I WONDER—
COUSIN DONALD IS GOING TO BE MOST UNHAPPY TO SEE HIS GUEST FLY IN FOR DINNER!
A LITTLE MORE SPEED, YOU GLORIFIED CROWS! I'M HUNGRY!
DINNERTIME!
WE'VE SEEN THE SIGHTS! SHALL WE GO ASHORE AND HAVE OUR THANKSGIVING TURKEY?
YES, UNCA DONALD!
YES!
AND YES!

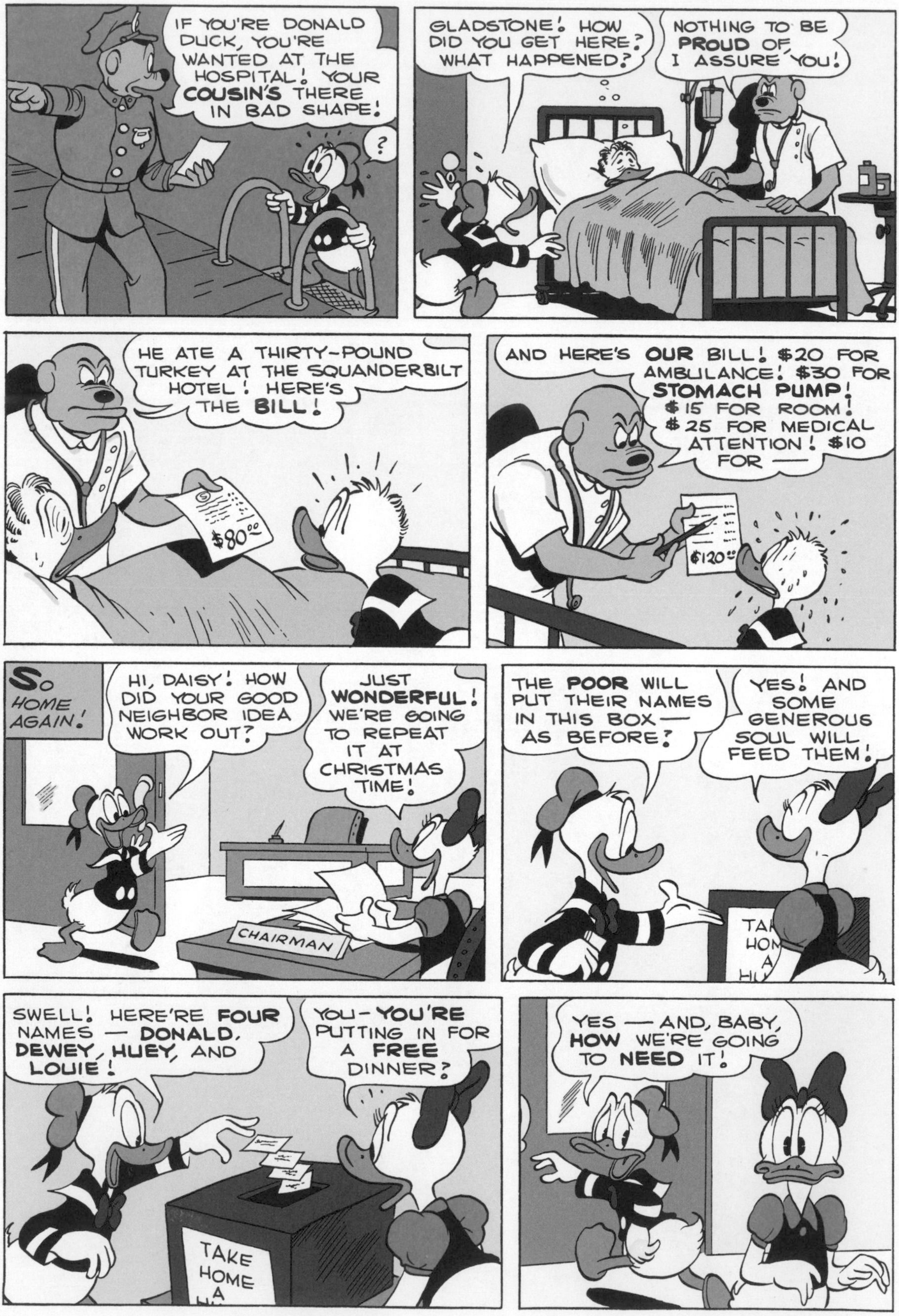
IF YOU'RE DONALD DUCK, YOU'RE WANTED AT THE HOSPITAL! YOUR COUSIN'S THERE IN BAD SHAPE!
?
GLADSTONE! HOW DID YOU GET HERE? WHAT HAPPENED?
NOTHING TO BE PROUD OF, I ASSURE YOU!
HE ATE A THIRTY-POUND TURKEY AT THE SQUANDERBILT HOTEL! HERE'S THE BILL!
$80.00
AND HERE'S OUR BILL! $20 FOR AMBULANCE! $30 FOR STOMACH PUMP! $15 FOR ROOM! $25 FOR MEDICAL ATTENTION! $10 FOR —
$120.00
SO HOME AGAIN!
HI, DAISY! HOW DID YOUR GOOD NEIGHBOR IDEA WORK OUT?
JUST WONDERFUL! WE'RE GOING TO REPEAT IT AT CHRISTMAS TIME!
CHAIRMAN
THE POOR WILL PUT THEIR NAMES IN THIS BOX — AS BEFORE?
YES! AND SOME GENEROUS SOUL WILL FEED THEM!
SWELL! HERE'RE FOUR NAMES — DONALD, DEWEY, HUEY, AND LOUIE!
YOU-YOU'RE PUTTING IN FOR A FREE DINNER?
TAKE HOME A
YES — AND, BABY, HOW WE'RE GOING TO NEED IT!

WALT DISNEY
Donald Duck
CHRISTMAS DAY IS ALWAYS A BUSY DAY AT DONALD'S HOUSE!
RING!
THAT MUST BE THE DELIVERY MAN WITH THE KIDS' PRESENTS!
IT IS!
$27.50 C.O.D.!
GOTTA PUT THESE UNDER THE TREE! OOP! THE PHONE!
BUZZ!
YES, YES! I'LL SEE THAT THE KIDS GET STARTED RIGHT AWAY!
HAVE YOU LOAFERS FORGOTTEN THAT YOU'RE HAVING CHRISTMAS DINNER WITH THE JUNIOR WOODCHUCKS?
MESSENGER BOY! DROP THIS DONATION OFF AT THE FRIENDS OF THE POOR CHARITY CLUB!
DONALD DUCK
STOP ON YOUR WAY DOWNTOWN, KIDS, AND PAY FOR THE CHRISTMAS TREE!
RING!

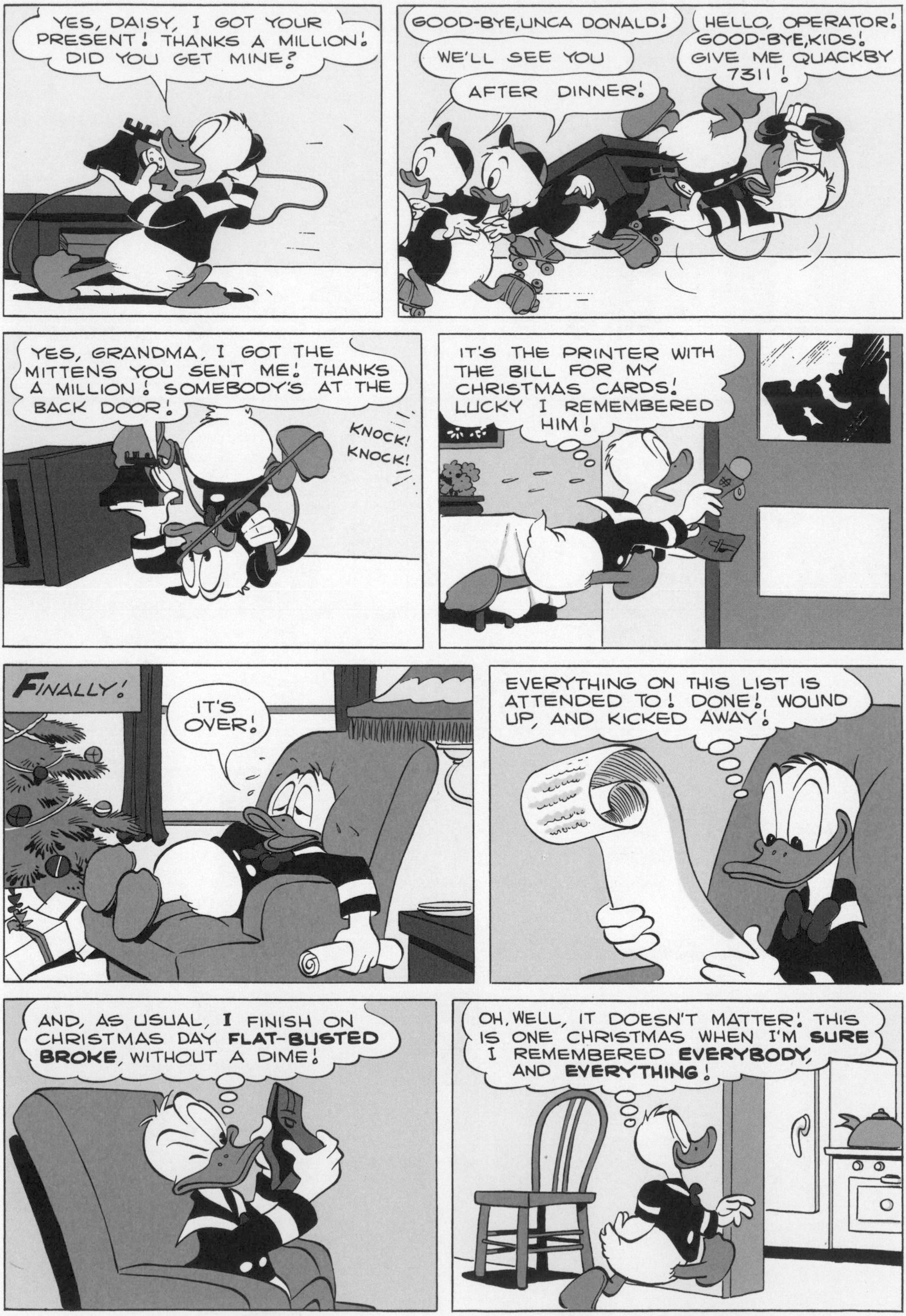
YES, DAISY, I GOT YOUR PRESENT! THANKS A MILLION! DID YOU GET MINE?
GOOD-BYE, UNCA DONALD!
WE'LL SEE YOU
AFTER DINNER!
HELLO, OPERATOR! GOOD-BYE, KIDS! GIVE ME QUACKBY 7311!
YES, GRANDMA, I GOT THE MITTENS YOU SENT ME! THANKS A MILLION! SOMEBODY'S AT THE BACK DOOR!
KNOCK! KNOCK!
IT'S THE PRINTER WITH THE BILL FOR MY CHRISTMAS CARDS! LUCKY I REMEMBERED HIM!
FINALLY!
IT'S OVER!
EVERYTHING ON THIS LIST IS ATTENDED TO! DONE! WOUND UP, AND KICKED AWAY!
AND, AS USUAL, I FINISH ON CHRISTMAS DAY FLAT-BUSTED BROKE, WITHOUT A DIME!
OH, WELL, IT DOESN'T MATTER! THIS IS ONE CHRISTMAS WHEN I'M SURE I REMEMBERED EVERYBODY, AND EVERYTHING!

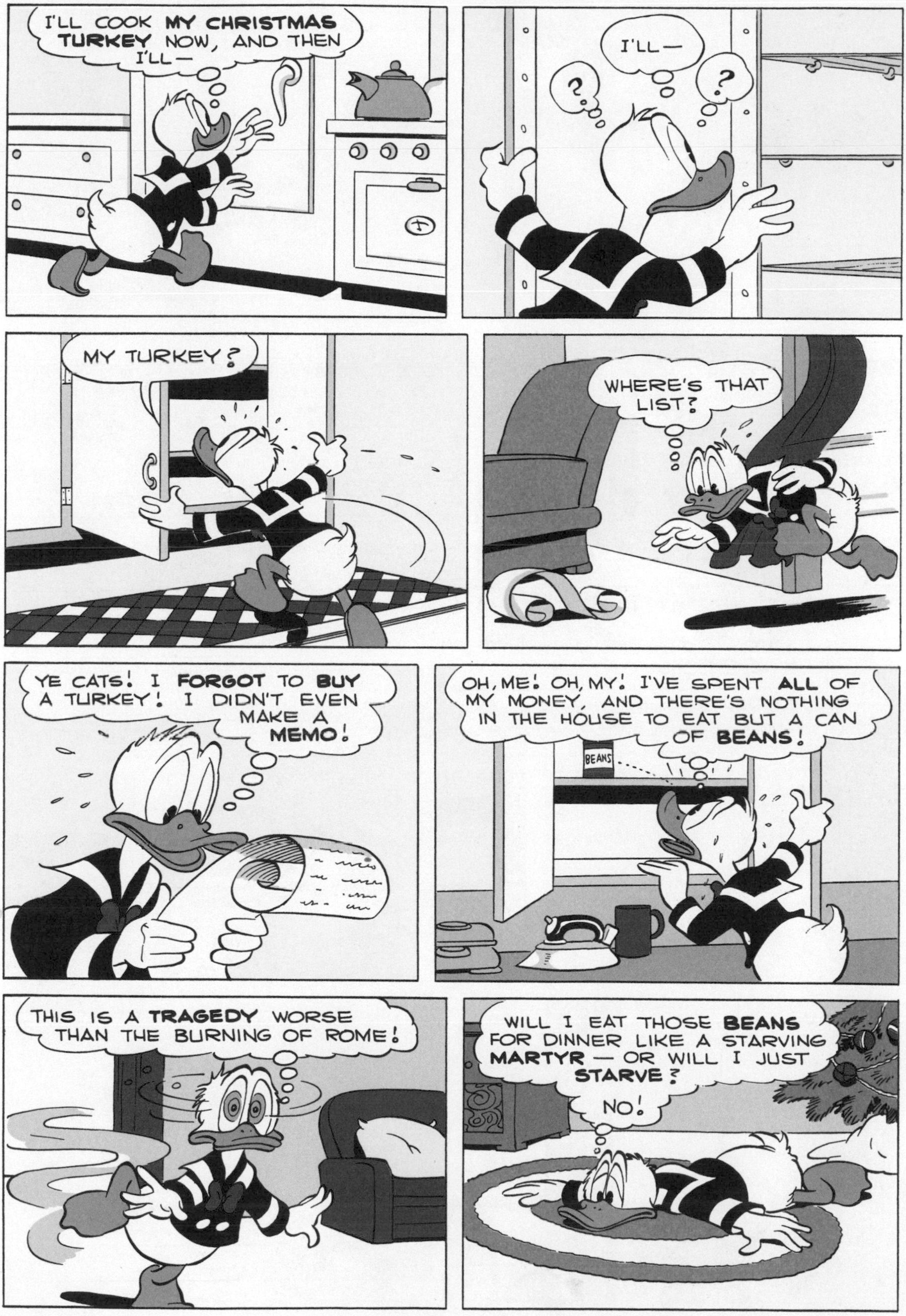
I'LL COOK MY CHRISTMAS TURKEY NOW, AND THEN I'LL—
I'LL—
?
?
MY TURKEY?
WHERE'S THAT LIST?
YE CATS! I FORGOT TO BUY A TURKEY! I DIDN'T EVEN MAKE A MEMO!
OH, ME! OH, MY! I'VE SPENT ALL OF MY MONEY, AND THERE'S NOTHING IN THE HOUSE TO EAT BUT A CAN OF BEANS!
BEANS
THIS IS A TRAGEDY WORSE THAN THE BURNING OF ROME!
WILL I EAT THOSE BEANS FOR DINNER LIKE A STARVING MARTYR — OR WILL I JUST STARVE?
NO!

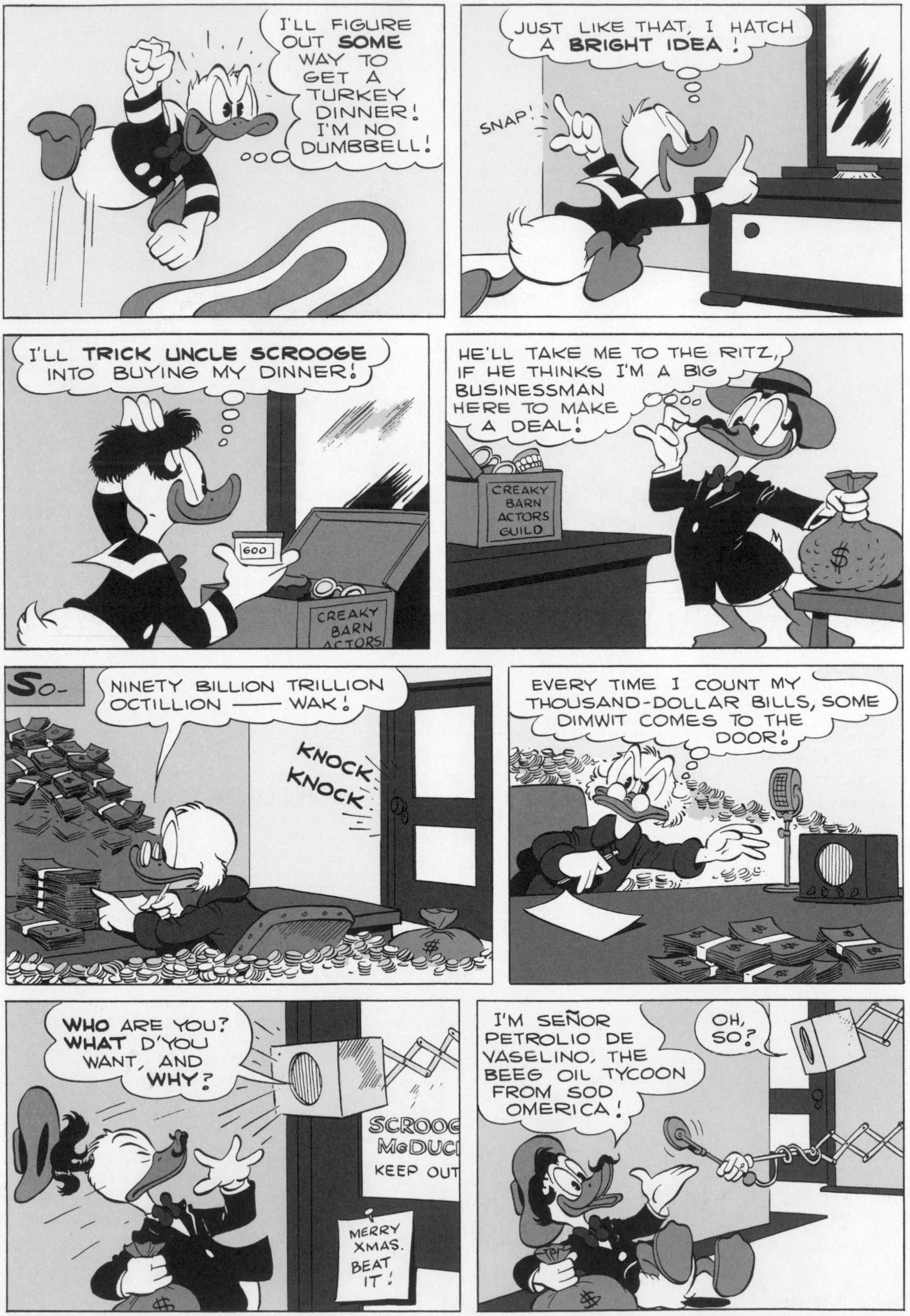

I'LL FIGURE OUT SOME WAY TO GET A TURKEY DINNER! I'M NO DUMBBELL!
JUST LIKE THAT, I HATCH A BRIGHT IDEA!
SNAP!
I'LL TRICK UNCLE SCROOGE INTO BUYING MY DINNER!
600
CREAKY BARN ACTORS
HE'LL TAKE ME TO THE RITZ, IF HE THINKS I'M A BIG BUSINESSMAN HERE TO MAKE A DEAL!
CREAKY BARN ACTORS GUILD
SO-
NINETY BILLION TRILLION OCTILLION — WAK!
KNOCK KNOCK
EVERY TIME I COUNT MY THOUSAND-DOLLAR BILLS, SOME DIMWIT COMES TO THE DOOR!
WHO ARE YOU? WHAT D'YOU WANT, AND WHY?
SCROOG McDUC KEEP OUT
MERRY XMAS. BEAT IT!
I'M SEÑOR PETROLIO DE VASELINO, THE BEEG OIL TYCOON FROM SOD OMERICA!
OH, SO?

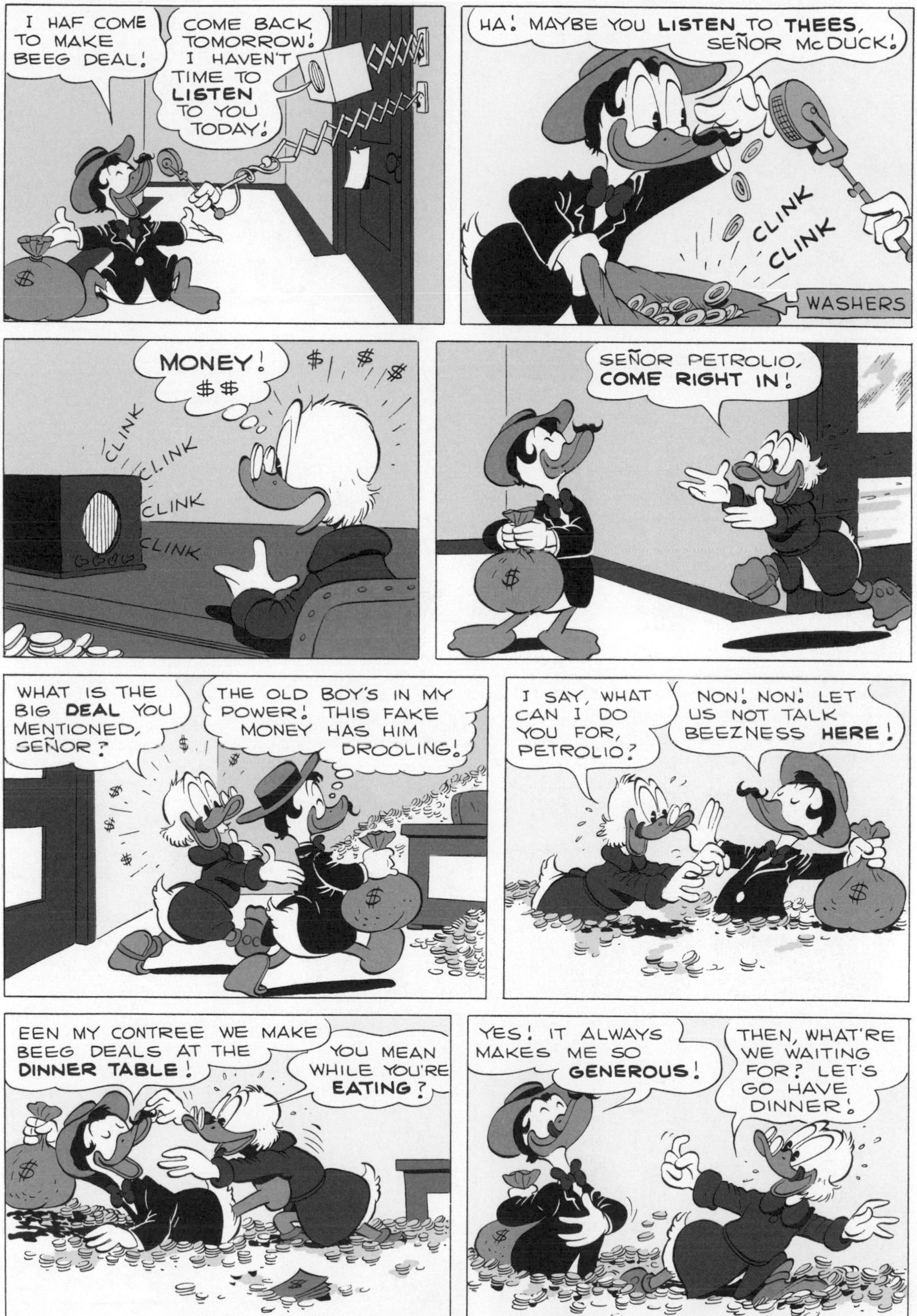
I HAF COME TO MAKE BEEG DEAL!
COME BACK TOMORROW! I HAVEN'T TIME TO LISTEN TO YOU TODAY!
HA! MAYBE YOU LISTEN TO THEES, SEÑOR McDUCK!
CLINK
CLINK
WASHERS
MONEY! $$
CLINK
CLINK
CLINK
CLINK
SEÑOR PETROLIO, COME RIGHT IN!
WHAT IS THE BIG DEAL YOU MENTIONED, SEÑOR?
THE OLD BOY'S IN MY POWER! THIS FAKE MONEY HAS HIM DROOLING!
I SAY, WHAT CAN I DO YOU FOR, PETROLIO?
NON! NON! LET US NOT TALK BEEZNESS HERE!
EEN MY CONTREE WE MAKE BEEG DEALS AT THE DINNER TABLE!
YOU MEAN WHILE YOU'RE EATING?
YES! IT ALWAYS MAKES ME SO GENEROUS!
THEN, WHAT'RE WE WAITING FOR? LET'S GO HAVE DINNER!

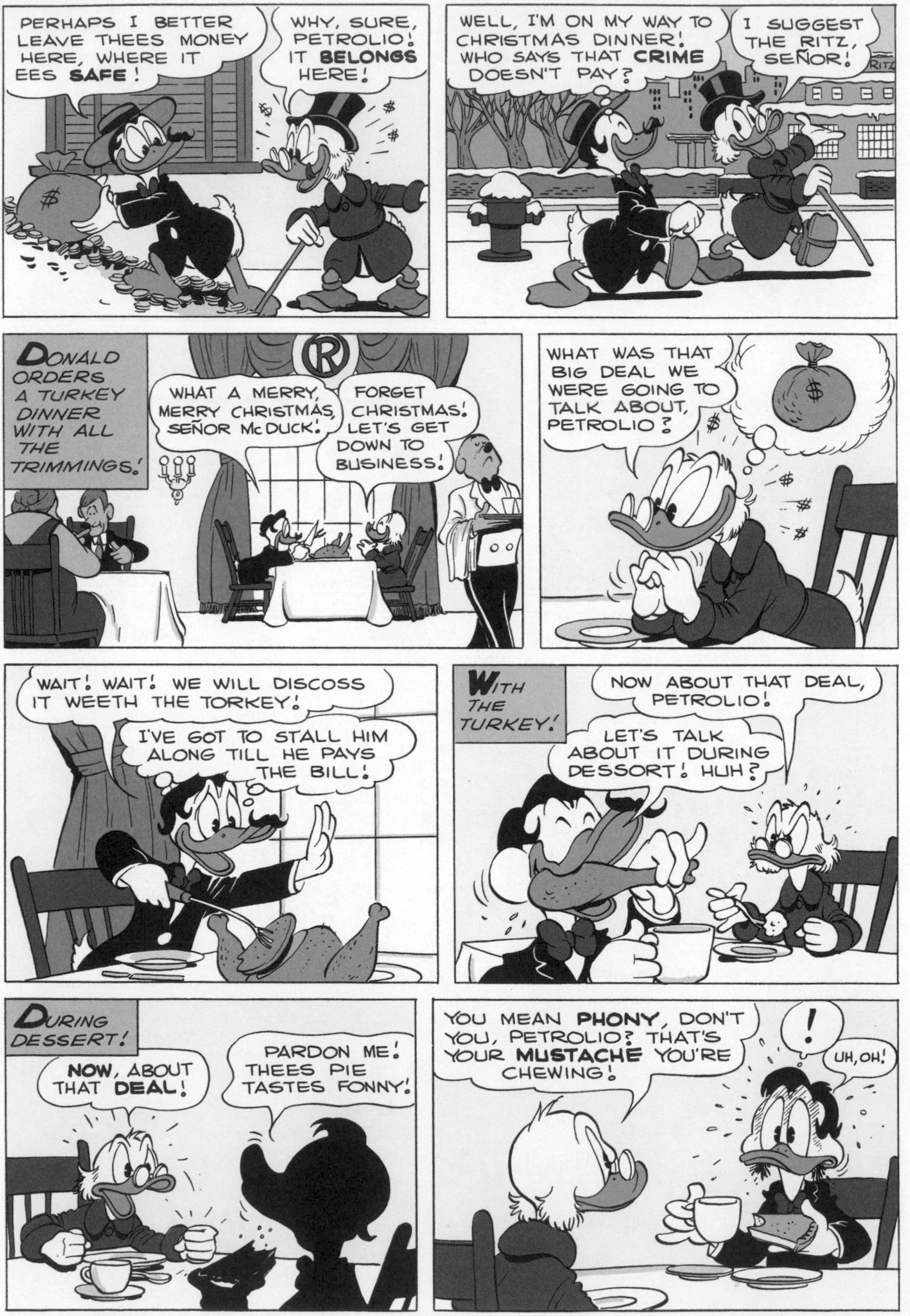
PERHAPS I BETTER LEAVE THEES MONEY HERE, WHERE IT EES SAFE!
WHY, SURE, PETROLIO! IT BELONGS HERE!
WELL, I'M ON MY WAY TO CHRISTMAS DINNER! WHO SAYS THAT CRIME DOESN'T PAY?
I SUGGEST THE RITZ, SEÑOR!
RITZ
DONALD ORDERS A TURKEY DINNER WITH ALL THE TRIMMINGS!
WHAT A MERRY, MERRY CHRISTMAS, SEÑOR McDUCK!
FORGET CHRISTMAS! LET'S GET DOWN TO BUSINESS!
WHAT WAS THAT BIG DEAL WE WERE GOING TO TALK ABOUT, PETROLIO?
WAIT! WAIT! WE WILL DISCOSS IT WEETH THE TORKEY!
I'VE GOT TO STALL HIM ALONG TILL HE PAYS THE BILL!
WITH THE TURKEY!
NOW ABOUT THAT DEAL, PETROLIO!
LET'S TALK ABOUT IT DURING DESSORT! HUH?
DURING DESSERT!
NOW, ABOUT THAT DEAL!
PARDON ME! THEES PIE TASTES FONNY!
YOU MEAN PHONY, DON'T YOU, PETROLIO? THAT'S YOUR MUSTACHE YOU'RE CHEWING!
!
UH, OH!

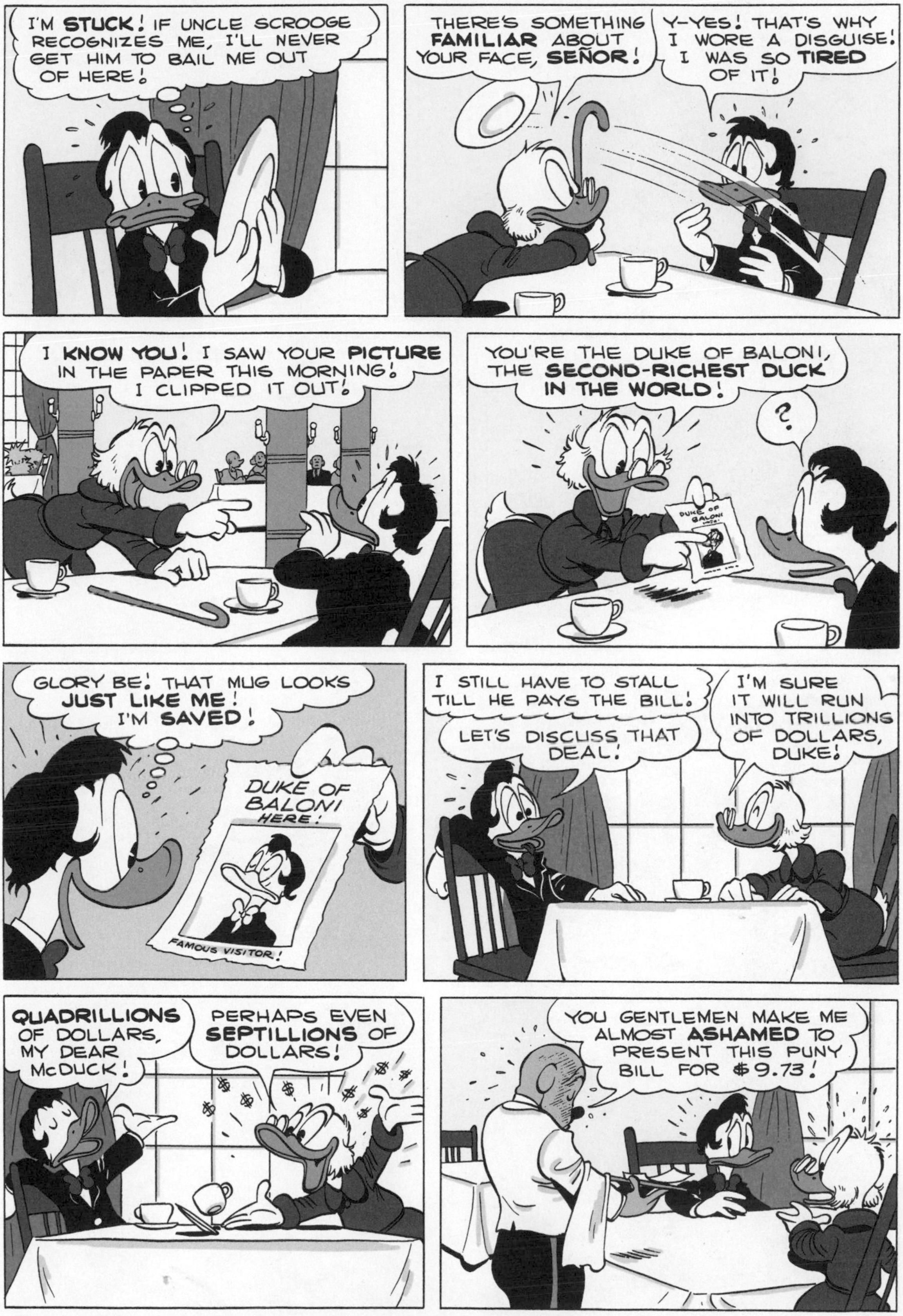

I'M STUCK! IF UNCLE SCROOGE RECOGNIZES ME, I'LL NEVER GET HIM TO BAIL ME OUT OF HERE!
THERE'S SOMETHING FAMILIAR ABOUT YOUR FACE, SEÑOR!
Y-YES! THAT'S WHY I WORE A DISGUISE! I WAS SO TIRED OF IT!
I KNOW YOU! I SAW YOUR PICTURE IN THE PAPER THIS MORNING! I CLIPPED IT OUT!
YOU'RE THE DUKE OF BALONI, THE SECOND-RICHEST DUCK IN THE WORLD!
?
GLORY BE! THAT MUG LOOKS JUST LIKE ME! I'M SAVED!
DUKE OF BALONI HERE!
FAMOUS VISITOR!
I STILL HAVE TO STALL TILL HE PAYS THE BILL!
LET'S DISCUSS THAT DEAL!
I'M SURE IT WILL RUN INTO TRILLIONS OF DOLLARS, DUKE!
QUADRILLIONS OF DOLLARS, MY DEAR McDUCK!
PERHAPS EVEN SEPTILLIONS OF DOLLARS!
YOU GENTLEMEN MAKE ME ALMOST ASHAMED TO PRESENT THIS PUNY BILL FOR $9.73!

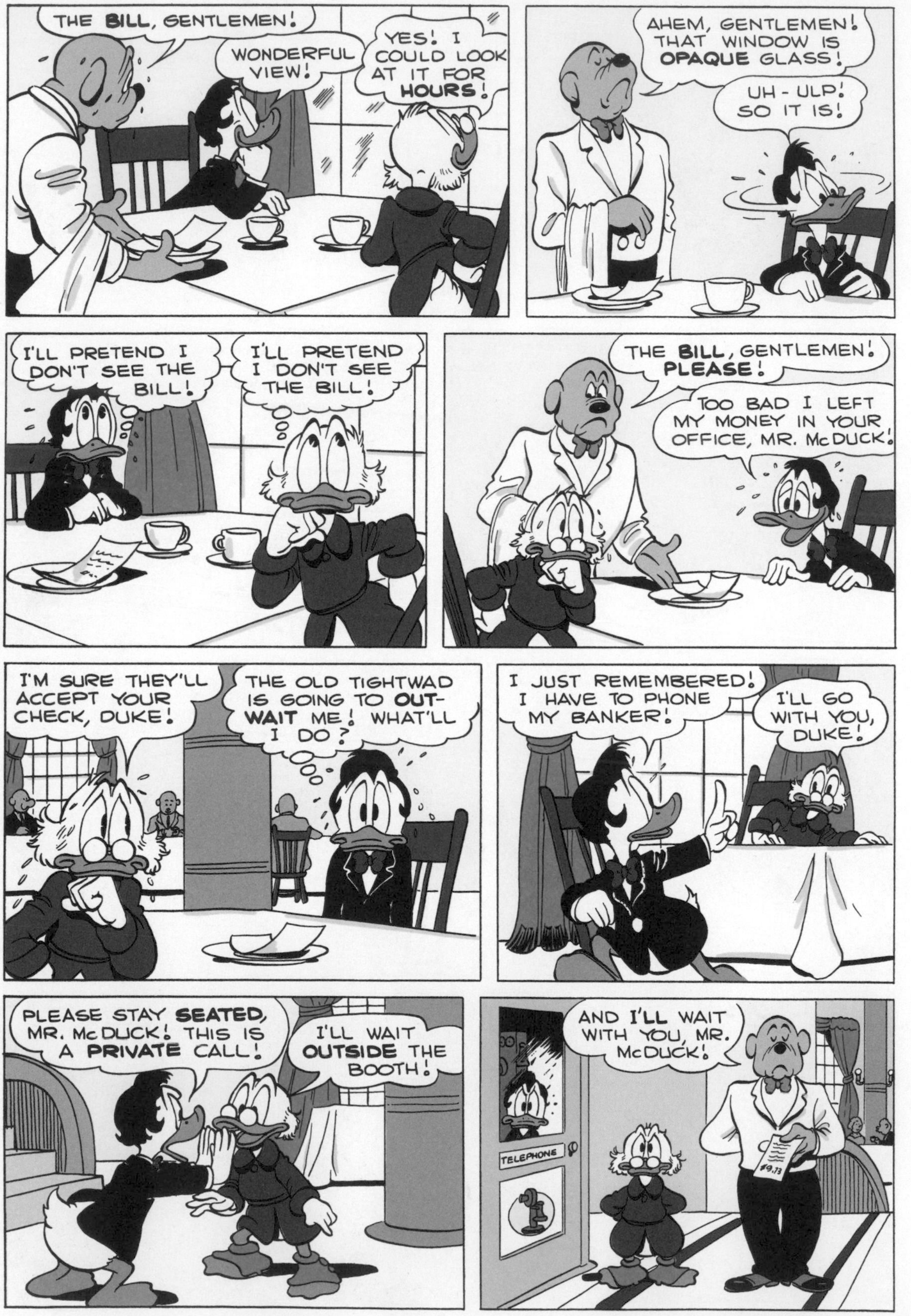
THE BILL, GENTLEMEN!
WONDERFUL VIEW!
YES! I COULD LOOK AT IT FOR HOURS!
AHEM, GENTLEMEN! THAT WINDOW IS OPAQUE GLASS!
UH-ULP! SO IT IS!
I'LL PRETEND I DON'T SEE THE BILL!
I'LL PRETEND I DON'T SEE THE BILL!
THE BILL, GENTLEMEN! PLEASE!
TOO BAD I LEFT MY MONEY IN YOUR OFFICE, MR. McDUCK!
I'M SURE THEY'LL ACCEPT YOUR CHECK, DUKE!
THE OLD TIGHTWAD IS GOING TO OUT-WAIT ME! WHAT'LL I DO?
I JUST REMEMBERED! I HAVE TO PHONE MY BANKER!
I'LL GO WITH YOU, DUKE!
PLEASE STAY SEATED, MR. McDUCK! THIS IS A PRIVATE CALL!
I'LL WAIT OUTSIDE THE BOOTH!
AND I'LL WAIT WITH YOU, MR. McDUCK!
TELEPHONE
$9.13

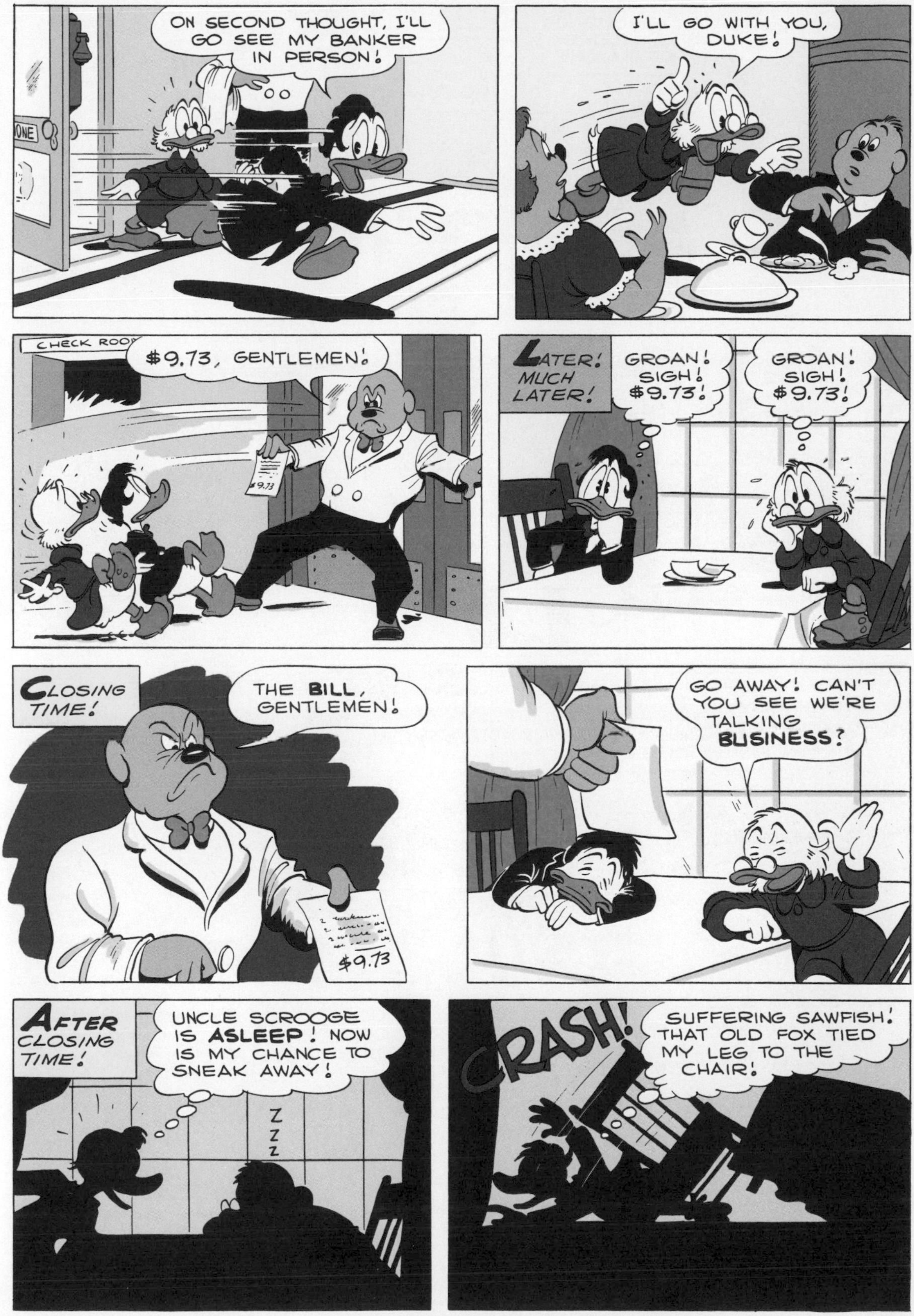
ON SECOND THOUGHT, I'LL GO SEE MY BANKER IN PERSON!
ONE
I'LL GO WITH YOU, DUKE!
CHECK ROO
$9.73, GENTLEMEN!
$9.73
LATER! MUCH LATER!
GROAN! SIGH! $9.73!
GROAN! SIGH! $9.73!
CLOSING TIME!
THE BILL, GENTLEMEN!
$9.73
GO AWAY! CAN'T YOU SEE WE'RE TALKING BUSINESS?
AFTER CLOSING TIME!
UNCLE SCROOGE IS ASLEEP! NOW IS MY CHANCE TO SNEAK AWAY!
Z Z Z
CRASH!
SUFFERING SAWFISH! THAT OLD FOX TIED MY LEG TO THE CHAIR!

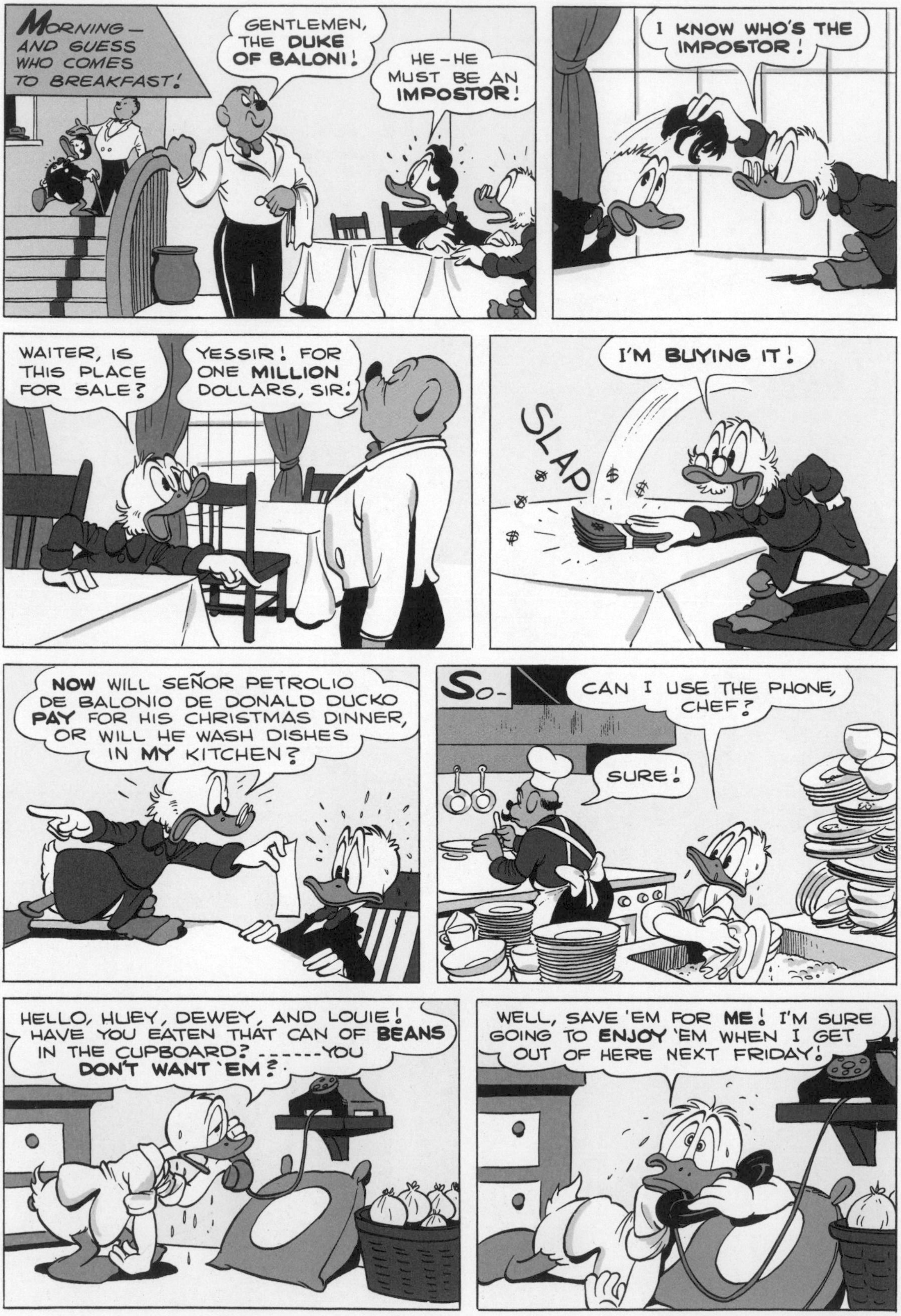

MORNING— AND GUESS WHO COMES TO BREAKFAST!
GENTLEMEN, THE DUKE OF BALONI!
HE—HE MUST BE AN IMPOSTOR!
I KNOW WHO'S THE IMPOSTOR!
WAITER, IS THIS PLACE FOR SALE?
YESSIR! FOR ONE MILLION DOLLARS, SIR!
I'M BUYING IT!
SLAP
NOW WILL SEÑOR PETROLIO DE BALONIO DE DONALD DUCKO PAY FOR HIS CHRISTMAS DINNER, OR WILL HE WASH DISHES IN MY KITCHEN?
SO—
CAN I USE THE PHONE, CHEF?
SURE!
HELLO, HUEY, DEWEY, AND LOUIE! HAVE YOU EATEN THAT CAN OF BEANS IN THE CUPBOARD? ------YOU DON'T WANT 'EM?
WELL, SAVE 'EM FOR ME! I'M SURE GOING TO ENJOY 'EM WHEN I GET OUT OF HERE NEXT FRIDAY!

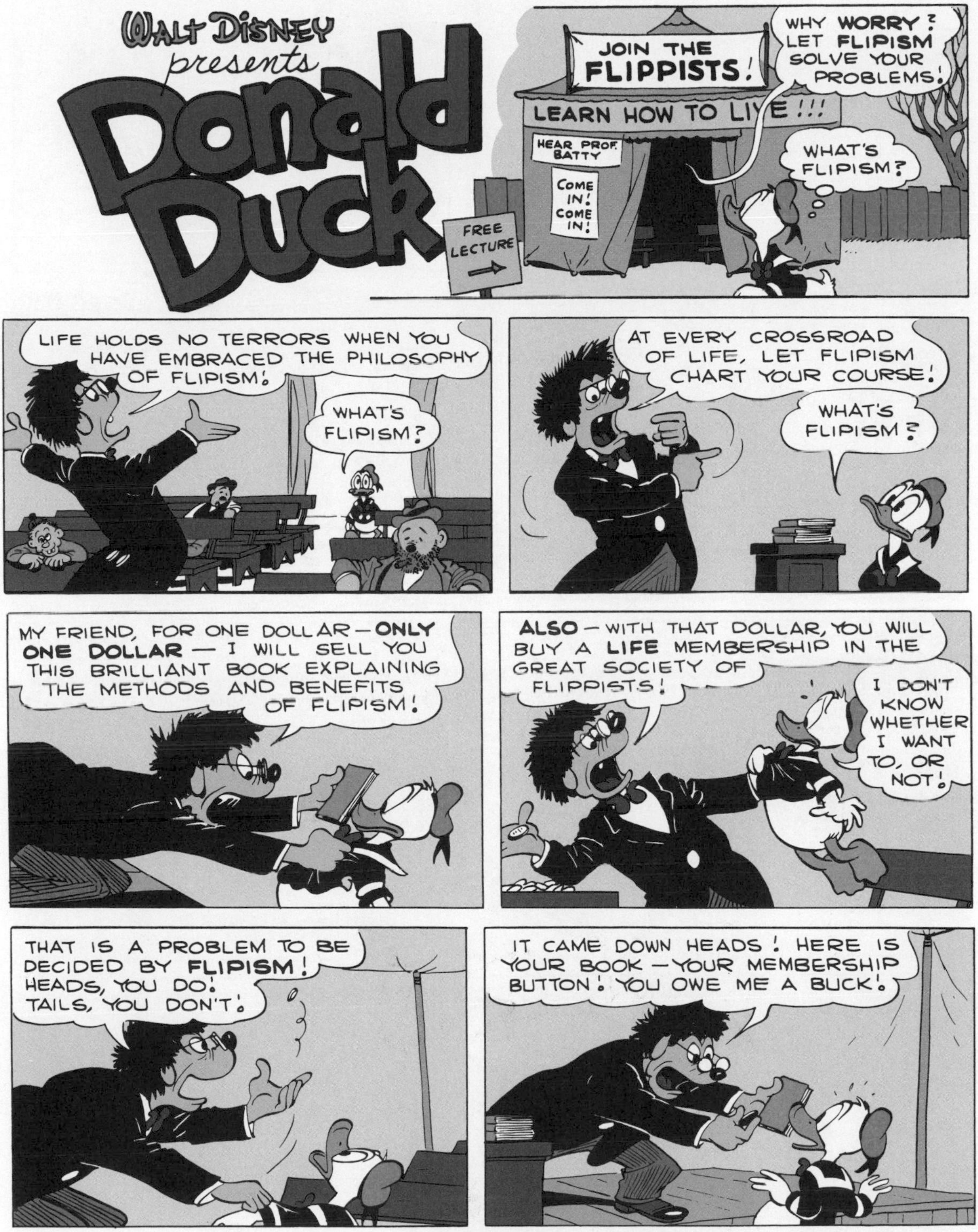
WALT DISNEY presents Donald Duck
JOIN THE FLIPPISTS!
WHY WORRY? LET FLIPISM SOLVE YOUR PROBLEMS!
LEARN HOW TO LIVE!!!
HEAR PROF. BATTY
COME IN! COME IN!
FREE LECTURE
WHAT'S FLIPISM?
LIFE HOLDS NO TERRORS WHEN YOU HAVE EMBRACED THE PHILOSOPHY OF FLIPISM!
WHAT'S FLIPISM?
AT EVERY CROSSROAD OF LIFE, LET FLIPISM CHART YOUR COURSE!
WHAT'S FLIPISM?
MY FRIEND, FOR ONE DOLLAR—ONLY ONE DOLLAR—I WILL SELL YOU THIS BRILLIANT BOOK EXPLAINING THE METHODS AND BENEFITS OF FLIPISM!
ALSO—WITH THAT DOLLAR, YOU WILL BUY A LIFE MEMBERSHIP IN THE GREAT SOCIETY OF FLIPPISTS!
I DON'T KNOW WHETHER I WANT TO, OR NOT!
THAT IS A PROBLEM TO BE DECIDED BY FLIPISM! HEADS, YOU DO! TAILS, YOU DON'T!
IT CAME DOWN HEADS! HERE IS YOUR BOOK—YOUR MEMBERSHIP BUTTON! YOU OWE ME A BUCK!

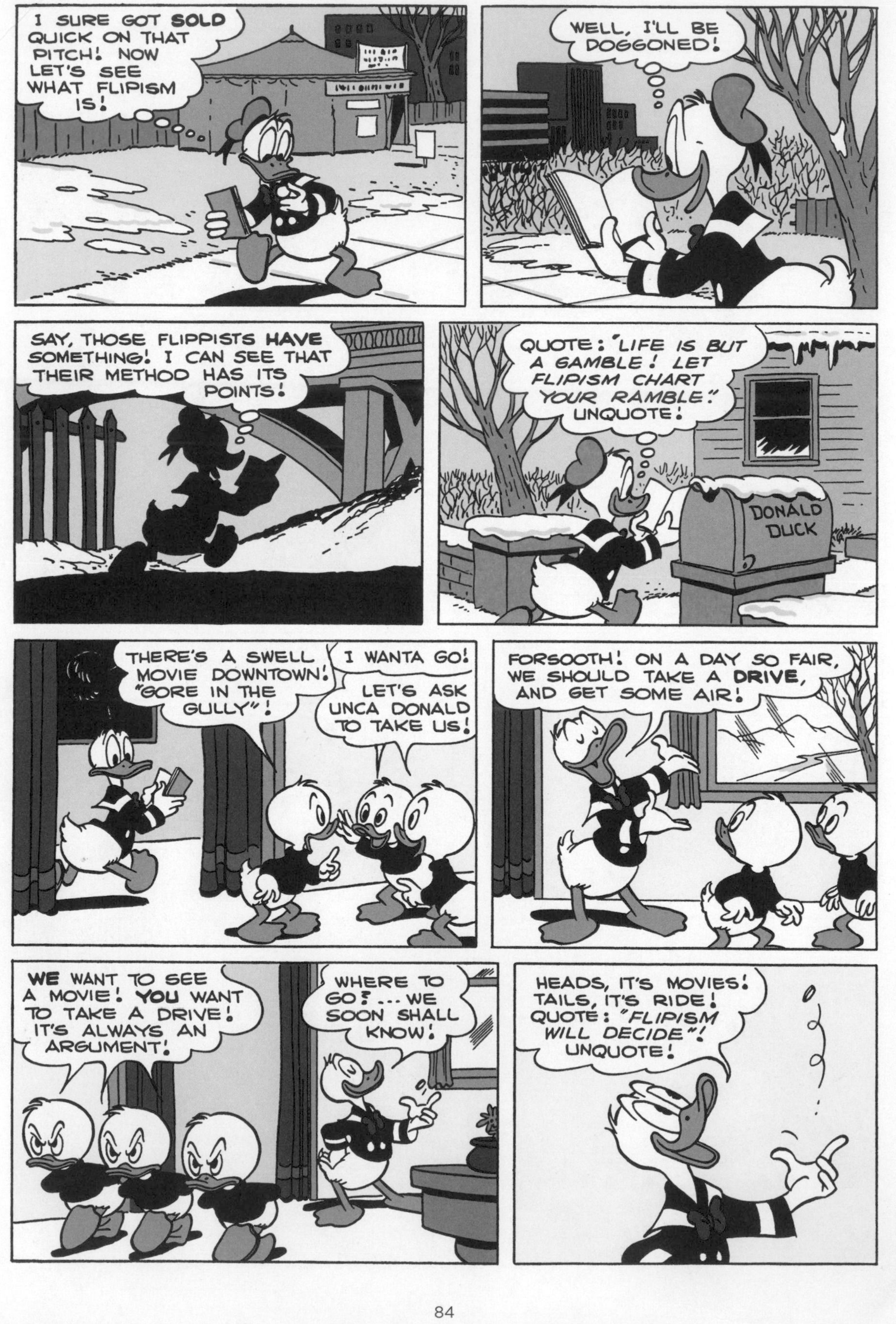
I SURE GOT SOLD QUICK ON THAT PITCH! NOW LET'S SEE WHAT FLIPISM IS!
WELL, I'LL BE DOGGONED!
SAY, THOSE FLIPPISTS HAVE SOMETHING! I CAN SEE THAT THEIR METHOD HAS ITS POINTS!
QUOTE: "LIFE IS BUT A GAMBLE! LET FLIPISM CHART YOUR RAMBLE!" UNQUOTE!
DONALD DUCK
THERE'S A SWELL MOVIE DOWNTOWN! "GORE IN THE GULLY"!
I WANTA GO!
LET'S ASK UNCA DONALD TO TAKE US!
FORSOOTH! ON A DAY SO FAIR, WE SHOULD TAKE A DRIVE, AND GET SOME AIR!
WE WANT TO SEE A MOVIE! YOU WANT TO TAKE A DRIVE! IT'S ALWAYS AN ARGUMENT!
WHERE TO GO? ... WE SOON SHALL KNOW!
HEADS, IT'S MOVIES! TAILS, IT'S RIDE! QUOTE: "FLIPISM WILL DECIDE"! UNQUOTE!

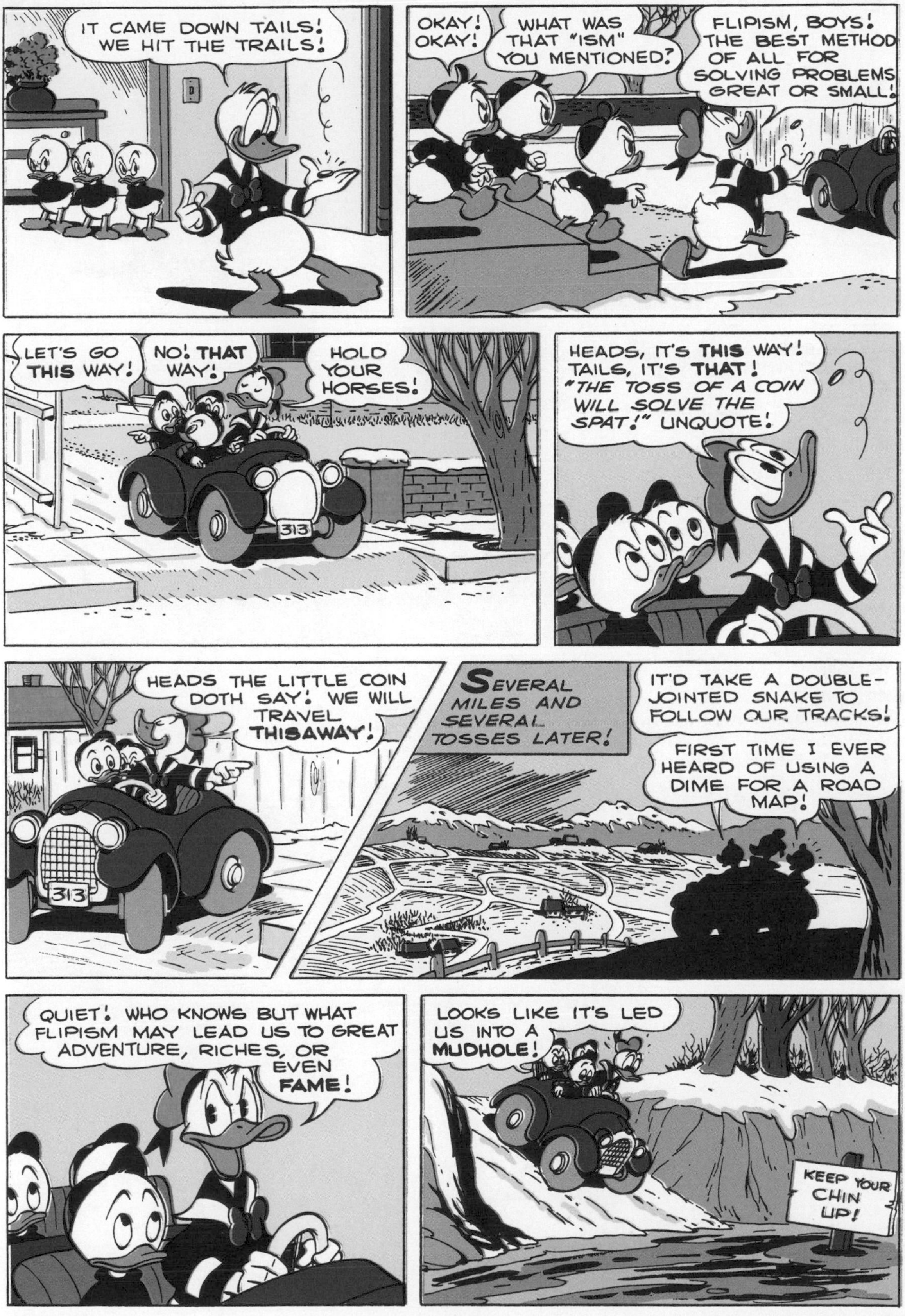

IT CAME DOWN TAILS! WE HIT THE TRAILS!
OKAY! OKAY!
WHAT WAS THAT "ISM" YOU MENTIONED?
FLIPISM, BOYS! THE BEST METHOD OF ALL FOR SOLVING PROBLEMS GREAT OR SMALL!
LET'S GO THIS WAY!
NO! THAT WAY!
HOLD YOUR HORSES!
313
HEADS, IT'S THIS WAY! TAILS, IT'S THAT! "THE TOSS OF A COIN WILL SOLVE THE SPAT!" UNQUOTE!
HEADS THE LITTLE COIN DOTH SAY! WE WILL TRAVEL THISAWAY!
313
SEVERAL MILES AND SEVERAL TOSSES LATER!
IT'D TAKE A DOUBLE-JOINTED SNAKE TO FOLLOW OUR TRACKS!
FIRST TIME I EVER HEARD OF USING A DIME FOR A ROAD MAP!
QUIET! WHO KNOWS BUT WHAT FLIPISM MAY LEAD US TO GREAT ADVENTURE, RICHES, OR EVEN FAME!
LOOKS LIKE IT'S LED US INTO A MUDHOLE!
KEEP YOUR CHIN UP!

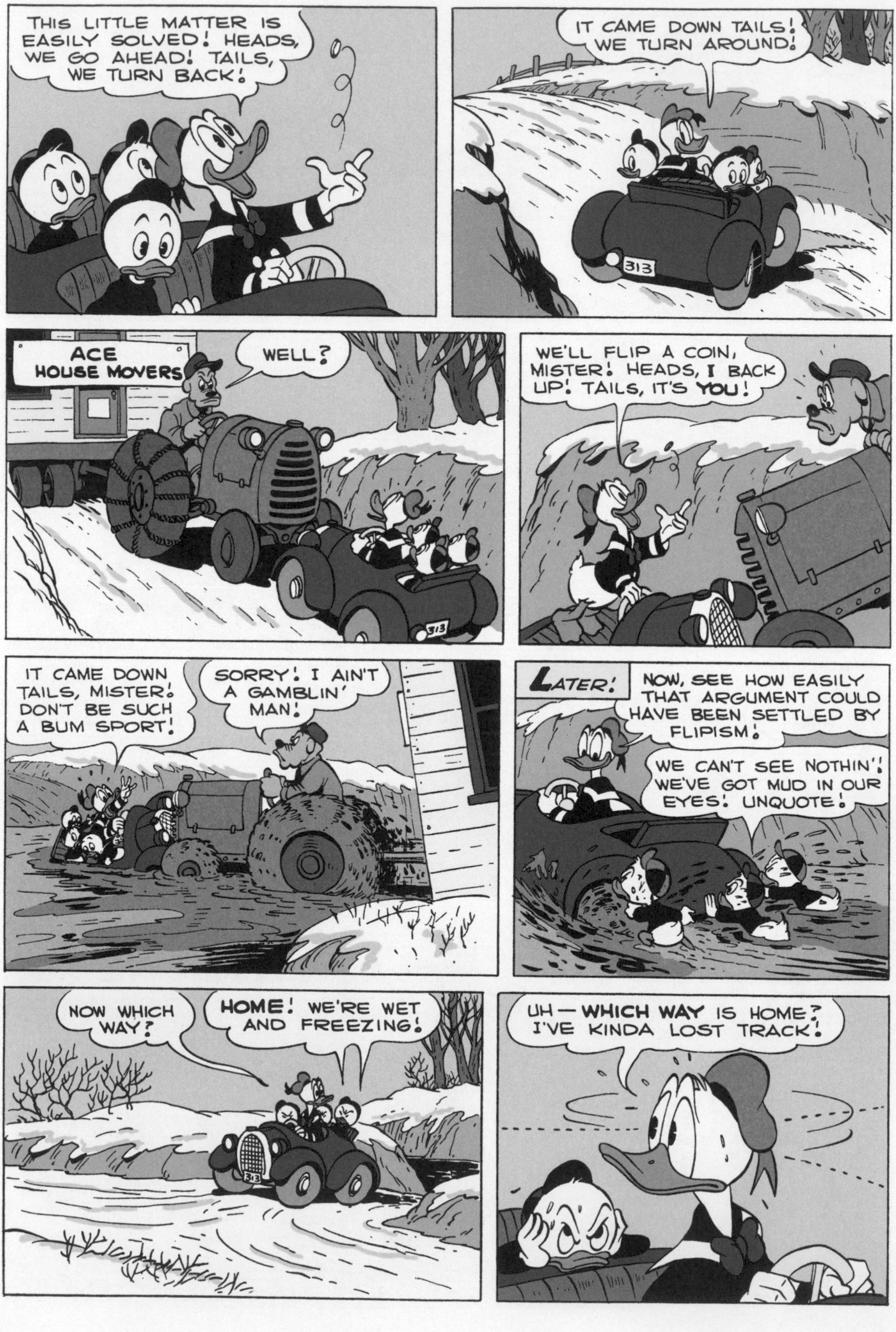
THIS LITTLE MATTER IS EASILY SOLVED! HEADS, WE GO AHEAD! TAILS, WE TURN BACK!
IT CAME DOWN TAILS! WE TURN AROUND!
313
ACE HOUSE MOVERS
WELL?
313
WE'LL FLIP A COIN, MISTER! HEADS, I BACK UP! TAILS, IT'S YOU!
IT CAME DOWN TAILS, MISTER! DON'T BE SUCH A BUM SPORT!
SORRY! I AIN'T A GAMBLIN' MAN!
LATER!
NOW, SEE HOW EASILY THAT ARGUMENT COULD HAVE BEEN SETTLED BY FLIPISM!
WE CAN'T SEE NOTHIN'! WE'VE GOT MUD IN OUR EYES! UNQUOTE!
NOW WHICH WAY?
HOME! WE'RE WET AND FREEZING!
313
UH—WHICH WAY IS HOME? I'VE KINDA LOST TRACK!

OH, WELL, WHY WORRY WHEN THERE'S FLIPISM TO TELL US THE WAY!
THE COIN SAYS HOME IS DOWN THIS ROAD!
IF IT'S RIGHT, THEN THEY'VE STARTED PRINTING HOMING PIGEONS ON THE DIMES!
SEE? WE'RE COMING TO A MAIN HIGHWAY!
YES! BUT WHERE DOES THE HIGHWAY GO?
OH, MY HEAVENLY DAYS!
WE CAN SEE THAT HERE IS WHERE FLIPISM GETS THE ACID TEST!
SEVEN ROUTE INTERCHANGE OBEY RULES

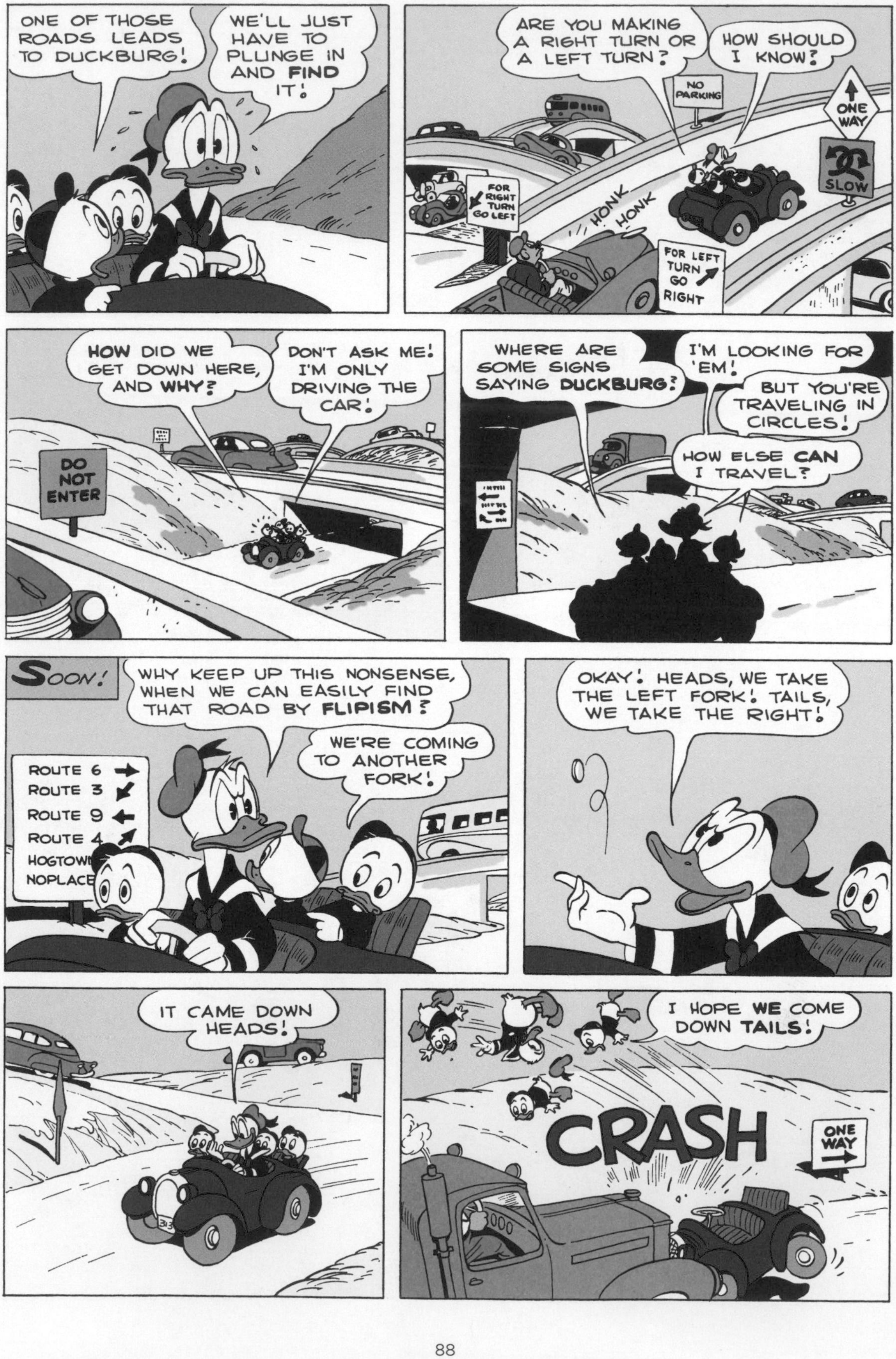
ONE OF THOSE ROADS LEADS TO DUCKBURG!
WE'LL JUST HAVE TO PLUNGE IN AND FIND IT!
ARE YOU MAKING A RIGHT TURN OR A LEFT TURN?
HOW SHOULD I KNOW?
NO PARKING
ONE WAY
SLOW
FOR RIGHT TURN GO LEFT
HONK HONK
FOR LEFT TURN GO RIGHT
HOW DID WE GET DOWN HERE, AND WHY?
DON'T ASK ME! I'M ONLY DRIVING THE CAR!
DO NOT ENTER
WHERE ARE SOME SIGNS SAYING DUCKBURG?
I'M LOOKING FOR 'EM!
BUT YOU'RE TRAVELING IN CIRCLES!
HOW ELSE CAN I TRAVEL?
SOON!
WHY KEEP UP THIS NONSENSE, WHEN WE CAN EASILY FIND THAT ROAD BY FLIPISM?
WE'RE COMING TO ANOTHER FORK!
ROUTE 6
ROUTE 3
ROUTE 9
ROUTE 4
HOGTOWN
NOPLACE
OKAY! HEADS, WE TAKE THE LEFT FORK! TAILS, WE TAKE THE RIGHT!
IT CAME DOWN HEADS!
313
I HOPE WE COME DOWN TAILS!
CRASH
ONE WAY
3000

THE DUCKS REACH DUCKBURG OKAY — IN A POLICE CAR!

YOU HAVEN'T A CHANCE! THE CITY IS BROKE, AND THE JUDGE WANTS A RAISE!

SO YOU DROVE THE WRONG WAY ON A ONE-WAY ROAD?

YES, YOUR HONOR!

IT WAS LIKE THIS — I'M A **FLIPPIST**! I TOSSED A DIME TO SEE **WHICH** WAY I'D GO!

YOU **DID**! ----WELL, THAT MAKES THESE CHARGES AGAINST YOU SEEM RATHER **SILLY**!

I'M NOT GOING TO FINE YOU THE USUAL $5.00 FOR WRONG-WAY DRIVING, NOR THE USUAL $10.00 FOR DISRUPTING TRAFFIC!

THANKS, JUDGE!

BUT I **AM** GOING TO FINE YOU **FIFTY** DOLLARS FOR LETTING A DIME DO YOUR **THINKING** FOR YOU!

PLOP

HEY! AREN'T YOU GOING HOME, UNCA DONALD?

NO! I'M GOING TO SEE A MAN ABOUT A BOOK!

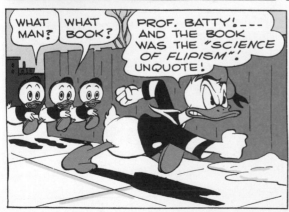

WHAT MAN?

WHAT BOOK?

PROF. BATTY! --- AND THE BOOK WAS THE "SCIENCE OF FLIPISM"! UNQUOTE!

THE **FAKE**! HE'S GONE! HIS TENT WAS STANDING RIGHT **HERE**!

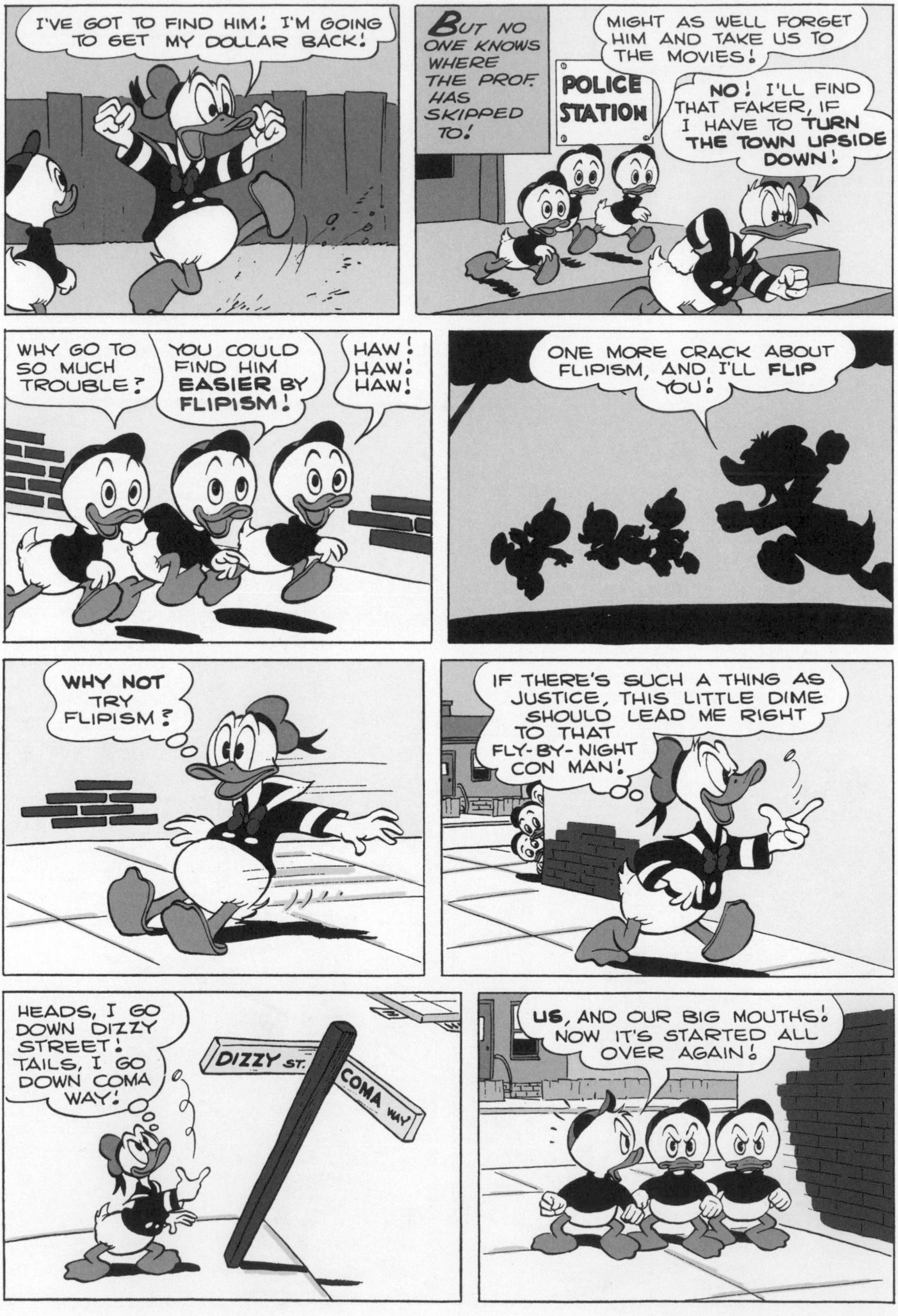

I'VE GOT TO FIND HIM! I'M GOING TO GET MY DOLLAR BACK!
BUT NO ONE KNOWS WHERE THE PROF. HAS SKIPPED TO!
MIGHT AS WELL FORGET HIM AND TAKE US TO THE MOVIES!
POLICE STATION
NO! I'LL FIND THAT FAKER, IF I HAVE TO TURN THE TOWN UPSIDE DOWN!
WHY GO TO SO MUCH TROUBLE?
YOU COULD FIND HIM EASIER BY FLIPISM!
HAW! HAW! HAW!
ONE MORE CRACK ABOUT FLIPISM, AND I'LL FLIP YOU!
WHY NOT TRY FLIPISM?
IF THERE'S SUCH A THING AS JUSTICE, THIS LITTLE DIME SHOULD LEAD ME RIGHT TO THAT FLY-BY-NIGHT CON MAN!
HEADS, I GO DOWN DIZZY STREET! TAILS, I GO DOWN COMA WAY!
DIZZY ST.
COMA WAY
US, AND OUR BIG MOUTHS! NOW IT'S STARTED ALL OVER AGAIN!

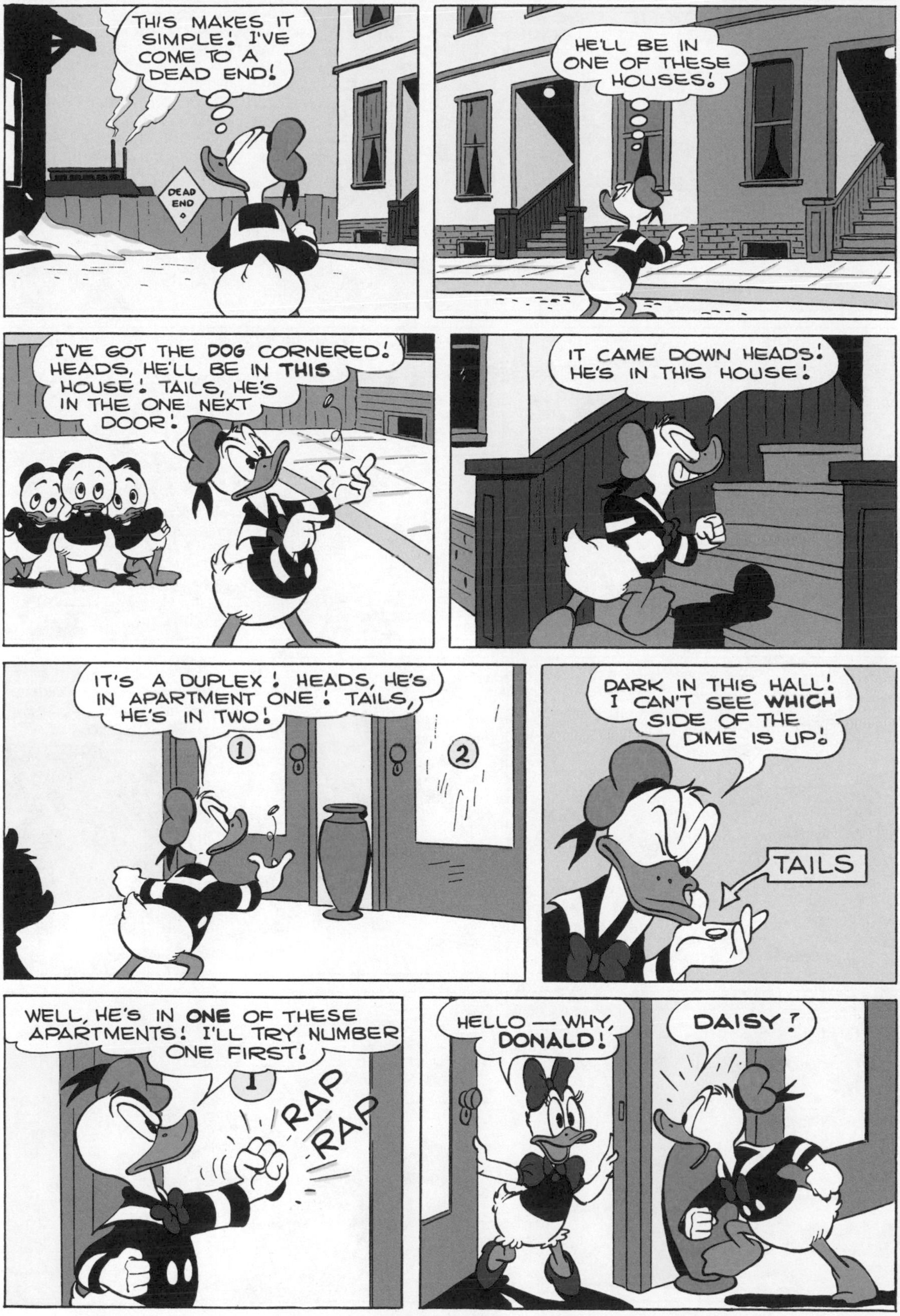
THIS MAKES IT SIMPLE! I'VE COME TO A DEAD END!
DEAD END
HE'LL BE IN ONE OF THESE HOUSES!
I'VE GOT THE DOG CORNERED! HEADS, HE'LL BE IN THIS HOUSE! TAILS, HE'S IN THE ONE NEXT DOOR!
IT CAME DOWN HEADS! HE'S IN THIS HOUSE!
IT'S A DUPLEX! HEADS, HE'S IN APARTMENT ONE! TAILS, HE'S IN TWO!
1
2
DARK IN THIS HALL! I CAN'T SEE WHICH SIDE OF THE DIME IS UP!
TAILS
WELL, HE'S IN ONE OF THESE APARTMENTS! I'LL TRY NUMBER ONE FIRST!
1
RAP RAP
HELLO — WHY, DONALD!
DAISY?

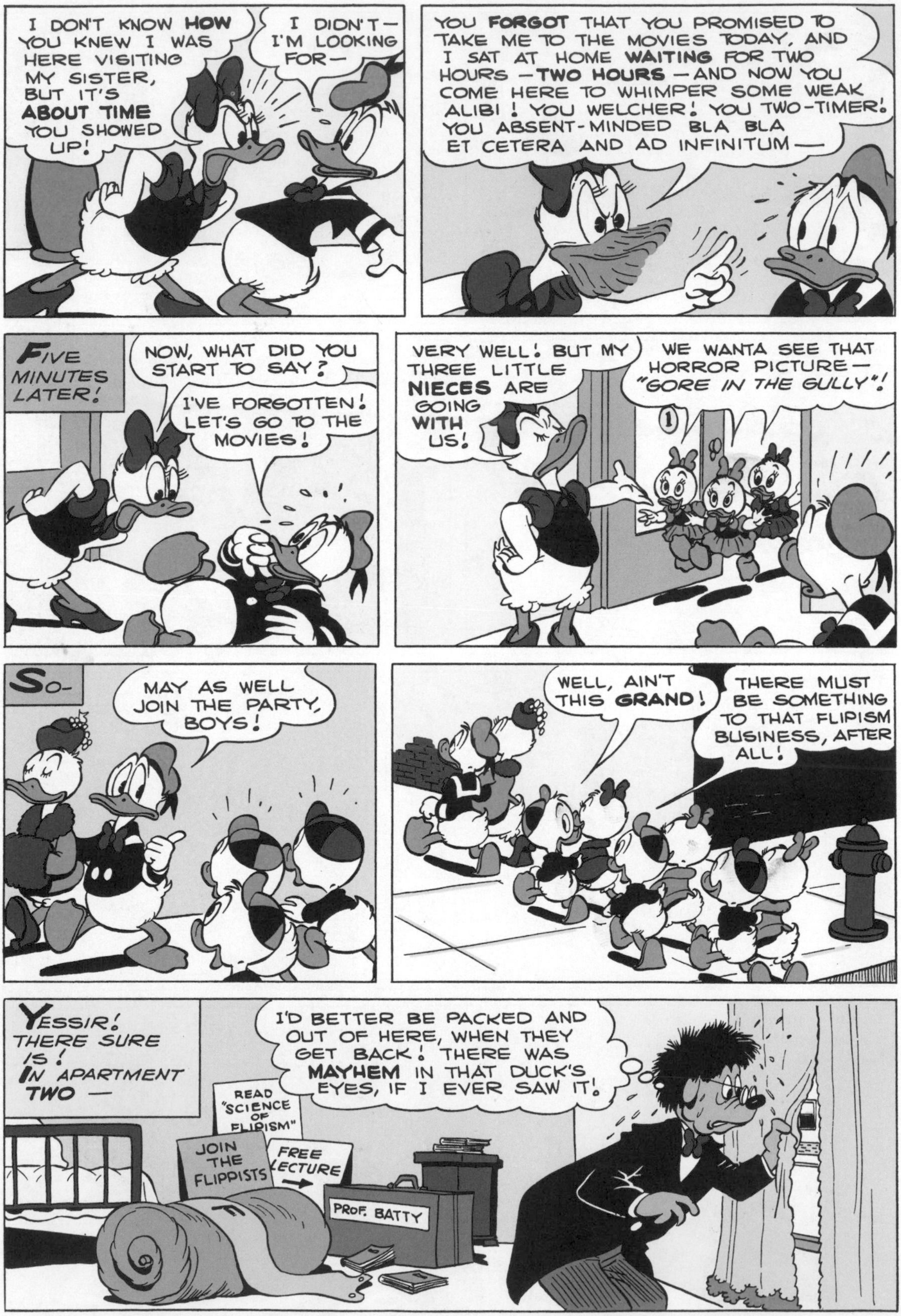

I DON'T KNOW HOW YOU KNEW I WAS HERE VISITING MY SISTER, BUT IT'S ABOUT TIME YOU SHOWED UP!
I DIDN'T— I'M LOOKING FOR—
YOU FORGOT THAT YOU PROMISED TO TAKE ME TO THE MOVIES TODAY, AND I SAT AT HOME WAITING FOR TWO HOURS —TWO HOURS— AND NOW YOU COME HERE TO WHIMPER SOME WEAK ALIBI! YOU WELCHER! YOU TWO-TIMER! YOU ABSENT-MINDED BLA BLA ET CETERA AND AD INFINITUM—
FIVE MINUTES LATER!
NOW, WHAT DID YOU START TO SAY?
I'VE FORGOTTEN! LET'S GO TO THE MOVIES!
VERY WELL! BUT MY THREE LITTLE NIECES ARE GOING WITH US!
WE WANTA SEE THAT HORROR PICTURE— "GORE IN THE GULLY"!
1
SO-
MAY AS WELL JOIN THE PARTY, BOYS!
WELL, AIN'T THIS GRAND!
THERE MUST BE SOMETHING TO THAT FLIPISM BUSINESS, AFTER ALL!
YESSIR! THERE SURE IS! IN APARTMENT TWO—
I'D BETTER BE PACKED AND OUT OF HERE, WHEN THEY GET BACK! THERE WAS MAYHEM IN THAT DUCK'S EYES, IF I EVER SAW IT!
READ "SCIENCE OF FLIPISM"
JOIN THE FLIPPISTS
FREE LECTURE
PROF. BATTY

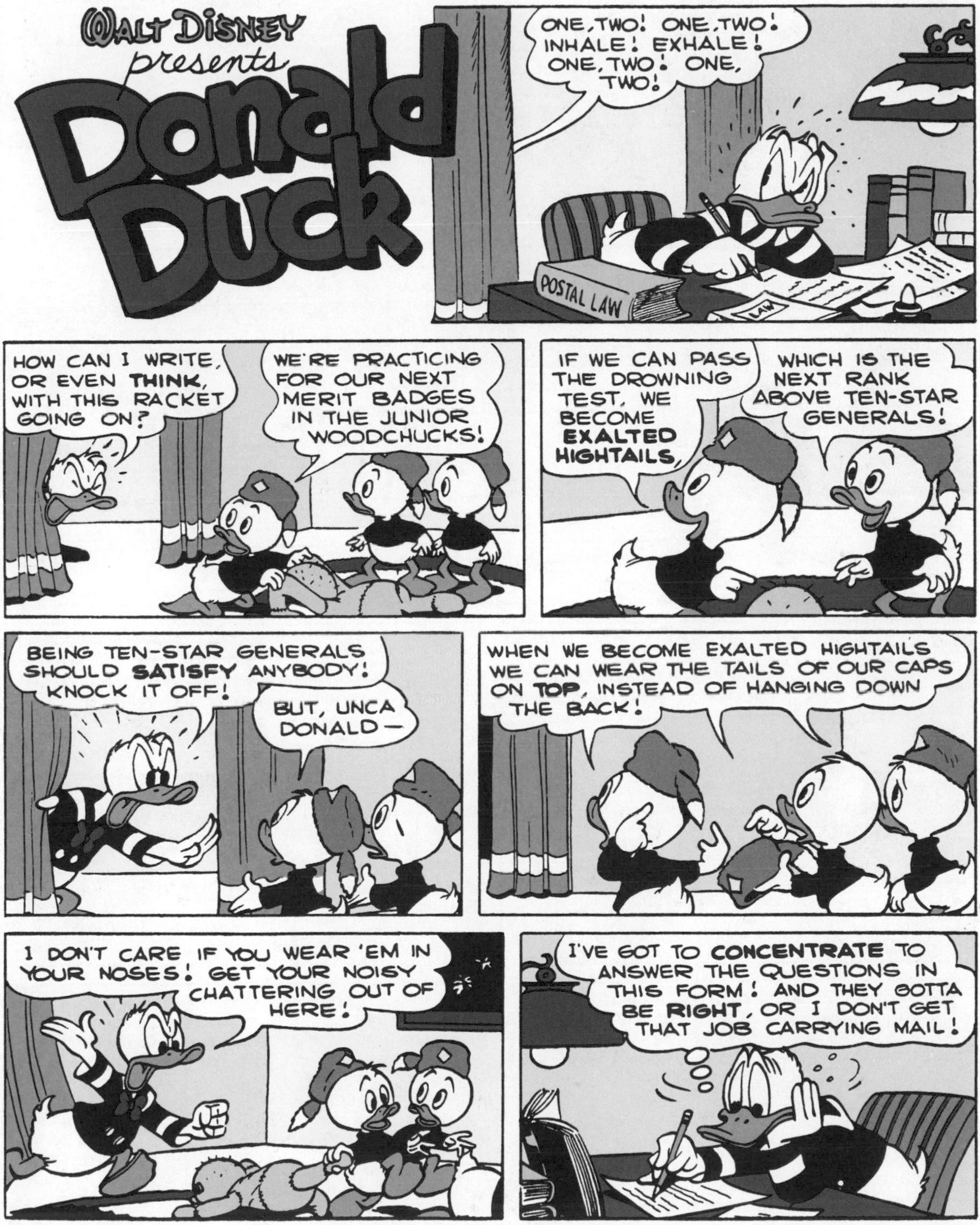
WALT DISNEY presents
Donald Duck
ONE, TWO! ONE, TWO! INHALE! EXHALE! ONE, TWO! ONE, TWO!
POSTAL LAW
LAW
HOW CAN I WRITE, OR EVEN THINK, WITH THIS RACKET GOING ON?
WE'RE PRACTICING FOR OUR NEXT MERIT BADGES IN THE JUNIOR WOODCHUCKS!
IF WE CAN PASS THE DROWNING TEST, WE BECOME EXALTED HIGHTAILS,
WHICH IS THE NEXT RANK ABOVE TEN-STAR GENERALS!
BEING TEN-STAR GENERALS SHOULD SATISFY ANYBODY! KNOCK IT OFF!
BUT, UNCA DONALD—
WHEN WE BECOME EXALTED HIGHTAILS WE CAN WEAR THE TAILS OF OUR CAPS ON TOP, INSTEAD OF HANGING DOWN THE BACK!
I DON'T CARE IF YOU WEAR 'EM IN YOUR NOSES! GET YOUR NOISY CHATTERING OUT OF HERE!
I'VE GOT TO CONCENTRATE TO ANSWER THE QUESTIONS IN THIS FORM! AND THEY GOTTA BE RIGHT, OR I DON'T GET THAT JOB CARRYING MAIL!

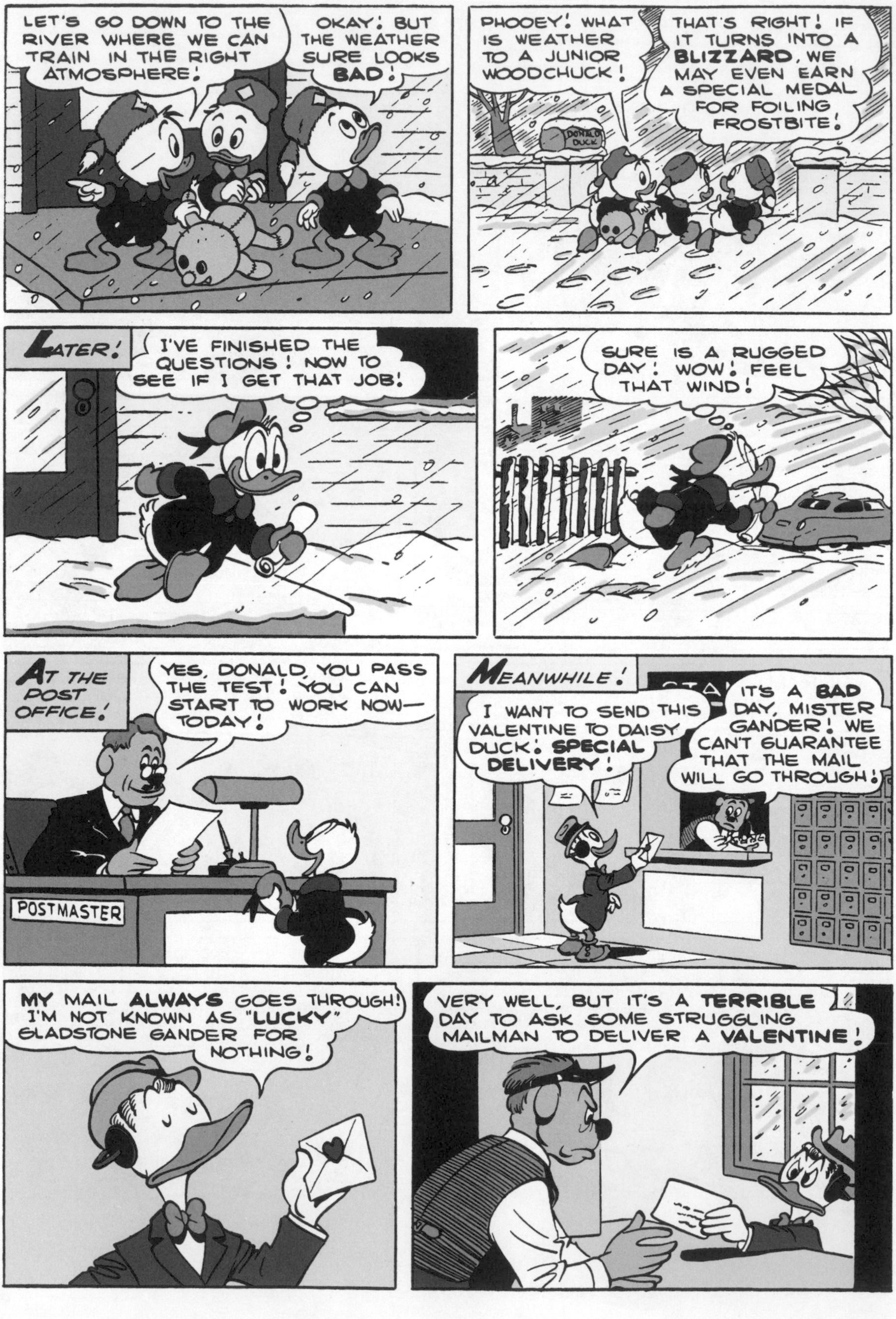
LET'S GO DOWN TO THE RIVER WHERE WE CAN TRAIN IN THE RIGHT ATMOSPHERE!
OKAY! BUT THE WEATHER SURE LOOKS BAD!
PHOOEY! WHAT IS WEATHER TO A JUNIOR WOODCHUCK!
THAT'S RIGHT! IF IT TURNS INTO A BLIZZARD, WE MAY EVEN EARN A SPECIAL MEDAL FOR FOILING FROSTBITE!
DONALD DUCK
LATER!
I'VE FINISHED THE QUESTIONS! NOW TO SEE IF I GET THAT JOB!
SURE IS A RUGGED DAY! WOW! FEEL THAT WIND!
AT THE POST OFFICE!
YES, DONALD, YOU PASS THE TEST! YOU CAN START TO WORK NOW—TODAY!
POSTMASTER
MEANWHILE!
I WANT TO SEND THIS VALENTINE TO DAISY DUCK! SPECIAL DELIVERY!
IT'S A BAD DAY, MISTER GANDER! WE CAN'T GUARANTEE THAT THE MAIL WILL GO THROUGH!
MY MAIL ALWAYS GOES THROUGH! I'M NOT KNOWN AS "LUCKY" GLADSTONE GANDER FOR NOTHING!
VERY WELL, BUT IT'S A TERRIBLE DAY TO ASK SOME STRUGGLING MAILMAN TO DELIVER A VALENTINE!

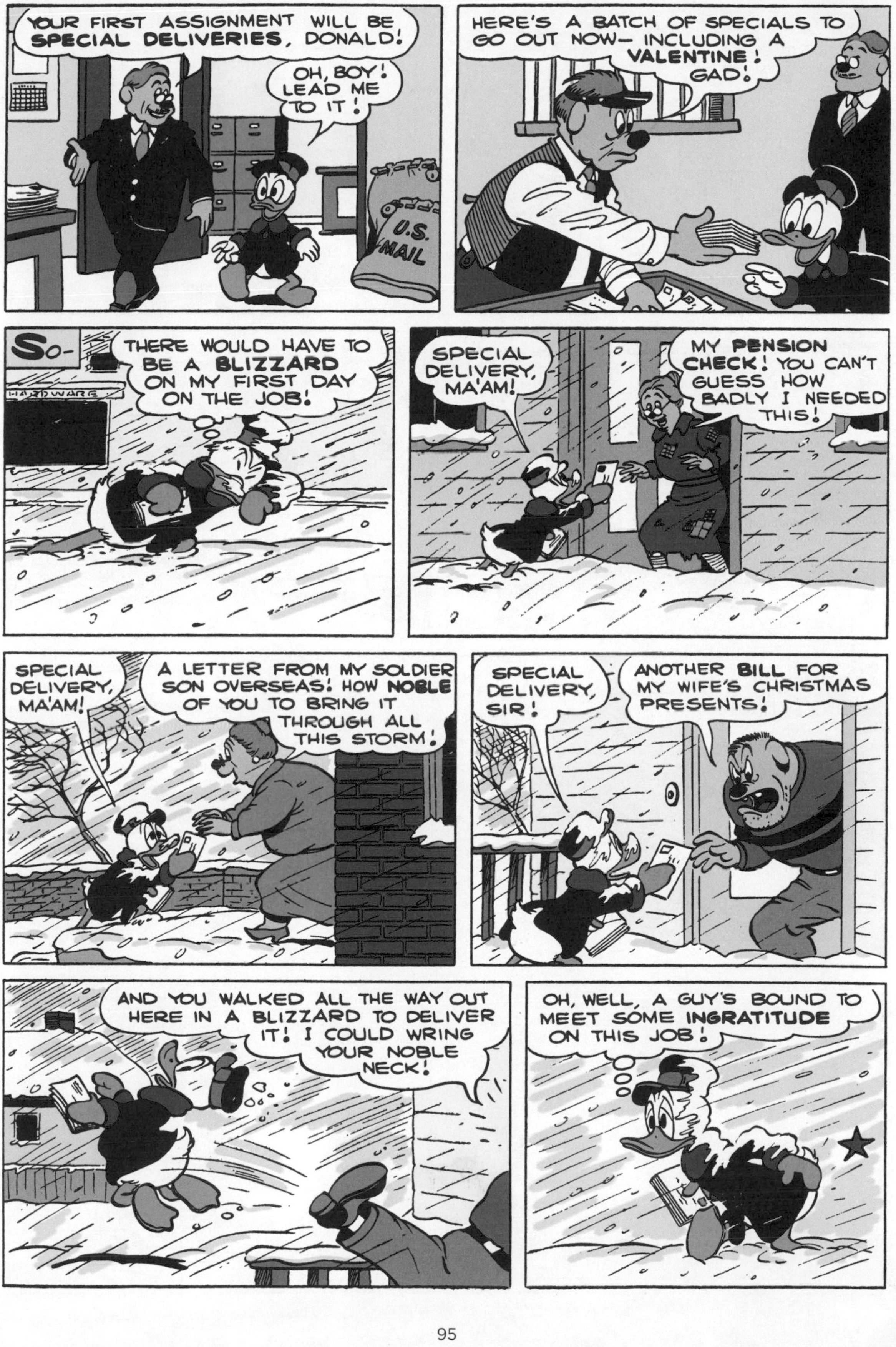
YOUR FIRST ASSIGNMENT WILL BE SPECIAL DELIVERIES, DONALD!
OH, BOY! LEAD ME TO IT!
U.S. MAIL
HERE'S A BATCH OF SPECIALS TO GO OUT NOW— INCLUDING A VALENTINE! GAD!
SO—
THERE WOULD HAVE TO BE A BLIZZARD ON MY FIRST DAY ON THE JOB!
HARDWARE
SPECIAL DELIVERY, MA'AM!
MY PENSION CHECK! YOU CAN'T GUESS HOW BADLY I NEEDED THIS!
SPECIAL DELIVERY, MA'AM!
A LETTER FROM MY SOLDIER SON OVERSEAS! HOW NOBLE OF YOU TO BRING IT THROUGH ALL THIS STORM!
SPECIAL DELIVERY, SIR!
ANOTHER BILL FOR MY WIFE'S CHRISTMAS PRESENTS!
AND YOU WALKED ALL THE WAY OUT HERE IN A BLIZZARD TO DELIVER IT! I COULD WRING YOUR NOBLE NECK!
OH, WELL, A GUY'S BOUND TO MEET SOME INGRATITUDE ON THIS JOB!

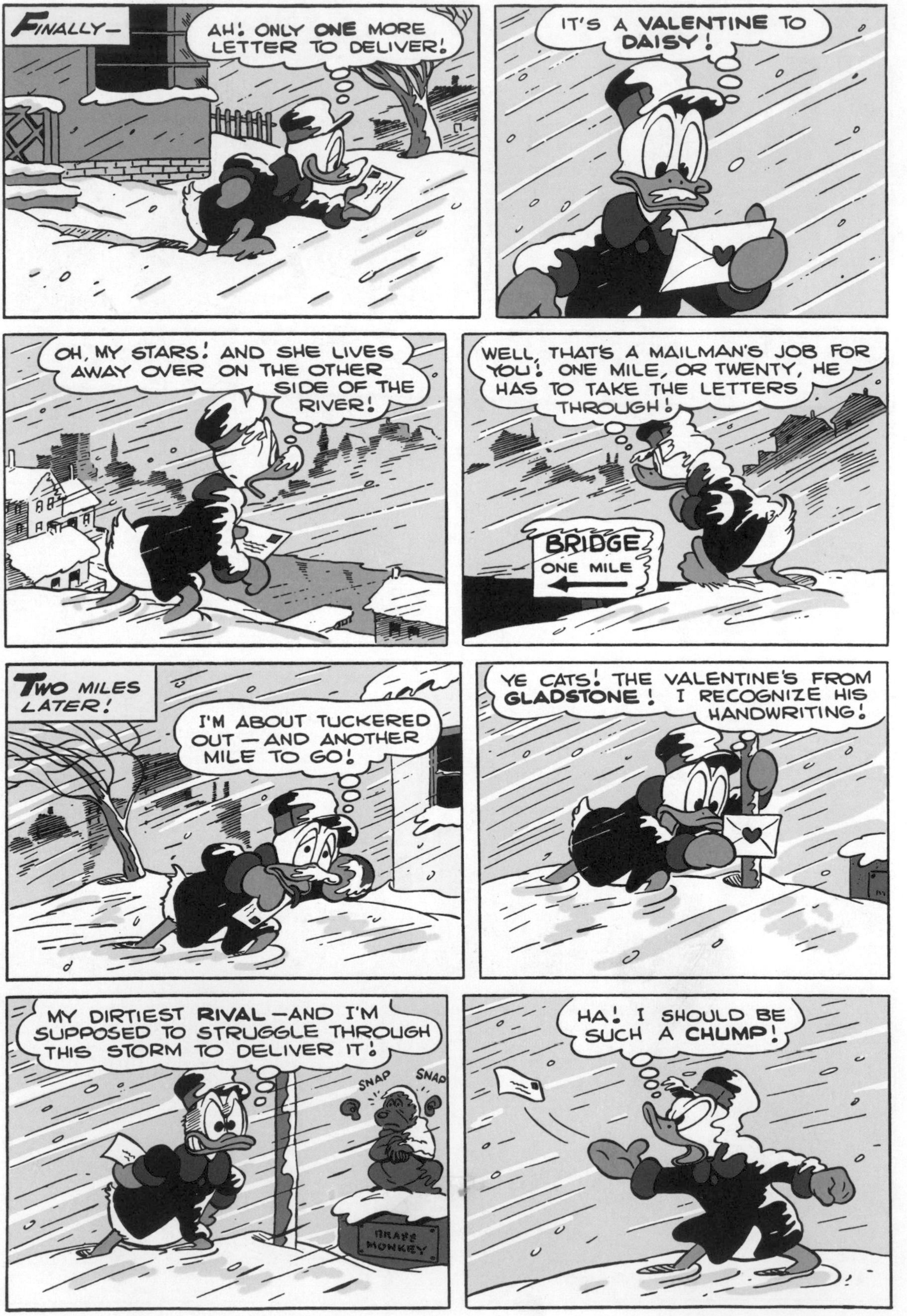
FINALLY—
AH! ONLY ONE MORE LETTER TO DELIVER!
IT'S A VALENTINE TO DAISY!
OH, MY STARS! AND SHE LIVES AWAY OVER ON THE OTHER SIDE OF THE RIVER!
WELL, THAT'S A MAILMAN'S JOB FOR YOU! ONE MILE, OR TWENTY, HE HAS TO TAKE THE LETTERS THROUGH!
BRIDGE
ONE MILE
TWO MILES LATER!
I'M ABOUT TUCKERED OUT—AND ANOTHER MILE TO GO!
YE CATS! THE VALENTINE'S FROM GLADSTONE! I RECOGNIZE HIS HANDWRITING!
MY DIRTIEST RIVAL—AND I'M SUPPOSED TO STRUGGLE THROUGH THIS STORM TO DELIVER IT!
SNAP
SNAP
BRASS MONKEY
HA! I SHOULD BE SUCH A CHUMP!

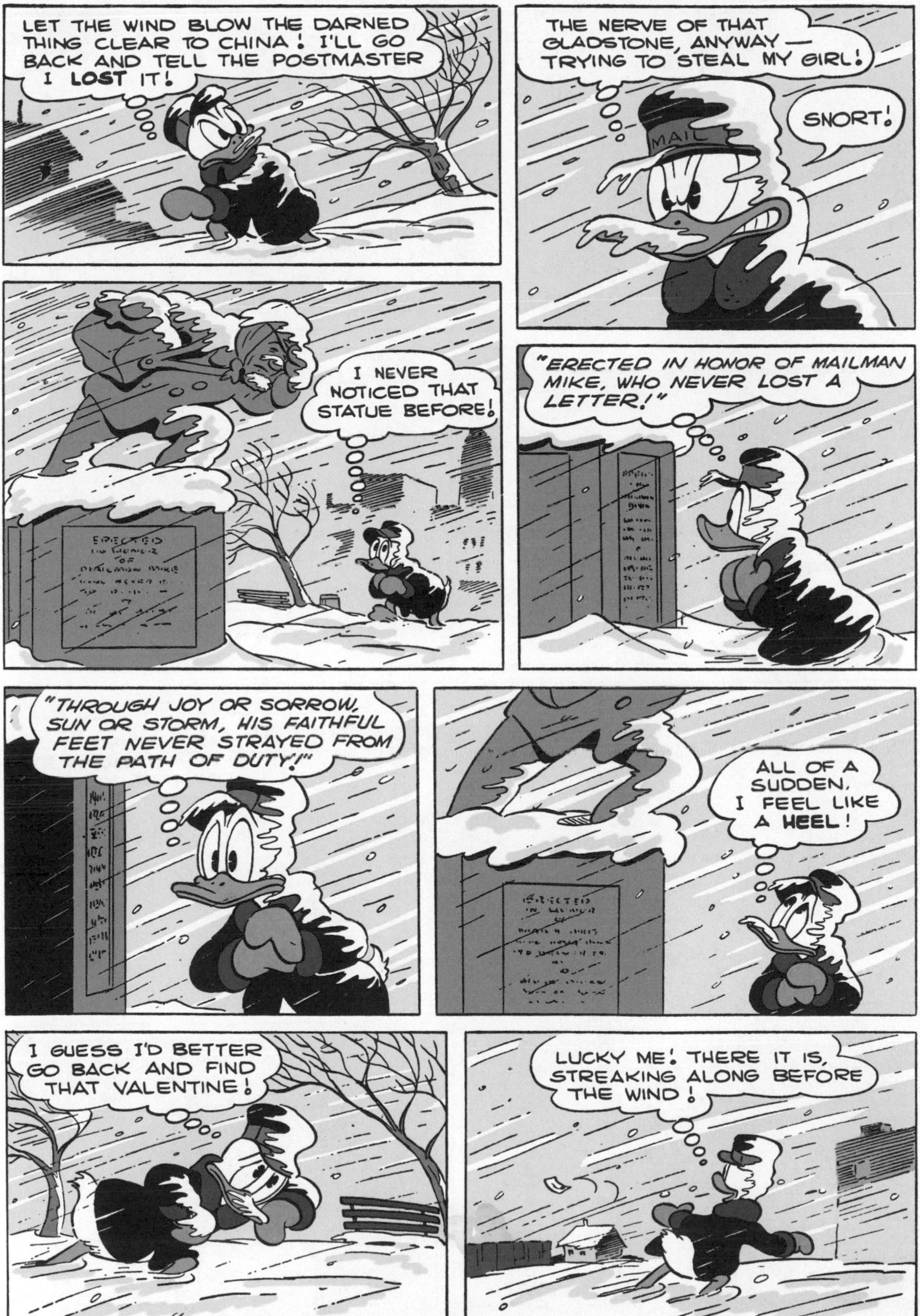
LET THE WIND BLOW THE DARNED THING CLEAR TO CHINA! I'LL GO BACK AND TELL THE POSTMASTER I LOST IT!
THE NERVE OF THAT GLADSTONE, ANYWAY — TRYING TO STEAL MY GIRL!
MAIL
SNORT!
I NEVER NOTICED THAT STATUE BEFORE!
"ERECTED IN HONOR OF MAILMAN MIKE, WHO NEVER LOST A LETTER!"
"THROUGH JOY OR SORROW, SUN OR STORM, HIS FAITHFUL FEET NEVER STRAYED FROM THE PATH OF DUTY!"
ALL OF A SUDDEN, I FEEL LIKE A HEEL!
I GUESS I'D BETTER GO BACK AND FIND THAT VALENTINE!
LUCKY ME! THERE IT IS, STREAKING ALONG BEFORE THE WIND!

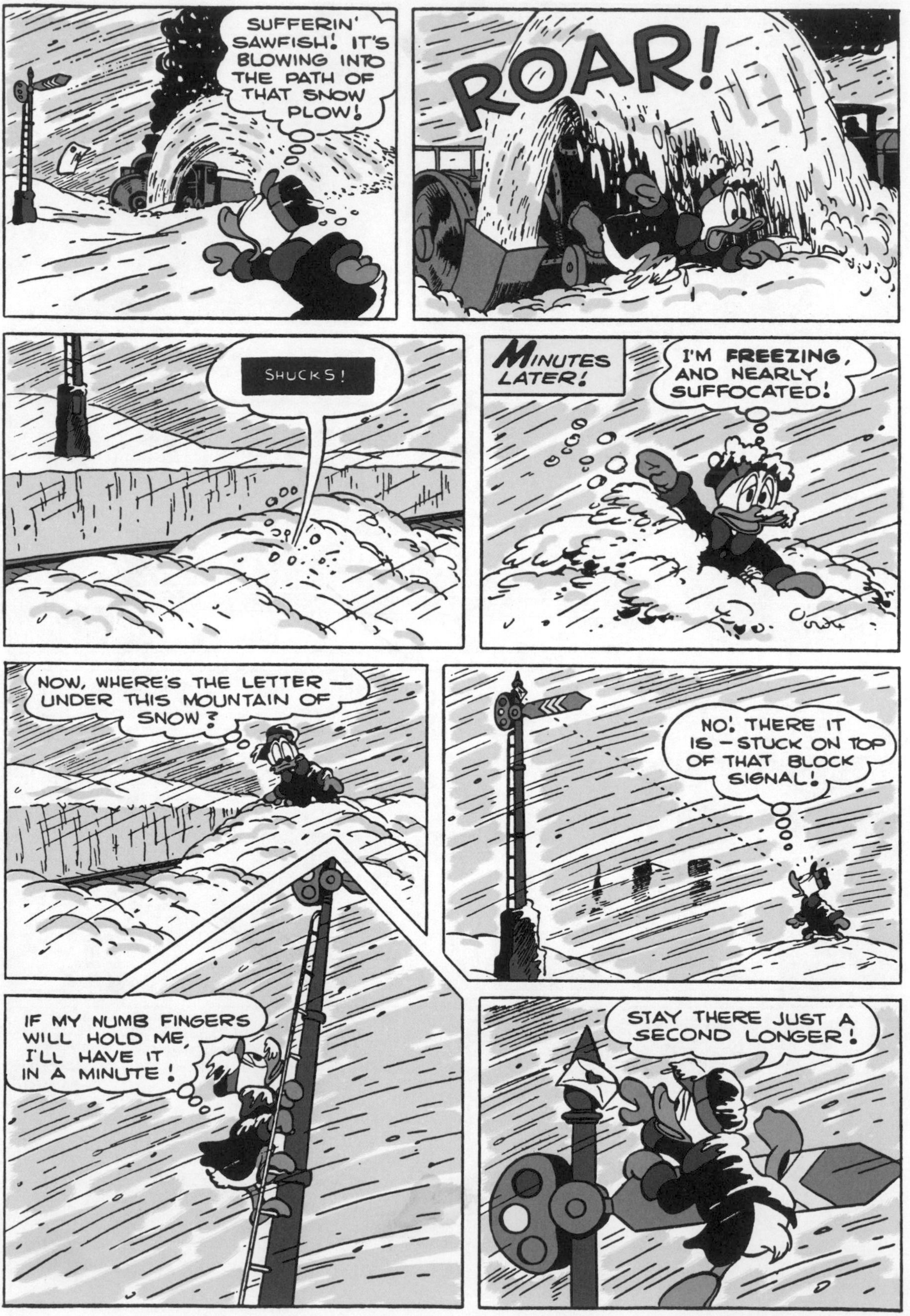
SUFFERIN' SAWFISH! IT'S BLOWING INTO THE PATH OF THAT SNOW PLOW!
ROAR!
SHUCKS!
MINUTES LATER!
I'M FREEZING, AND NEARLY SUFFOCATED!
NOW, WHERE'S THE LETTER — UNDER THIS MOUNTAIN OF SNOW?
NO! THERE IT IS — STUCK ON TOP OF THAT BLOCK SIGNAL!
IF MY NUMB FINGERS WILL HOLD ME, I'LL HAVE IT IN A MINUTE!
STAY THERE JUST A SECOND LONGER!

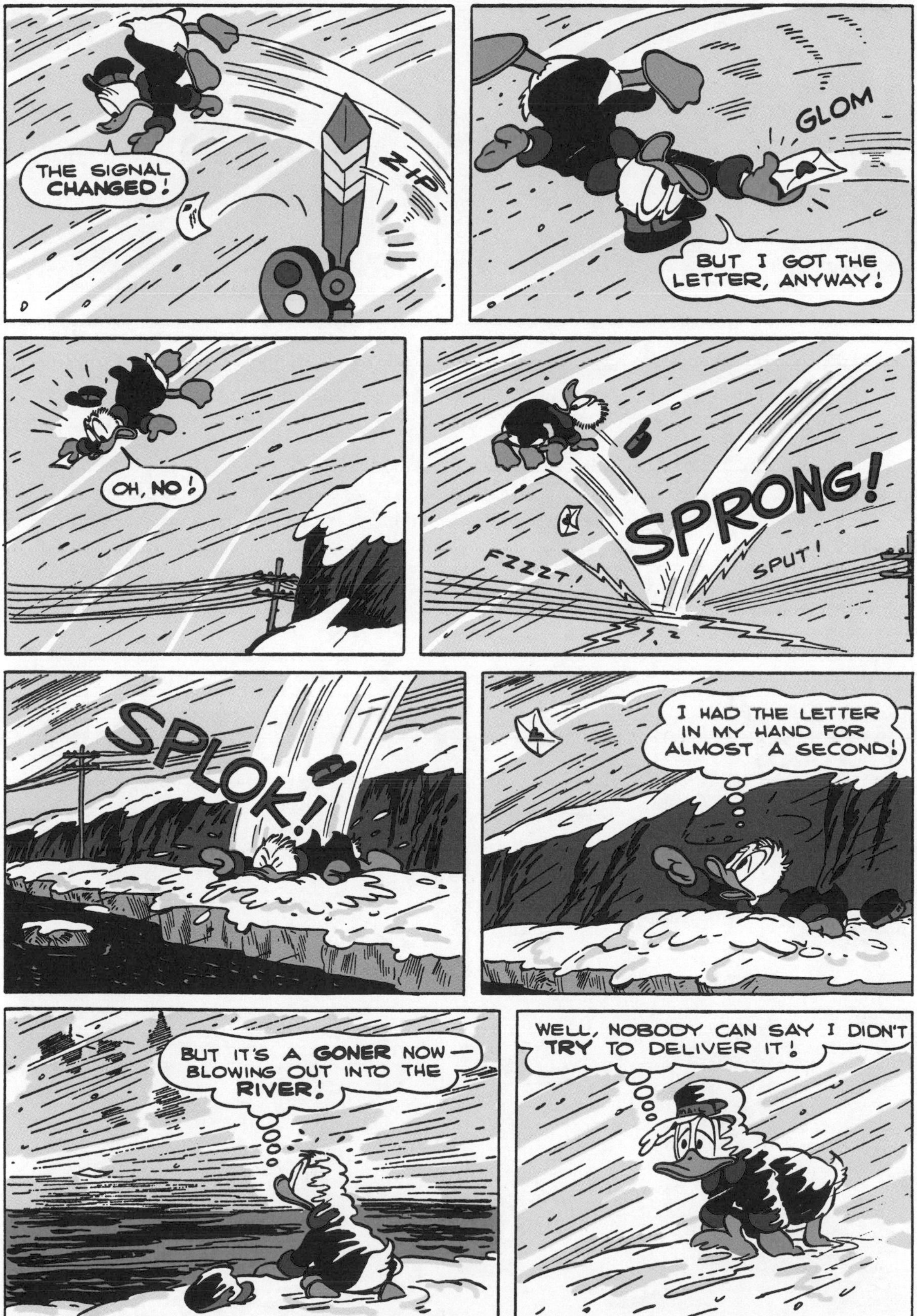

THE SIGNAL CHANGED!
ZIP
GLOM
BUT I GOT THE LETTER, ANYWAY!
OH, NO!
SPRONG!
FZZZZT!
SPUT!
SPLOK!
I HAD THE LETTER IN MY HAND FOR ALMOST A SECOND!
BUT IT'S A GONER NOW— BLOWING OUT INTO THE RIVER!
WELL, NOBODY CAN SAY I DIDN'T TRY TO DELIVER IT!
MAIL

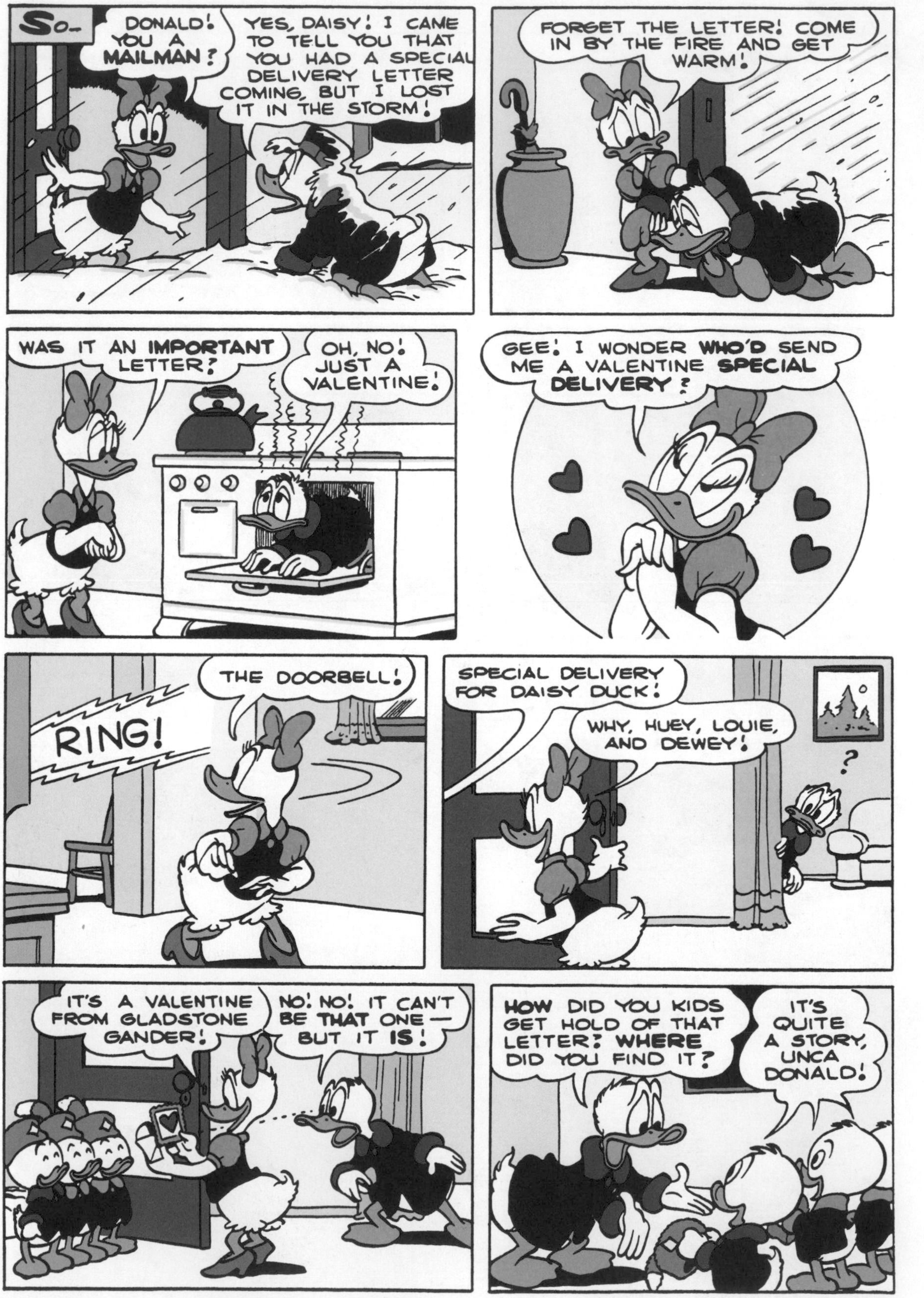
SO–
DONALD! YOU A MAILMAN?
YES, DAISY! I CAME TO TELL YOU THAT YOU HAD A SPECIAL DELIVERY LETTER COMING, BUT I LOST IT IN THE STORM!
FORGET THE LETTER! COME IN BY THE FIRE AND GET WARM!
WAS IT AN IMPORTANT LETTER?
OH, NO! JUST A VALENTINE!
GEE! I WONDER WHO'D SEND ME A VALENTINE SPECIAL DELIVERY?
RING!
THE DOORBELL!
SPECIAL DELIVERY FOR DAISY DUCK!
WHY, HUEY, LOUIE, AND DEWEY!
?
IT'S A VALENTINE FROM GLADSTONE GANDER!
NO! NO! IT CAN'T BE THAT ONE— BUT IT IS!
HOW DID YOU KIDS GET HOLD OF THAT LETTER? WHERE DID YOU FIND IT?
IT'S QUITE A STORY, UNCA DONALD!

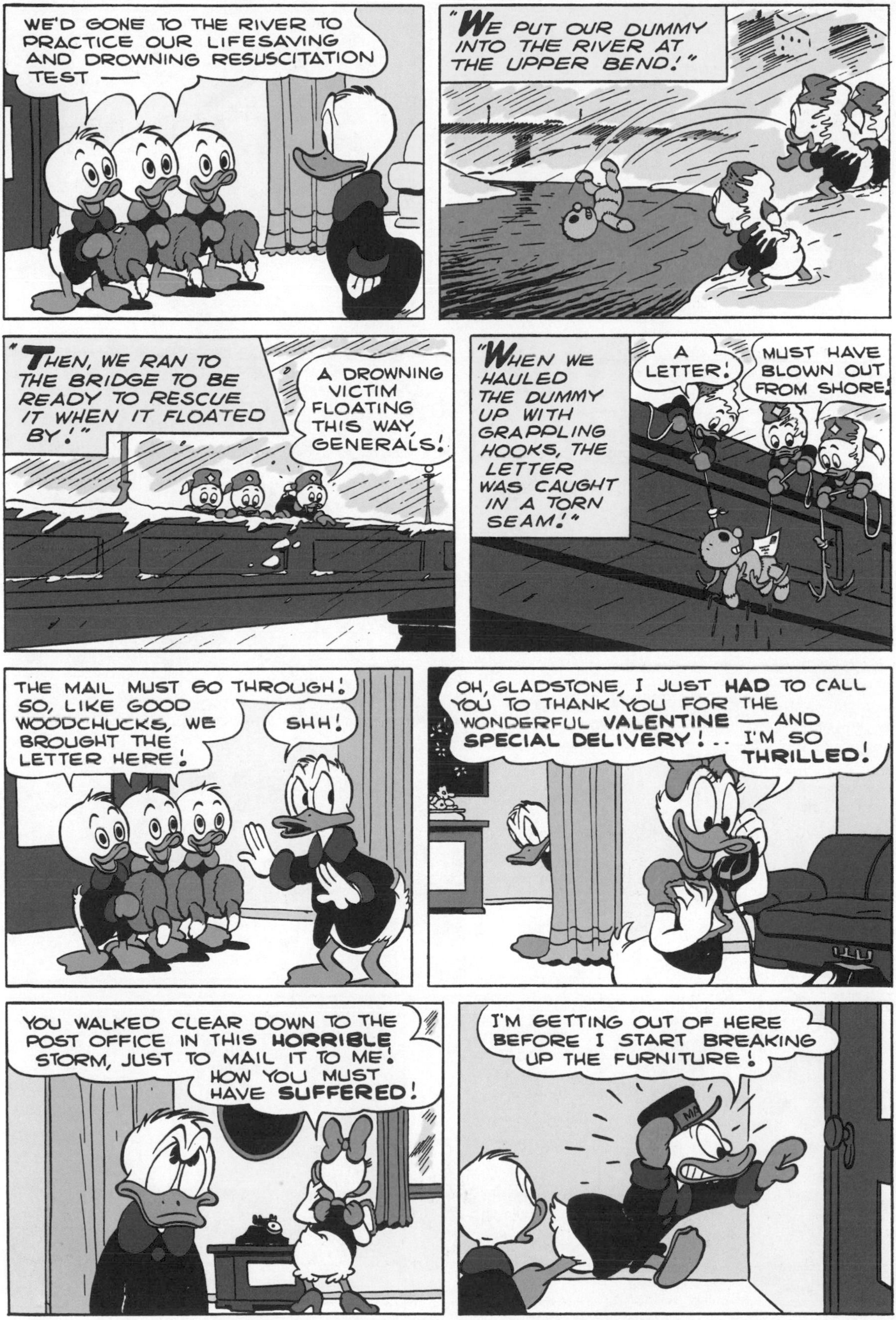
WE'D GONE TO THE RIVER TO PRACTICE OUR LIFESAVING AND DROWNING RESUSCITATION TEST —
"WE PUT OUR DUMMY INTO THE RIVER AT THE UPPER BEND!"
"THEN, WE RAN TO THE BRIDGE TO BE READY TO RESCUE IT WHEN IT FLOATED BY!"
A DROWNING VICTIM FLOATING THIS WAY, GENERALS!
"WHEN WE HAULED THE DUMMY UP WITH GRAPPLING HOOKS, THE LETTER WAS CAUGHT IN A TORN SEAM!"
A LETTER!
MUST HAVE BLOWN OUT FROM SHORE!
THE MAIL MUST GO THROUGH! SO, LIKE GOOD WOODCHUCKS, WE BROUGHT THE LETTER HERE!
SHH!
OH, GLADSTONE, I JUST HAD TO CALL YOU TO THANK YOU FOR THE WONDERFUL VALENTINE — AND SPECIAL DELIVERY!.. I'M SO THRILLED!
YOU WALKED CLEAR DOWN TO THE POST OFFICE IN THIS HORRIBLE STORM, JUST TO MAIL IT TO ME! HOW YOU MUST HAVE SUFFERED!
I'M GETTING OUT OF HERE BEFORE I START BREAKING UP THE FURNITURE!

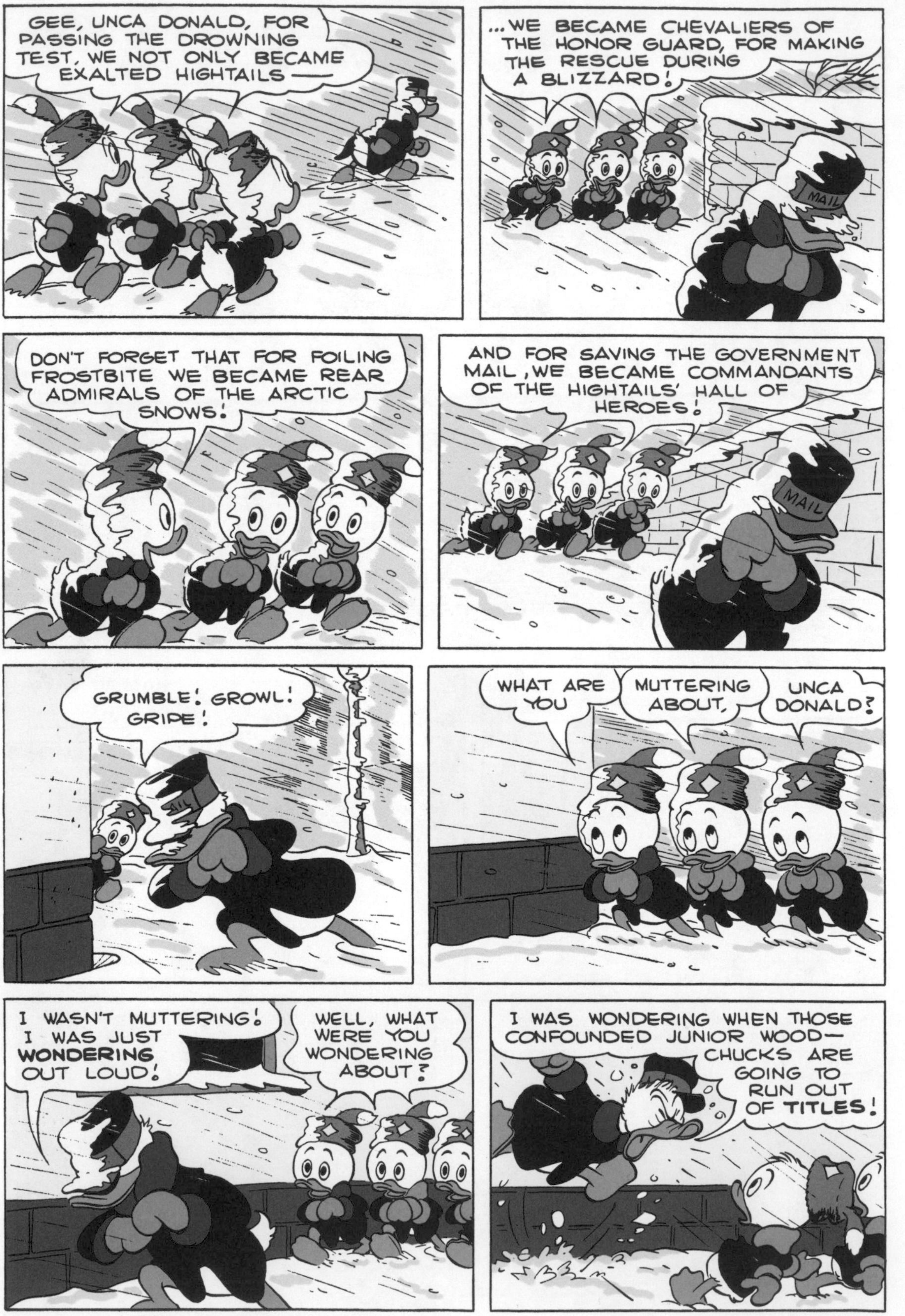
GEE, UNCA DONALD, FOR PASSING THE DROWNING TEST, WE NOT ONLY BECAME EXALTED HIGHTAILS —
...WE BECAME CHEVALIERS OF THE HONOR GUARD, FOR MAKING THE RESCUE DURING A BLIZZARD!
MAIL
DON'T FORGET THAT FOR FOILING FROSTBITE WE BECAME REAR ADMIRALS OF THE ARCTIC SNOWS!
AND FOR SAVING THE GOVERNMENT MAIL, WE BECAME COMMANDANTS OF THE HIGHTAILS' HALL OF HEROES!
MAIL
GRUMBLE! GROWL! GRIPE!
WHAT ARE YOU
MUTTERING ABOUT,
UNCA DONALD?
I WASN'T MUTTERING! I WAS JUST **WONDERING** OUT LOUD!
WELL, WHAT WERE YOU WONDERING ABOUT?
I WAS WONDERING WHEN THOSE CONFOUNDED JUNIOR WOOD-CHUCKS ARE GOING TO RUN OUT OF **TITLES**!

Walt Disney presents Donald Duck

THERE IS GREAT EXCITEMENT IN DUCKBURG! DAISY DUCK'S CLUB HAS PLANNED A GIGANTIC EASTER PARADE!

THERE'S GOING TO BE FLOATS, AND KIDS IN COSTUMES, AND BANDS, AND EVERYTHING!

AND THERE'S GOING TO BE A POPULARITY CONTEST TO CHOOSE A **GRAND MARSHAL** FOR THE PARADE!

A **GRAND MARSHAL!**

YES! THE WINNER WILL BE CHOSEN BY THE APPLAUSE OF THE KIDS THE DAY BEFORE THE PARADE!

WHY DON'T **YOU** TRY TO BE GRAND MARSHAL, UNCA DONALD?

SAY! THAT WOULDN'T BE HARD TO TAKE! I'LL GO DOWN RIGHT NOW AND FILE FOR THE OFFICE!

SO— YOU'LL HAVE TO CAMPAIGN HARD, DONALD! THE CHILDREN OF DUCKBURG MUST BE CONVINCED THAT YOU ARE WORTHY!

I'LL MAKE THEM LOVE ME LIKE A BROTHER!

EASTER PROGRAM

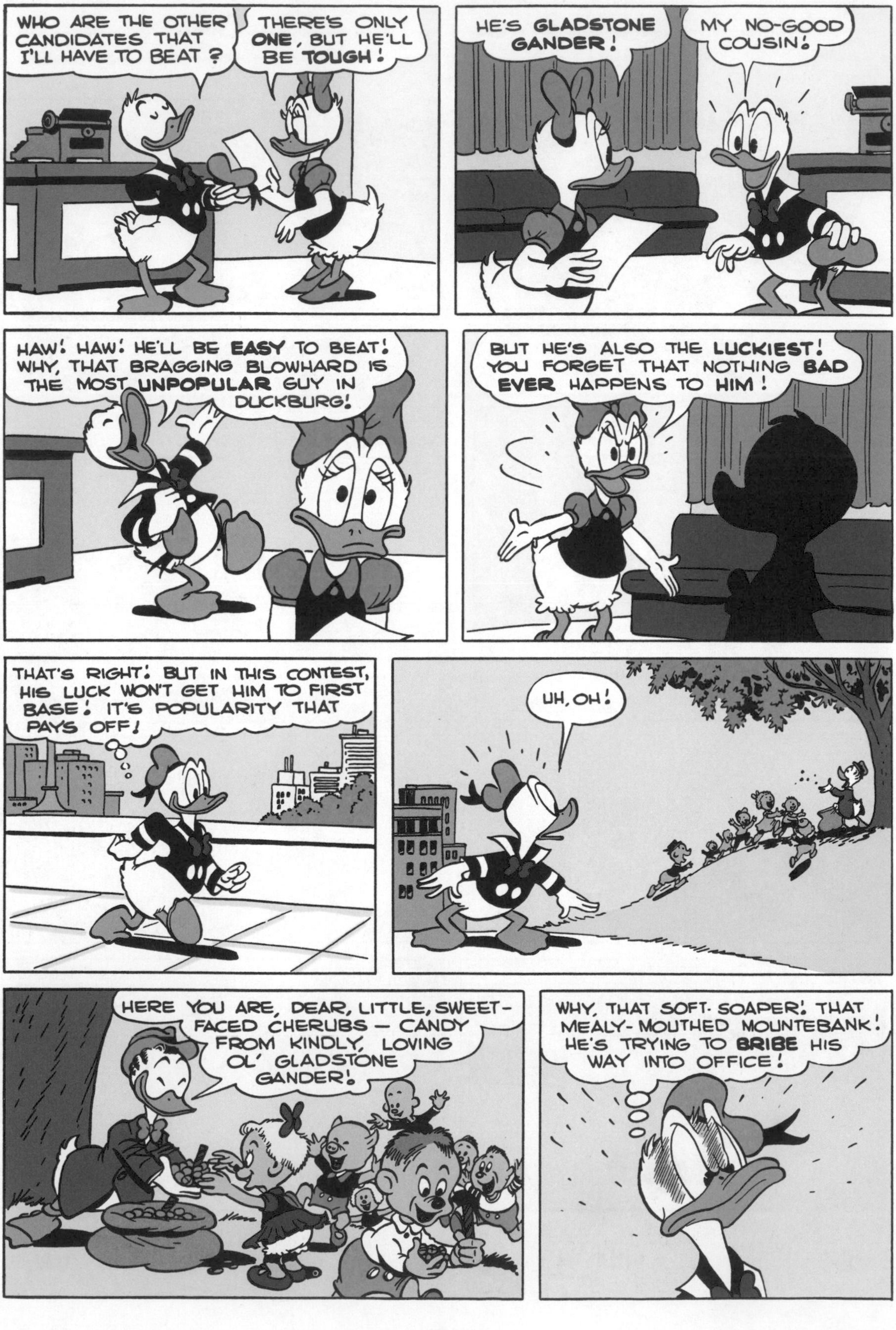
WHO ARE THE OTHER CANDIDATES THAT I'LL HAVE TO BEAT ?
THERE'S ONLY ONE, BUT HE'LL BE TOUGH!
HE'S GLADSTONE GANDER!
MY NO-GOOD COUSIN!
HAW! HAW! HE'LL BE EASY TO BEAT! WHY, THAT BRAGGING BLOWHARD IS THE MOST UNPOPULAR GUY IN DUCKBURG!
BUT HE'S ALSO THE LUCKIEST! YOU FORGET THAT NOTHING BAD EVER HAPPENS TO HIM!
THAT'S RIGHT! BUT IN THIS CONTEST, HIS LUCK WON'T GET HIM TO FIRST BASE! IT'S POPULARITY THAT PAYS OFF!
UH, OH!
HERE YOU ARE, DEAR, LITTLE, SWEET-FACED CHERUBS — CANDY FROM KINDLY, LOVING OL' GLADSTONE GANDER!
WHY, THAT SOFT-SOAPER! THAT MEALY-MOUTHED MOUNTEBANK! HE'S TRYING TO BRIBE HIS WAY INTO OFFICE!

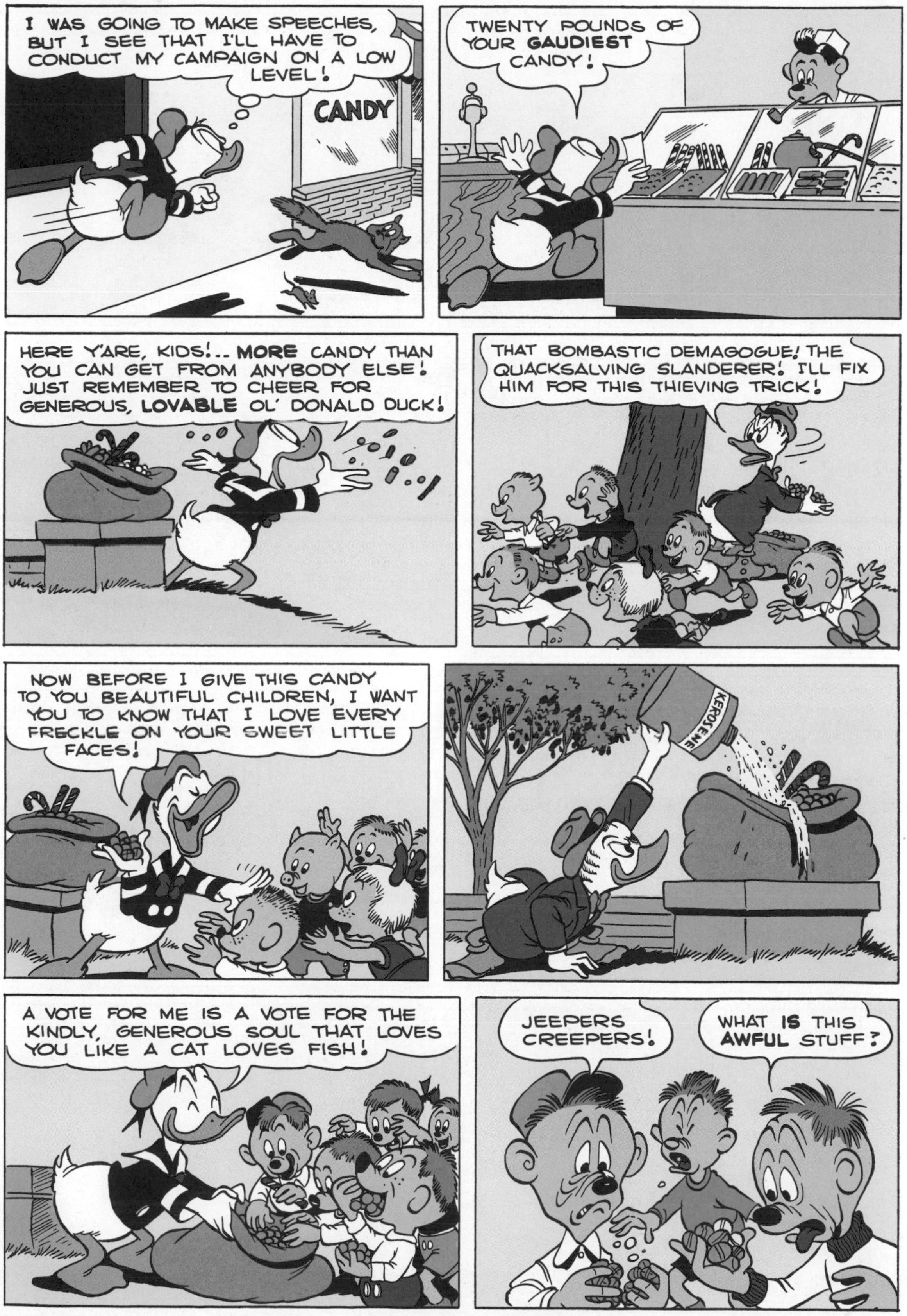

I WAS GOING TO MAKE SPEECHES, BUT I SEE THAT I'LL HAVE TO CONDUCT MY CAMPAIGN ON A LOW LEVEL!
CANDY
TWENTY POUNDS OF YOUR GAUDIEST CANDY!
HERE Y'ARE, KIDS!.. MORE CANDY THAN YOU CAN GET FROM ANYBODY ELSE! JUST REMEMBER TO CHEER FOR GENEROUS, LOVABLE OL' DONALD DUCK!
THAT BOMBASTIC DEMAGOGUE! THE QUACKSALVING SLANDERER! I'LL FIX HIM FOR THIS THIEVING TRICK!
NOW BEFORE I GIVE THIS CANDY TO YOU BEAUTIFUL CHILDREN, I WANT YOU TO KNOW THAT I LOVE EVERY FRECKLE ON YOUR SWEET LITTLE FACES!
KEROSENE
A VOTE FOR ME IS A VOTE FOR THE KINDLY, GENEROUS SOUL THAT LOVES YOU LIKE A CAT LOVES FISH!
JEEPERS CREEPERS!
WHAT IS THIS AWFUL STUFF?

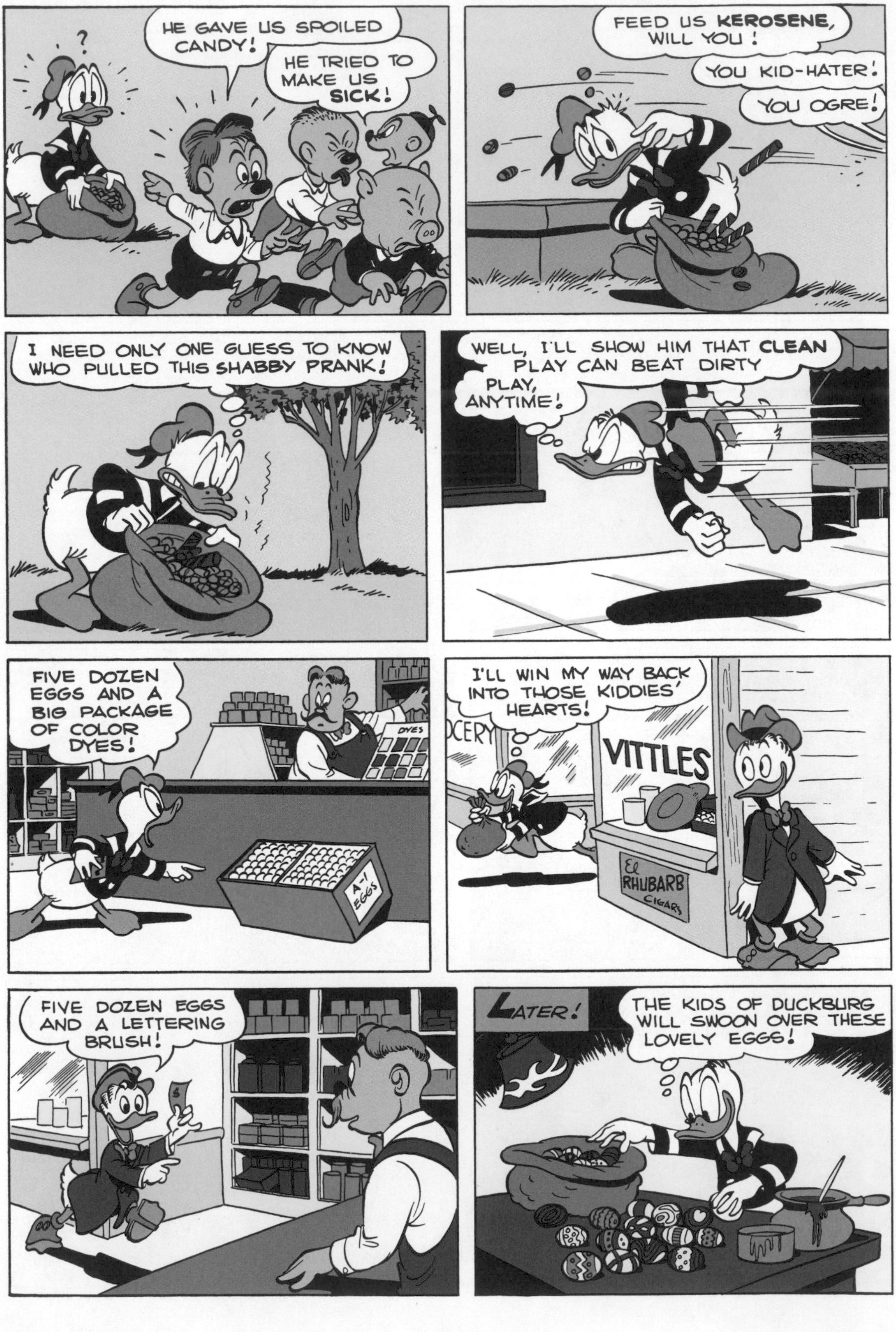
HE GAVE US SPOILED CANDY!
HE TRIED TO MAKE US SICK!
FEED US KEROSENE, WILL YOU!
YOU KID-HATER!
YOU OGRE!
I NEED ONLY ONE GUESS TO KNOW WHO PULLED THIS SHABBY PRANK!
WELL, I'LL SHOW HIM THAT CLEAN PLAY CAN BEAT DIRTY PLAY, ANYTIME!
FIVE DOZEN EGGS AND A BIG PACKAGE OF COLOR DYES!
DYES
A-1 EGGS
I'LL WIN MY WAY BACK INTO THOSE KIDDIES' HEARTS!
VITTLES
El RHUBARB CIGARS
FIVE DOZEN EGGS AND A LETTERING BRUSH!
LATER!
THE KIDS OF DUCKBURG WILL SWOON OVER THESE LOVELY EGGS!

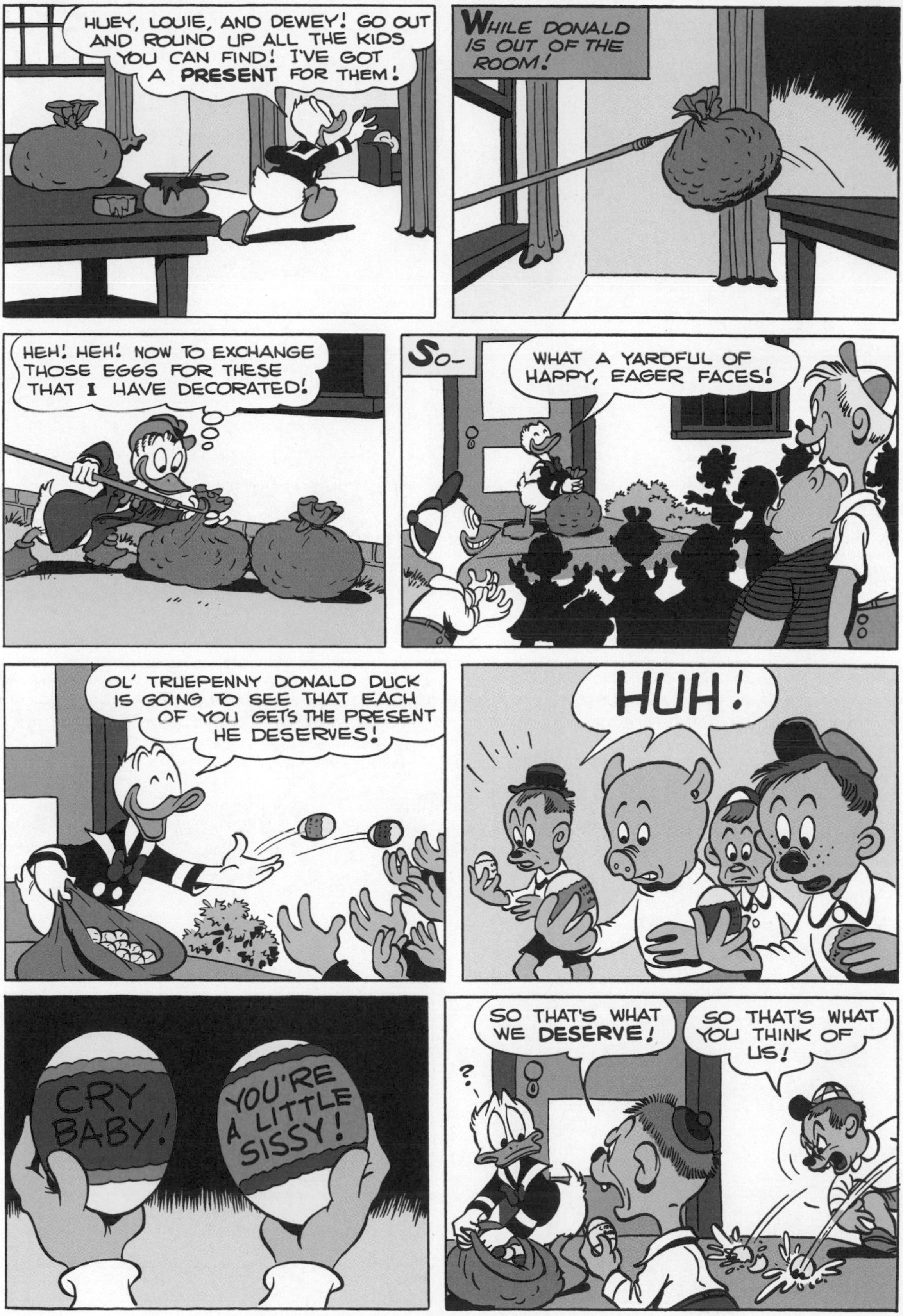

HUEY, LOUIE, AND DEWEY! GO OUT AND ROUND UP ALL THE KIDS YOU CAN FIND! I'VE GOT A **PRESENT** FOR THEM!
WHILE DONALD IS OUT OF THE ROOM!
HEH! HEH! NOW TO EXCHANGE THOSE EGGS FOR THESE THAT **I** HAVE DECORATED!
SO–
WHAT A YARDFUL OF HAPPY, EAGER FACES!
OL' TRUEPENNY DONALD DUCK IS GOING TO SEE THAT EACH OF YOU GETS THE PRESENT HE DESERVES!
HUH!
CRY BABY!
YOU'RE A LITTLE SISSY!
SO THAT'S WHAT WE **DESERVE**!
SO THAT'S WHAT YOU THINK OF US!

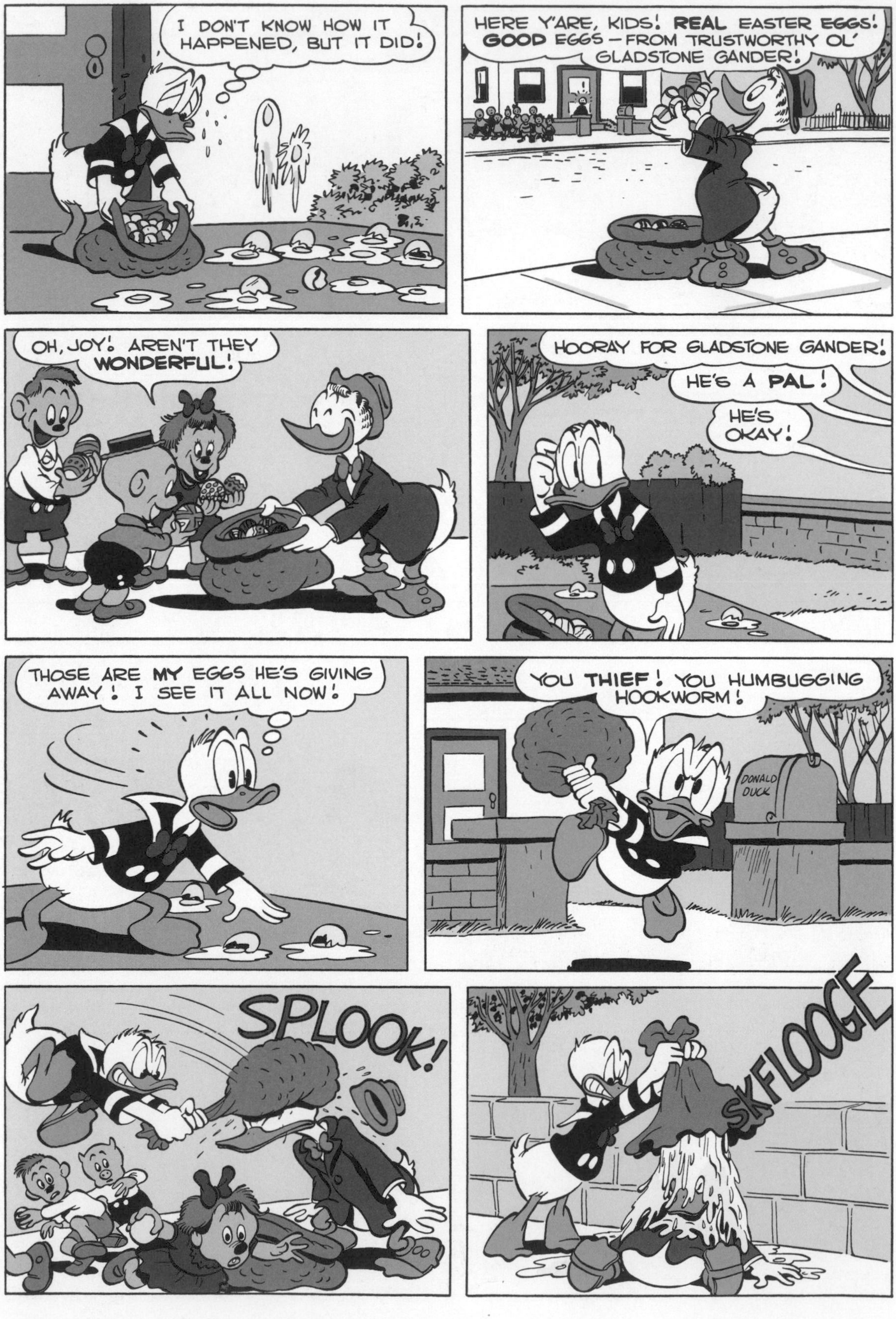
I DON'T KNOW HOW IT HAPPENED, BUT IT DID!
HERE Y'ARE, KIDS! REAL EASTER EGGS! GOOD EGGS — FROM TRUSTWORTHY OL' GLADSTONE GANDER!
OH, JOY! AREN'T THEY WONDERFUL!
HOORAY FOR GLADSTONE GANDER!
HE'S A PAL!
HE'S OKAY!
THOSE ARE MY EGGS HE'S GIVING AWAY! I SEE IT ALL NOW!
YOU THIEF! YOU HUMBUGGING HOOKWORM!
DONALD DUCK
SPLOOK!
SKFLOOGE

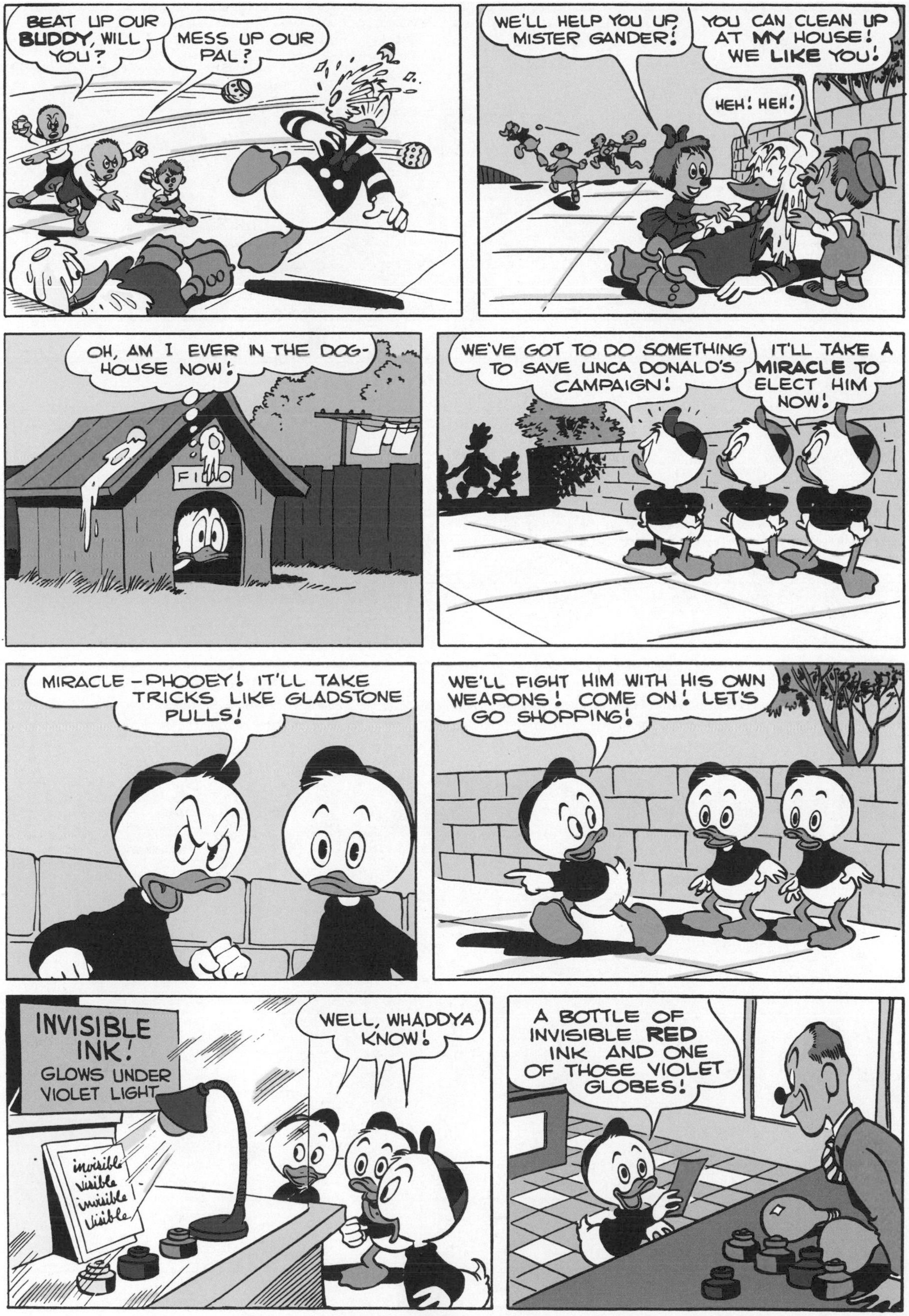
BEAT UP OUR BUDDY, WILL YOU?
MESS UP OUR PAL?
WE'LL HELP YOU UP MISTER GANDER!
YOU CAN CLEAN UP AT MY HOUSE! WE LIKE YOU!
HEH! HEH!
OH, AM I EVER IN THE DOG-HOUSE NOW!
FIDO
WE'VE GOT TO DO SOMETHING TO SAVE UNCA DONALD'S CAMPAIGN!
IT'LL TAKE A MIRACLE TO ELECT HIM NOW!
MIRACLE—PHOOEY! IT'LL TAKE TRICKS LIKE GLADSTONE PULLS!
WE'LL FIGHT HIM WITH HIS OWN WEAPONS! COME ON! LET'S GO SHOPPING!
INVISIBLE INK! GLOWS UNDER VIOLET LIGHT
invisible visible invisible visible
WELL, WHADDYA KNOW!
A BOTTLE OF INVISIBLE RED INK AND ONE OF THOSE VIOLET GLOBES!

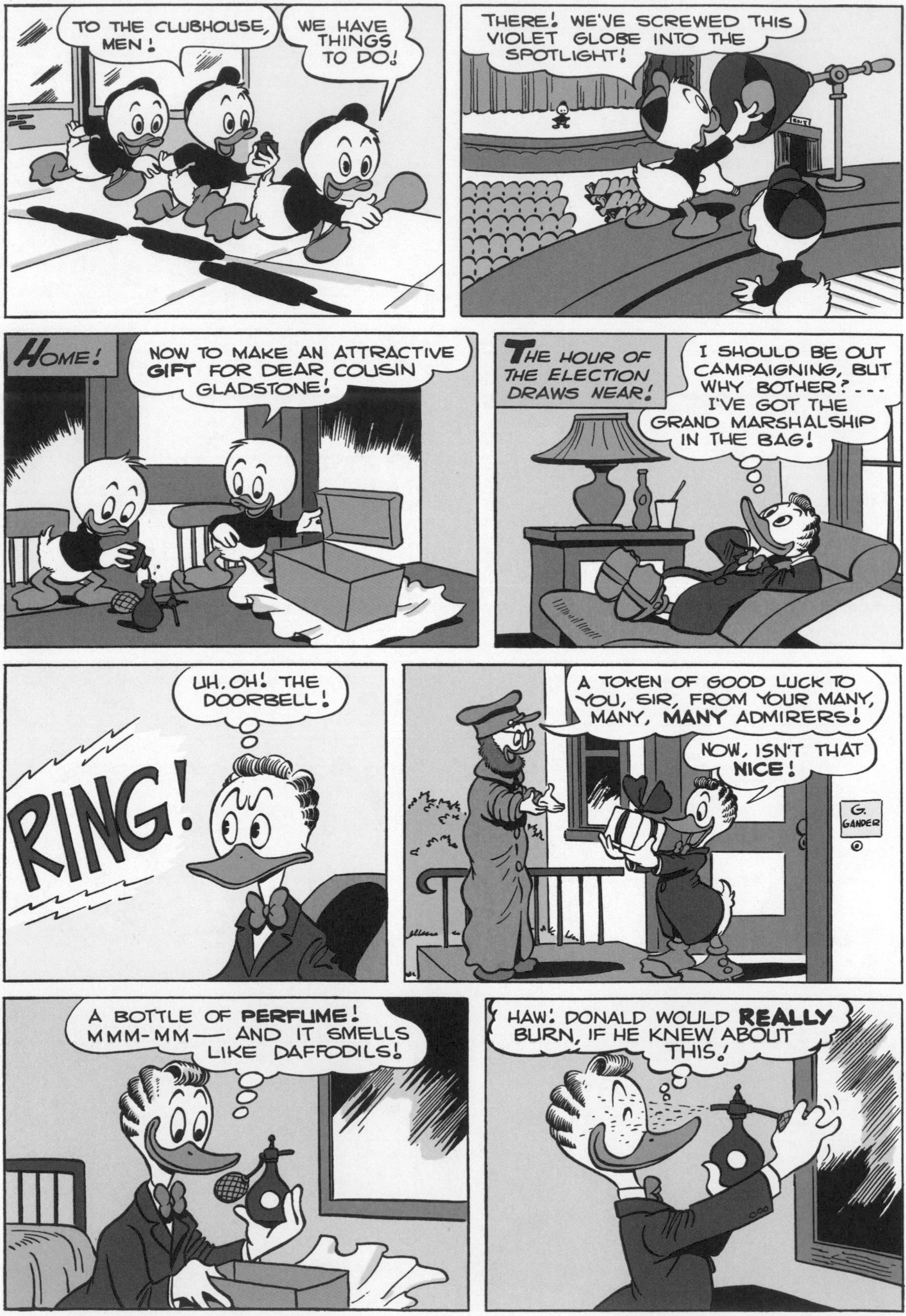
TO THE CLUBHOUSE, MEN!
WE HAVE THINGS TO DO!
THERE! WE'VE SCREWED THIS VIOLET GLOBE INTO THE SPOTLIGHT!
HOME!
NOW TO MAKE AN ATTRACTIVE GIFT FOR DEAR COUSIN GLADSTONE!
THE HOUR OF THE ELECTION DRAWS NEAR!
I SHOULD BE OUT CAMPAIGNING, BUT WHY BOTHER?... I'VE GOT THE GRAND MARSHALSHIP IN THE BAG!
UH, OH! THE DOORBELL!
RING!
A TOKEN OF GOOD LUCK TO YOU, SIR, FROM YOUR MANY, MANY, MANY ADMIRERS!
NOW, ISN'T THAT NICE!
G. GANDER
A BOTTLE OF PERFUME! MMM-MM— AND IT SMELLS LIKE DAFFODILS!
HAW! DONALD WOULD REALLY BURN, IF HE KNEW ABOUT THIS!

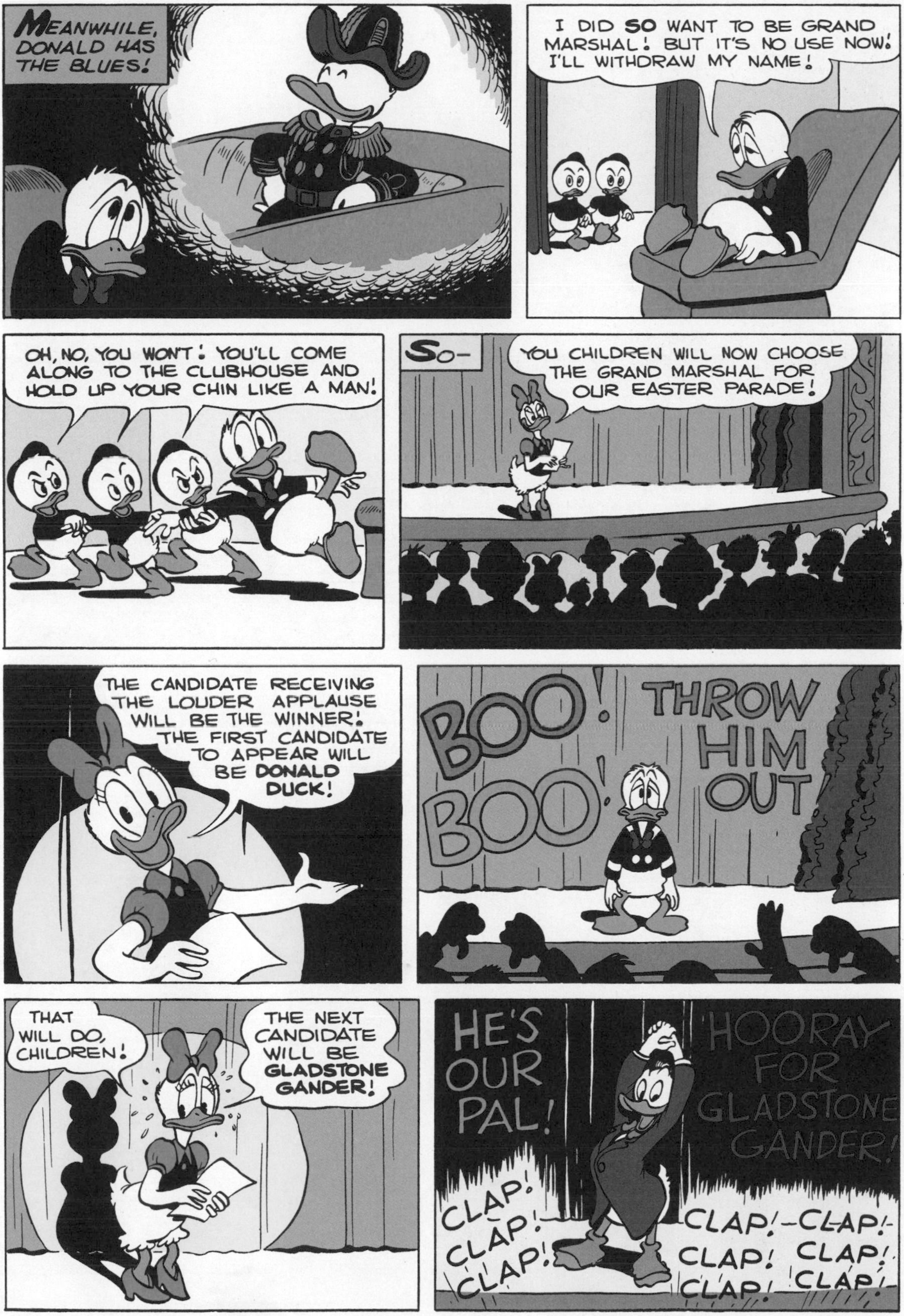
MEANWHILE, DONALD HAS THE BLUES!
I DID SO WANT TO BE GRAND MARSHAL! BUT IT'S NO USE NOW! I'LL WITHDRAW MY NAME!
OH, NO, YOU WON'T! YOU'LL COME ALONG TO THE CLUBHOUSE AND HOLD UP YOUR CHIN LIKE A MAN!
SO-
YOU CHILDREN WILL NOW CHOOSE THE GRAND MARSHAL FOR OUR EASTER PARADE!
THE CANDIDATE RECEIVING THE LOUDER APPLAUSE WILL BE THE WINNER! THE FIRST CANDIDATE TO APPEAR WILL BE DONALD DUCK!
BOO! BOO!
THROW HIM OUT!
THAT WILL DO, CHILDREN!
THE NEXT CANDIDATE WILL BE GLADSTONE GANDER!
HE'S OUR PAL!
HOORAY FOR GLADSTONE GANDER!
CLAP! CLAP! CLAP!
CLAP! -CLAP! CLAP! CLAP! CLAP! CLAP!

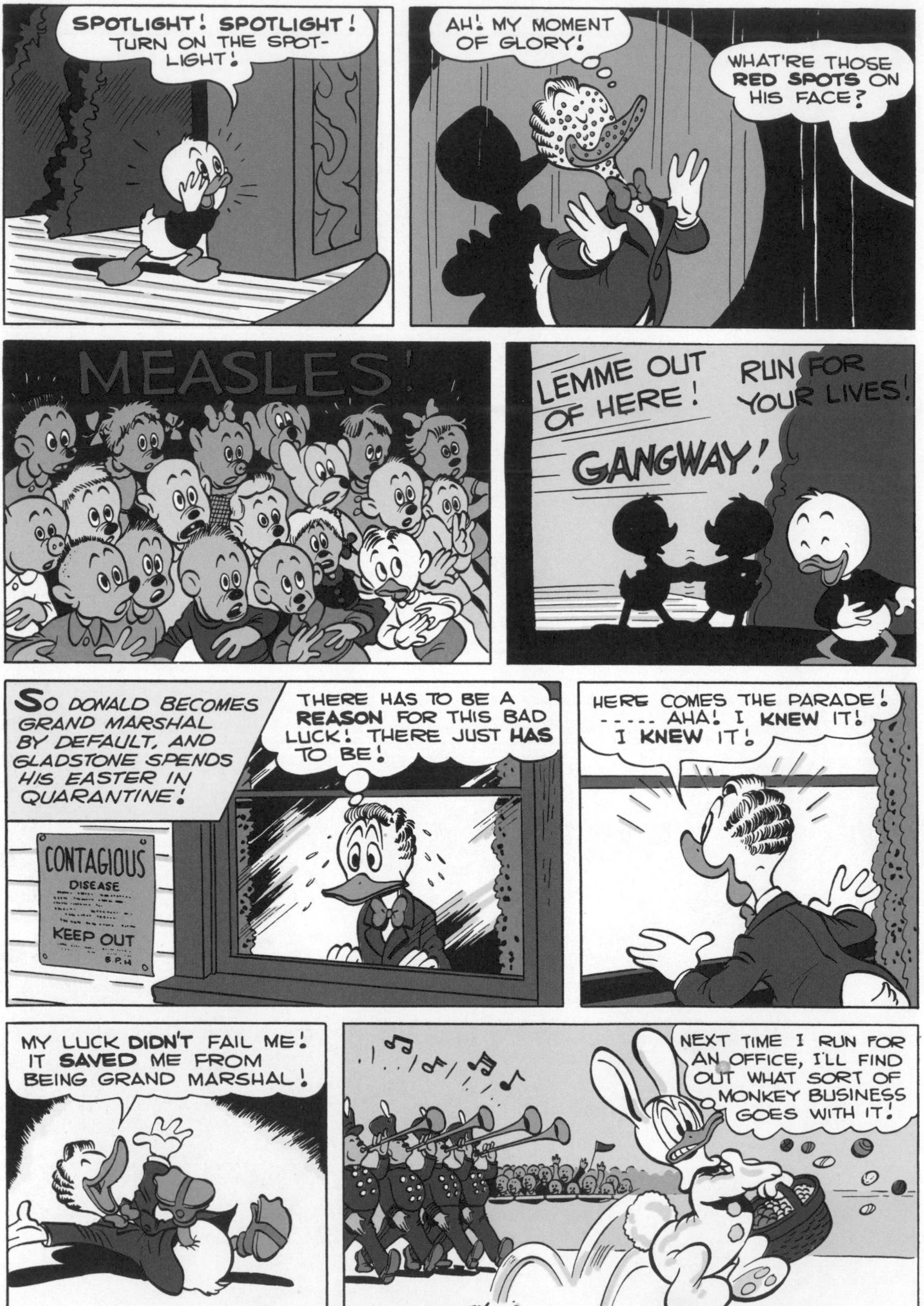

SPOTLIGHT! SPOTLIGHT! TURN ON THE SPOT-LIGHT!
AH! MY MOMENT OF GLORY!
WHAT'RE THOSE RED SPOTS ON HIS FACE?
MEASLES!
LEMME OUT OF HERE!
RUN FOR YOUR LIVES!
GANGWAY!
SO DONALD BECOMES GRAND MARSHAL BY DEFAULT, AND GLADSTONE SPENDS HIS EASTER IN QUARANTINE!
THERE HAS TO BE A REASON FOR THIS BAD LUCK! THERE JUST HAS TO BE!
CONTAGIOUS
DISEASE
KEEP OUT
HERE COMES THE PARADE! ----- AHA! I KNEW IT! I KNEW IT!
MY LUCK DIDN'T FAIL ME! IT SAVED ME FROM BEING GRAND MARSHAL!
NEXT TIME I RUN FOR AN OFFICE, I'LL FIND OUT WHAT SORT OF MONKEY BUSINESS GOES WITH IT!
HOPPITY
HOP

WALT DISNEY presents
Donald Duck
UNCA DONALD, WILL YOU BUY US A TALKING DOG?
QUIET! CAN'T YOU SEE THAT I'M LISTENING TO THIS QUIZ PROGRAM?
BUT, UNCA DONALD! WE'LL ONLY TAKE A MINUTE!
YOU KNOW DOGGONED WELL THERE'S NO SUCH THING AS A DOG THAT TALKS! NOW SCRAM!
PHOOEY!
HOW MANY STATES IN THE 50 STATES?
UH — UK — GUK! ------ ------- 50, I SUPPOSE!
THAT IS RIGHT! THIS BRILLIANT CONTESTANT WINS THE GRAND TOTAL OF ONE THOUSAND DOLLARS!
THAT GOES ON EVERY DAY! SOME SQUARE WINS A THOUSAND FOR ANSWERING A QUESTION THAT ANSWERS ITSELF!
I'VE GOT TO GET ON THAT PROGRAM!

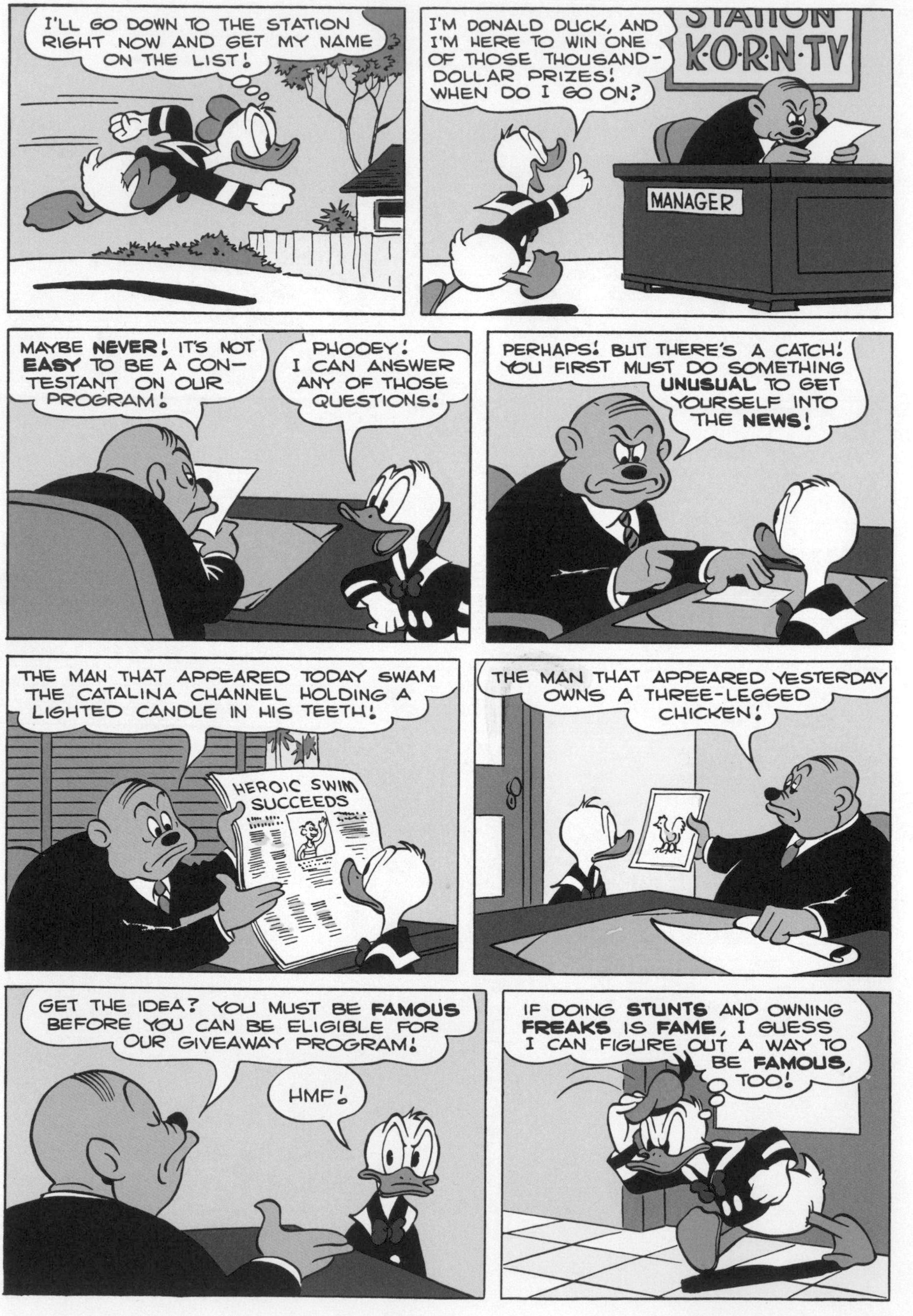
I'LL GO DOWN TO THE STATION RIGHT NOW AND GET MY NAME ON THE LIST!
STATION K·O·R·N·TV
I'M DONALD DUCK, AND I'M HERE TO WIN ONE OF THOSE THOUSAND-DOLLAR PRIZES! WHEN DO I GO ON?
MANAGER
MAYBE NEVER! IT'S NOT EASY TO BE A CONTESTANT ON OUR PROGRAM!
PHOOEY! I CAN ANSWER ANY OF THOSE QUESTIONS!
PERHAPS! BUT THERE'S A CATCH! YOU FIRST MUST DO SOMETHING UNUSUAL TO GET YOURSELF INTO THE NEWS!
THE MAN THAT APPEARED TODAY SWAM THE CATALINA CHANNEL HOLDING A LIGHTED CANDLE IN HIS TEETH!
HEROIC SWIM SUCCEEDS
THE MAN THAT APPEARED YESTERDAY OWNS A THREE-LEGGED CHICKEN!
GET THE IDEA? YOU MUST BE FAMOUS BEFORE YOU CAN BE ELIGIBLE FOR OUR GIVEAWAY PROGRAM!
HMF!
IF DOING STUNTS AND OWNING FREAKS IS FAME, I GUESS I CAN FIGURE OUT A WAY TO BE FAMOUS, TOO!

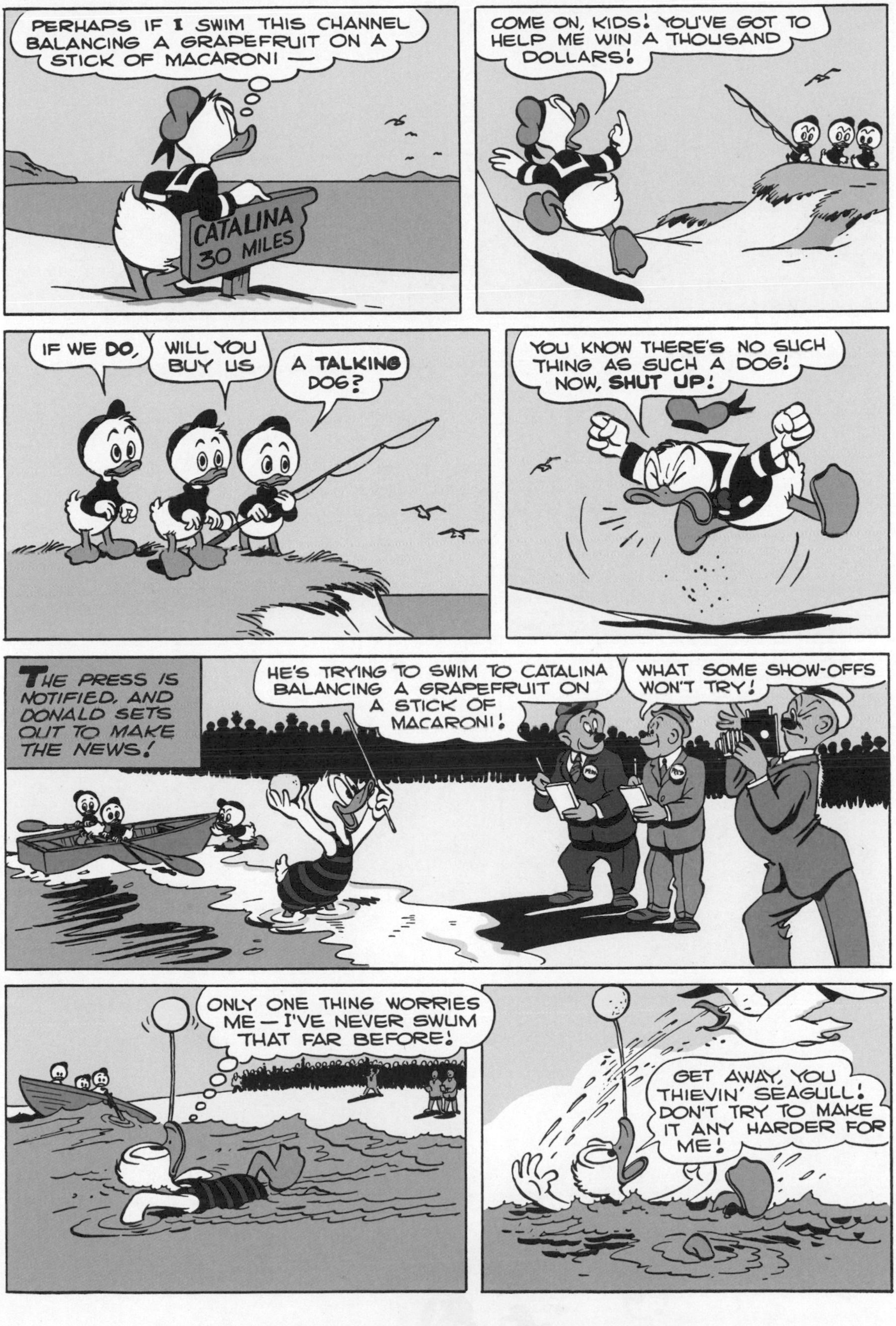
PERHAPS IF I SWIM THIS CHANNEL BALANCING A GRAPEFRUIT ON A STICK OF MACARONI —
CATALINA 30 MILES
COME ON, KIDS! YOU'VE GOT TO HELP ME WIN A THOUSAND DOLLARS!
IF WE DO,
WILL YOU BUY US
A TALKING DOG?
YOU KNOW THERE'S NO SUCH THING AS SUCH A DOG! NOW, SHUT UP!
THE PRESS IS NOTIFIED, AND DONALD SETS OUT TO MAKE THE NEWS!
HE'S TRYING TO SWIM TO CATALINA BALANCING A GRAPEFRUIT ON A STICK OF MACARONI!
WHAT SOME SHOW-OFFS WON'T TRY!
ONLY ONE THING WORRIES ME — I'VE NEVER SWUM THAT FAR BEFORE!
GET AWAY, YOU THIEVIN' SEAGULL! DON'T TRY TO MAKE IT ANY HARDER FOR ME!

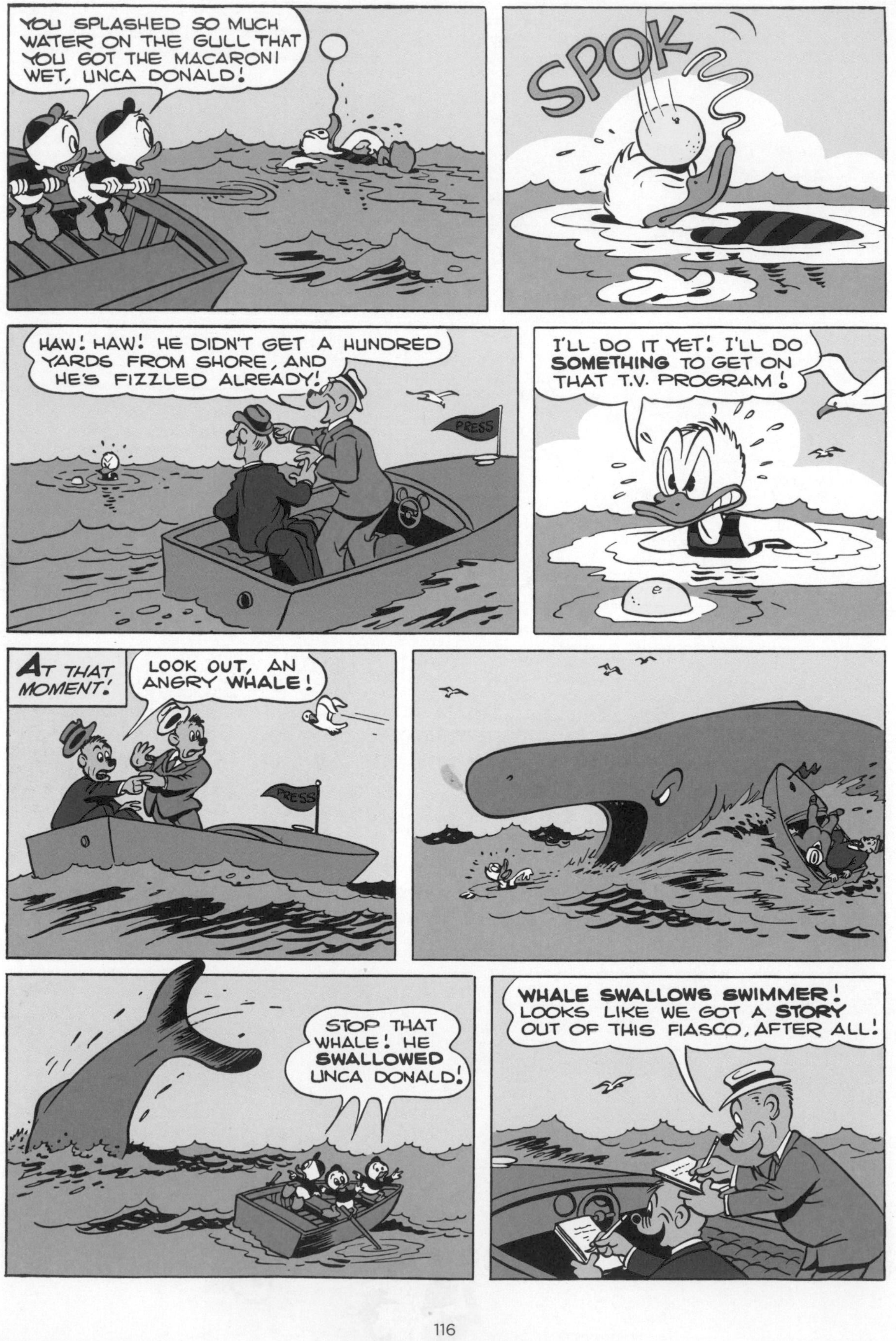
YOU SPLASHED SO MUCH WATER ON THE GULL THAT YOU GOT THE MACARONI WET, UNCA DONALD!
SPOK
HAW! HAW! HE DIDN'T GET A HUNDRED YARDS FROM SHORE, AND HE'S FIZZLED ALREADY!
PRESS
I'LL DO IT YET! I'LL DO **SOMETHING** TO GET ON THAT T.V. PROGRAM!
AT THAT MOMENT!
LOOK OUT, AN ANGRY **WHALE**!
PRESS
STOP THAT WHALE! HE **SWALLOWED** UNCA DONALD!
WHALE SWALLOWS SWIMMER! LOOKS LIKE WE GOT A **STORY** OUT OF THIS FIASCO, AFTER ALL!

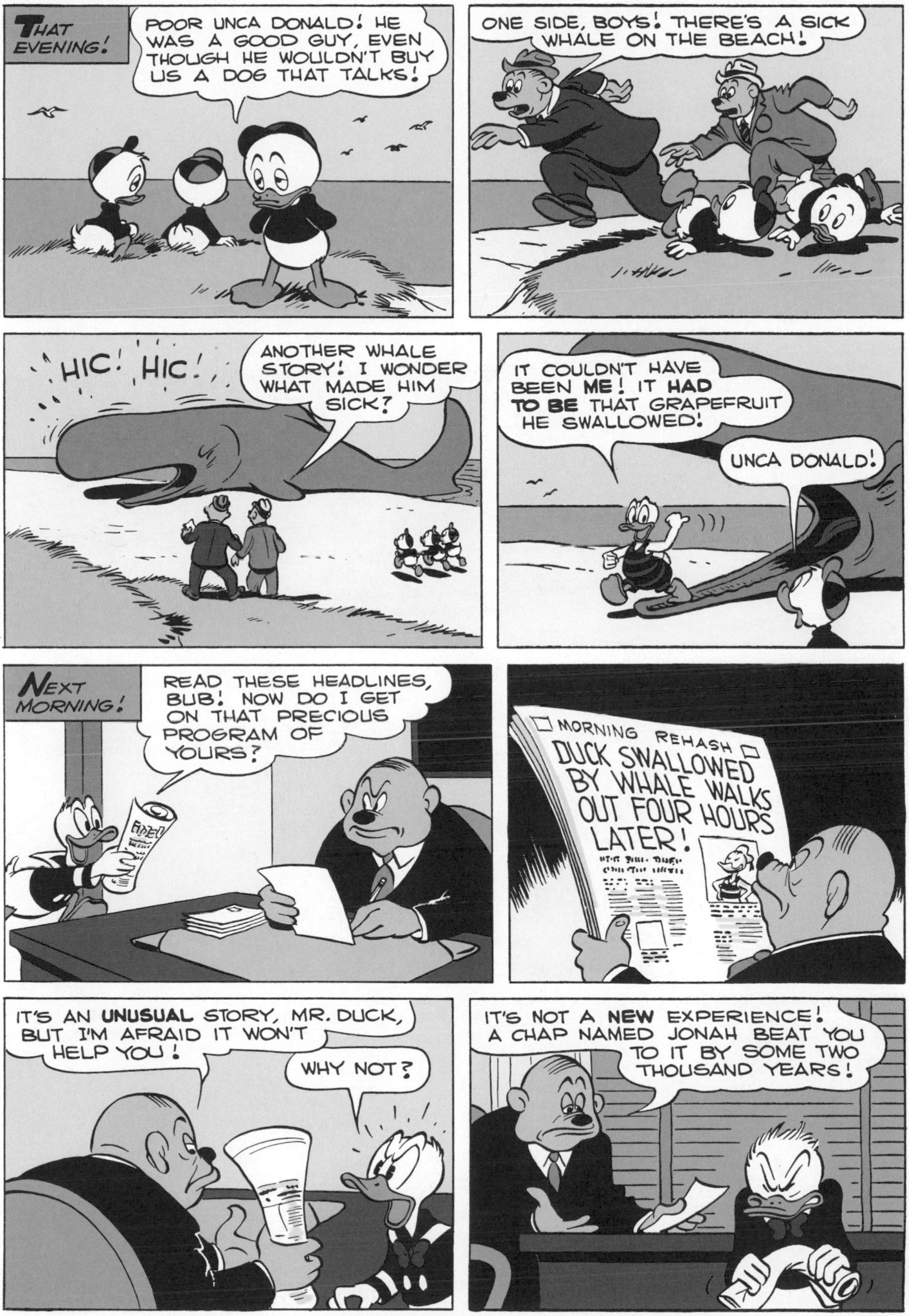
THAT EVENING!
POOR UNCA DONALD! HE WAS A GOOD GUY, EVEN THOUGH HE WOULDN'T BUY US A DOG THAT TALKS!
ONE SIDE, BOYS! THERE'S A SICK WHALE ON THE BEACH!
HIC! HIC!
ANOTHER WHALE STORY! I WONDER WHAT MADE HIM SICK?
IT COULDN'T HAVE BEEN ME! IT HAD TO BE THAT GRAPEFRUIT HE SWALLOWED!
UNCA DONALD!
NEXT MORNING!
READ THESE HEADLINES, BUB! NOW DO I GET ON THAT PRECIOUS PROGRAM OF YOURS?
MORNING REHASH
DUCK SWALLOWED BY WHALE WALKS OUT FOUR HOURS LATER!
IT'S AN UNUSUAL STORY, MR. DUCK, BUT I'M AFRAID IT WON'T HELP YOU!
WHY NOT?
IT'S NOT A NEW EXPERIENCE! A CHAP NAMED JONAH BEAT YOU TO IT BY SOME TWO THOUSAND YEARS!

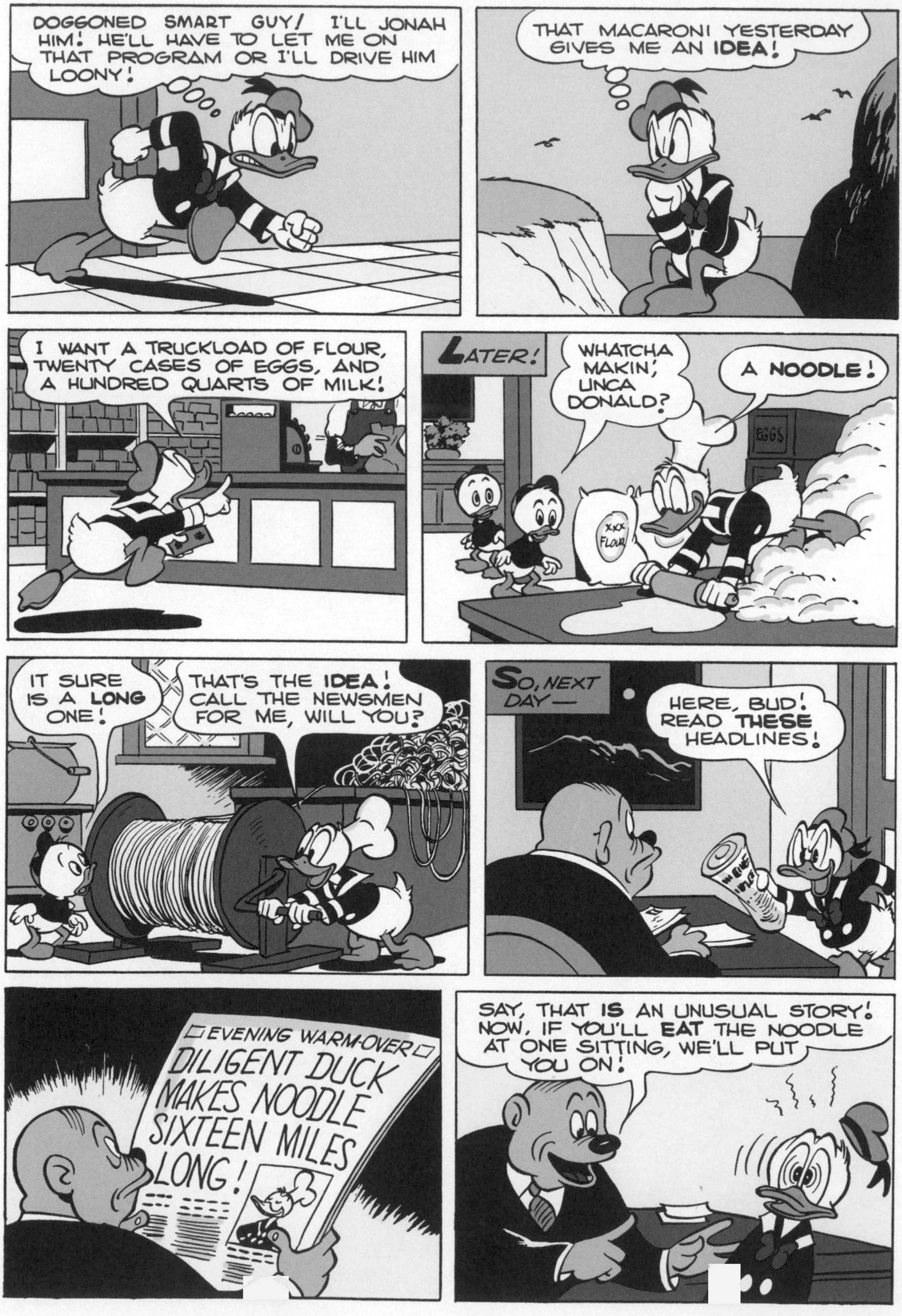

DOGGONED SMART GUY! I'LL JONAH HIM! HE'LL HAVE TO LET ME ON THAT PROGRAM OR I'LL DRIVE HIM LOONY!
THAT MACARONI YESTERDAY GIVES ME AN IDEA!
I WANT A TRUCKLOAD OF FLOUR, TWENTY CASES OF EGGS, AND A HUNDRED QUARTS OF MILK!
LATER!
WHATCHA MAKIN', UNCA DONALD?
A NOODLE!
EGGS
XXX FLOUR
IT SURE IS A LONG ONE!
THAT'S THE IDEA! CALL THE NEWSMEN FOR ME, WILL YOU?
SO, NEXT DAY—
HERE, BUD! READ THESE HEADLINES!
EVENING WARM-OVER
DILIGENT DUCK MAKES NOODLE SIXTEEN MILES LONG!
SAY, THAT IS AN UNUSUAL STORY! NOW, IF YOU'LL EAT THE NOODLE AT ONE SITTING, WE'LL PUT YOU ON!

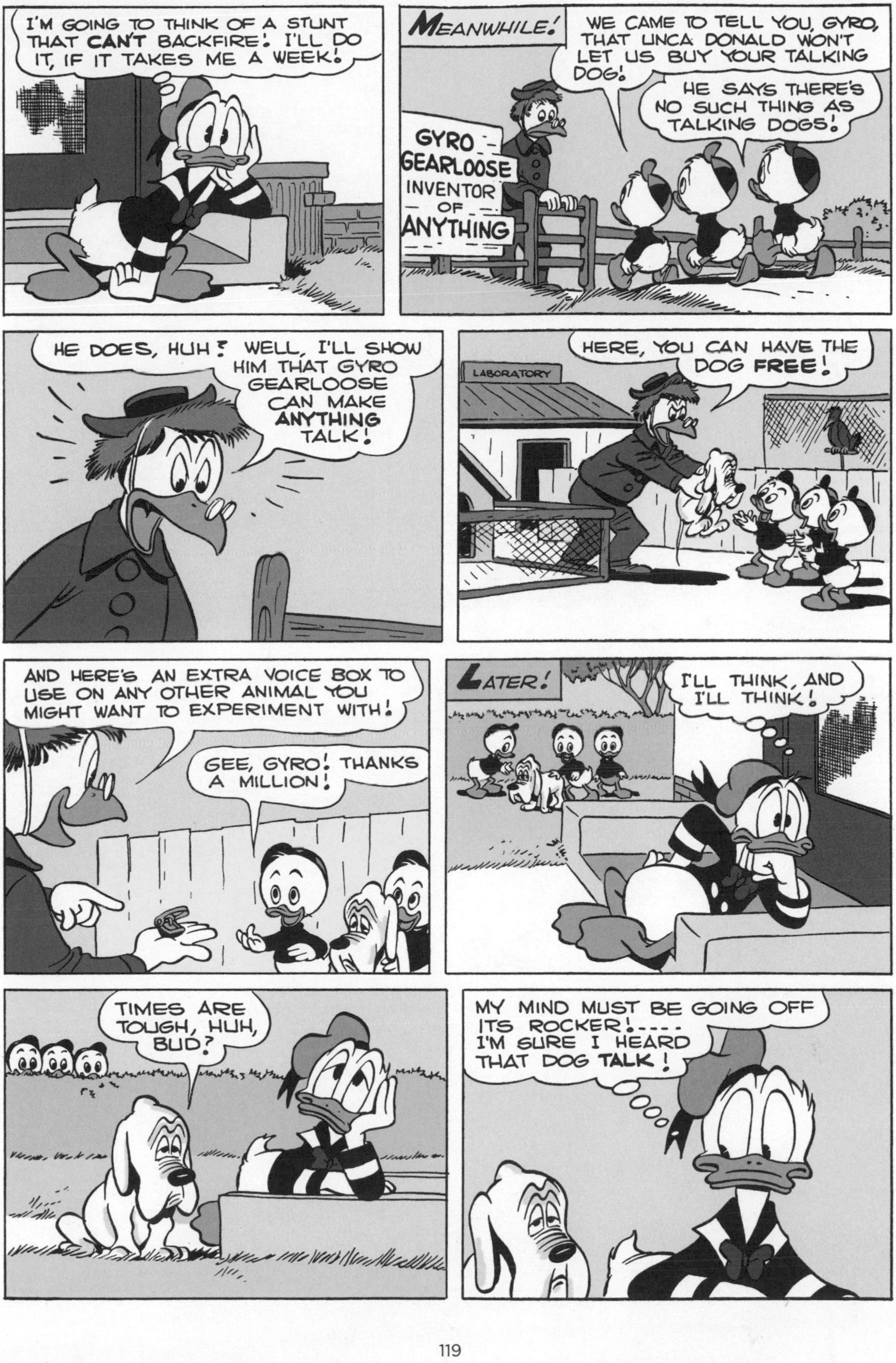
I'M GOING TO THINK OF A STUNT THAT CAN'T BACKFIRE! I'LL DO IT, IF IT TAKES ME A WEEK!
MEANWHILE!
WE CAME TO TELL YOU, GYRO, THAT UNCA DONALD WON'T LET US BUY YOUR TALKING DOG!
HE SAYS THERE'S NO SUCH THING AS TALKING DOGS!
GYRO GEARLOOSE INVENTOR OF ANYTHING
HE DOES, HUH? WELL, I'LL SHOW HIM THAT GYRO GEARLOOSE CAN MAKE ANYTHING TALK!
LABORATORY
HERE, YOU CAN HAVE THE DOG FREE!
AND HERE'S AN EXTRA VOICE BOX TO USE ON ANY OTHER ANIMAL YOU MIGHT WANT TO EXPERIMENT WITH!
GEE, GYRO! THANKS A MILLION!
LATER!
I'LL THINK, AND I'LL THINK!
TIMES ARE TOUGH, HUH, BUD?
MY MIND MUST BE GOING OFF ITS ROCKER!.... I'M SURE I HEARD THAT DOG TALK!

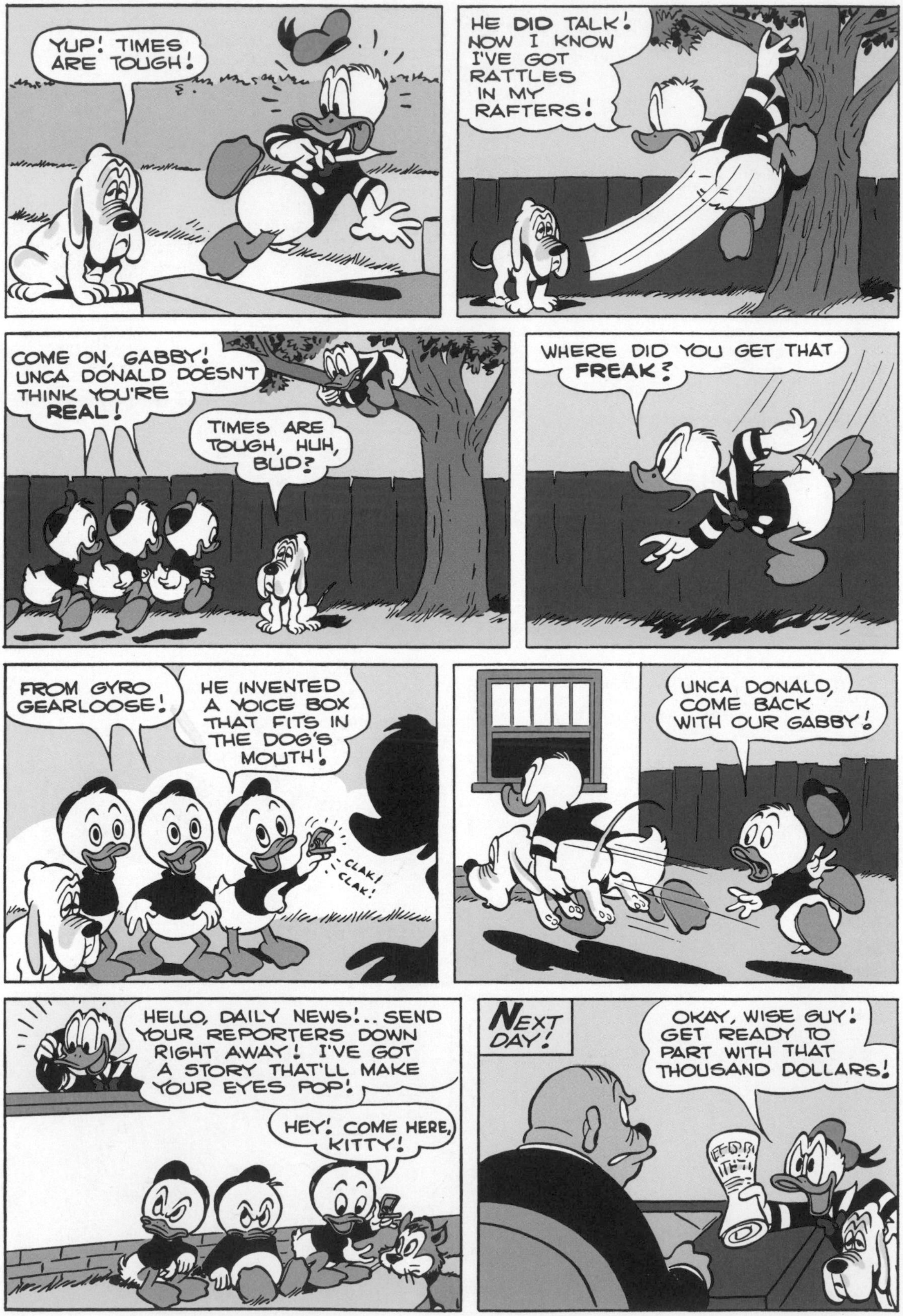

YUP! TIMES ARE TOUGH!
HE **DID** TALK! NOW I KNOW I'VE GOT RATTLES IN MY RAFTERS!
COME ON, GABBY! UNCA DONALD DOESN'T THINK YOU'RE **REAL**!
TIMES ARE TOUGH, HUH, BUD?
WHERE DID YOU GET THAT **FREAK**?
FROM GYRO GEARLOOSE!
HE INVENTED A VOICE BOX THAT FITS IN THE DOG'S MOUTH!
CLAK! CLAK!
UNCA DONALD, COME BACK WITH OUR GABBY!
HELLO, DAILY NEWS!.. SEND YOUR REPORTERS DOWN RIGHT AWAY! I'VE GOT A STORY THAT'LL MAKE YOUR EYES POP!
HEY! COME HERE, KITTY!
NEXT DAY!
OKAY, WISE GUY! GET READY TO PART WITH THAT THOUSAND DOLLARS!

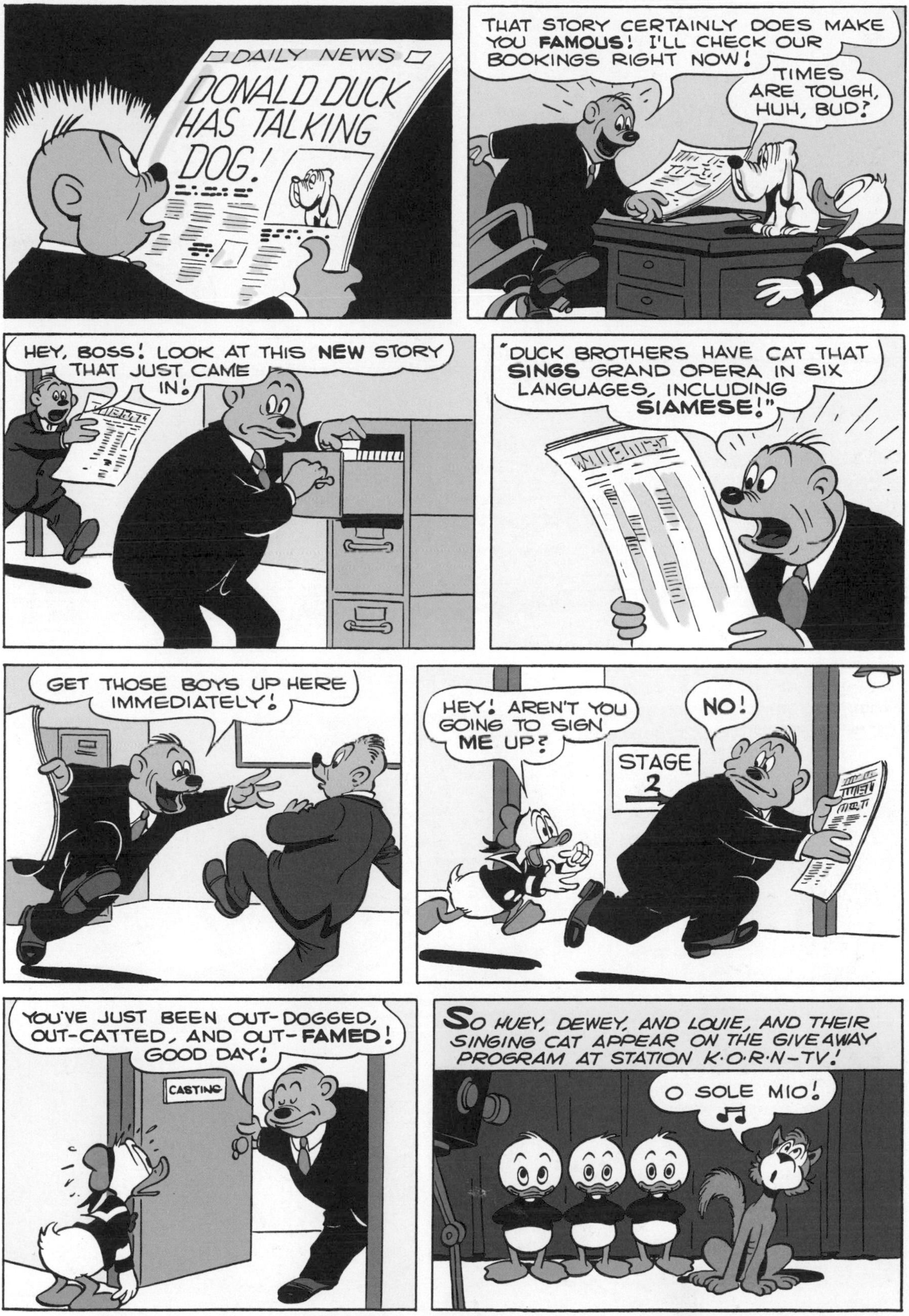
DAILY NEWS
DONALD DUCK HAS TALKING DOG!
THAT STORY CERTAINLY DOES MAKE YOU FAMOUS! I'LL CHECK OUR BOOKINGS RIGHT NOW!
TIMES ARE TOUGH, HUH, BUD?
HEY, BOSS! LOOK AT THIS NEW STORY THAT JUST CAME IN!
"DUCK BROTHERS HAVE CAT THAT SINGS GRAND OPERA IN SIX LANGUAGES, INCLUDING SIAMESE!"
GET THOSE BOYS UP HERE IMMEDIATELY!
HEY! AREN'T YOU GOING TO SIGN ME UP?
NO!
STAGE 2
YOU'VE JUST BEEN OUT-DOGGED, OUT-CATTED, AND OUT-FAMED! GOOD DAY!
CASTING
SO HUEY, DEWEY, AND LOUIE, AND THEIR SINGING CAT APPEAR ON THE GIVEAWAY PROGRAM AT STATION K·O·R·N–TV!
O SOLE MIO!

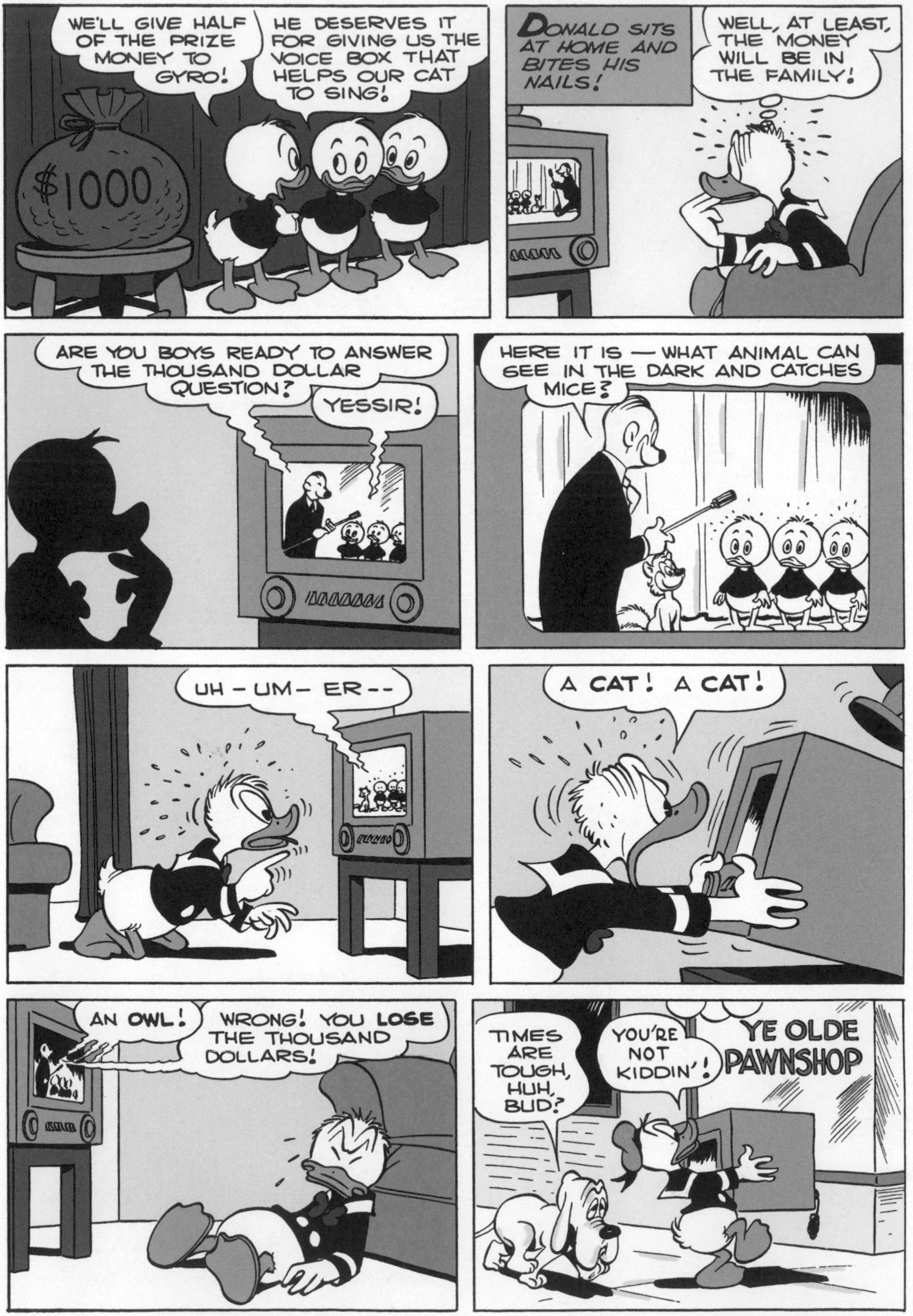

WE'LL GIVE HALF OF THE PRIZE MONEY TO GYRO!
HE DESERVES IT FOR GIVING US THE VOICE BOX THAT HELPS OUR CAT TO SING!
$1000
DONALD SITS AT HOME AND BITES HIS NAILS!
WELL, AT LEAST, THE MONEY WILL BE IN THE FAMILY!
ARE YOU BOYS READY TO ANSWER THE THOUSAND DOLLAR QUESTION?
YESSIR!
HERE IT IS — WHAT ANIMAL CAN SEE IN THE DARK AND CATCHES MICE?
UH – UM – ER --
A CAT! A CAT!
AN OWL!
WRONG! YOU LOSE THE THOUSAND DOLLARS!
TIMES ARE TOUGH, HUH, BUD?
YOU'RE NOT KIDDIN'!
YE OLDE PAWNSHOP

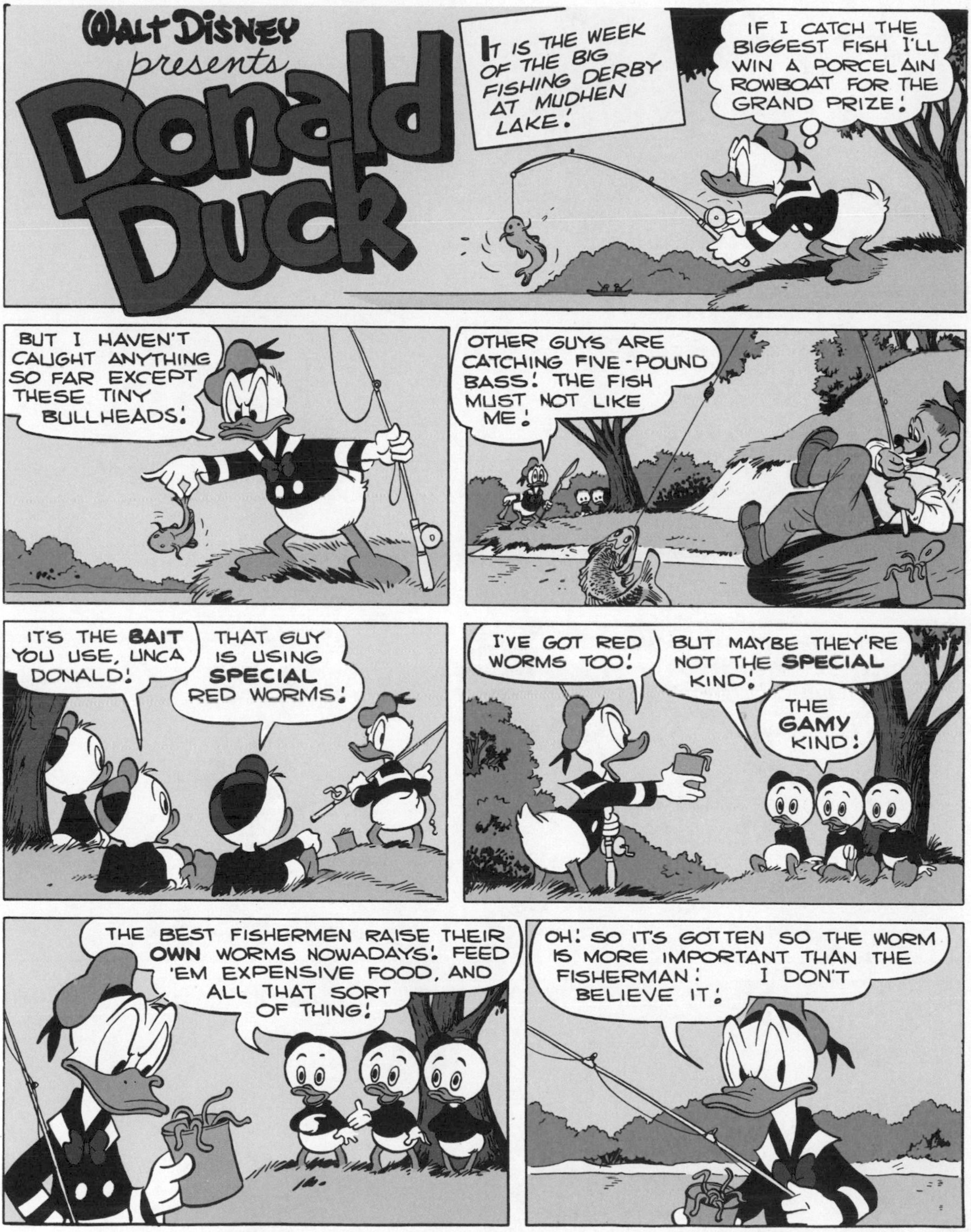
WALT DISNEY presents
Donald Duck
IT IS THE WEEK OF THE BIG FISHING DERBY AT MUDHEN LAKE!
IF I CATCH THE BIGGEST FISH I'LL WIN A PORCELAIN ROWBOAT FOR THE GRAND PRIZE!
BUT I HAVEN'T CAUGHT ANYTHING SO FAR EXCEPT THESE TINY BULLHEADS!
OTHER GUYS ARE CATCHING FIVE-POUND BASS! THE FISH MUST NOT LIKE ME!
IT'S THE BAIT YOU USE, UNCA DONALD!
THAT GUY IS USING SPECIAL RED WORMS!
I'VE GOT RED WORMS TOO!
BUT MAYBE THEY'RE NOT THE SPECIAL KIND!
THE GAMY KIND!
THE BEST FISHERMEN RAISE THEIR OWN WORMS NOWADAYS! FEED 'EM EXPENSIVE FOOD, AND ALL THAT SORT OF THING!
OH! SO IT'S GOTTEN SO THE WORM IS MORE IMPORTANT THAN THE FISHERMAN! I DON'T BELIEVE IT!

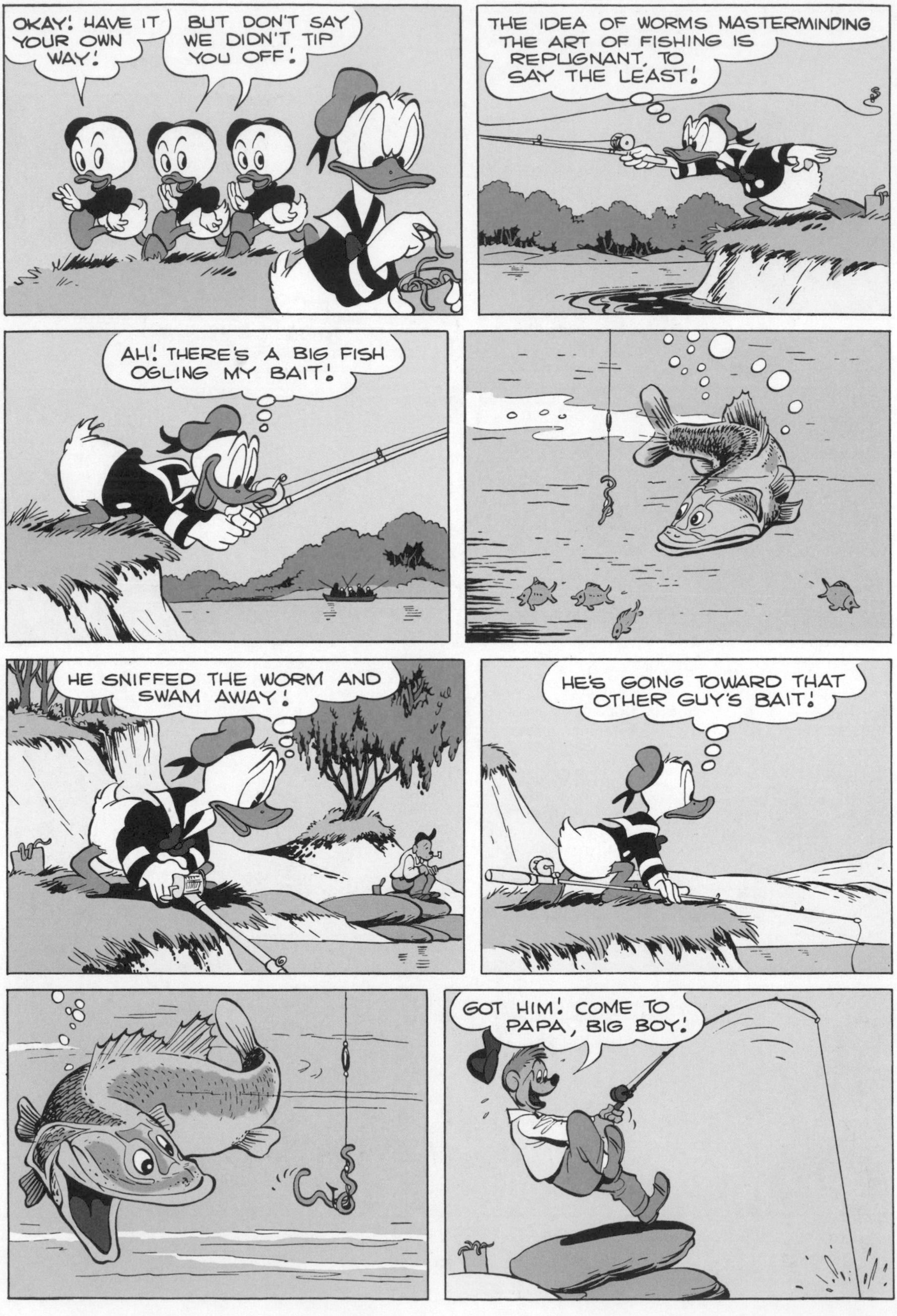
OKAY! HAVE IT YOUR OWN WAY!
BUT DON'T SAY WE DIDN'T TIP YOU OFF!
THE IDEA OF WORMS MASTERMINDING THE ART OF FISHING IS REPUGNANT, TO SAY THE LEAST!
AH! THERE'S A BIG FISH OGLING MY BAIT!
HE SNIFFED THE WORM AND SWAM AWAY!
HE'S GOING TOWARD THAT OTHER GUY'S BAIT!
GOT HIM! COME TO PAPA, BIG BOY!

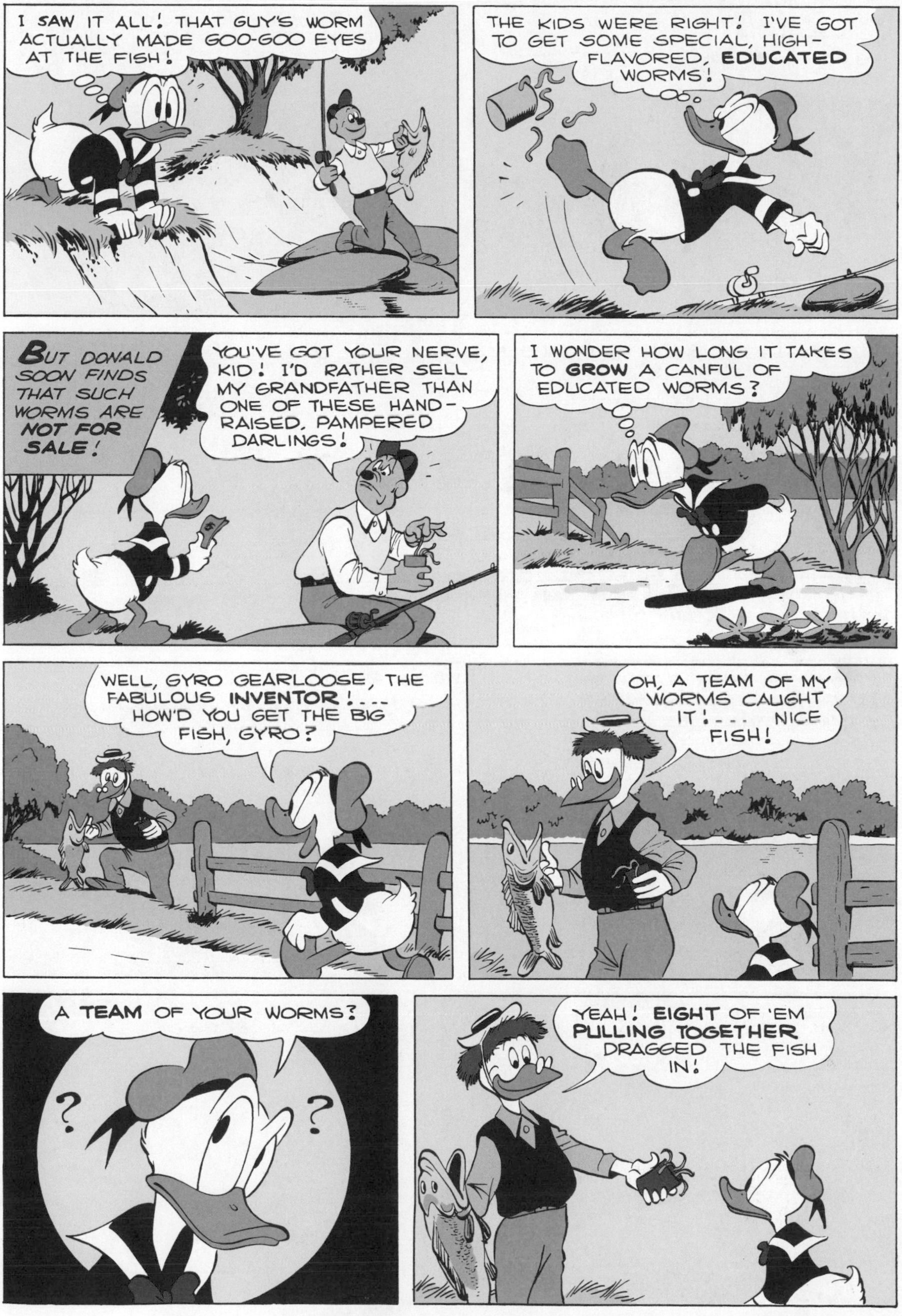
I SAW IT ALL! THAT GUY'S WORM ACTUALLY MADE GOO-GOO EYES AT THE FISH!
THE KIDS WERE RIGHT! I'VE GOT TO GET SOME SPECIAL, HIGH-FLAVORED, EDUCATED WORMS!
BUT DONALD SOON FINDS THAT SUCH WORMS ARE NOT FOR SALE!
YOU'VE GOT YOUR NERVE, KID! I'D RATHER SELL MY GRANDFATHER THAN ONE OF THESE HAND-RAISED, PAMPERED DARLINGS!
I WONDER HOW LONG IT TAKES TO GROW A CANFUL OF EDUCATED WORMS?
WELL, GYRO GEARLOOSE, THE FABULOUS INVENTOR!... HOW'D YOU GET THE BIG FISH, GYRO?
OH, A TEAM OF MY WORMS CAUGHT IT!... NICE FISH!
A TEAM OF YOUR WORMS?
YEAH! EIGHT OF 'EM PULLING TOGETHER DRAGGED THE FISH IN!

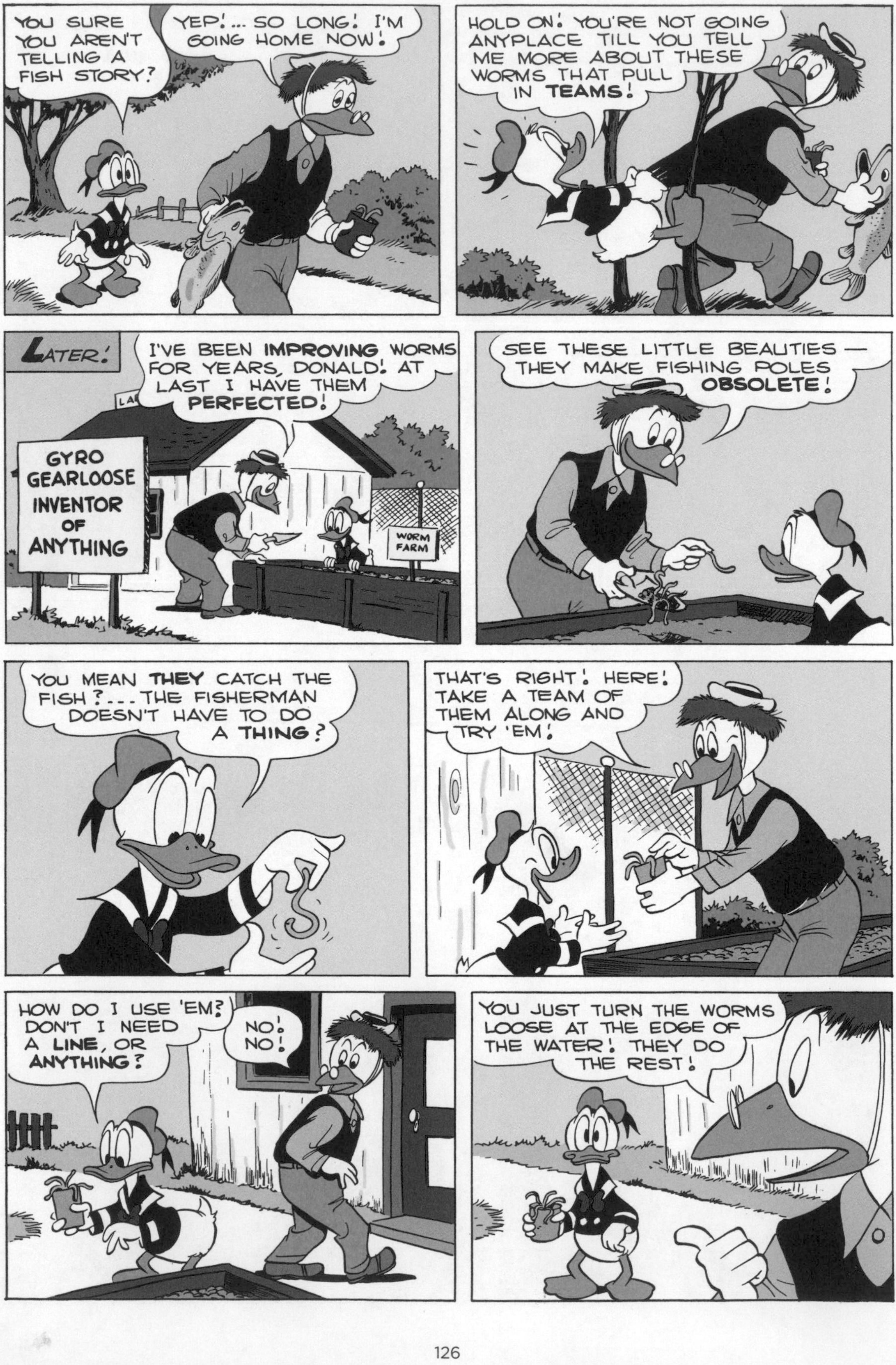
YOU SURE YOU AREN'T TELLING A FISH STORY?
YEP! ... SO LONG! I'M GOING HOME NOW!
HOLD ON! YOU'RE NOT GOING ANYPLACE TILL YOU TELL ME MORE ABOUT THESE WORMS THAT PULL IN TEAMS!
LATER!
I'VE BEEN IMPROVING WORMS FOR YEARS, DONALD! AT LAST I HAVE THEM PERFECTED!
GYRO GEARLOOSE INVENTOR OF ANYTHING
WORM FARM
SEE THESE LITTLE BEAUTIES — THEY MAKE FISHING POLES OBSOLETE!
YOU MEAN THEY CATCH THE FISH? . . . THE FISHERMAN DOESN'T HAVE TO DO A THING?
THAT'S RIGHT! HERE! TAKE A TEAM OF THEM ALONG AND TRY 'EM!
HOW DO I USE 'EM? DON'T I NEED A LINE, OR ANYTHING?
NO! NO!
YOU JUST TURN THE WORMS LOOSE AT THE EDGE OF THE WATER! THEY DO THE REST!

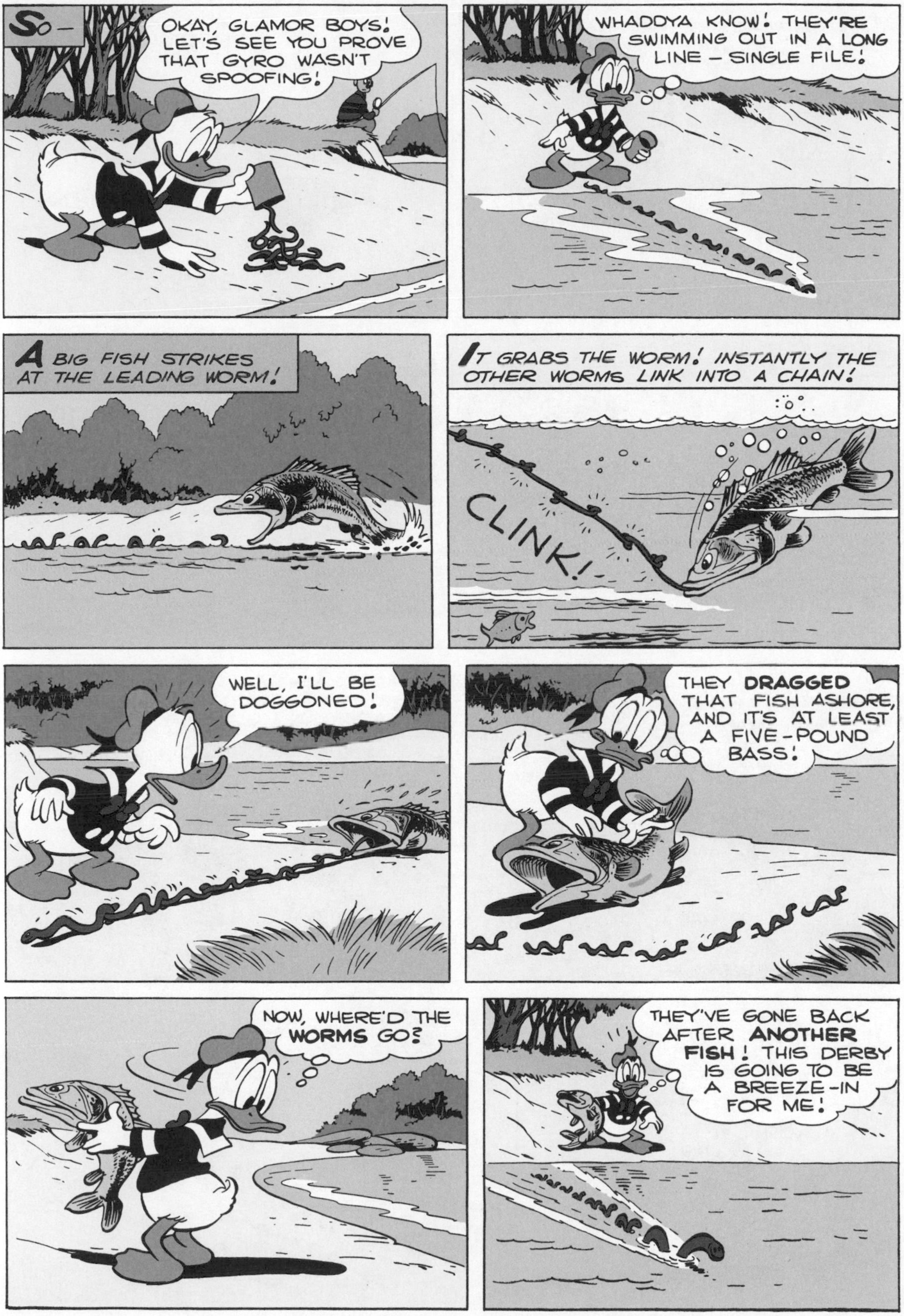
SO—
OKAY, GLAMOR BOYS! LET'S SEE YOU PROVE THAT GYRO WASN'T SPOOFING!
WHADDYA KNOW! THEY'RE SWIMMING OUT IN A LONG LINE — SINGLE FILE!
A BIG FISH STRIKES AT THE LEADING WORM!
IT GRABS THE WORM! INSTANTLY THE OTHER WORMS LINK INTO A CHAIN!
CLINK!
WELL, I'LL BE DOGGONED!
THEY **DRAGGED** THAT FISH ASHORE, AND IT'S AT LEAST A FIVE-POUND BASS!
NOW, WHERE'D THE **WORMS** GO?
THEY'VE GONE BACK AFTER **ANOTHER FISH**! THIS DERBY IS GOING TO BE A BREEZE-IN FOR ME!

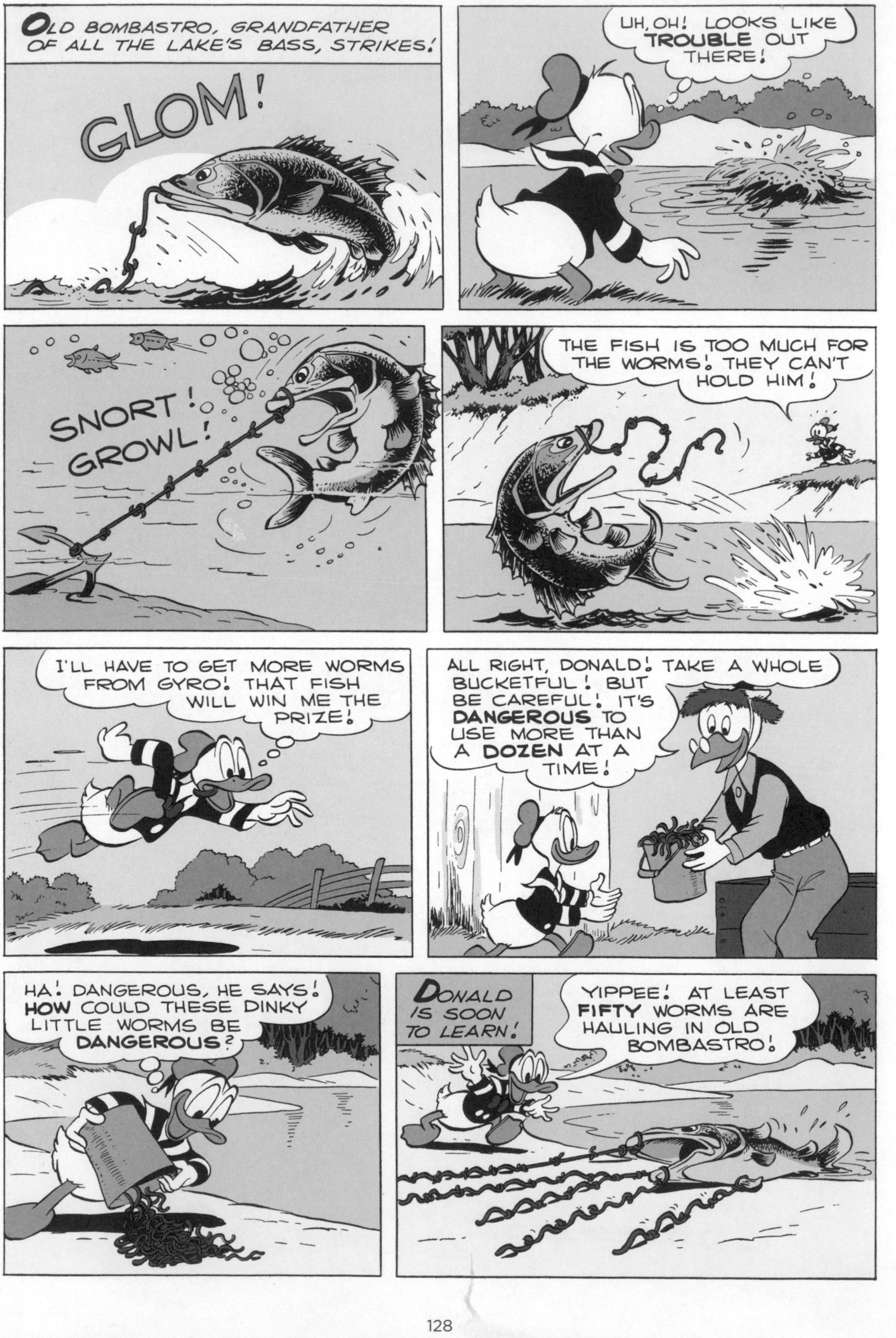
OLD BOMBASTRO, GRANDFATHER OF ALL THE LAKE'S BASS, STRIKES!
GLOM!
UH, OH! LOOKS LIKE TROUBLE OUT THERE!
SNORT! GROWL!
THE FISH IS TOO MUCH FOR THE WORMS! THEY CAN'T HOLD HIM!
I'LL HAVE TO GET MORE WORMS FROM GYRO! THAT FISH WILL WIN ME THE PRIZE!
ALL RIGHT, DONALD! TAKE A WHOLE BUCKETFUL! BUT BE CAREFUL! IT'S DANGEROUS TO USE MORE THAN A DOZEN AT A TIME!
HA! DANGEROUS, HE SAYS! HOW COULD THESE DINKY LITTLE WORMS BE DANGEROUS?
DONALD IS SOON TO LEARN!
YIPPEE! AT LEAST FIFTY WORMS ARE HAULING IN OLD BOMBASTRO!

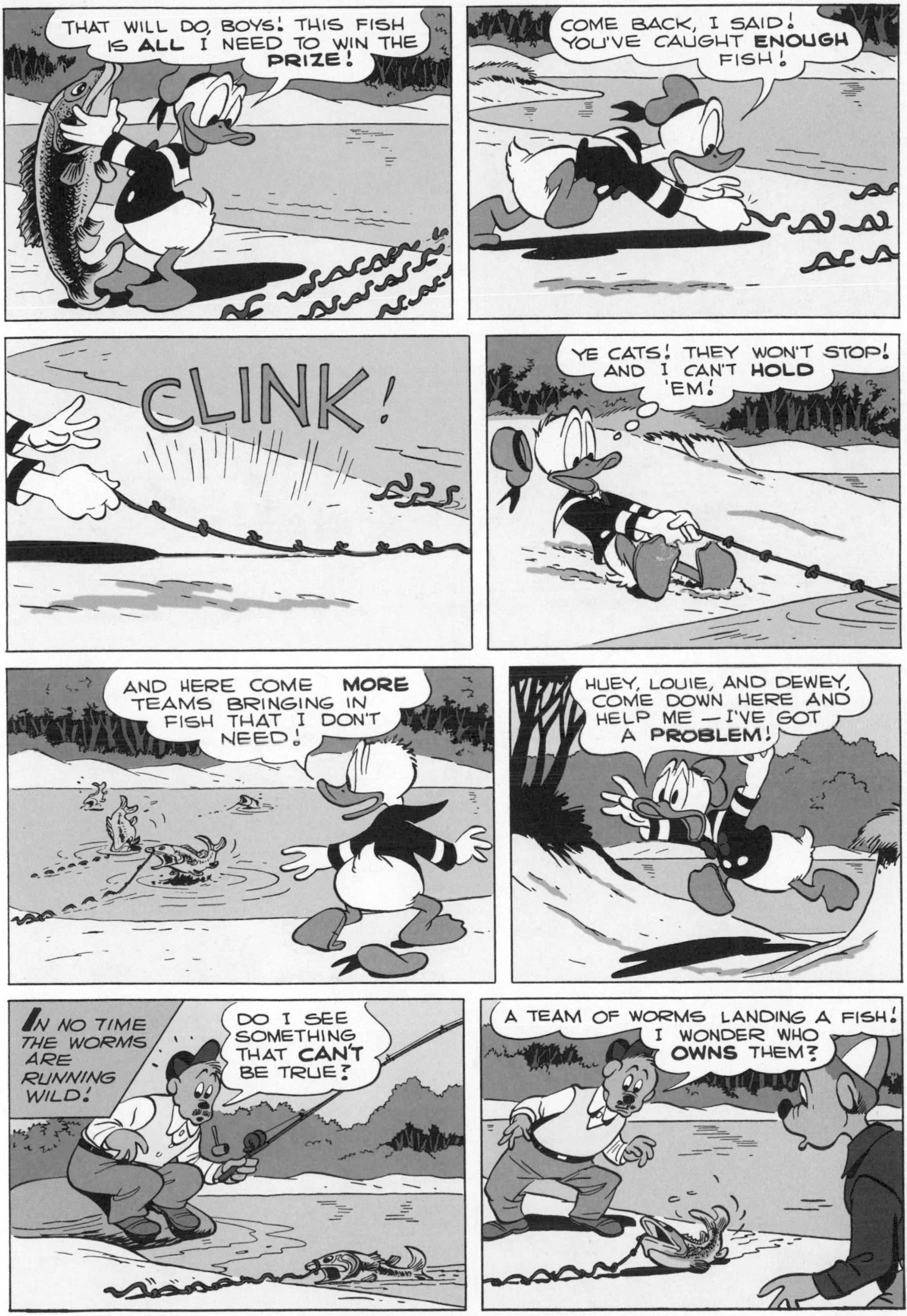
THAT WILL DO, BOYS! THIS FISH IS ALL I NEED TO WIN THE PRIZE!
COME BACK, I SAID! YOU'VE CAUGHT ENOUGH FISH!
CLINK!
YE CATS! THEY WON'T STOP! AND I CAN'T HOLD 'EM!
AND HERE COME MORE TEAMS BRINGING IN FISH THAT I DON'T NEED!
HUEY, LOUIE, AND DEWEY, COME DOWN HERE AND HELP ME — I'VE GOT A PROBLEM!
IN NO TIME THE WORMS ARE RUNNING WILD!
DO I SEE SOMETHING THAT CAN'T BE TRUE?
A TEAM OF WORMS LANDING A FISH! I WONDER WHO OWNS THEM?

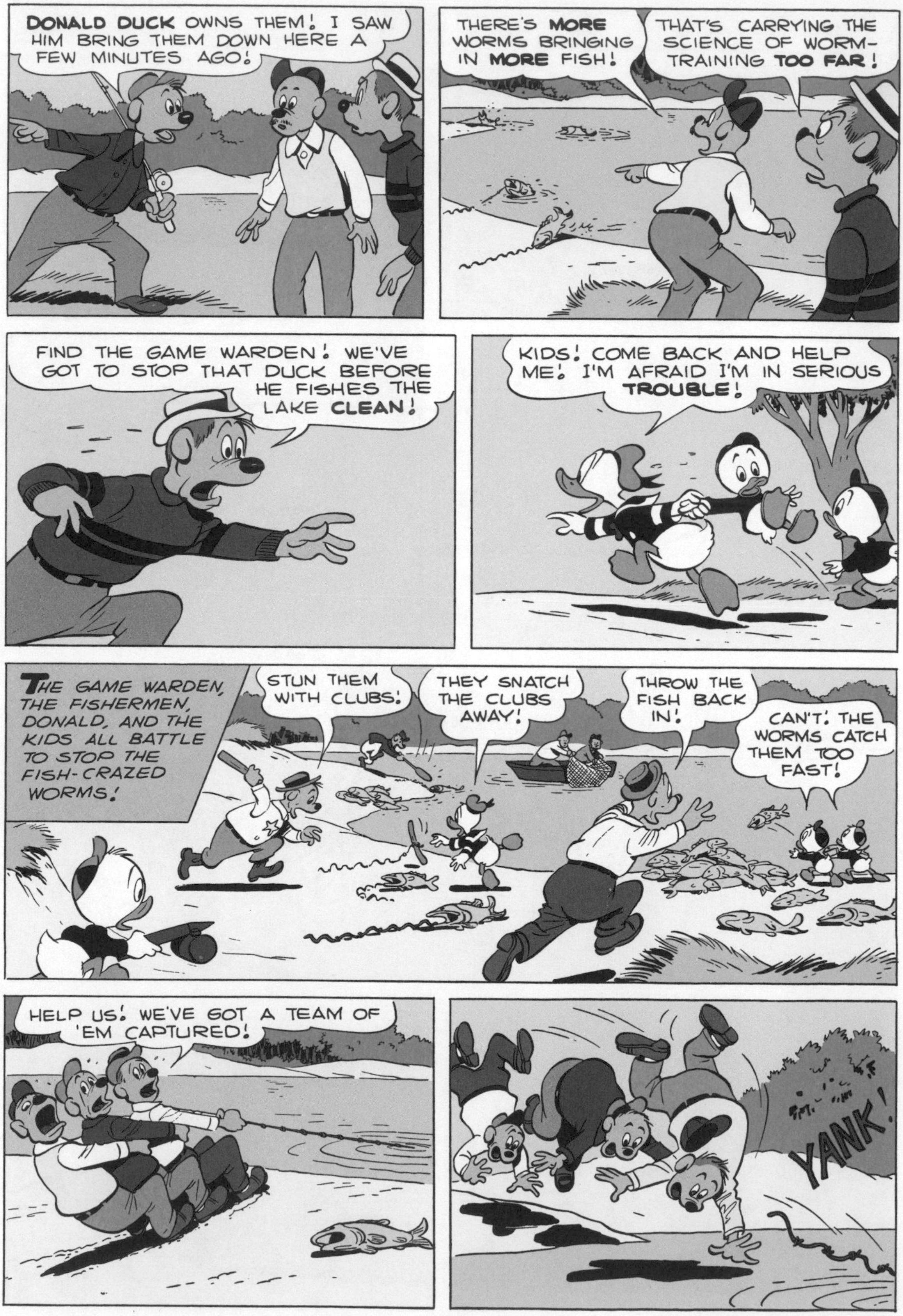
DONALD DUCK OWNS THEM! I SAW HIM BRING THEM DOWN HERE A FEW MINUTES AGO!
THERE'S MORE WORMS BRINGING IN MORE FISH!
THAT'S CARRYING THE SCIENCE OF WORM-TRAINING TOO FAR!
FIND THE GAME WARDEN! WE'VE GOT TO STOP THAT DUCK BEFORE HE FISHES THE LAKE CLEAN!
KIDS! COME BACK AND HELP ME! I'M AFRAID I'M IN SERIOUS TROUBLE!
THE GAME WARDEN, THE FISHERMEN, DONALD, AND THE KIDS ALL BATTLE TO STOP THE FISH-CRAZED WORMS!
STUN THEM WITH CLUBS!
THEY SNATCH THE CLUBS AWAY!
THROW THE FISH BACK IN!
CAN'T! THE WORMS CATCH THEM TOO FAST!
HELP US! WE'VE GOT A TEAM OF 'EM CAPTURED!
YANK!

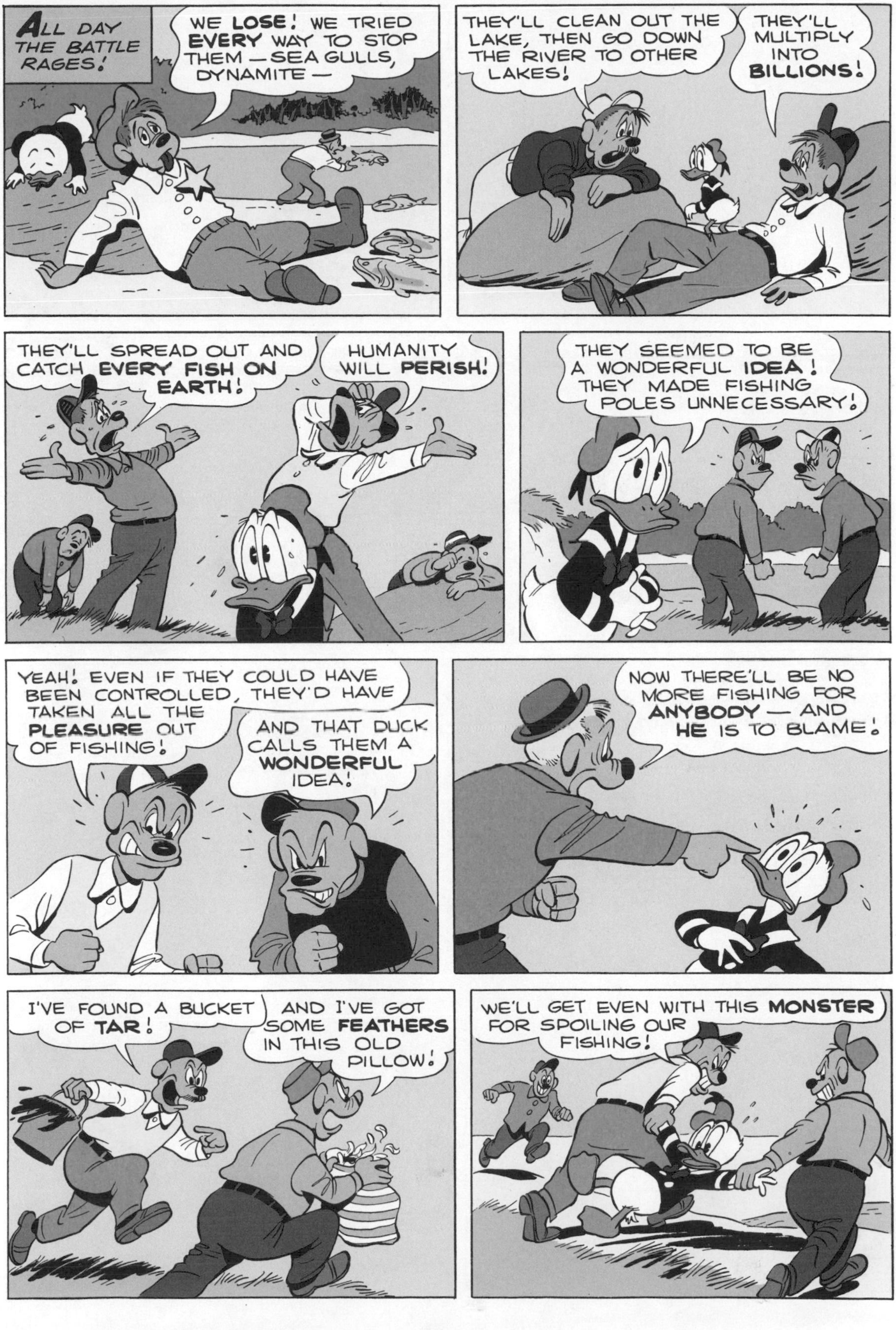
ALL DAY THE BATTLE RAGES!
WE LOSE! WE TRIED EVERY WAY TO STOP THEM — SEA GULLS, DYNAMITE —
THEY'LL CLEAN OUT THE LAKE, THEN GO DOWN THE RIVER TO OTHER LAKES!
THEY'LL MULTIPLY INTO BILLIONS!
THEY'LL SPREAD OUT AND CATCH EVERY FISH ON EARTH!
HUMANITY WILL PERISH!
THEY SEEMED TO BE A WONDERFUL IDEA! THEY MADE FISHING POLES UNNECESSARY!
YEAH! EVEN IF THEY COULD HAVE BEEN CONTROLLED, THEY'D HAVE TAKEN ALL THE PLEASURE OUT OF FISHING!
AND THAT DUCK CALLS THEM A WONDERFUL IDEA!
NOW THERE'LL BE NO MORE FISHING FOR ANYBODY — AND HE IS TO BLAME!
I'VE FOUND A BUCKET OF TAR!
AND I'VE GOT SOME FEATHERS IN THIS OLD PILLOW!
WE'LL GET EVEN WITH THIS MONSTER FOR SPOILING OUR FISHING!

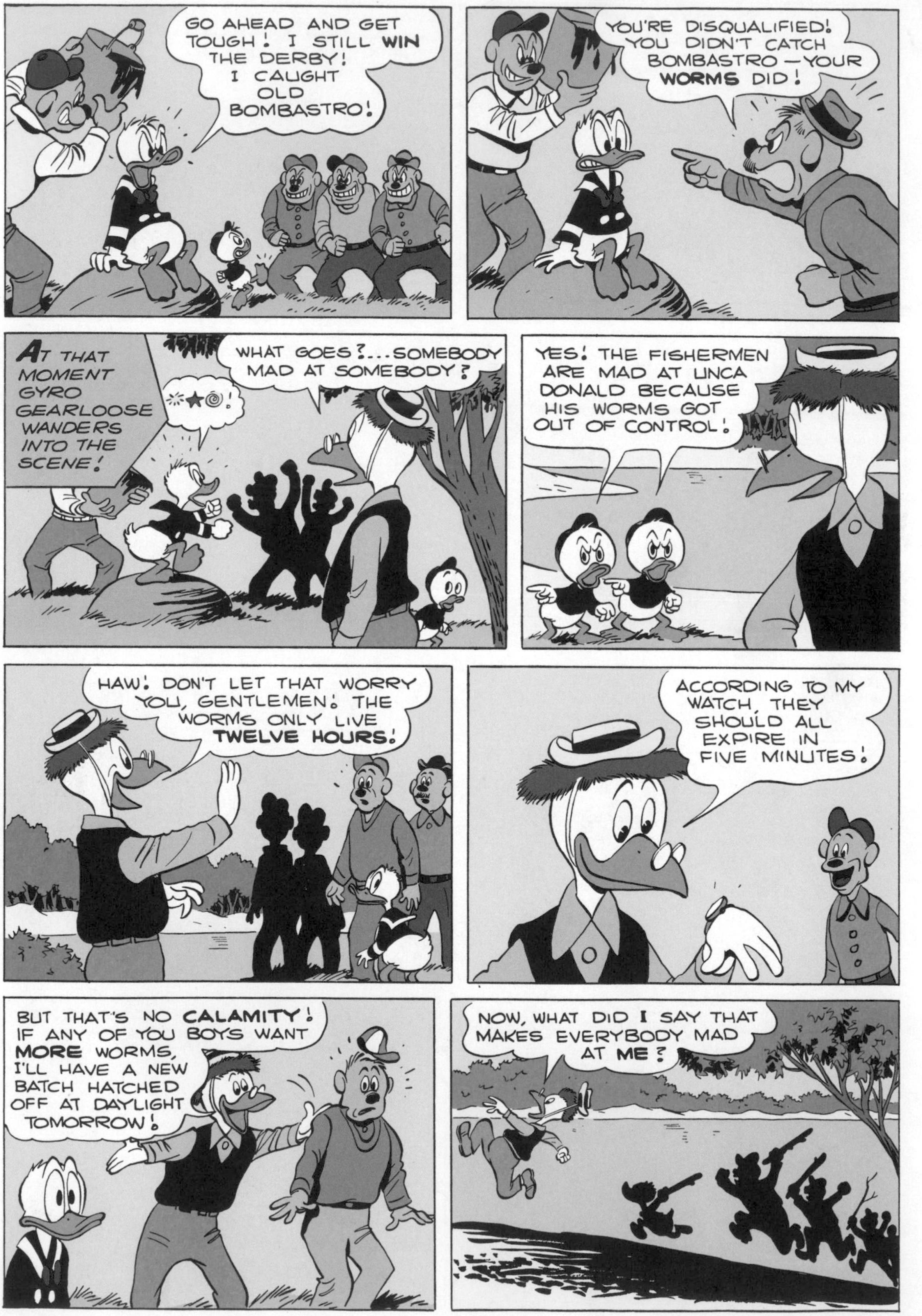
GO AHEAD AND GET TOUGH! I STILL WIN THE DERBY! I CAUGHT OLD BOMBASTRO!
YOU'RE DISQUALIFIED! YOU DIDN'T CATCH BOMBASTRO—YOUR WORMS DID!
AT THAT MOMENT GYRO GEARLOOSE WANDERS INTO THE SCENE!
WHAT GOES?...SOMEBODY MAD AT SOMEBODY?
YES! THE FISHERMEN ARE MAD AT UNCA DONALD BECAUSE HIS WORMS GOT OUT OF CONTROL!
HAW! DON'T LET THAT WORRY YOU, GENTLEMEN! THE WORMS ONLY LIVE TWELVE HOURS!
ACCORDING TO MY WATCH, THEY SHOULD ALL EXPIRE IN FIVE MINUTES!
BUT THAT'S NO CALAMITY! IF ANY OF YOU BOYS WANT MORE WORMS, I'LL HAVE A NEW BATCH HATCHED OFF AT DAYLIGHT TOMORROW!
NOW, WHAT DID I SAY THAT MAKES EVERYBODY MAD AT ME?

Walt Disney presents **Donald Duck**

FOR YEARS AND YEARS THE OLD QUACKLY PLACE HAS STOOD DESERTED ON THE HILL ABOVE DUCKBURG!

FOR SALE
SEE
DONALD DUCK
REALTOR

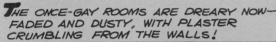

THE ONCE-GAY ROOMS ARE DREARY NOW— FADED AND DUSTY, WITH PLASTER CRUMBLING FROM THE WALLS!

THE FORMAL GARDEN IS RANK WITH WEEDS! THE LILY POND TEEMS WITH FROGS!

ONLY GRASSHOPPERS PASTURE IN THE ROLLING FIELD WHERE CARRIAGE HORSES ONCE MUNCHED IN CLOVER AS HIGH AS THEIR KNEES!

THE WHOLE WORKS HAS FINALLY BEEN PUT ON THE MARKET BY THE QUACKLY HEIRS! BUT **WHO** WILL BUY IT?

FOR SALE
SEE
DONALD DUCK
REALTOR

IT'S TOO OLD-FASHIONED FOR A HOME, TOO HILLY FOR A FARM! I'LL NEVER FIND ANYBODY DUMB ENOUGH TO WANT IT!

TO MAKE MATTERS WORSE FOR DONALD, HIS NEPHEWS HAVE ADOPTED THE OLD PLACE FOR A CLUBHOUSE!

SO!

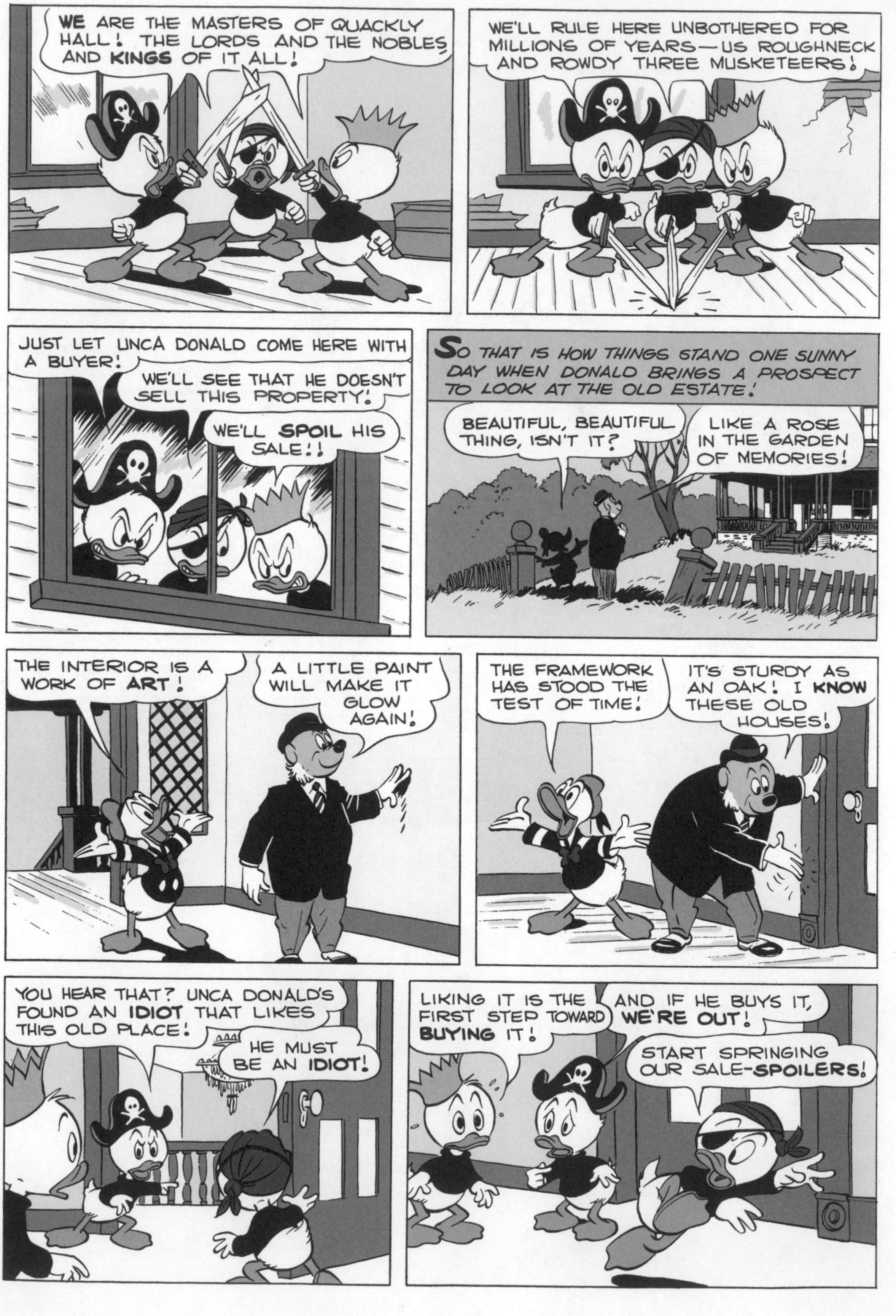

WE ARE THE MASTERS OF QUACKLY HALL! THE LORDS AND THE NOBLES AND KINGS OF IT ALL!
WE'LL RULE HERE UNBOTHERED FOR MILLIONS OF YEARS—US ROUGHNECK AND ROWDY THREE MUSKETEERS!
JUST LET UNCA DONALD COME HERE WITH A BUYER!
WE'LL SEE THAT HE DOESN'T SELL THIS PROPERTY!
WE'LL SPOIL HIS SALE!!
SO THAT IS HOW THINGS STAND ONE SUNNY DAY WHEN DONALD BRINGS A PROSPECT TO LOOK AT THE OLD ESTATE!
BEAUTIFUL, BEAUTIFUL THING, ISN'T IT?
LIKE A ROSE IN THE GARDEN OF MEMORIES!
THE INTERIOR IS A WORK OF ART!
A LITTLE PAINT WILL MAKE IT GLOW AGAIN!
THE FRAMEWORK HAS STOOD THE TEST OF TIME!
IT'S STURDY AS AN OAK! I KNOW THESE OLD HOUSES!
YOU HEAR THAT? UNCA DONALD'S FOUND AN IDIOT THAT LIKES THIS OLD PLACE!
HE MUST BE AN IDIOT!
LIKING IT IS THE FIRST STEP TOWARD BUYING IT!
AND IF HE BUYS IT, WE'RE OUT!
START SPRINGING OUR SALE-SPOILERS!

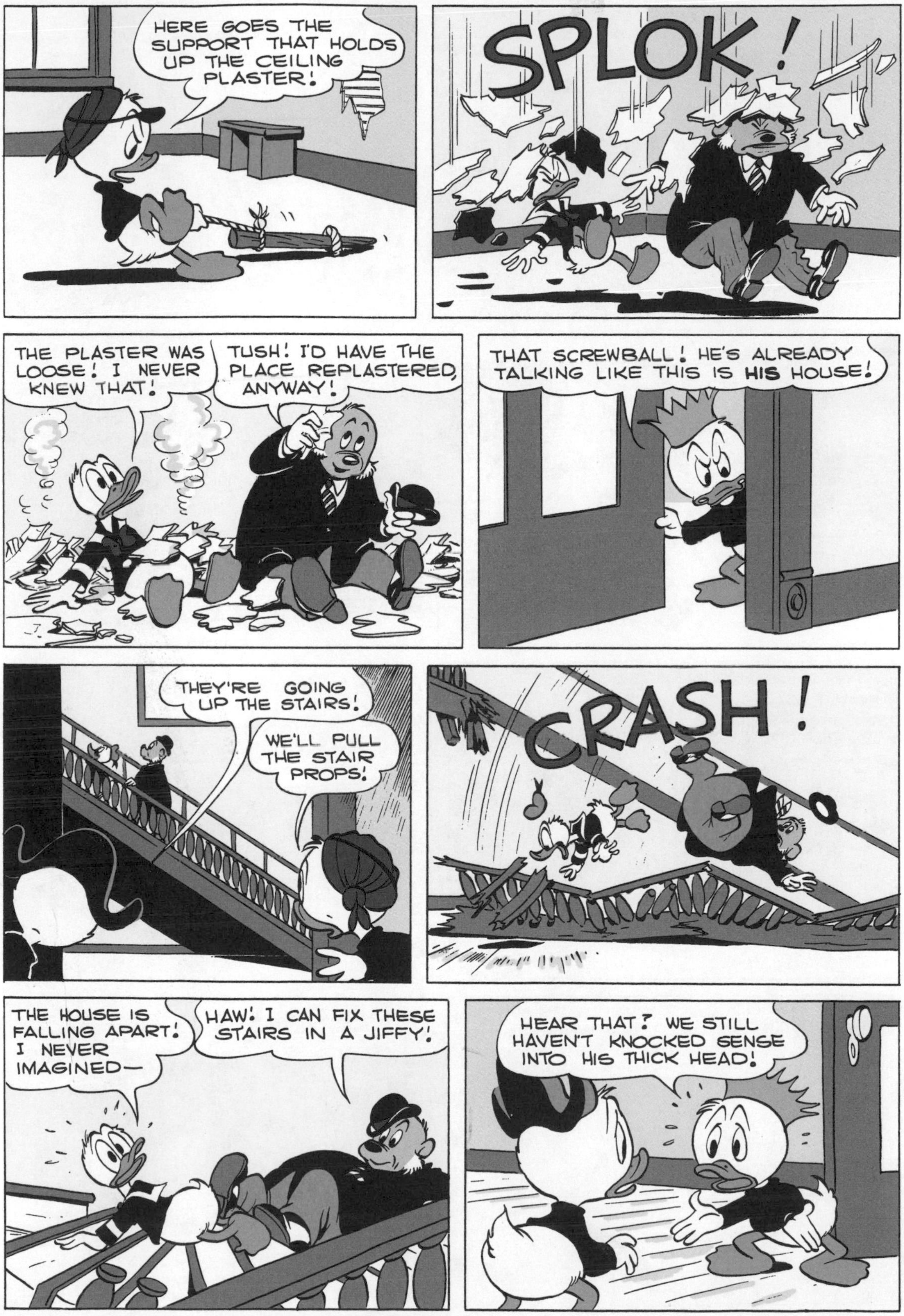
HERE GOES THE SUPPORT THAT HOLDS UP THE CEILING PLASTER!
SPLOK!
THE PLASTER WAS LOOSE! I NEVER KNEW THAT!
TUSH! I'D HAVE THE PLACE REPLASTERED, ANYWAY!
THAT SCREWBALL! HE'S ALREADY TALKING LIKE THIS IS HIS HOUSE!
THEY'RE GOING UP THE STAIRS!
WE'LL PULL THE STAIR PROPS!
CRASH!
THE HOUSE IS FALLING APART! I NEVER IMAGINED—
HAW! I CAN FIX THESE STAIRS IN A JIFFY!
HEAR THAT? WE STILL HAVEN'T KNOCKED SENSE INTO HIS THICK HEAD!

NOW THE OLD TRESPASSER'S GOING INTO THE KITCHEN!
HA! THAT'S WHERE WE CAN CLOBBER HIM!
WHEN THE FLOOR COLLAPSES, HE'LL KNOW HIS DREAM HOUSE IS A NIGHTMARE!
AWK!
I'M SORRY, MR. WINTERBEARD! I NEVER KNEW THIS RUIN WAS IN SUCH AWFUL CONDITION!
IT'S UNSAFE, ALL RIGHT!
BUT THAT MERELY WHETS MY INTEREST! I LOVE TO REPAIR OLD HOUSES!
HE'S BUGHOUSE LOONEY!
NOBODY COULD WANT THIS OLD PLACE THAT BAD, UNLESS HE WAS WACKY IN THE RAFTERS!
MY WORD! WHAT A PERFECT SETUP FOR A SWIMMING POOL!
YE CATS! NOW HE WANTS OUR FROG POND!
HE'S UP TO NO GOOD!
HE'S A BIG CROOK, I BET!

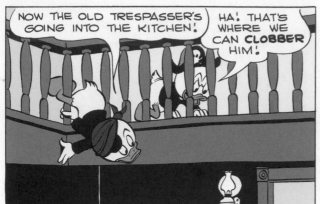

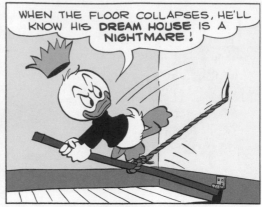

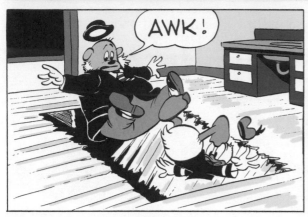

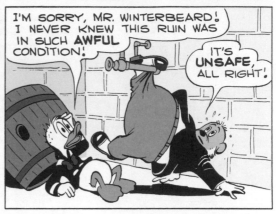

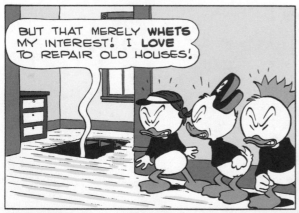

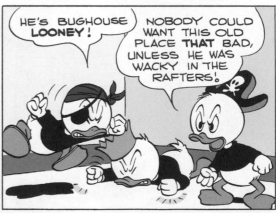

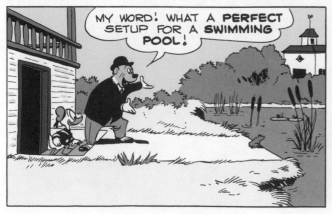

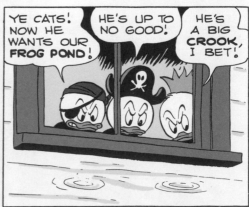

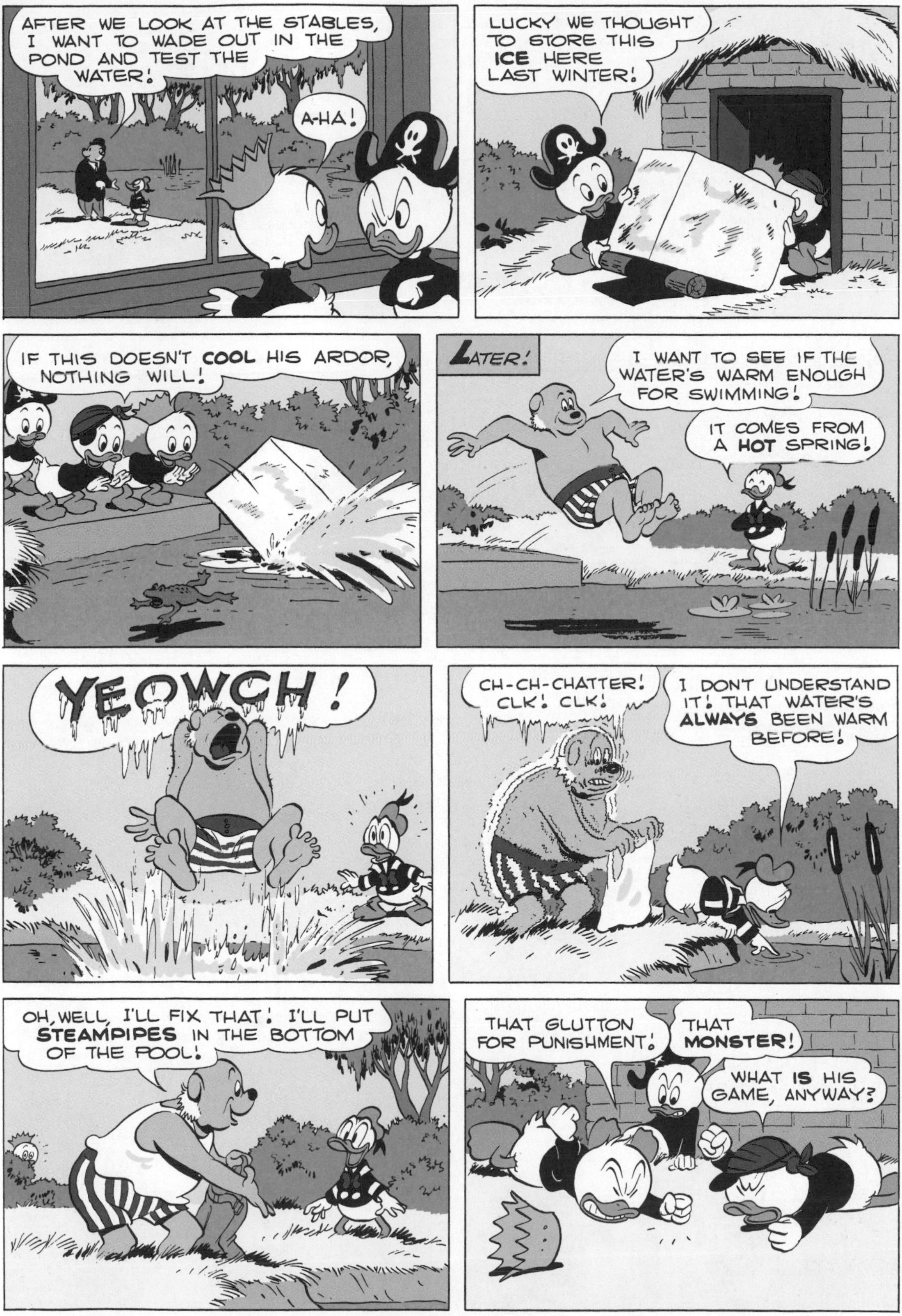
AFTER WE LOOK AT THE STABLES, I WANT TO WADE OUT IN THE POND AND TEST THE WATER!
A-HA!
LUCKY WE THOUGHT TO STORE THIS ICE HERE LAST WINTER!
IF THIS DOESN'T COOL HIS ARDOR, NOTHING WILL!
LATER!
I WANT TO SEE IF THE WATER'S WARM ENOUGH FOR SWIMMING!
IT COMES FROM A HOT SPRING!
YEOWCH!
CH-CH-CHATTER! CLK! CLK!
I DON'T UNDERSTAND IT! THAT WATER'S ALWAYS BEEN WARM BEFORE!
OH, WELL, I'LL FIX THAT! I'LL PUT STEAMPIPES IN THE BOTTOM OF THE POOL!
THAT GLUTTON FOR PUNISHMENT!
THAT MONSTER!
WHAT IS HIS GAME, ANYWAY?

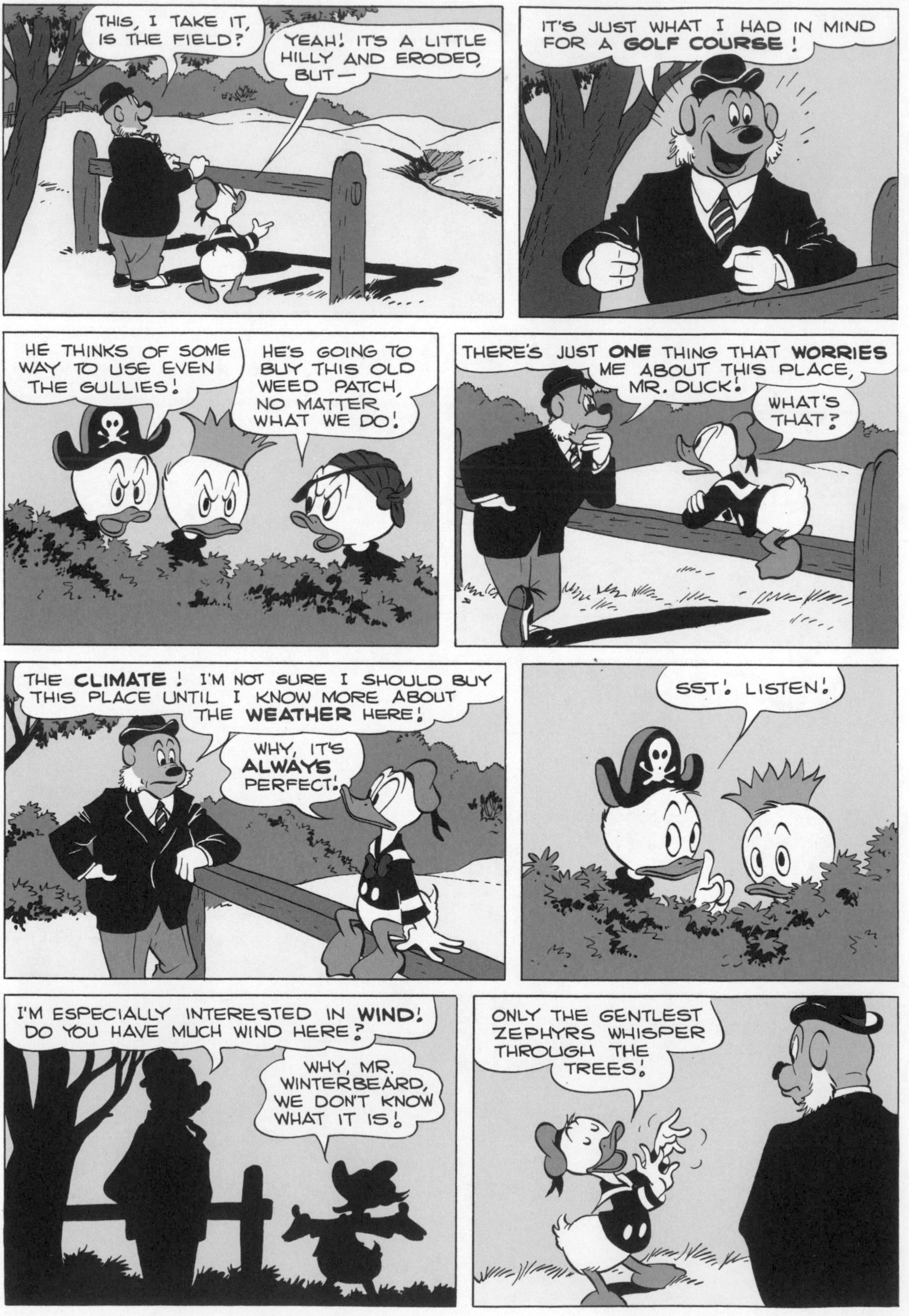
THIS, I TAKE IT, IS THE FIELD?
YEAH! IT'S A LITTLE HILLY AND ERODED, BUT—
IT'S JUST WHAT I HAD IN MIND FOR A **GOLF COURSE**!
HE THINKS OF SOME WAY TO USE EVEN THE GULLIES!
HE'S GOING TO BUY THIS OLD WEED PATCH, NO MATTER WHAT WE DO!
THERE'S JUST **ONE** THING THAT **WORRIES** ME ABOUT THIS PLACE, MR. DUCK!
WHAT'S THAT?
THE **CLIMATE**! I'M NOT SURE I SHOULD BUY THIS PLACE UNTIL I KNOW MORE ABOUT THE **WEATHER** HERE!
WHY, IT'S **ALWAYS** PERFECT!
SST! LISTEN!
I'M ESPECIALLY INTERESTED IN **WIND**! DO YOU HAVE MUCH WIND HERE?
WHY, MR. WINTERBEARD, WE DON'T KNOW WHAT IT IS!
ONLY THE GENTLEST ZEPHYRS WHISPER THROUGH THE TREES!

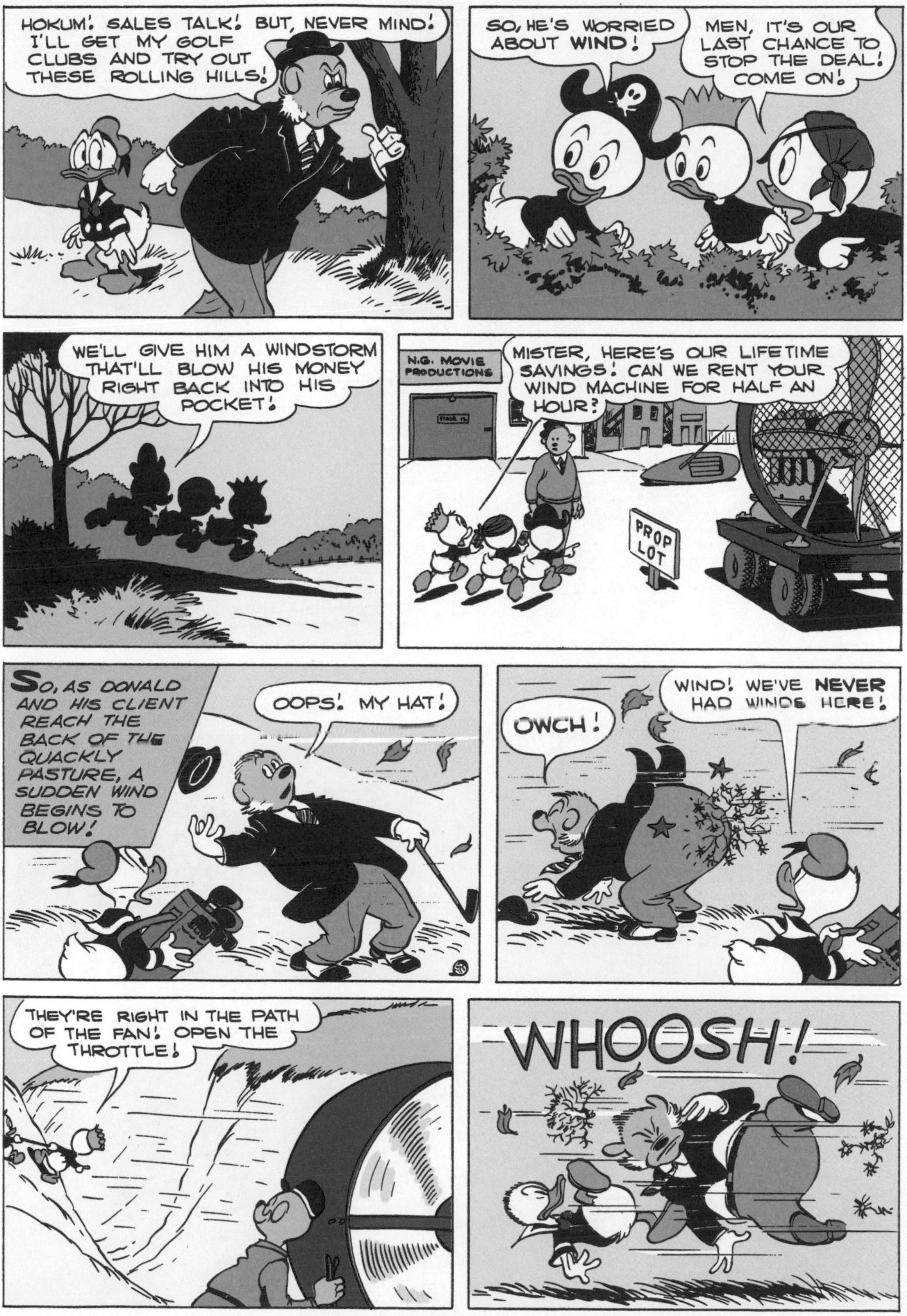
HOKUM! SALES TALK! BUT, NEVER MIND! I'LL GET MY GOLF CLUBS AND TRY OUT THESE ROLLING HILLS!
SO, HE'S WORRIED ABOUT **WIND**!
MEN, IT'S OUR LAST CHANCE TO STOP THE DEAL! COME ON!
WE'LL GIVE HIM A WINDSTORM THAT'LL BLOW HIS MONEY RIGHT BACK INTO HIS POCKET!
N.G. MOVIE PRODUCTIONS
MISTER, HERE'S OUR LIFETIME SAVINGS! CAN WE RENT YOUR WIND MACHINE FOR HALF AN HOUR?
PROP LOT
SO, AS DONALD AND HIS CLIENT REACH THE BACK OF THE QUACKLY PASTURE, A SUDDEN WIND BEGINS TO BLOW!
OOPS! MY HAT!
OWCH!
WIND! WE'VE **NEVER** HAD WINDS HERE!
THEY'RE RIGHT IN THE PATH OF THE FAN! OPEN THE THROTTLE!
WHOOSH!

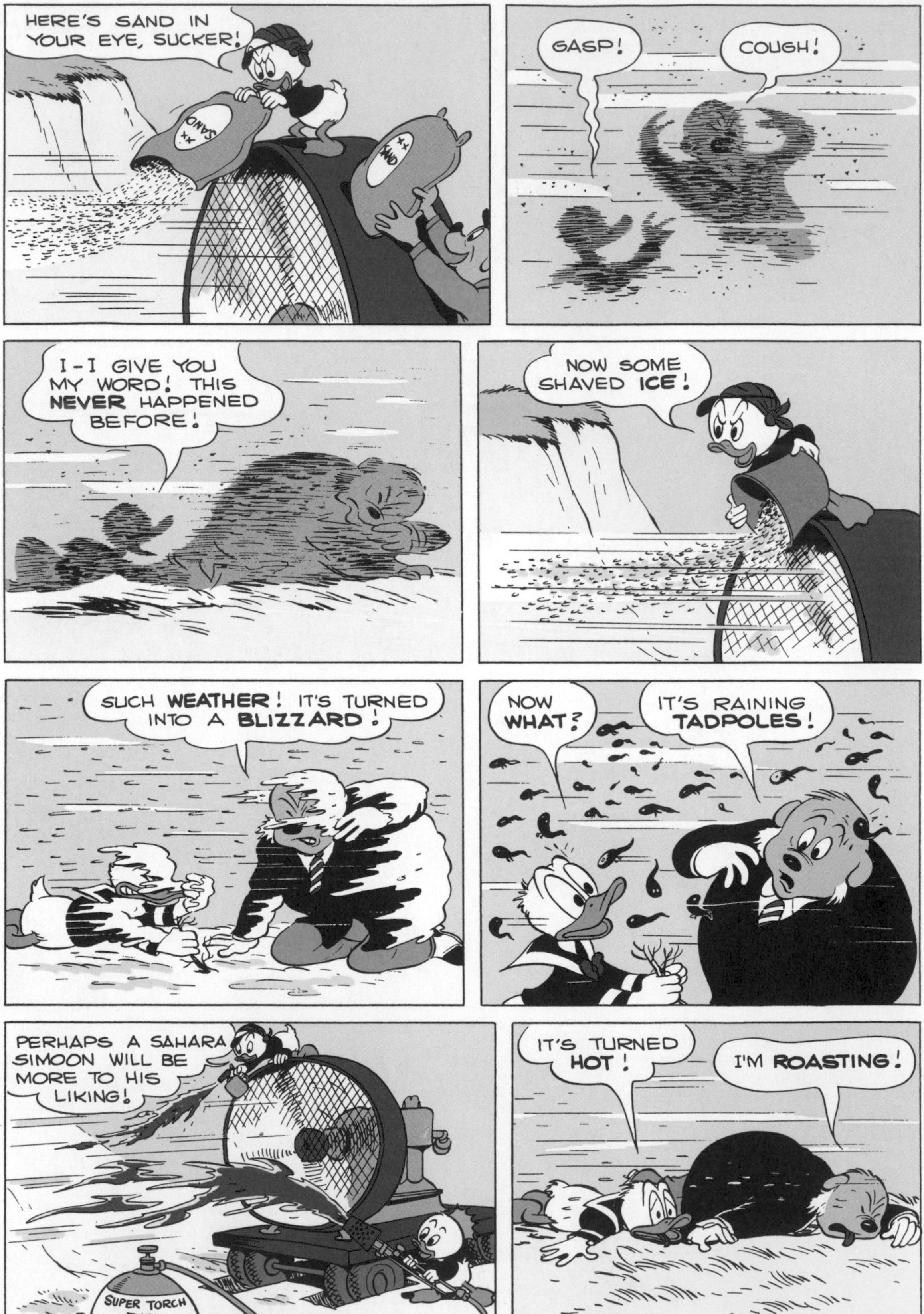

HERE'S SAND IN YOUR EYE, SUCKER!
SAND XX
SAND XX
GASP!
COUGH!
I-I GIVE YOU MY WORD! THIS **NEVER** HAPPENED BEFORE!
NOW SOME SHAVED **ICE**!
SUCH **WEATHER**! IT'S TURNED INTO A **BLIZZARD**!
NOW **WHAT**?
IT'S RAINING **TADPOLES**!
PERHAPS A SAHARA SIMOON WILL BE MORE TO HIS LIKING!
SUPER TORCH FUEL
IT'S TURNED **HOT**!
I'M **ROASTING**!

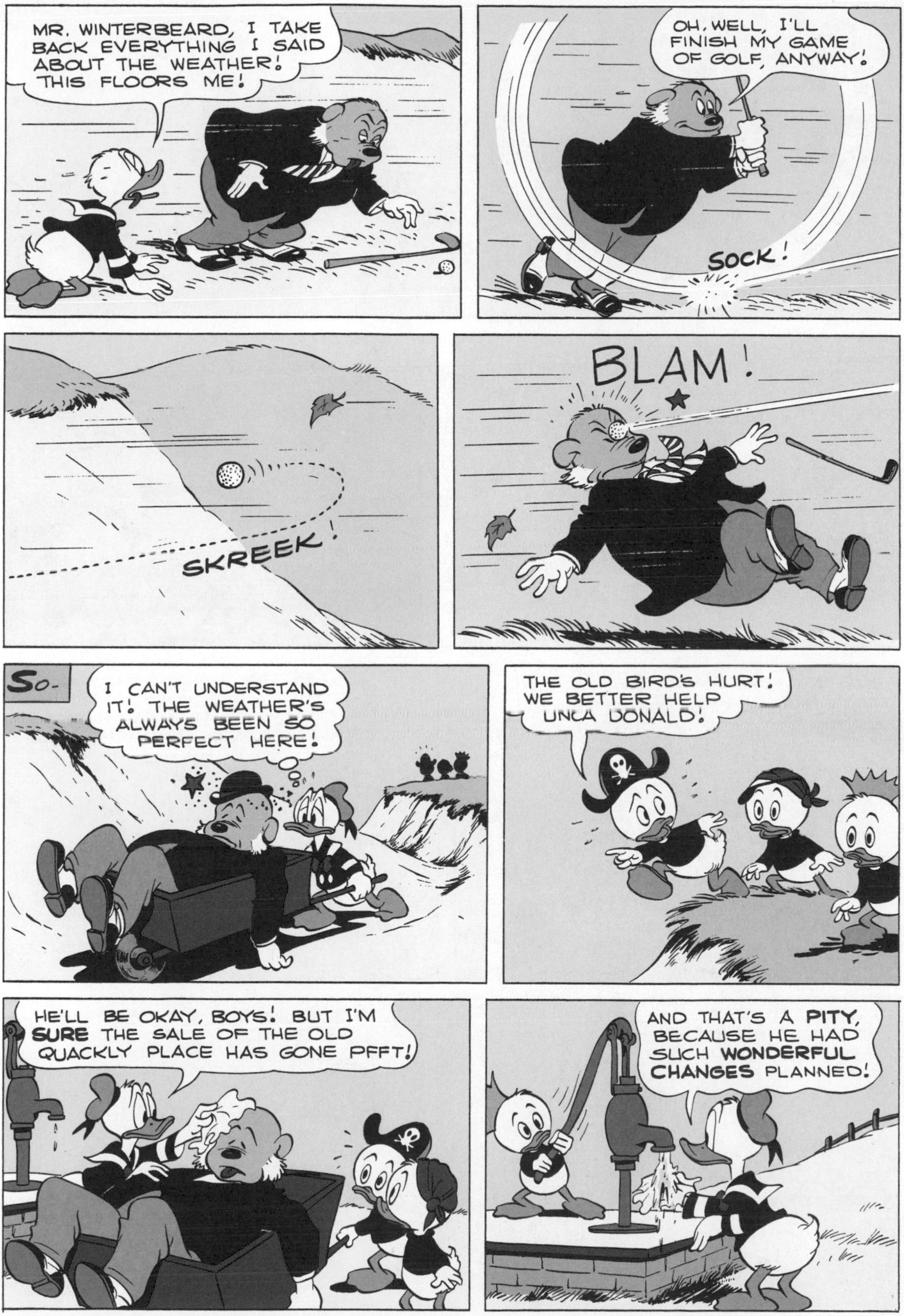
MR. WINTERBEARD, I TAKE BACK EVERYTHING I SAID ABOUT THE WEATHER! THIS FLOORS ME!
OH, WELL, I'LL FINISH MY GAME OF GOLF, ANYWAY!
SOCK!
SKREEK!
BLAM!
SO-
I CAN'T UNDERSTAND IT! THE WEATHER'S ALWAYS BEEN SO PERFECT HERE!
THE OLD BIRD'S HURT! WE BETTER HELP UNCA DONALD!
HE'LL BE OKAY, BOYS! BUT I'M SURE THE SALE OF THE OLD QUACKLY PLACE HAS GONE PFFT!
AND THAT'S A PITY, BECAUSE HE HAD SUCH WONDERFUL CHANGES PLANNED!

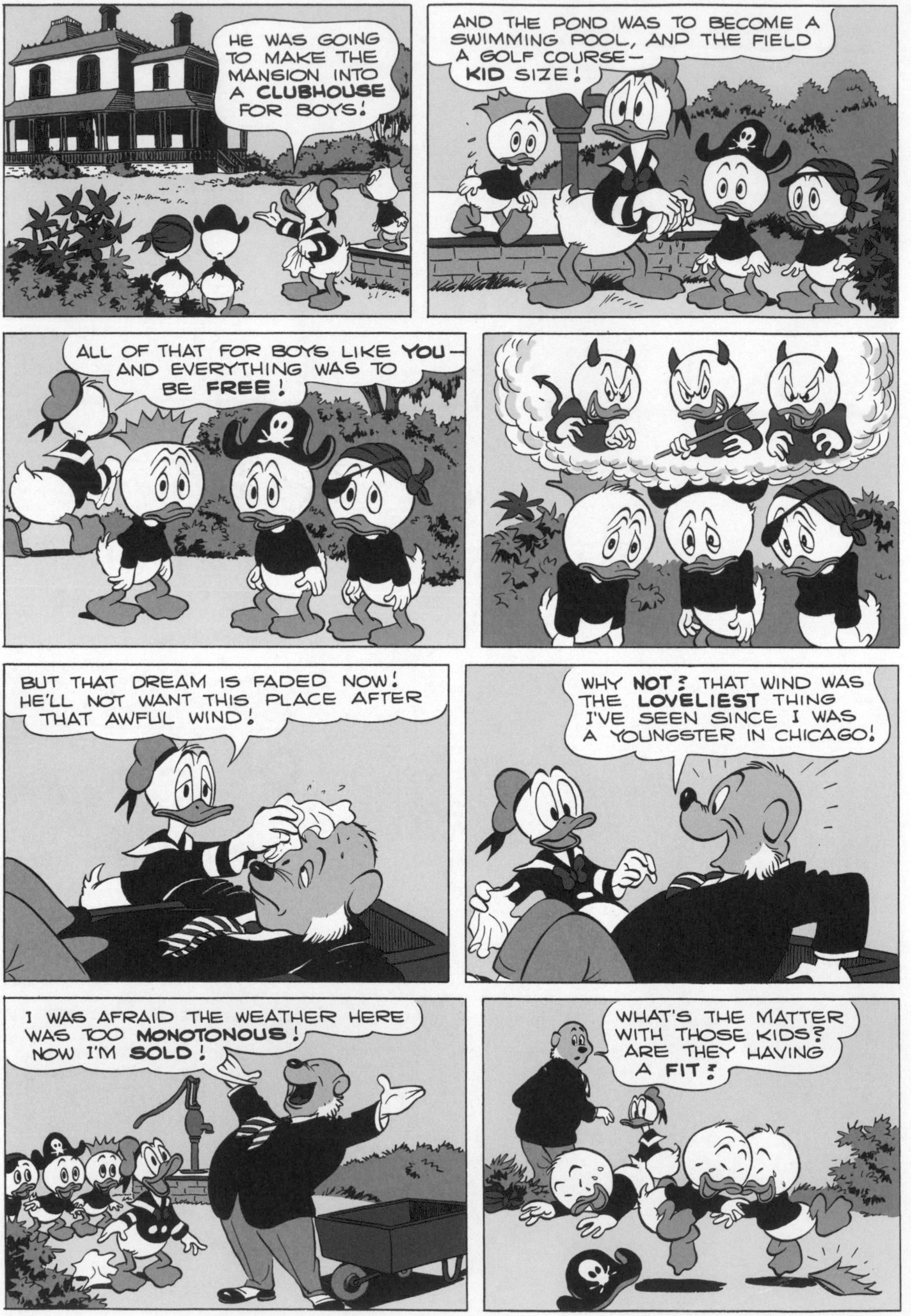
HE WAS GOING TO MAKE THE MANSION INTO A CLUBHOUSE FOR BOYS!
AND THE POND WAS TO BECOME A SWIMMING POOL, AND THE FIELD A GOLF COURSE— KID SIZE!
ALL OF THAT FOR BOYS LIKE YOU— AND EVERYTHING WAS TO BE FREE!
BUT THAT DREAM IS FADED NOW! HE'LL NOT WANT THIS PLACE AFTER THAT AWFUL WIND!
WHY NOT? THAT WIND WAS THE LOVELIEST THING I'VE SEEN SINCE I WAS A YOUNGSTER IN CHICAGO!
I WAS AFRAID THE WEATHER HERE WAS TOO MONOTONOUS! NOW I'M SOLD!
WHAT'S THE MATTER WITH THOSE KIDS? ARE THEY HAVING A FIT?

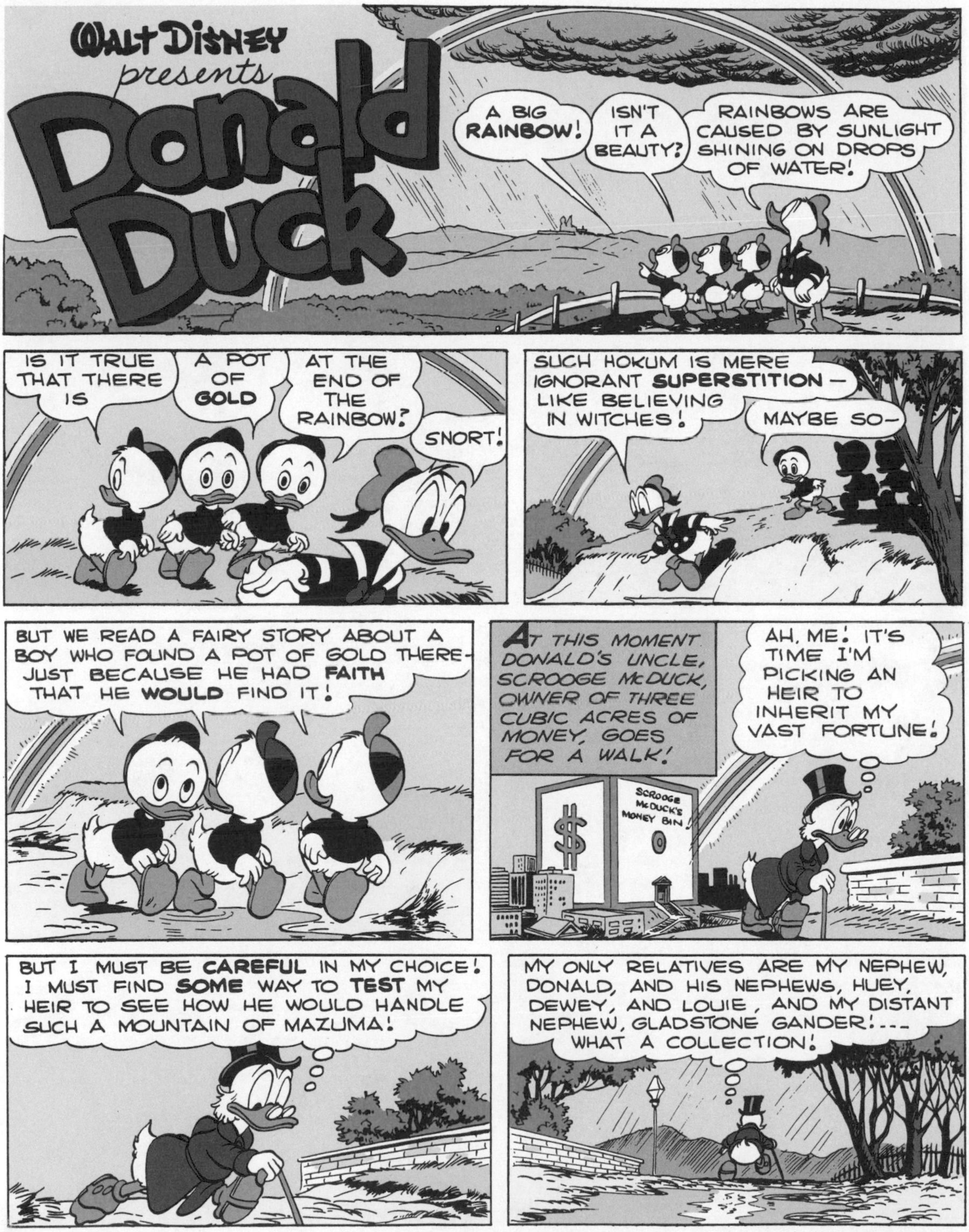
WALT DISNEY
presents
Donald Duck
A BIG RAINBOW!
ISN'T IT A BEAUTY?
RAINBOWS ARE CAUSED BY SUNLIGHT SHINING ON DROPS OF WATER!
IS IT TRUE THAT THERE IS
A POT OF GOLD
AT THE END OF THE RAINBOW?
SNORT!
SUCH HOKUM IS MERE IGNORANT SUPERSTITION — LIKE BELIEVING IN WITCHES!
MAYBE SO—
BUT WE READ A FAIRY STORY ABOUT A BOY WHO FOUND A POT OF GOLD THERE— JUST BECAUSE HE HAD FAITH THAT HE WOULD FIND IT!
AT THIS MOMENT DONALD'S UNCLE, SCROOGE McDUCK, OWNER OF THREE CUBIC ACRES OF MONEY, GOES FOR A WALK!
AH, ME! IT'S TIME I'M PICKING AN HEIR TO INHERIT MY VAST FORTUNE!
SCROOGE McDUCK'S MONEY BIN
BUT I MUST BE CAREFUL IN MY CHOICE! I MUST FIND SOME WAY TO TEST MY HEIR TO SEE HOW HE WOULD HANDLE SUCH A MOUNTAIN OF MAZUMA!
MY ONLY RELATIVES ARE MY NEPHEW, DONALD, AND HIS NEPHEWS, HUEY, DEWEY, AND LOUIE, AND MY DISTANT NEPHEW, GLADSTONE GANDER!... WHAT A COLLECTION!

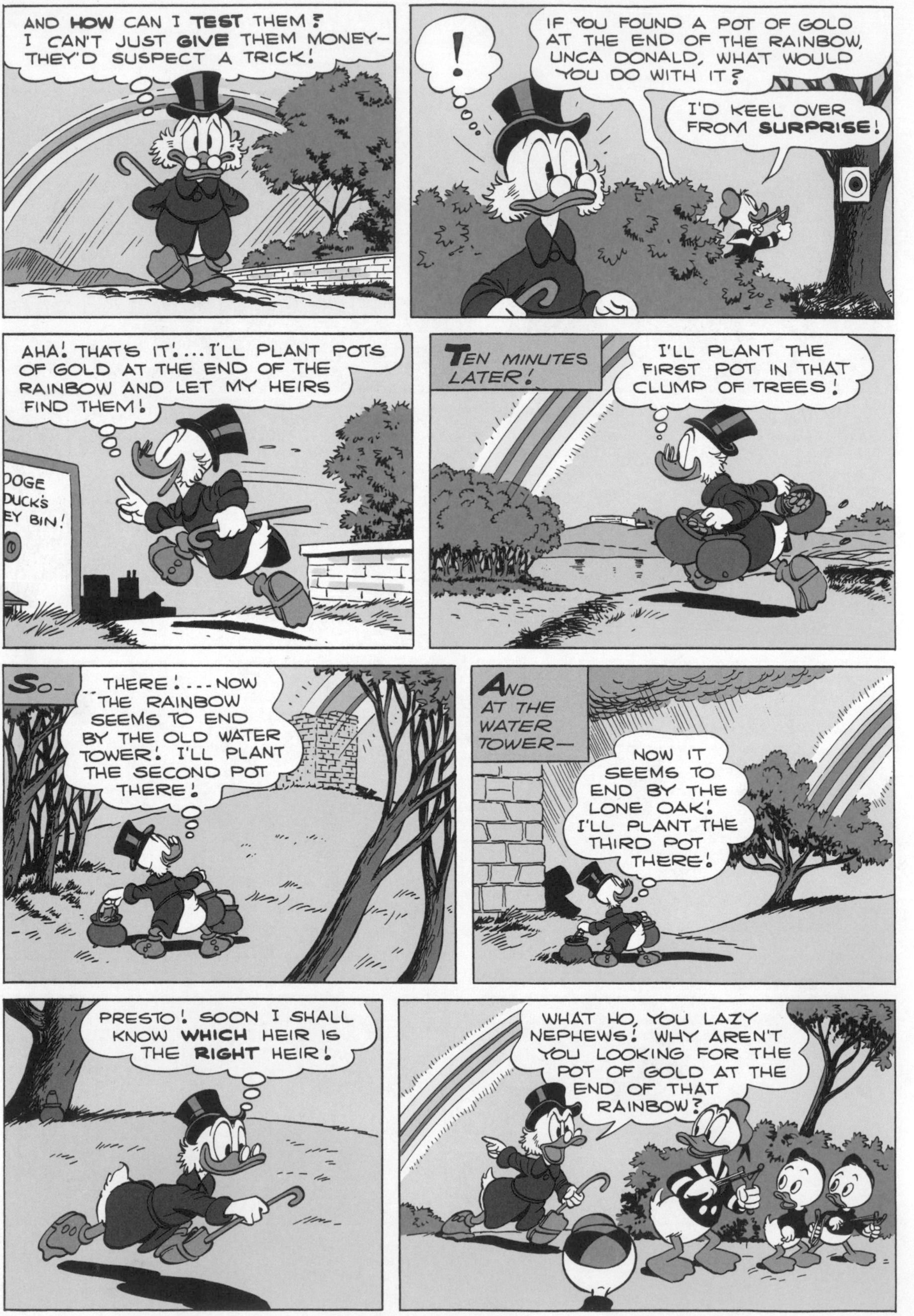
AND HOW CAN I TEST THEM? I CAN'T JUST GIVE THEM MONEY— THEY'D SUSPECT A TRICK!
!
IF YOU FOUND A POT OF GOLD AT THE END OF THE RAINBOW, UNCA DONALD, WHAT WOULD YOU DO WITH IT?
I'D KEEL OVER FROM SURPRISE!
AHA! THAT'S IT!... I'LL PLANT POTS OF GOLD AT THE END OF THE RAINBOW AND LET MY HEIRS FIND THEM!
DOGE DUCK'S EY BIN!
TEN MINUTES LATER!
I'LL PLANT THE FIRST POT IN THAT CLUMP OF TREES!
SO—
THERE!... NOW THE RAINBOW SEEMS TO END BY THE OLD WATER TOWER! I'LL PLANT THE SECOND POT THERE!
AND AT THE WATER TOWER—
NOW IT SEEMS TO END BY THE LONE OAK! I'LL PLANT THE THIRD POT THERE!
PRESTO! SOON I SHALL KNOW WHICH HEIR IS THE RIGHT HEIR!
WHAT HO, YOU LAZY NEPHEWS! WHY AREN'T YOU LOOKING FOR THE POT OF GOLD AT THE END OF THAT RAINBOW?

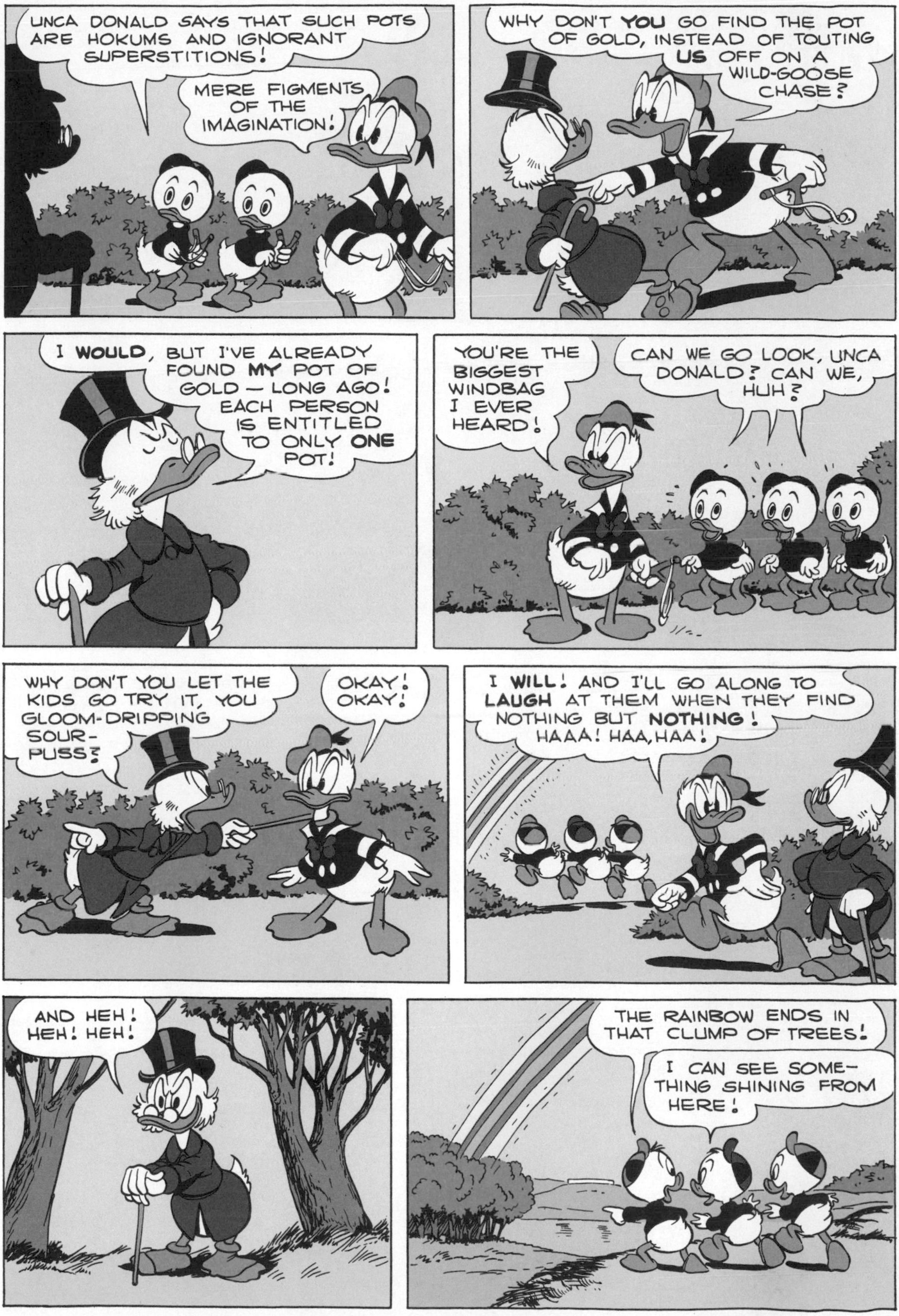
UNCA DONALD SAYS THAT SUCH POTS ARE HOKUMS AND IGNORANT SUPERSTITIONS!
MERE FIGMENTS OF THE IMAGINATION!
WHY DON'T **YOU** GO FIND THE POT OF GOLD, INSTEAD OF TOUTING **US** OFF ON A WILD-GOOSE CHASE?
I **WOULD**, BUT I'VE ALREADY FOUND **MY** POT OF GOLD — LONG AGO! EACH PERSON IS ENTITLED TO ONLY **ONE** POT!
YOU'RE THE BIGGEST WINDBAG I EVER HEARD!
CAN WE GO LOOK, UNCA DONALD? CAN WE, HUH?
WHY DON'T YOU LET THE KIDS GO TRY IT, YOU GLOOM-DRIPPING SOUR-PUSS?
OKAY! OKAY!
I **WILL**! AND I'LL GO ALONG TO **LAUGH** AT THEM WHEN THEY FIND NOTHING BUT **NOTHING**! HAAA! HAA, HAA!
AND HEH! HEH! HEH!
THE RAINBOW ENDS IN THAT CLUMP OF TREES!
I CAN SEE SOME-THING SHINING FROM HERE!

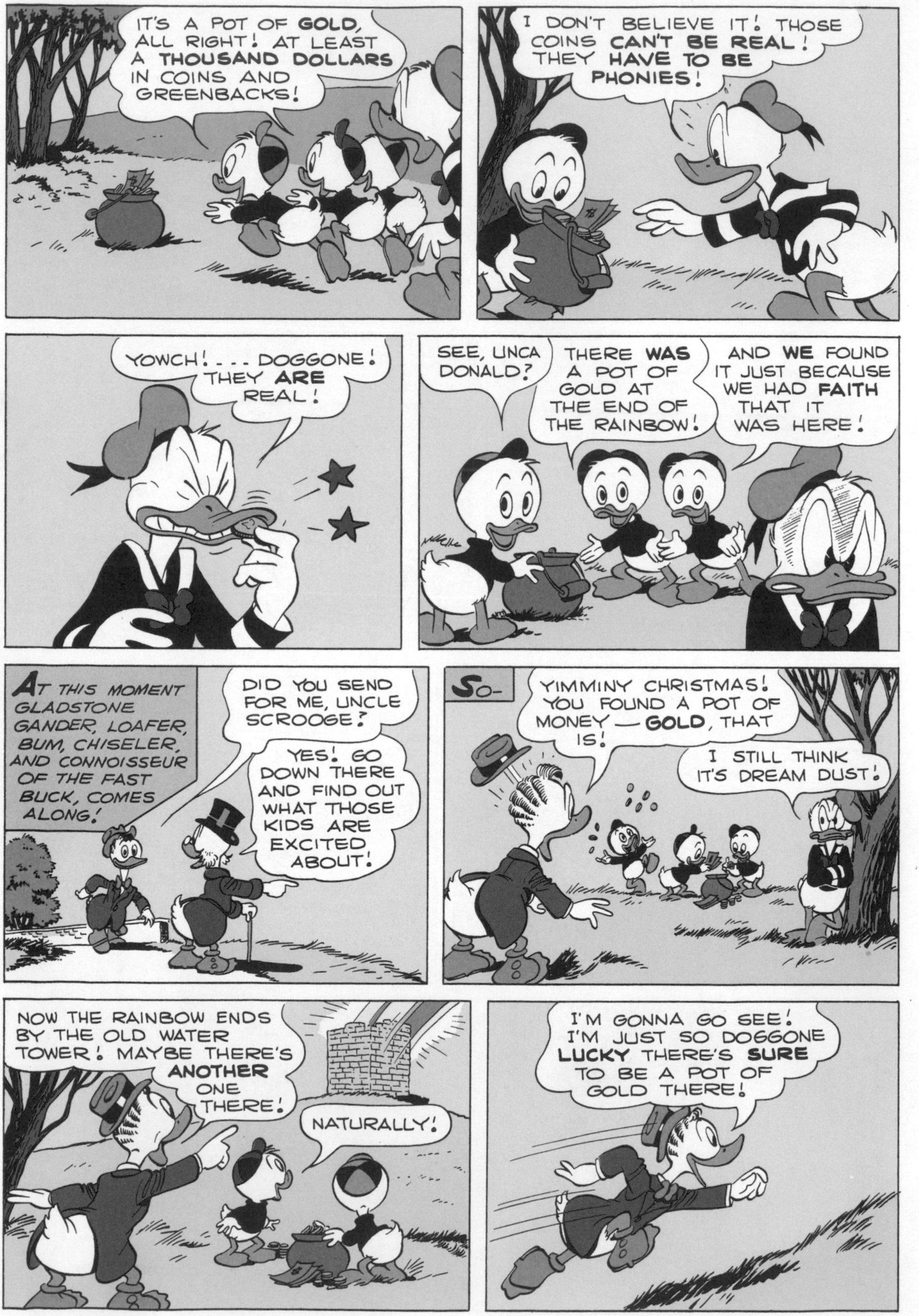
IT'S A POT OF **GOLD**, ALL RIGHT! AT LEAST A **THOUSAND DOLLARS** IN COINS AND GREENBACKS!
I DON'T BELIEVE IT! THOSE COINS **CAN'T BE REAL**! THEY **HAVE TO BE PHONIES**!
YOWCH! . . . DOGGONE! THEY **ARE** REAL!
SEE, UNCA DONALD?
THERE **WAS** A POT OF GOLD AT THE END OF THE RAINBOW!
AND **WE** FOUND IT JUST BECAUSE WE HAD **FAITH** THAT IT WAS HERE!
AT THIS MOMENT GLADSTONE GANDER, LOAFER, BUM, CHISELER, AND CONNOISSEUR OF THE FAST BUCK, COMES ALONG!
DID YOU SEND FOR ME, UNCLE SCROOGE?
YES! GO DOWN THERE AND FIND OUT WHAT THOSE KIDS ARE EXCITED ABOUT!
SO—
YIMMINY CHRISTMAS! YOU FOUND A POT OF MONEY — **GOLD**, THAT IS!
I STILL THINK IT'S DREAM DUST!
NOW THE RAINBOW ENDS BY THE OLD WATER TOWER! MAYBE THERE'S **ANOTHER** ONE THERE!
NATURALLY!
I'M GONNA GO SEE! I'M JUST SO DOGGONE **LUCKY** THERE'S **SURE** TO BE A POT OF GOLD THERE!

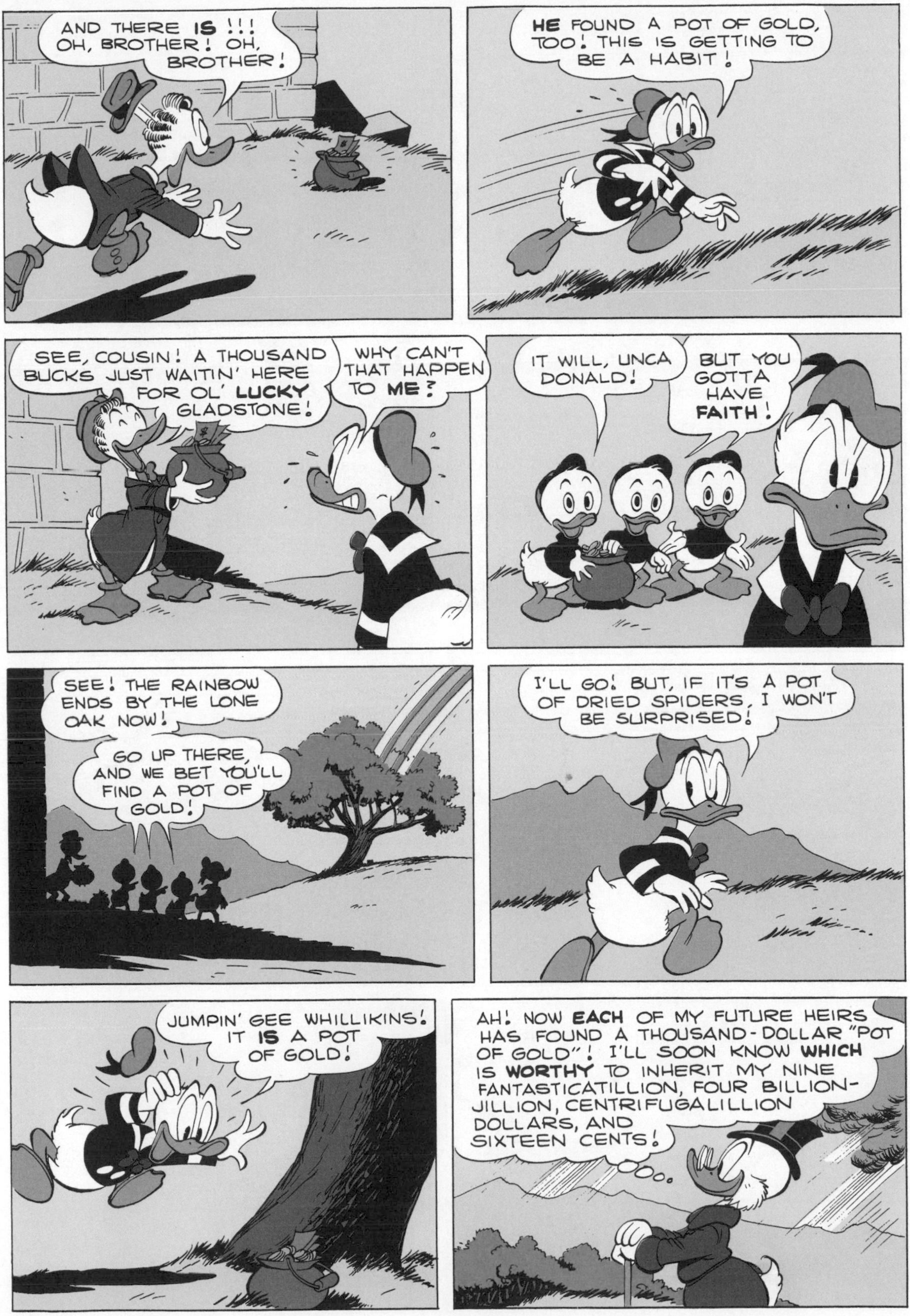
AND THERE IS !!! OH, BROTHER! OH, BROTHER!
HE FOUND A POT OF GOLD, TOO! THIS IS GETTING TO BE A HABIT!
SEE, COUSIN! A THOUSAND BUCKS JUST WAITIN' HERE FOR OL' LUCKY GLADSTONE!
WHY CAN'T THAT HAPPEN TO ME?
IT WILL, UNCA DONALD!
BUT YOU GOTTA HAVE FAITH!
SEE! THE RAINBOW ENDS BY THE LONE OAK NOW!
GO UP THERE, AND WE BET YOU'LL FIND A POT OF GOLD!
I'LL GO! BUT, IF IT'S A POT OF DRIED SPIDERS, I WON'T BE SURPRISED!
JUMPIN' GEE WHILLIKINS! IT IS A POT OF GOLD!
AH! NOW EACH OF MY FUTURE HEIRS HAS FOUND A THOUSAND-DOLLAR "POT OF GOLD"! I'LL SOON KNOW WHICH IS WORTHY TO INHERIT MY NINE FANTASTICATILLION, FOUR BILLION-JILLION, CENTRIFUGALILLION DOLLARS, AND SIXTEEN CENTS!

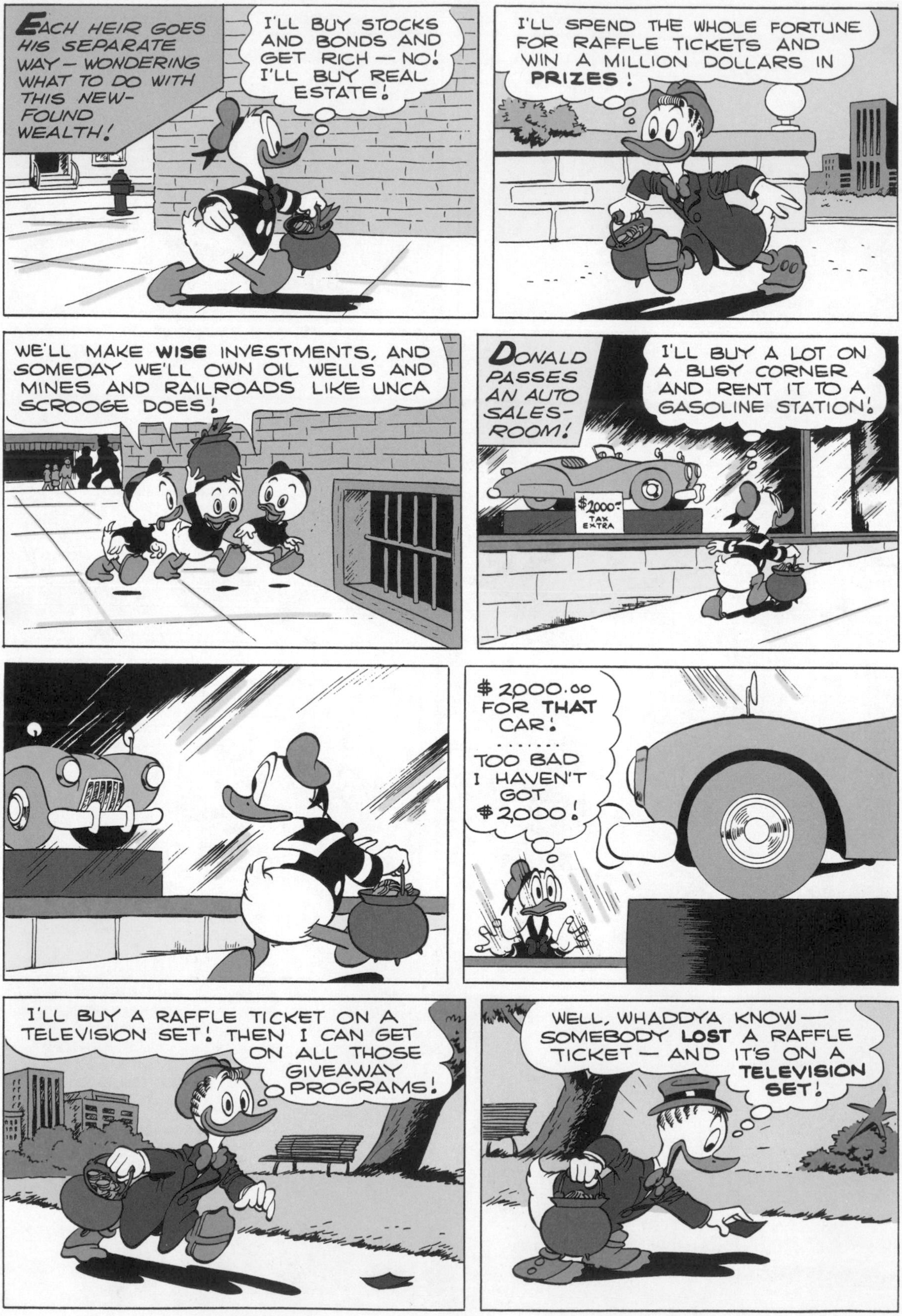

EACH HEIR GOES HIS SEPARATE WAY — WONDERING WHAT TO DO WITH THIS NEW-FOUND WEALTH!
I'LL BUY STOCKS AND BONDS AND GET RICH — NO! I'LL BUY REAL ESTATE!
I'LL SPEND THE WHOLE FORTUNE FOR RAFFLE TICKETS AND WIN A MILLION DOLLARS IN PRIZES!
WE'LL MAKE WISE INVESTMENTS, AND SOMEDAY WE'LL OWN OIL WELLS AND MINES AND RAILROADS LIKE UNCA SCROOGE DOES!
DONALD PASSES AN AUTO SALES-ROOM!
I'LL BUY A LOT ON A BUSY CORNER AND RENT IT TO A GASOLINE STATION!
$2000.— TAX EXTRA
$2000.00 FOR THAT CAR!
TOO BAD I HAVEN'T GOT $2000!
I'LL BUY A RAFFLE TICKET ON A TELEVISION SET! THEN I CAN GET ON ALL THOSE GIVEAWAY PROGRAMS!
WELL, WHADDYA KNOW — SOMEBODY LOST A RAFFLE TICKET — AND IT'S ON A TELEVISION SET!

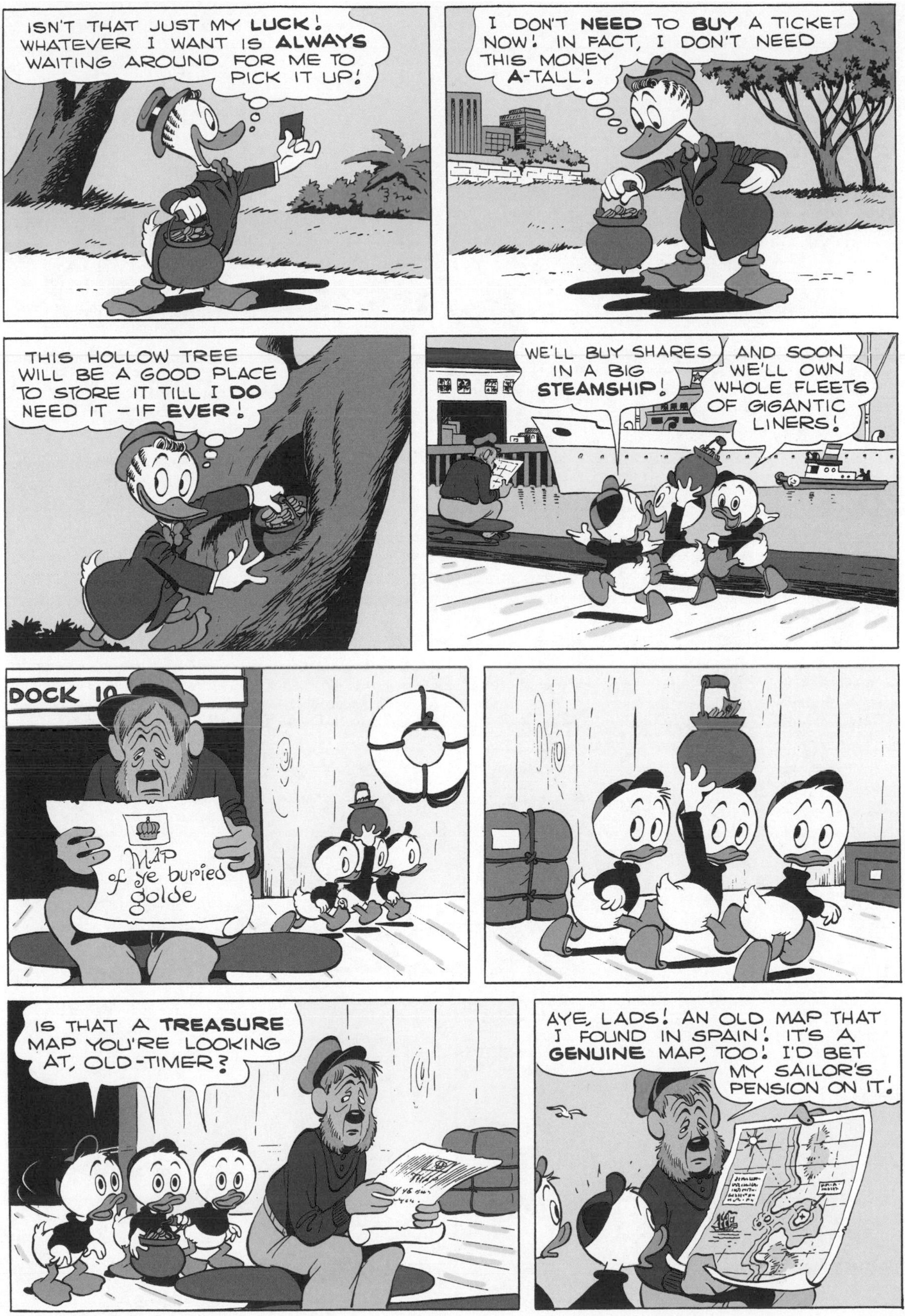
ISN'T THAT JUST MY LUCK! WHATEVER I WANT IS ALWAYS WAITING AROUND FOR ME TO PICK IT UP!
I DON'T NEED TO BUY A TICKET NOW! IN FACT, I DON'T NEED THIS MONEY A-TALL!
THIS HOLLOW TREE WILL BE A GOOD PLACE TO STORE IT TILL I DO NEED IT — IF EVER!
WE'LL BUY SHARES IN A BIG STEAMSHIP!
AND SOON WE'LL OWN WHOLE FLEETS OF GIGANTIC LINERS!
DOCK 10
Map of ye buried golde
IS THAT A TREASURE MAP YOU'RE LOOKING AT, OLD-TIMER?
AYE, LADS! AN OLD MAP THAT I FOUND IN SPAIN! IT'S A GENUINE MAP, TOO! I'D BET MY SAILOR'S PENSION ON IT!

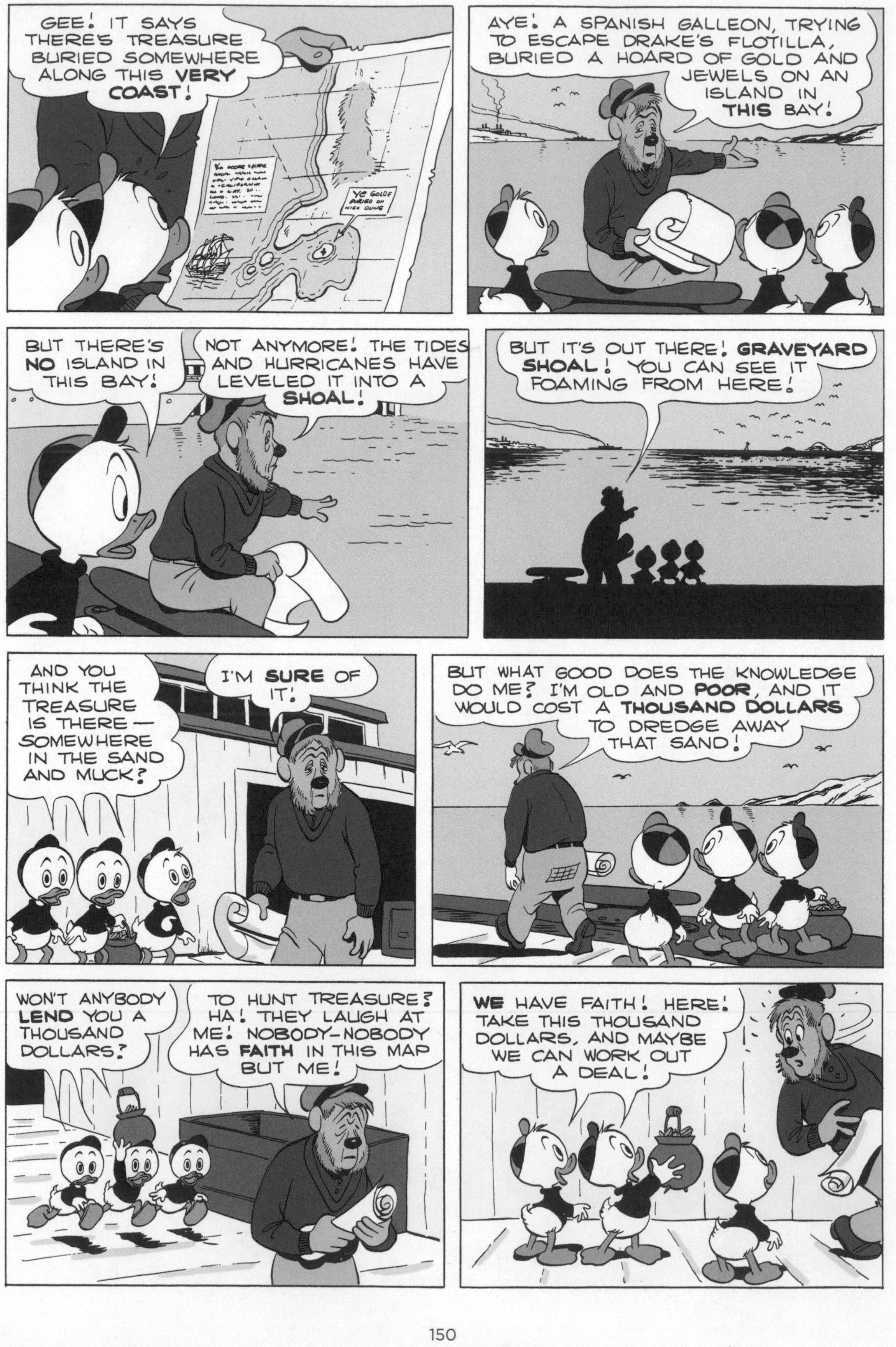
GEE! IT SAYS THERE'S TREASURE BURIED SOMEWHERE ALONG THIS VERY COAST!
AYE! A SPANISH GALLEON, TRYING TO ESCAPE DRAKE'S FLOTILLA, BURIED A HOARD OF GOLD AND JEWELS ON AN ISLAND IN THIS BAY!
BUT THERE'S NO ISLAND IN THIS BAY!
NOT ANYMORE! THE TIDES AND HURRICANES HAVE LEVELED IT INTO A SHOAL!
BUT IT'S OUT THERE! GRAVEYARD SHOAL! YOU CAN SEE IT FOAMING FROM HERE!
AND YOU THINK THE TREASURE IS THERE— SOMEWHERE IN THE SAND AND MUCK?
I'M SURE OF IT!
BUT WHAT GOOD DOES THE KNOWLEDGE DO ME? I'M OLD AND POOR, AND IT WOULD COST A THOUSAND DOLLARS TO DREDGE AWAY THAT SAND!
WON'T ANYBODY LEND YOU A THOUSAND DOLLARS?
TO HUNT TREASURE? HA! THEY LAUGH AT ME! NOBODY-NOBODY HAS FAITH IN THIS MAP BUT ME!
WE HAVE FAITH! HERE! TAKE THIS THOUSAND DOLLARS, AND MAYBE WE CAN WORK OUT A DEAL!

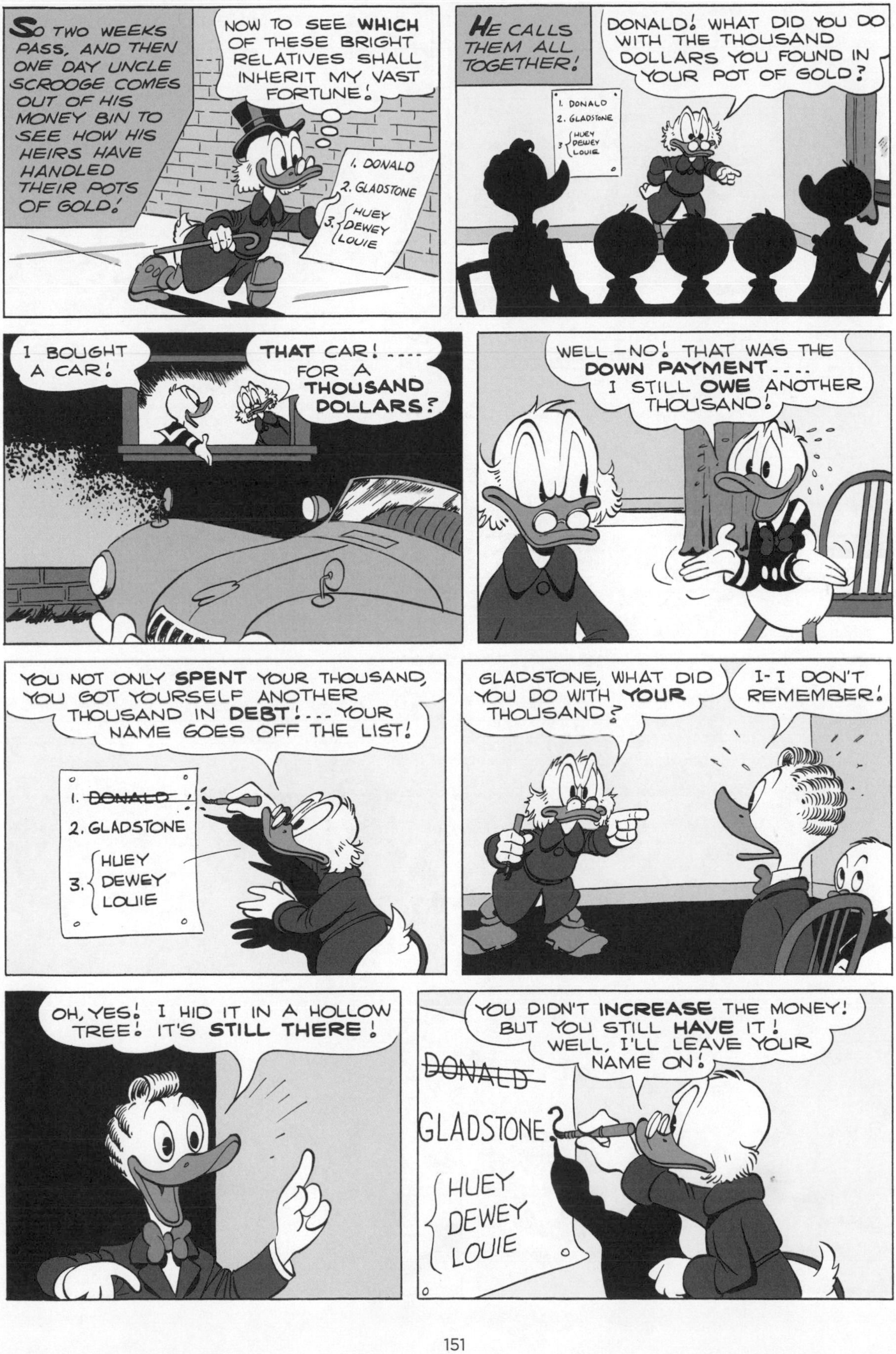
SO TWO WEEKS PASS, AND THEN ONE DAY UNCLE SCROOGE COMES OUT OF HIS MONEY BIN TO SEE HOW HIS HEIRS HAVE HANDLED THEIR POTS OF GOLD!
NOW TO SEE WHICH OF THESE BRIGHT RELATIVES SHALL INHERIT MY VAST FORTUNE!
1. DONALD
2. GLADSTONE
3. HUEY DEWEY LOUIE
HE CALLS THEM ALL TOGETHER!
DONALD! WHAT DID YOU DO WITH THE THOUSAND DOLLARS YOU FOUND IN YOUR POT OF GOLD?
1. DONALD
2. GLADSTONE
3. HUEY DEWEY LOUIE
I BOUGHT A CAR!
THAT CAR! .... FOR A THOUSAND DOLLARS?
WELL—NO! THAT WAS THE DOWN PAYMENT.... I STILL OWE ANOTHER THOUSAND!
YOU NOT ONLY SPENT YOUR THOUSAND, YOU GOT YOURSELF ANOTHER THOUSAND IN DEBT!... YOUR NAME GOES OFF THE LIST!
1. DONALD
2. GLADSTONE
3. HUEY DEWEY LOUIE
GLADSTONE, WHAT DID YOU DO WITH YOUR THOUSAND?
I-I DON'T REMEMBER!
OH, YES! I HID IT IN A HOLLOW TREE! IT'S STILL THERE!
YOU DIDN'T INCREASE THE MONEY! BUT YOU STILL HAVE IT! WELL, I'LL LEAVE YOUR NAME ON!
DONALD
GLADSTONE?
HUEY DEWEY LOUIE

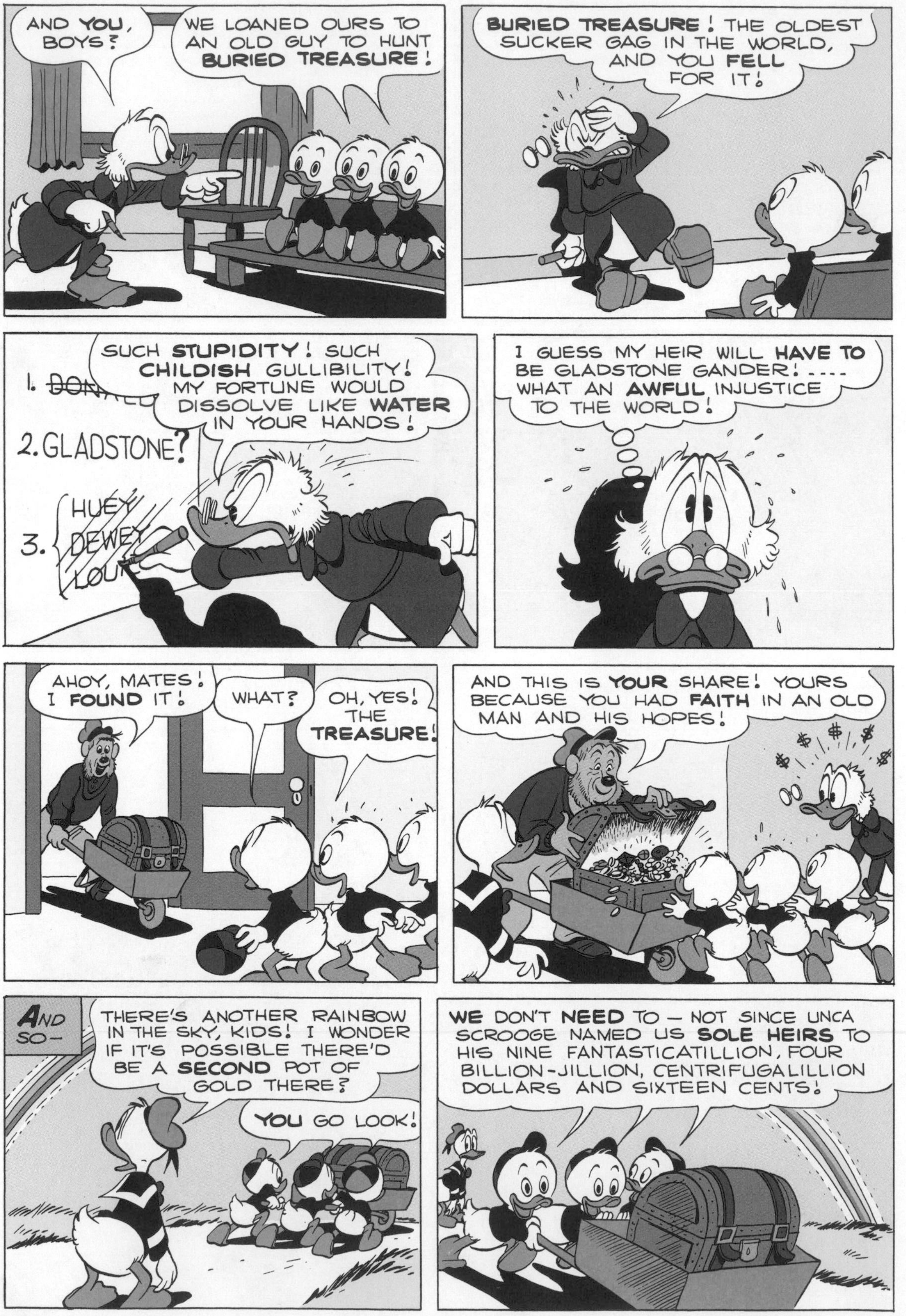
AND YOU, BOYS?
WE LOANED OURS TO AN OLD GUY TO HUNT BURIED TREASURE!
BURIED TREASURE! THE OLDEST SUCKER GAG IN THE WORLD, AND YOU FELL FOR IT!
SUCH STUPIDITY! SUCH CHILDISH GULLIBILITY! MY FORTUNE WOULD DISSOLVE LIKE WATER IN YOUR HANDS!
2. GLADSTONE?
3. HUEY DEWEY
I GUESS MY HEIR WILL HAVE TO BE GLADSTONE GANDER! ---- WHAT AN AWFUL INJUSTICE TO THE WORLD!
AHOY, MATES! I FOUND IT!
WHAT?
OH, YES! THE TREASURE!
AND THIS IS YOUR SHARE! YOURS BECAUSE YOU HAD FAITH IN AN OLD MAN AND HIS HOPES!
AND SO—
THERE'S ANOTHER RAINBOW IN THE SKY, KIDS! I WONDER IF IT'S POSSIBLE THERE'D BE A SECOND POT OF GOLD THERE?
YOU GO LOOK!
WE DON'T NEED TO — NOT SINCE UNCA SCROOGE NAMED US SOLE HEIRS TO HIS NINE FANTASTICATILLION, FOUR BILLION-JILLION, CENTRIFUGALILLION DOLLARS AND SIXTEEN CENTS!

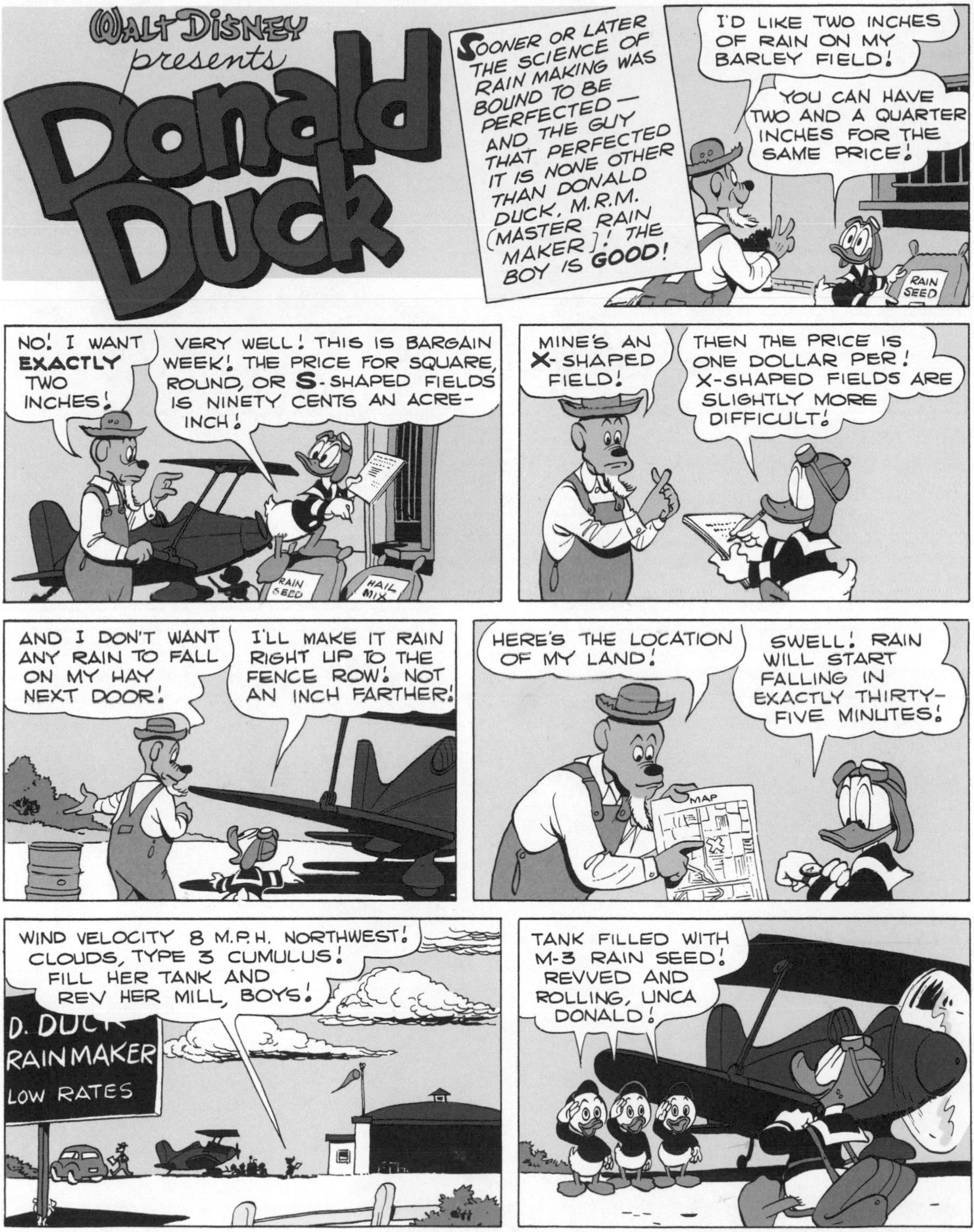
WALT DISNEY presents
Donald Duck
SOONER OR LATER THE SCIENCE OF RAIN MAKING WAS BOUND TO BE PERFECTED— AND THE GUY THAT PERFECTED IT IS NONE OTHER THAN DONALD DUCK, M.R.M. (MASTER RAIN MAKER)! THE BOY IS GOOD!
I'D LIKE TWO INCHES OF RAIN ON MY BARLEY FIELD!
YOU CAN HAVE TWO AND A QUARTER INCHES FOR THE SAME PRICE!
RAIN SEED
NO! I WANT EXACTLY TWO INCHES!
VERY WELL! THIS IS BARGAIN WEEK! THE PRICE FOR SQUARE, ROUND, OR S-SHAPED FIELDS IS NINETY CENTS AN ACRE-INCH!
RAIN SEED
HAIL MIX
MINE'S AN X-SHAPED FIELD!
THEN THE PRICE IS ONE DOLLAR PER! X-SHAPED FIELDS ARE SLIGHTLY MORE DIFFICULT!
AND I DON'T WANT ANY RAIN TO FALL ON MY HAY NEXT DOOR!
I'LL MAKE IT RAIN RIGHT UP TO THE FENCE ROW! NOT AN INCH FARTHER!
HERE'S THE LOCATION OF MY LAND!
SWELL! RAIN WILL START FALLING IN EXACTLY THIRTY-FIVE MINUTES!
MAP
WIND VELOCITY 8 M.P.H. NORTHWEST! CLOUDS, TYPE 3 CUMULUS! FILL HER TANK AND REV HER MILL, BOYS!
D. DUCK
RAINMAKER
LOW RATES
TANK FILLED WITH M-3 RAIN SEED! REVVED AND ROLLING, UNCA DONALD!

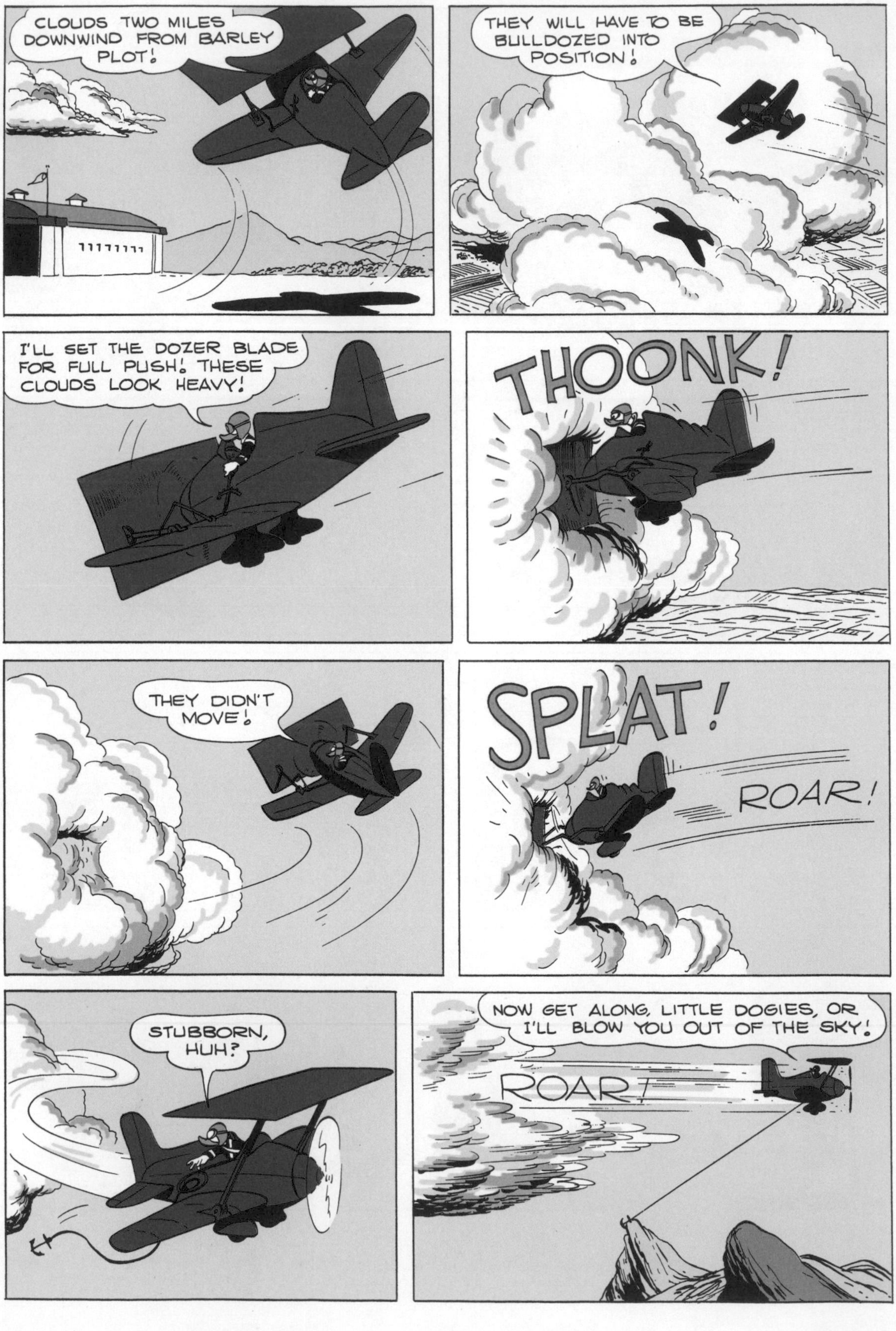

CLOUDS TWO MILES DOWNWIND FROM BARLEY PLOT!
THEY WILL HAVE TO BE BULLDOZED INTO POSITION!
I'LL SET THE DOZER BLADE FOR FULL PUSH! THESE CLOUDS LOOK HEAVY!
THOONK!
THEY DIDN'T MOVE!
SPLAT!
ROAR!
STUBBORN, HUH?
NOW GET ALONG, LITTLE DOGIES, OR I'LL BLOW YOU OUT OF THE SKY!
ROAR!

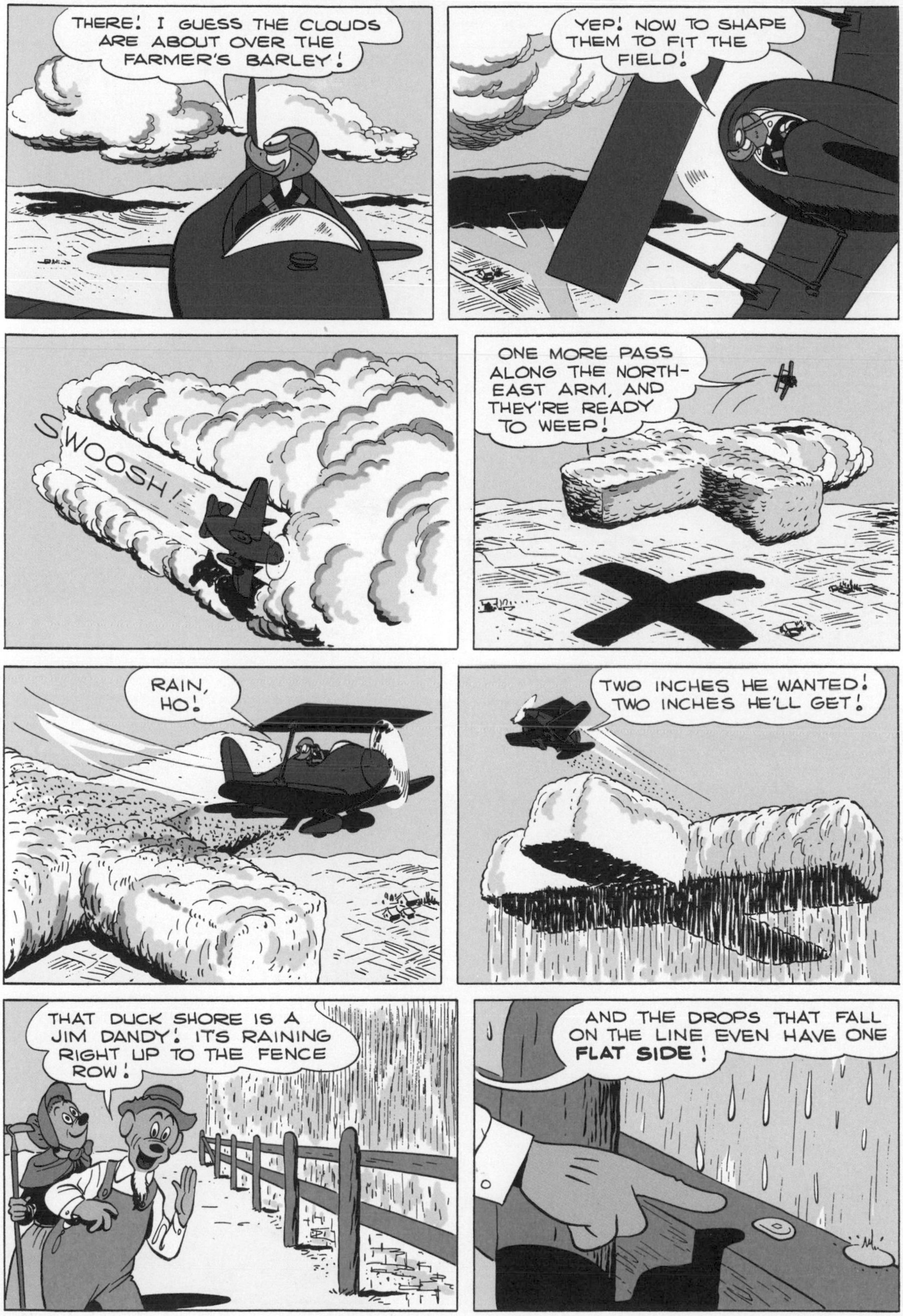
THERE! I GUESS THE CLOUDS ARE ABOUT OVER THE FARMER'S BARLEY!
YEP! NOW TO SHAPE THEM TO FIT THE FIELD!
SWOOSH!
ONE MORE PASS ALONG THE NORTH-EAST ARM, AND THEY'RE READY TO WEEP!
RAIN, HO!
TWO INCHES HE WANTED! TWO INCHES HE'LL GET!
THAT DUCK SHORE IS A JIM DANDY! IT'S RAINING RIGHT UP TO THE FENCE ROW!
AND THE DROPS THAT FALL ON THE LINE EVEN HAVE ONE **FLAT SIDE**!

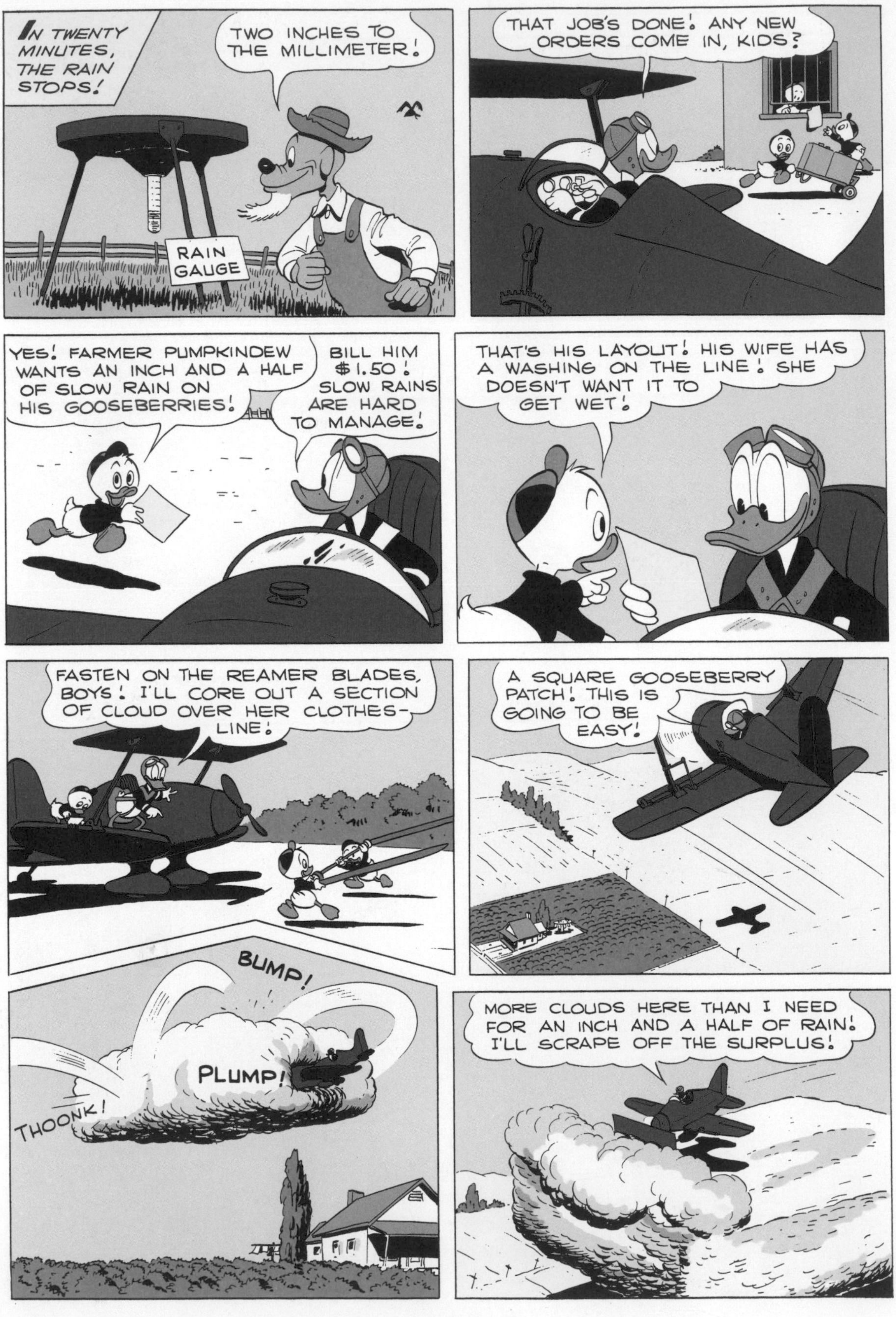
IN TWENTY MINUTES, THE RAIN STOPS!
TWO INCHES TO THE MILLIMETER!
RAIN GAUGE
THAT JOB'S DONE! ANY NEW ORDERS COME IN, KIDS?
YES! FARMER PUMPKINDEW WANTS AN INCH AND A HALF OF SLOW RAIN ON HIS GOOSEBERRIES!
BILL HIM $1.50! SLOW RAINS ARE HARD TO MANAGE!
THAT'S HIS LAYOUT! HIS WIFE HAS A WASHING ON THE LINE! SHE DOESN'T WANT IT TO GET WET!
FASTEN ON THE REAMER BLADES, BOYS! I'LL CORE OUT A SECTION OF CLOUD OVER HER CLOTHES-LINE!
A SQUARE GOOSEBERRY PATCH! THIS IS GOING TO BE EASY!
BUMP!
PLUMP!
THOONK!
MORE CLOUDS HERE THAN I NEED FOR AN INCH AND A HALF OF RAIN! I'LL SCRAPE OFF THE SURPLUS!

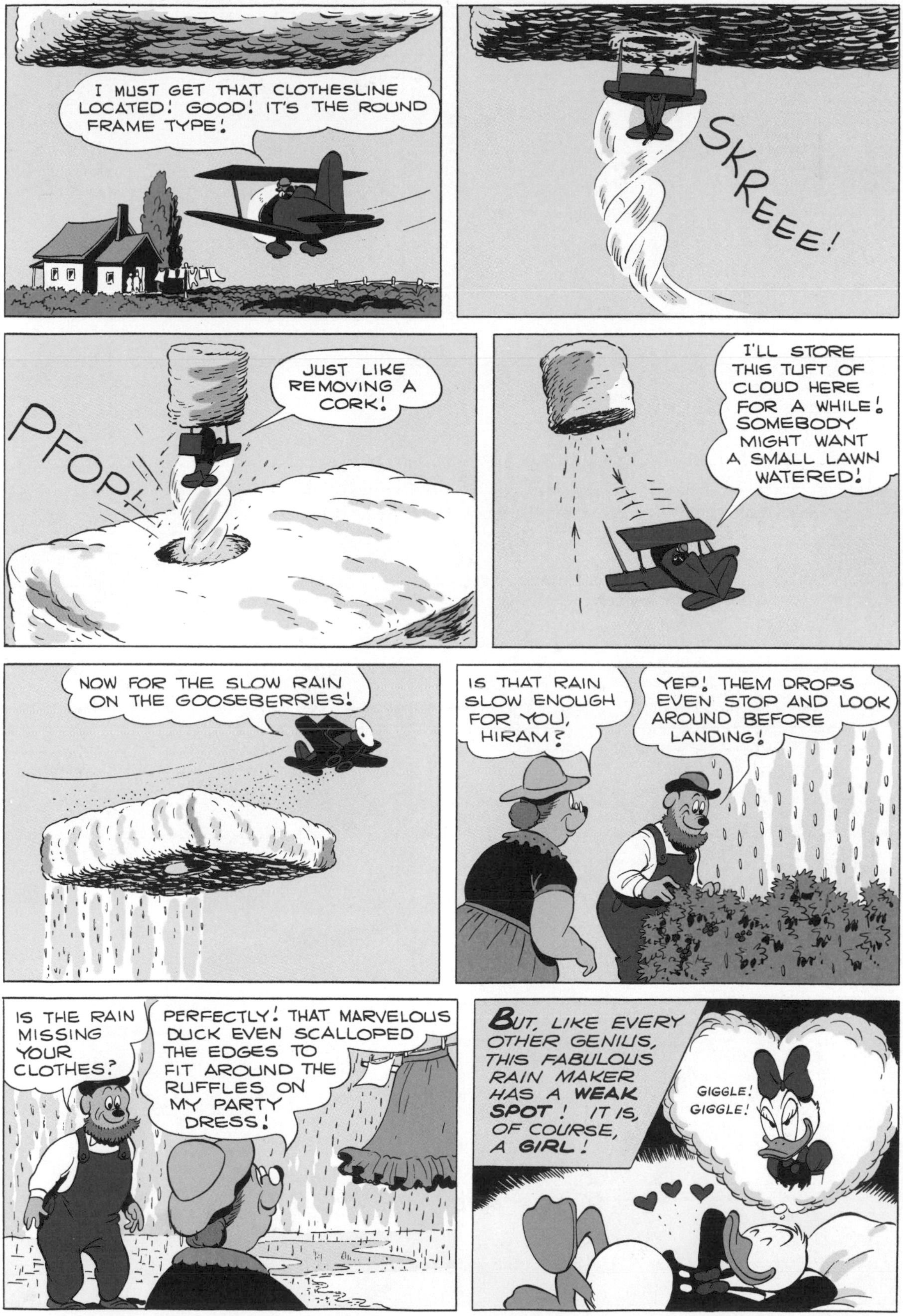
I MUST GET THAT CLOTHESLINE LOCATED! GOOD! IT'S THE ROUND FRAME TYPE!
SKREEEE!
PFOP!
JUST LIKE REMOVING A CORK!
I'LL STORE THIS TUFT OF CLOUD HERE FOR A WHILE! SOMEBODY MIGHT WANT A SMALL LAWN WATERED!
NOW FOR THE SLOW RAIN ON THE GOOSEBERRIES!
IS THAT RAIN SLOW ENOUGH FOR YOU, HIRAM?
YEP! THEM DROPS EVEN STOP AND LOOK AROUND BEFORE LANDING!
IS THE RAIN MISSING YOUR CLOTHES?
PERFECTLY! THAT MARVELOUS DUCK EVEN SCALLOPED THE EDGES TO FIT AROUND THE RUFFLES ON MY PARTY DRESS!
BUT, LIKE EVERY OTHER GENIUS, THIS FABULOUS RAIN MAKER HAS A WEAK SPOT! IT IS, OF COURSE, A GIRL!
GIGGLE! GIGGLE!

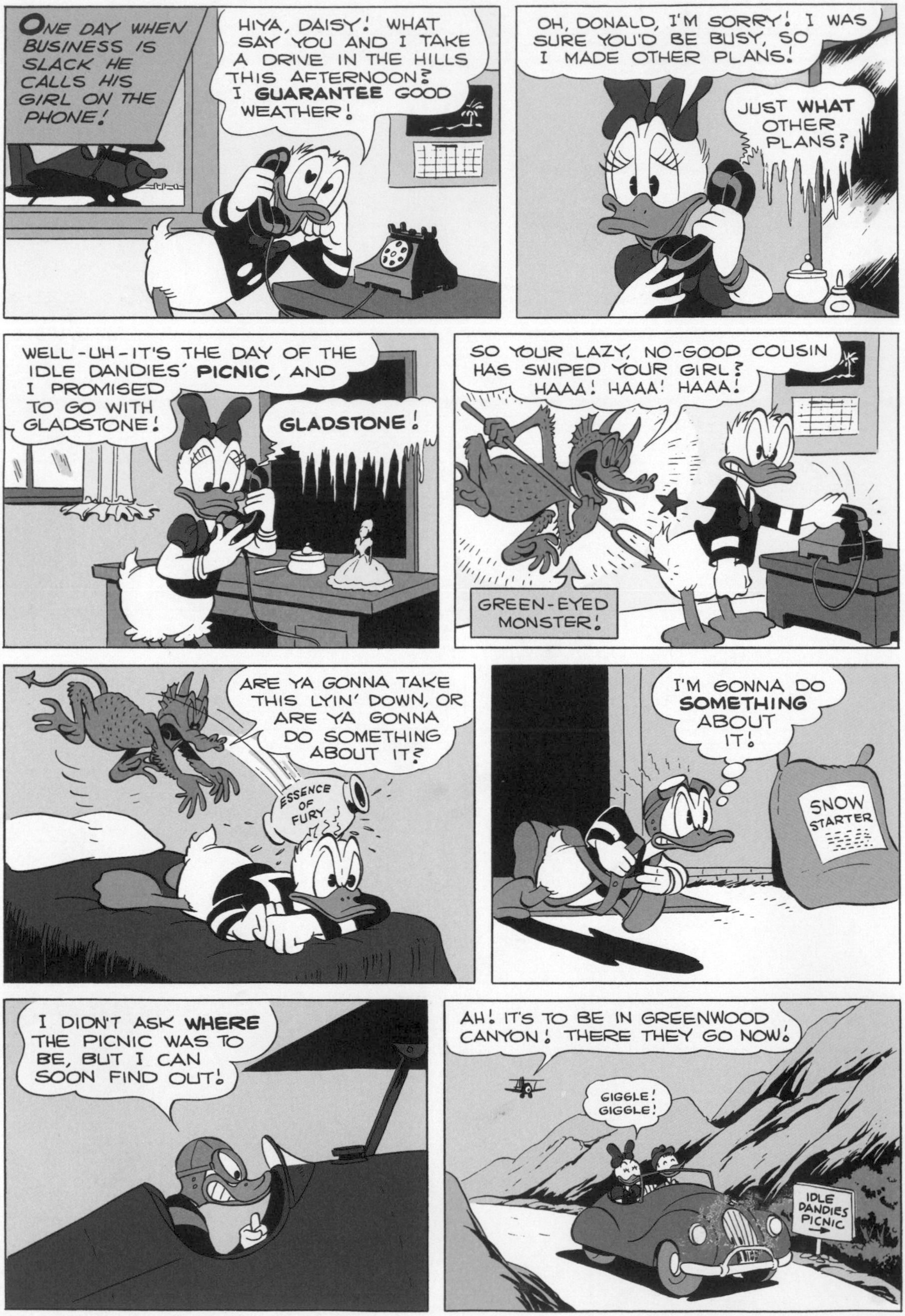
ONE DAY WHEN BUSINESS IS SLACK HE CALLS HIS GIRL ON THE PHONE!
HIYA, DAISY! WHAT SAY YOU AND I TAKE A DRIVE IN THE HILLS THIS AFTERNOON? I GUARANTEE GOOD WEATHER!
OH, DONALD, I'M SORRY! I WAS SURE YOU'D BE BUSY, SO I MADE OTHER PLANS!
JUST WHAT OTHER PLANS?
WELL-UH-IT'S THE DAY OF THE IDLE DANDIES' PICNIC, AND I PROMISED TO GO WITH GLADSTONE!
GLADSTONE!
SO YOUR LAZY, NO-GOOD COUSIN HAS SWIPED YOUR GIRL? HAAA! HAAA! HAAA!
GREEN-EYED MONSTER!
ARE YA GONNA TAKE THIS LYIN' DOWN, OR ARE YA GONNA DO SOMETHING ABOUT IT?
ESSENCE OF FURY
I'M GONNA DO SOMETHING ABOUT IT!
SNOW STARTER
I DIDN'T ASK WHERE THE PICNIC WAS TO BE, BUT I CAN SOON FIND OUT!
AH! IT'S TO BE IN GREENWOOD CANYON! THERE THEY GO NOW!
GIGGLE! GIGGLE!
IDLE DANDIES PICNIC

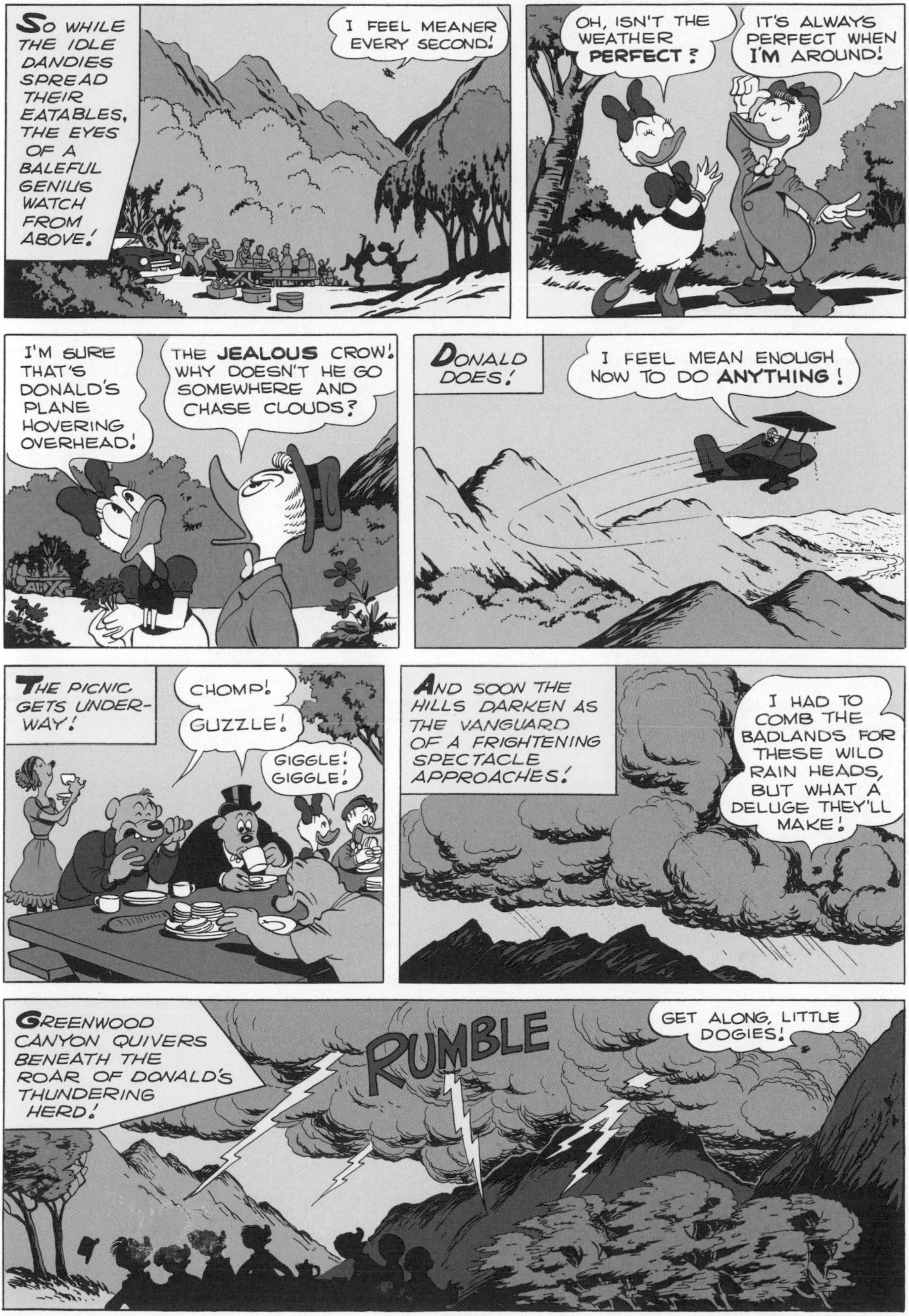
SO WHILE THE IDLE DANDIES SPREAD THEIR EATABLES, THE EYES OF A BALEFUL GENIUS WATCH FROM ABOVE!
I FEEL MEANER EVERY SECOND!
OH, ISN'T THE WEATHER PERFECT?
IT'S ALWAYS PERFECT WHEN I'M AROUND!
I'M SURE THAT'S DONALD'S PLANE HOVERING OVERHEAD!
THE JEALOUS CROW! WHY DOESN'T HE GO SOMEWHERE AND CHASE CLOUDS?
DONALD DOES!
I FEEL MEAN ENOUGH NOW TO DO ANYTHING!
THE PICNIC GETS UNDER-WAY!
CHOMP!
GUZZLE!
GIGGLE! GIGGLE!
AND SOON THE HILLS DARKEN AS THE VANGUARD OF A FRIGHTENING SPECTACLE APPROACHES!
I HAD TO COMB THE BADLANDS FOR THESE WILD RAIN HEADS, BUT WHAT A DELUGE THEY'LL MAKE!
GREENWOOD CANYON QUIVERS BENEATH THE ROAR OF DONALD'S THUNDERING HERD!
RUMBLE
GET ALONG, LITTLE DOGIES!

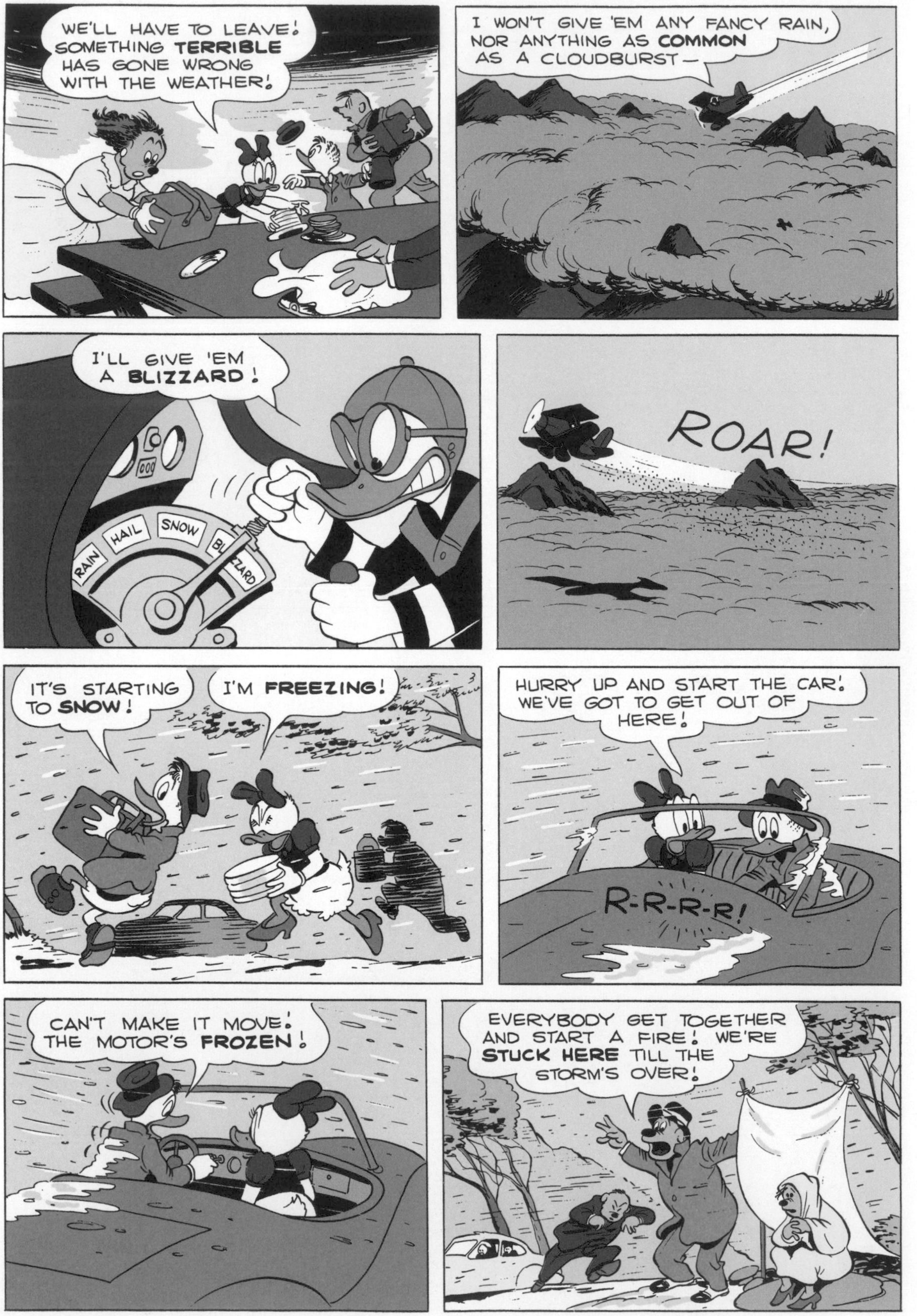
WE'LL HAVE TO LEAVE! SOMETHING TERRIBLE HAS GONE WRONG WITH THE WEATHER!
I WON'T GIVE 'EM ANY FANCY RAIN, NOR ANYTHING AS COMMON AS A CLOUDBURST—
I'LL GIVE 'EM A BLIZZARD!
RAIN
HAIL
SNOW
BLIZZARD
ROAR!
IT'S STARTING TO SNOW!
I'M FREEZING!
HURRY UP AND START THE CAR! WE'VE GOT TO GET OUT OF HERE!
R-R-R-R!
CAN'T MAKE IT MOVE! THE MOTOR'S FROZEN!
EVERYBODY GET TOGETHER AND START A FIRE! WE'RE STUCK HERE TILL THE STORM'S OVER!

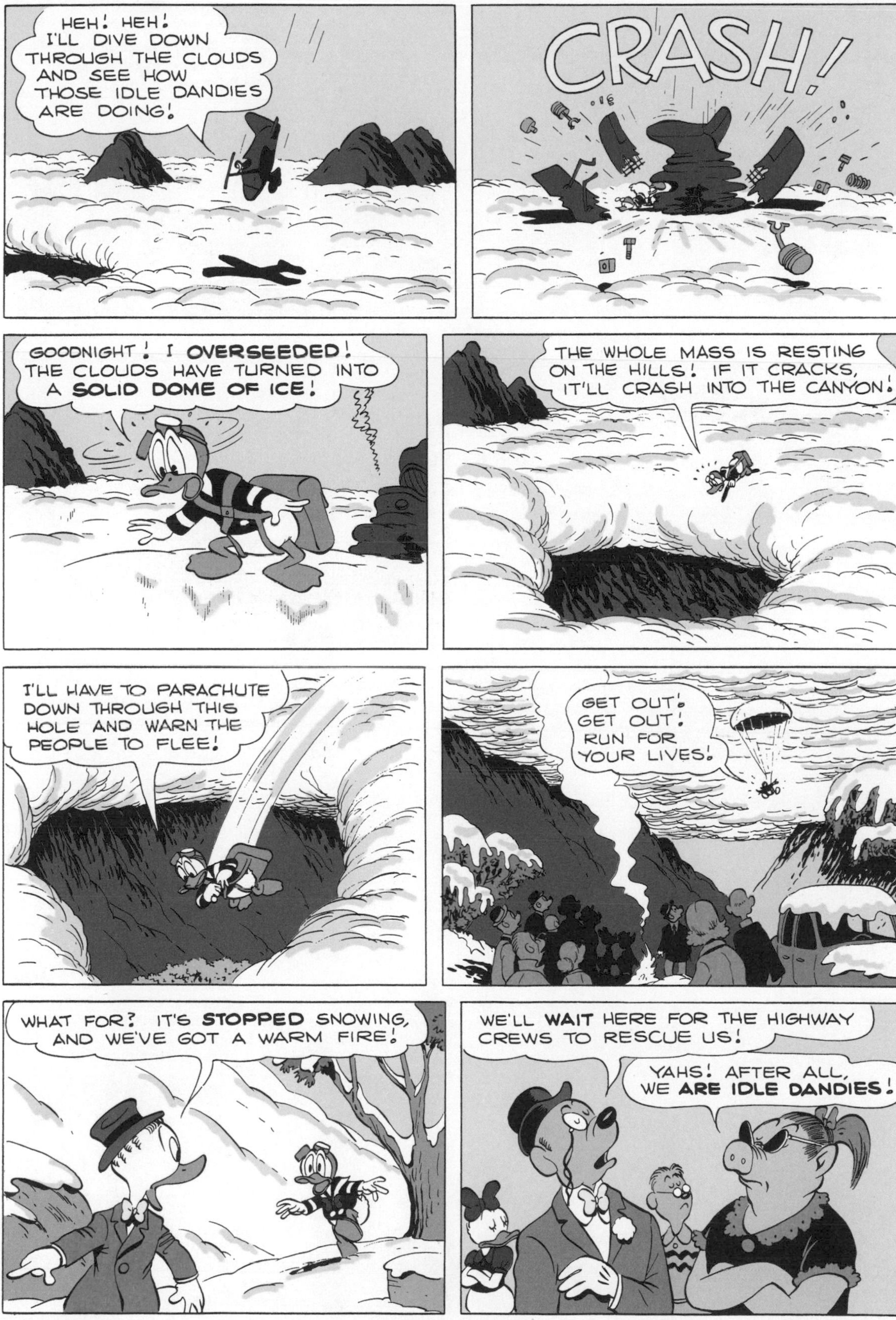
HEH! HEH! I'LL DIVE DOWN THROUGH THE CLOUDS AND SEE HOW THOSE IDLE DANDIES ARE DOING!
CRASH!
GOODNIGHT! I OVERSEEDED! THE CLOUDS HAVE TURNED INTO A SOLID DOME OF ICE!
THE WHOLE MASS IS RESTING ON THE HILLS! IF IT CRACKS, IT'LL CRASH INTO THE CANYON!
I'LL HAVE TO PARACHUTE DOWN THROUGH THIS HOLE AND WARN THE PEOPLE TO FLEE!
GET OUT! GET OUT! RUN FOR YOUR LIVES!
WHAT FOR? IT'S STOPPED SNOWING, AND WE'VE GOT A WARM FIRE!
WE'LL WAIT HERE FOR THE HIGHWAY CREWS TO RESCUE US!
YAHS! AFTER ALL, WE ARE IDLE DANDIES!

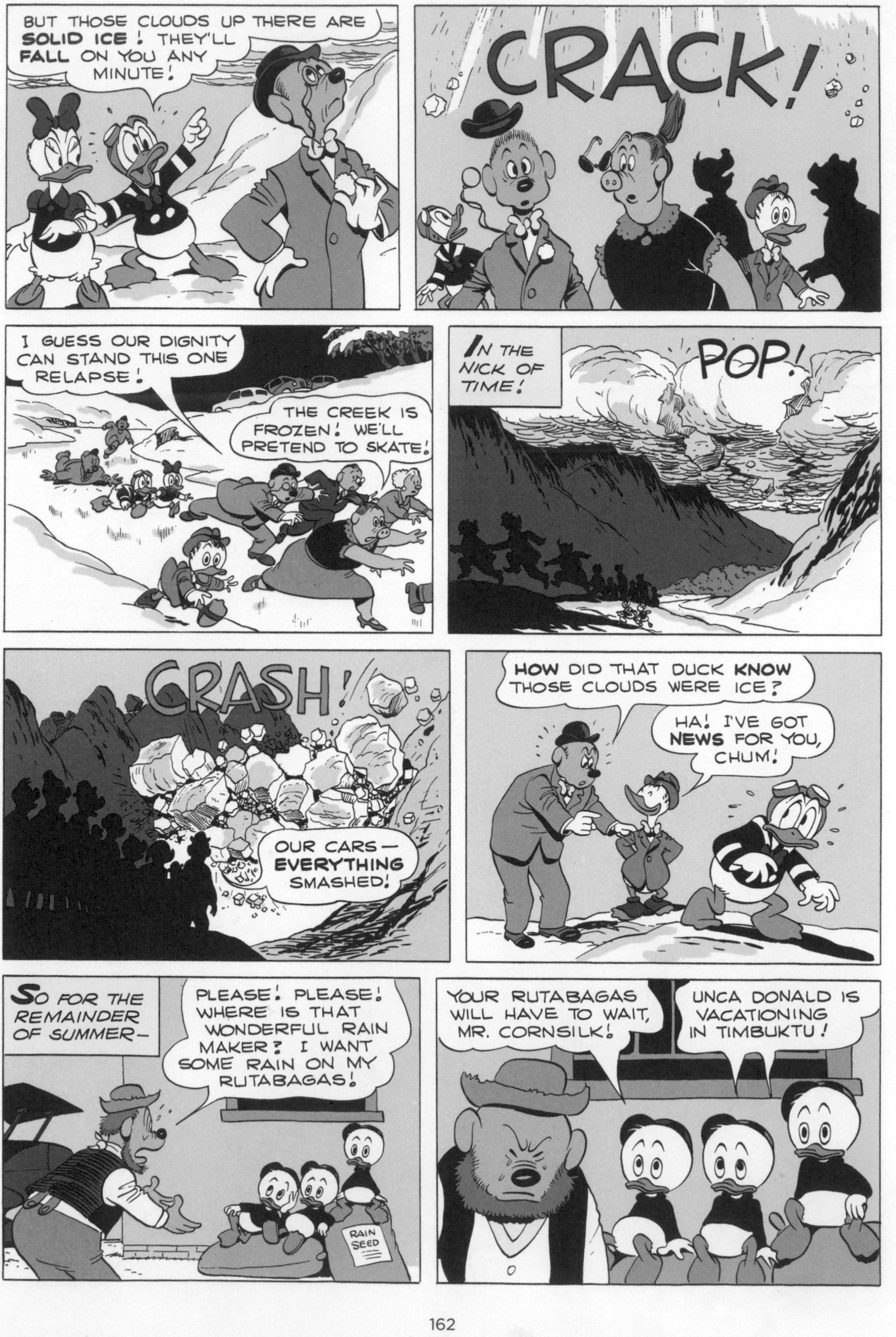
BUT THOSE CLOUDS UP THERE ARE SOLID ICE! THEY'LL FALL ON YOU ANY MINUTE!
CRACK!
I GUESS OUR DIGNITY CAN STAND THIS ONE RELAPSE!
THE CREEK IS FROZEN! WE'LL PRETEND TO SKATE!
IN THE NICK OF TIME!
POP!
CRASH!
OUR CARS— EVERYTHING SMASHED!
HOW DID THAT DUCK KNOW THOSE CLOUDS WERE ICE?
HA! I'VE GOT NEWS FOR YOU, CHUM!
SO FOR THE REMAINDER OF SUMMER—
PLEASE! PLEASE! WHERE IS THAT WONDERFUL RAIN MAKER? I WANT SOME RAIN ON MY RUTABAGAS!
RAIN SEED
YOUR RUTABAGAS WILL HAVE TO WAIT, MR. CORNSILK!
UNCA DONALD IS VACATIONING IN TIMBUKTU!

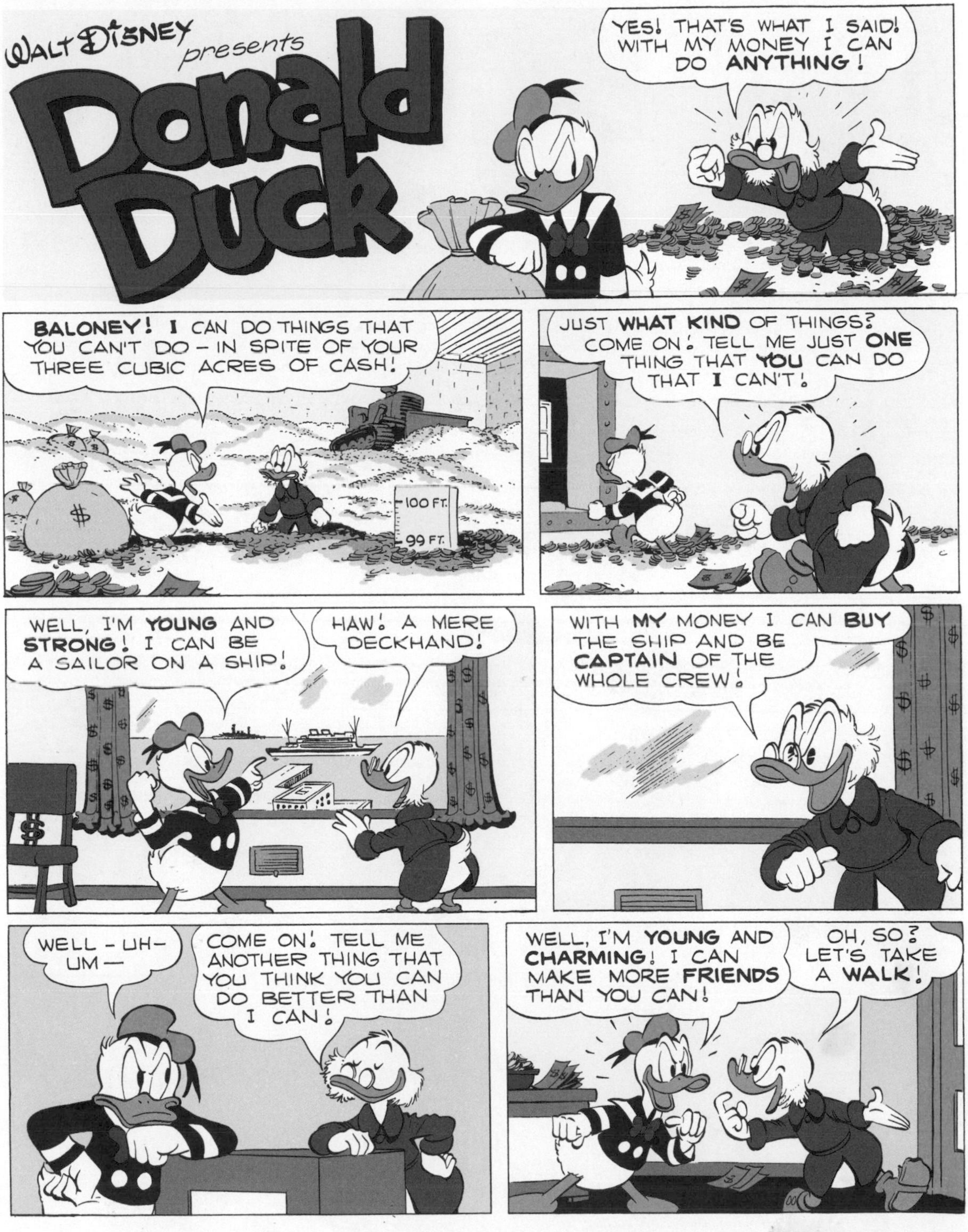
Walt Disney presents
Donald Duck
YES! THAT'S WHAT I SAID! WITH MY MONEY I CAN DO ANYTHING!
BALONEY! I CAN DO THINGS THAT YOU CAN'T DO – IN SPITE OF YOUR THREE CUBIC ACRES OF CASH!
100 FT.
99 FT.
JUST WHAT KIND OF THINGS? COME ON! TELL ME JUST ONE THING THAT YOU CAN DO THAT I CAN'T!
WELL, I'M YOUNG AND STRONG! I CAN BE A SAILOR ON A SHIP!
HAW! A MERE DECKHAND!
WITH MY MONEY I CAN BUY THE SHIP AND BE CAPTAIN OF THE WHOLE CREW!
WELL – UH– UM—
COME ON! TELL ME ANOTHER THING THAT YOU THINK YOU CAN DO BETTER THAN I CAN!
WELL, I'M YOUNG AND CHARMING! I CAN MAKE MORE FRIENDS THAN YOU CAN!
OH, SO? LET'S TAKE A WALK!

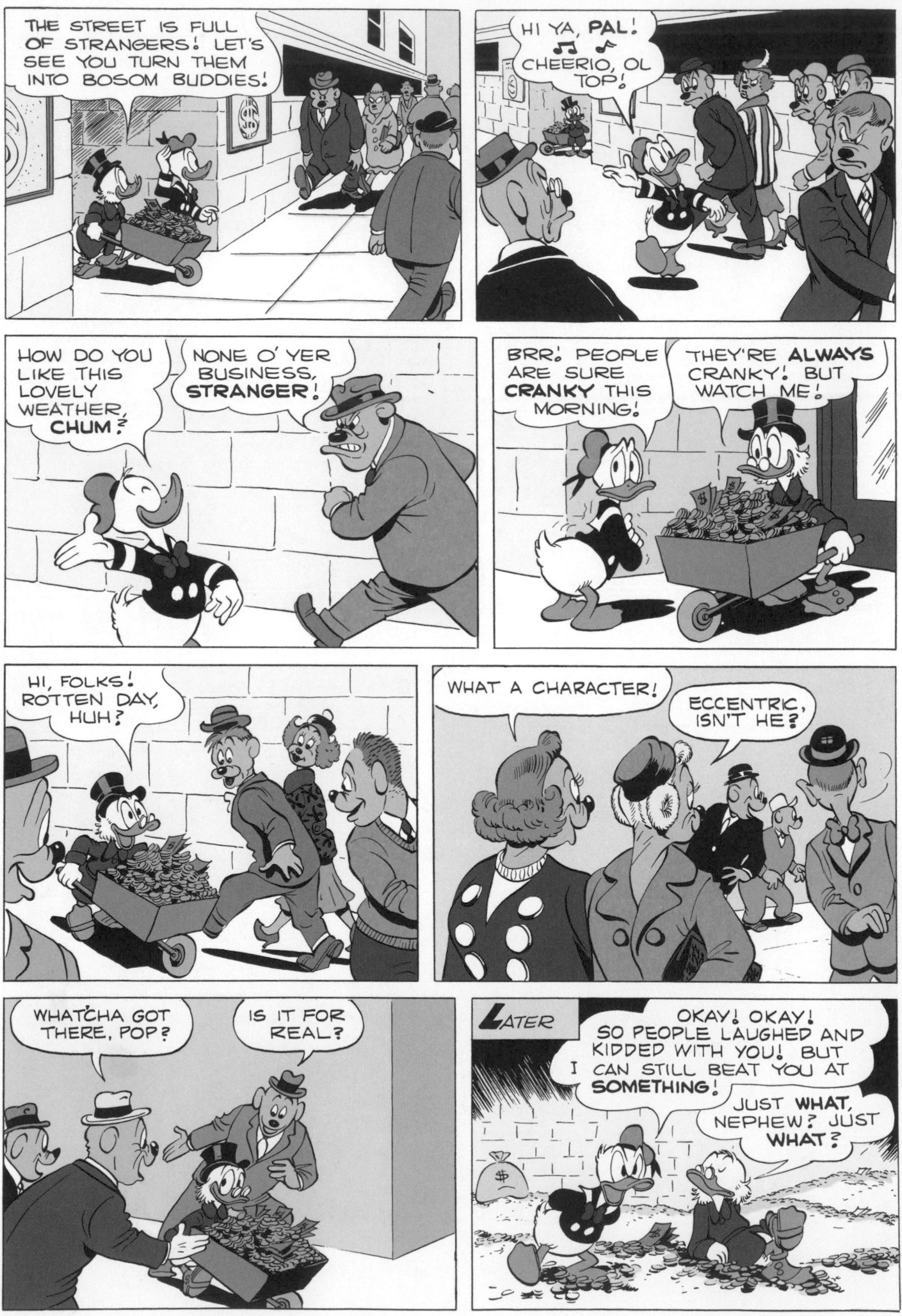
THE STREET IS FULL OF STRANGERS! LET'S SEE YOU TURN THEM INTO BOSOM BUDDIES!
HI YA, PAL! CHEERIO, OL TOP!
HOW DO YOU LIKE THIS LOVELY WEATHER, CHUM?
NONE O' YER BUSINESS, STRANGER!
BRR! PEOPLE ARE SURE CRANKY THIS MORNING!
THEY'RE ALWAYS CRANKY! BUT WATCH ME!
HI, FOLKS! ROTTEN DAY, HUH?
WHAT A CHARACTER!
ECCENTRIC, ISN'T HE?
WHATCHA GOT THERE, POP?
IS IT FOR REAL?
LATER
OKAY! OKAY! SO PEOPLE LAUGHED AND KIDDED WITH YOU! BUT I CAN STILL BEAT YOU AT SOMETHING!
JUST WHAT, NEPHEW? JUST WHAT?

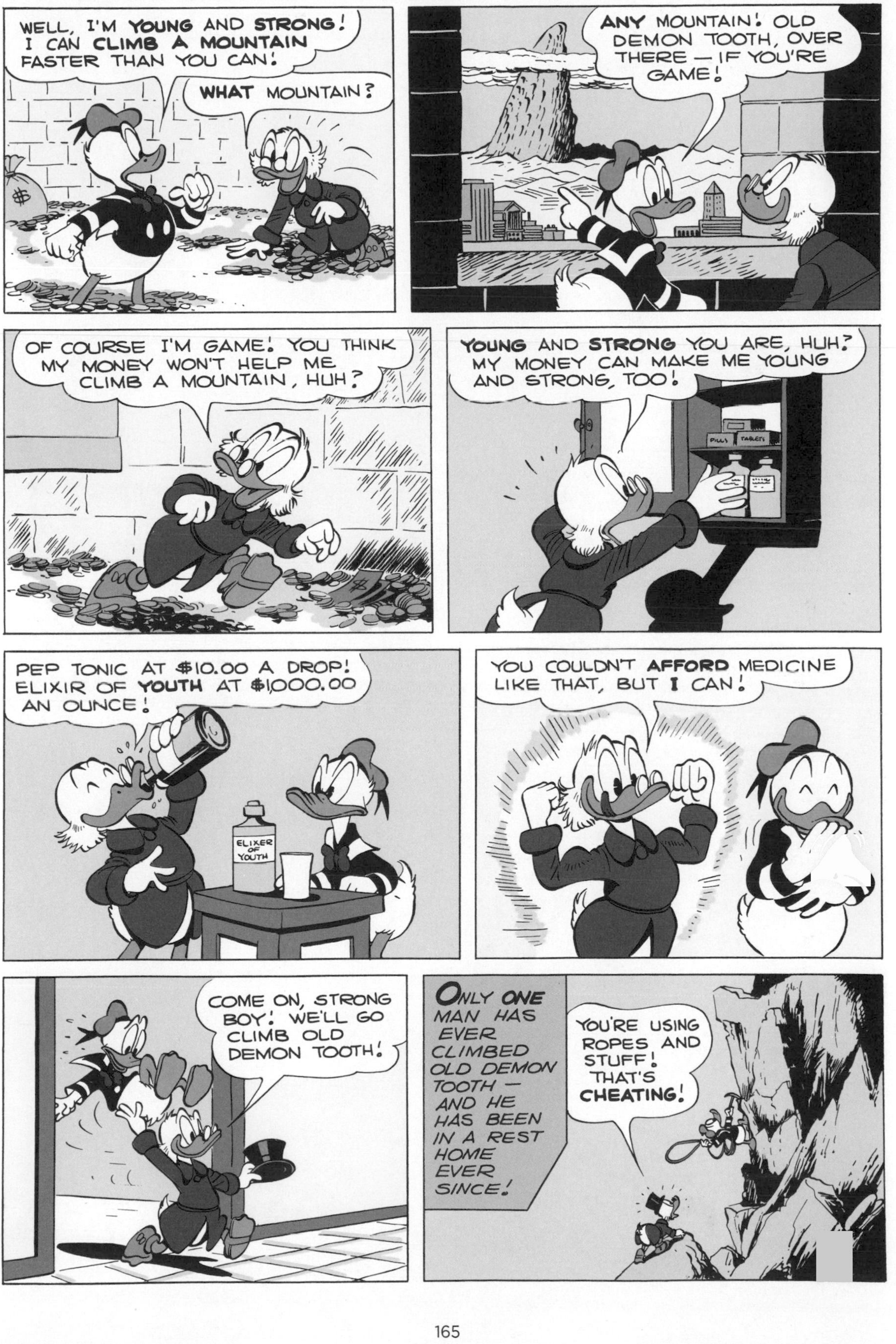

WELL, I'M YOUNG AND STRONG! I CAN CLIMB A MOUNTAIN FASTER THAN YOU CAN!
WHAT MOUNTAIN?
ANY MOUNTAIN! OLD DEMON TOOTH, OVER THERE — IF YOU'RE GAME!
OF COURSE I'M GAME! YOU THINK MY MONEY WON'T HELP ME CLIMB A MOUNTAIN, HUH?
YOUNG AND STRONG YOU ARE, HUH? MY MONEY CAN MAKE ME YOUNG AND STRONG, TOO!
PILLS
TABLETS
PEP TONIC AT $10.00 A DROP! ELIXIR OF YOUTH AT $1,000.00 AN OUNCE!
ELIXER OF YOUTH
YOU COULDN'T AFFORD MEDICINE LIKE THAT, BUT I CAN!
COME ON, STRONG BOY! WE'LL GO CLIMB OLD DEMON TOOTH!
ONLY ONE MAN HAS EVER CLIMBED OLD DEMON TOOTH — AND HE HAS BEEN IN A REST HOME EVER SINCE!
YOU'RE USING ROPES AND STUFF! THAT'S CHEATING!

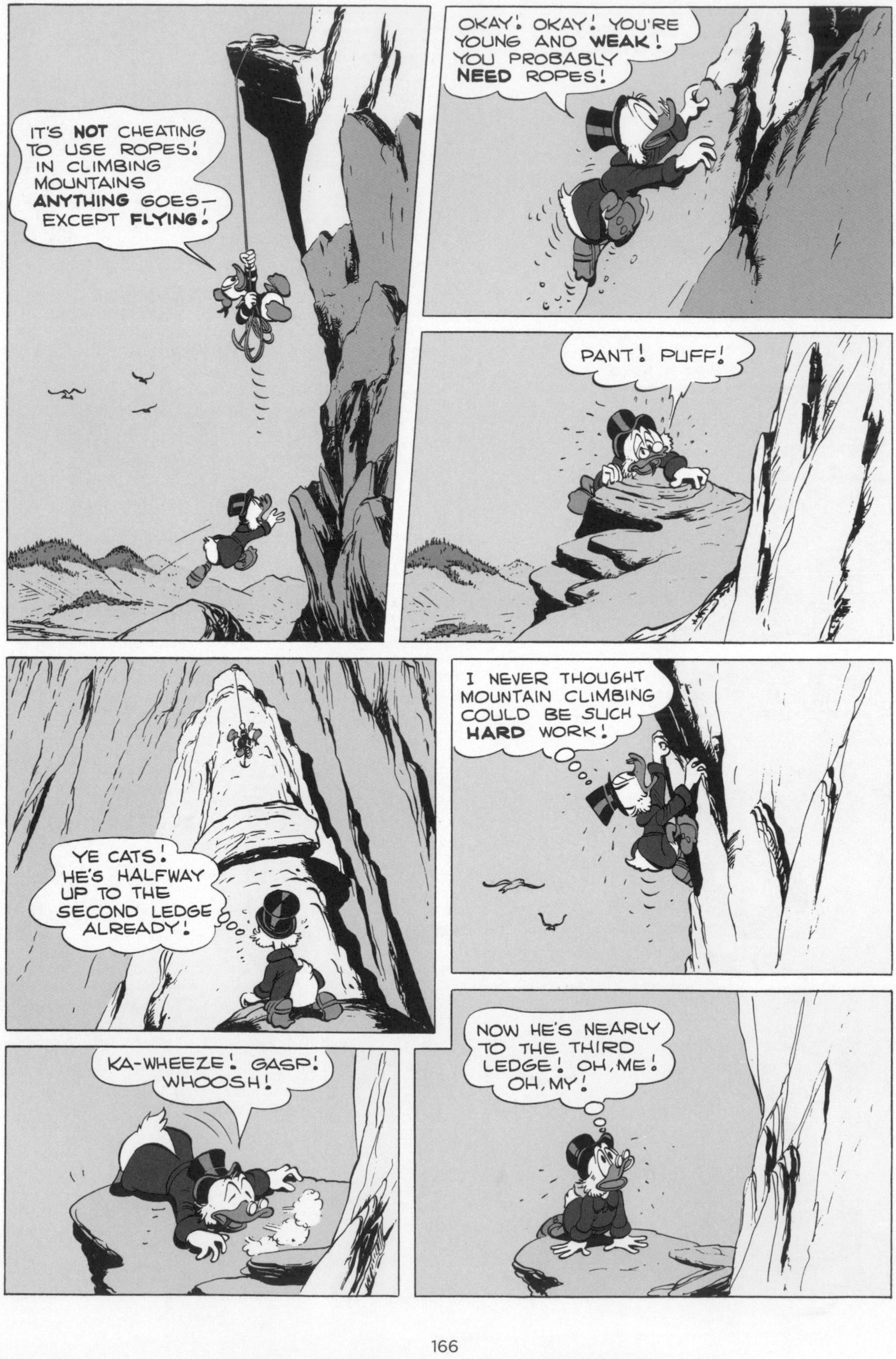
IT'S **NOT** CHEATING TO USE ROPES! IN CLIMBING MOUNTAINS **ANYTHING** GOES— EXCEPT **FLYING**!
OKAY! OKAY! YOU'RE YOUNG AND **WEAK**! YOU PROBABLY **NEED** ROPES!
PANT! PUFF!
YE CATS! HE'S HALFWAY UP TO THE SECOND LEDGE ALREADY!
I NEVER THOUGHT MOUNTAIN CLIMBING COULD BE SUCH **HARD** WORK!
KA-WHEEZE! GASP! WHOOSH!
NOW HE'S NEARLY TO THE THIRD LEDGE! OH, ME! OH, MY!

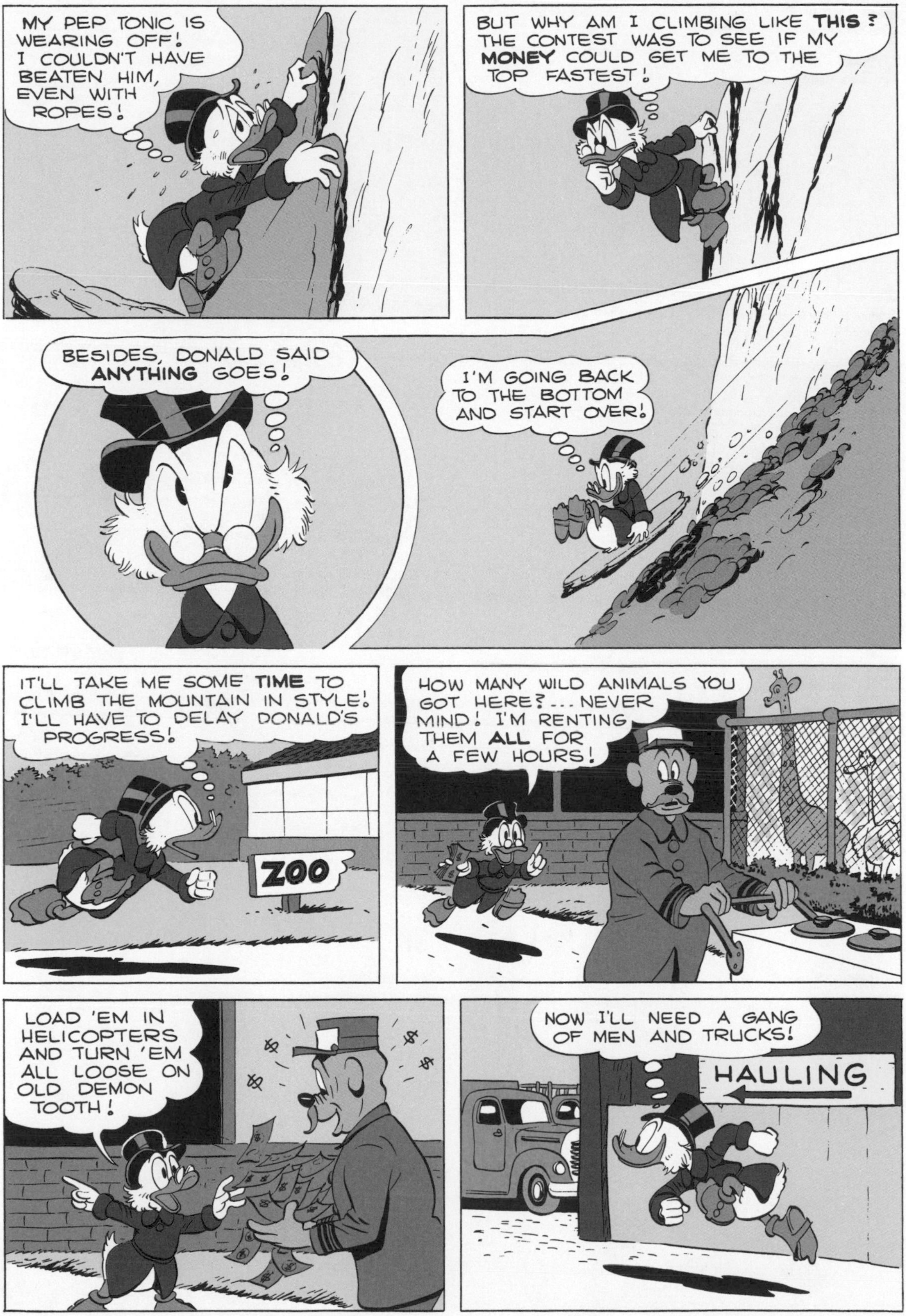
MY PEP TONIC IS WEARING OFF! I COULDN'T HAVE BEATEN HIM, EVEN WITH ROPES!
BUT WHY AM I CLIMBING LIKE THIS? THE CONTEST WAS TO SEE IF MY MONEY COULD GET ME TO THE TOP FASTEST!
BESIDES, DONALD SAID ANYTHING GOES!
I'M GOING BACK TO THE BOTTOM AND START OVER!
IT'LL TAKE ME SOME TIME TO CLIMB THE MOUNTAIN IN STYLE! I'LL HAVE TO DELAY DONALD'S PROGRESS!
ZOO
HOW MANY WILD ANIMALS YOU GOT HERE?... NEVER MIND! I'M RENTING THEM ALL FOR A FEW HOURS!
LOAD 'EM IN HELICOPTERS AND TURN 'EM ALL LOOSE ON OLD DEMON TOOTH!
NOW I'LL NEED A GANG OF MEN AND TRUCKS!
HAULING

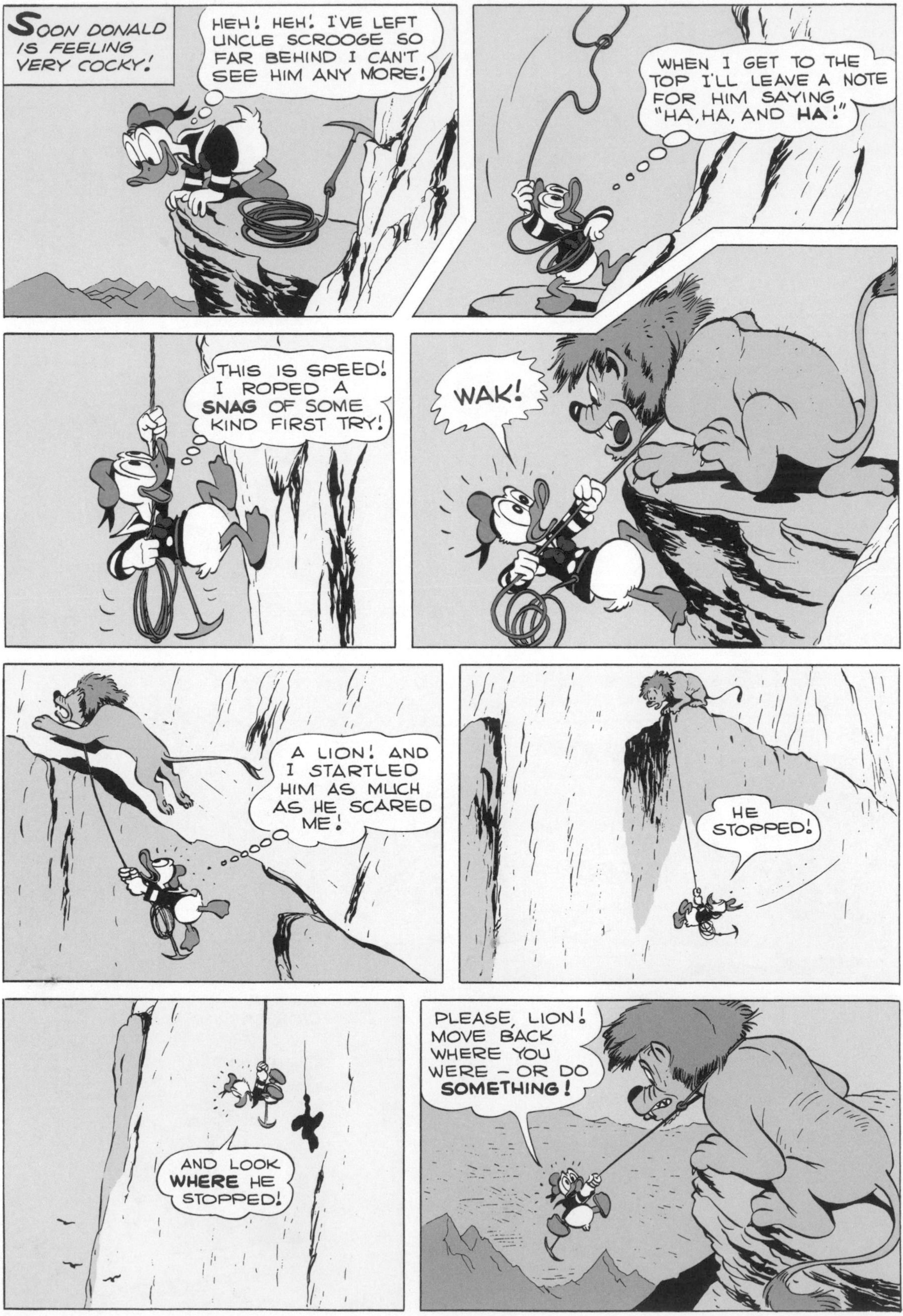
SOON DONALD IS FEELING VERY COCKY!
HEH! HEH! I'VE LEFT UNCLE SCROOGE SO FAR BEHIND I CAN'T SEE HIM ANY MORE!
WHEN I GET TO THE TOP I'LL LEAVE A NOTE FOR HIM SAYING "HA, HA, AND HA!"
THIS IS SPEED! I ROPED A SNAG OF SOME KIND FIRST TRY!
WAK!
A LION! AND I STARTLED HIM AS MUCH AS HE SCARED ME!
HE STOPPED!
AND LOOK WHERE HE STOPPED!
PLEASE, LION! MOVE BACK WHERE YOU WERE — OR DO SOMETHING!

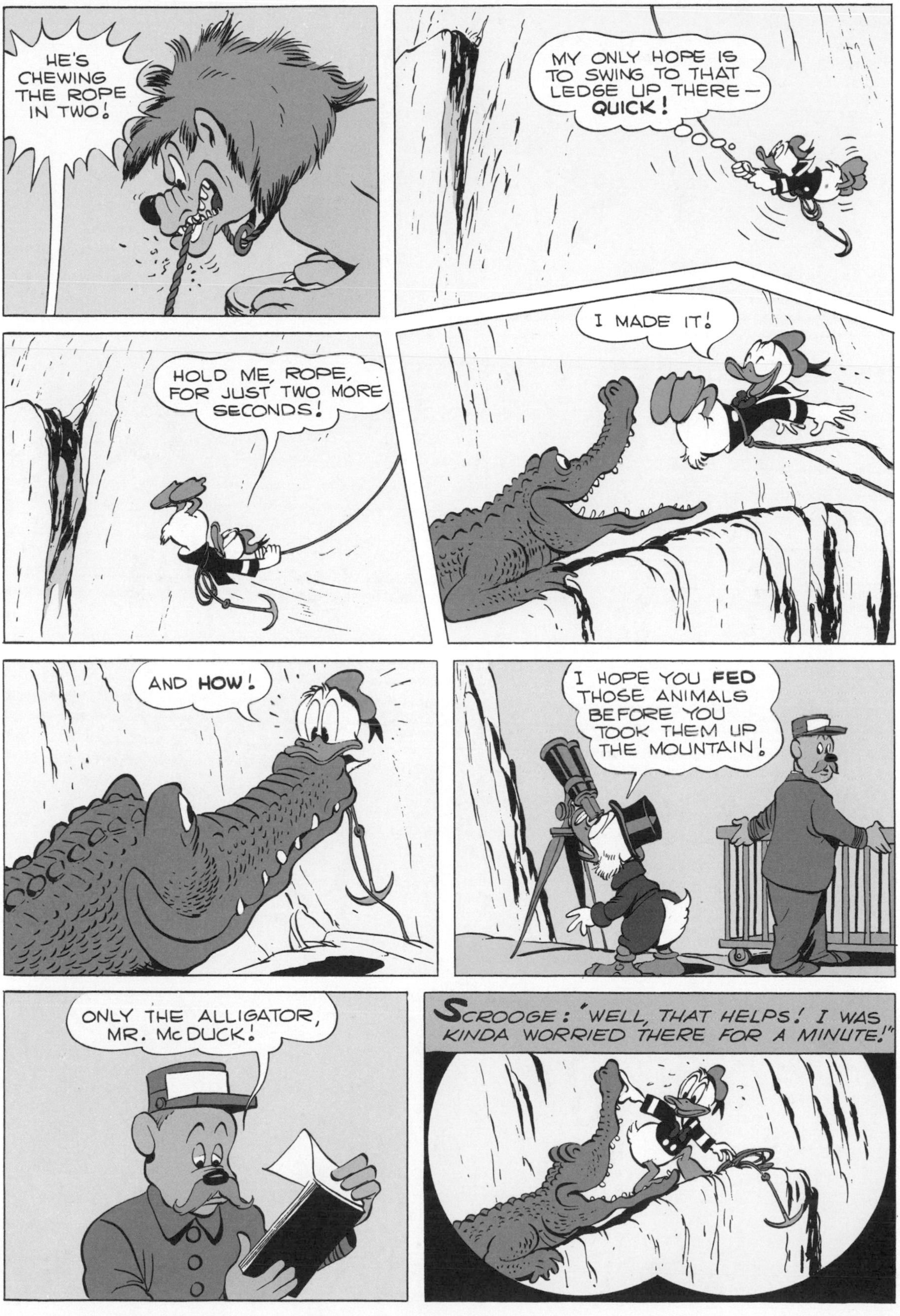

HE'S CHEWING THE ROPE IN TWO!
MY ONLY HOPE IS TO SWING TO THAT LEDGE UP THERE— **QUICK!**
HOLD ME, ROPE, FOR JUST TWO MORE SECONDS!
I MADE IT!
AND **HOW!**
I HOPE YOU **FED** THOSE ANIMALS BEFORE YOU TOOK THEM UP THE MOUNTAIN!
ONLY THE ALLIGATOR, MR. McDUCK!
SCROOGE: "WELL, THAT HELPS! I WAS KINDA WORRIED THERE FOR A MINUTE!"

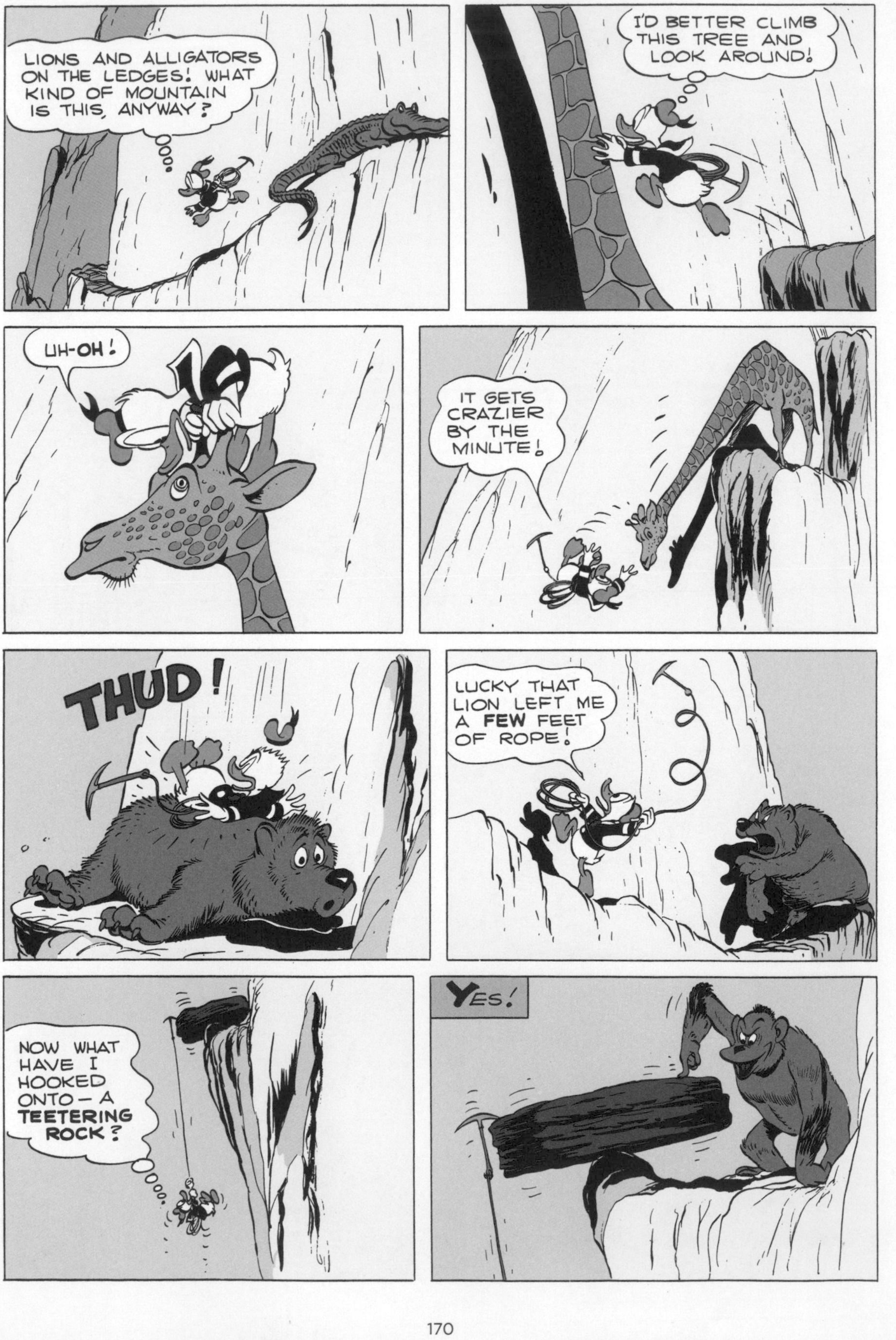
LIONS AND ALLIGATORS ON THE LEDGES! WHAT KIND OF MOUNTAIN IS THIS, ANYWAY?
I'D BETTER CLIMB THIS TREE AND LOOK AROUND!
UH-OH!
IT GETS CRAZIER BY THE MINUTE!
THUD!
LUCKY THAT LION LEFT ME A FEW FEET OF ROPE!
NOW WHAT HAVE I HOOKED ONTO — A TEETERING ROCK?
YES!

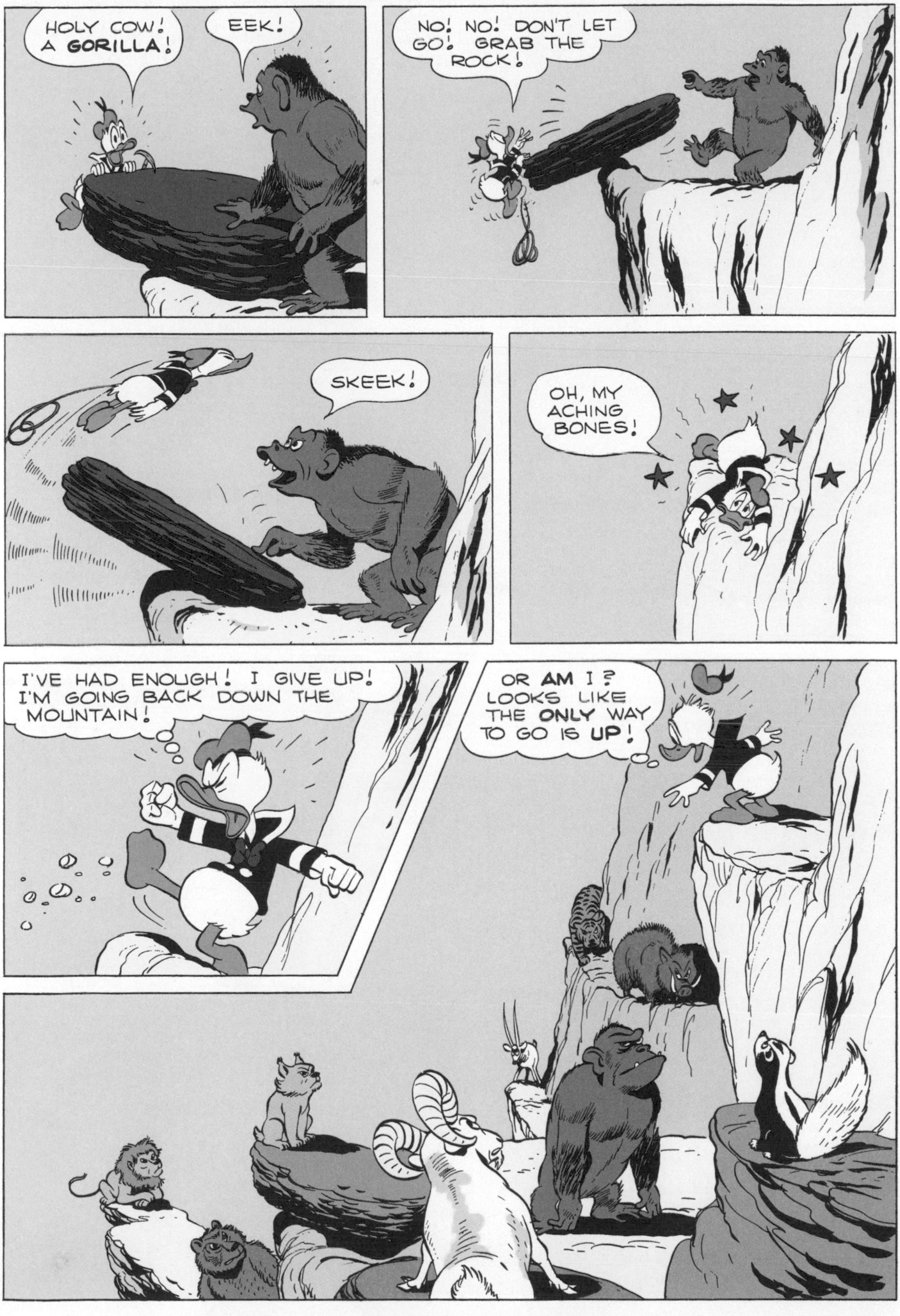
HOLY COW! A GORILLA!
EEK!
NO! NO! DON'T LET GO! GRAB THE ROCK!
SKEEK!
OH, MY ACHING BONES!
I'VE HAD ENOUGH! I GIVE UP! I'M GOING BACK DOWN THE MOUNTAIN!
OR AM I? LOOKS LIKE THE ONLY WAY TO GO IS UP!

MANY HOURS AND MANY ADVENTURES LATER, DONALD REACHES THE TOP OF OLD DEMON TOOTH!

UNCLE SCROOGE! HOW DID **YOU** GET HERE?

I CAME UP THE **EASY** WAY, NEPHEW! THE **EASY** WAY!

LIKE I SAID — WITH MY MONEY I CAN DO **ANYTHING**!

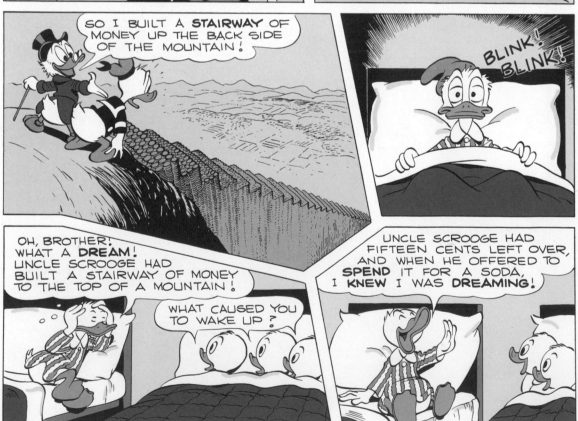

SO I BUILT A **STAIRWAY** OF MONEY UP THE BACK SIDE OF THE MOUNTAIN!

BLINK! BLINK!!

OH, BROTHER! WHAT A **DREAM**! UNCLE SCROOGE HAD BUILT A STAIRWAY OF MONEY TO THE TOP OF A MOUNTAIN!

WHAT CAUSED YOU TO WAKE UP?

UNCLE SCROOGE HAD FIFTEEN CENTS LEFT OVER, AND WHEN HE OFFERED TO **SPEND** IT FOR A SODA, I **KNEW** I WAS **DREAMING**!

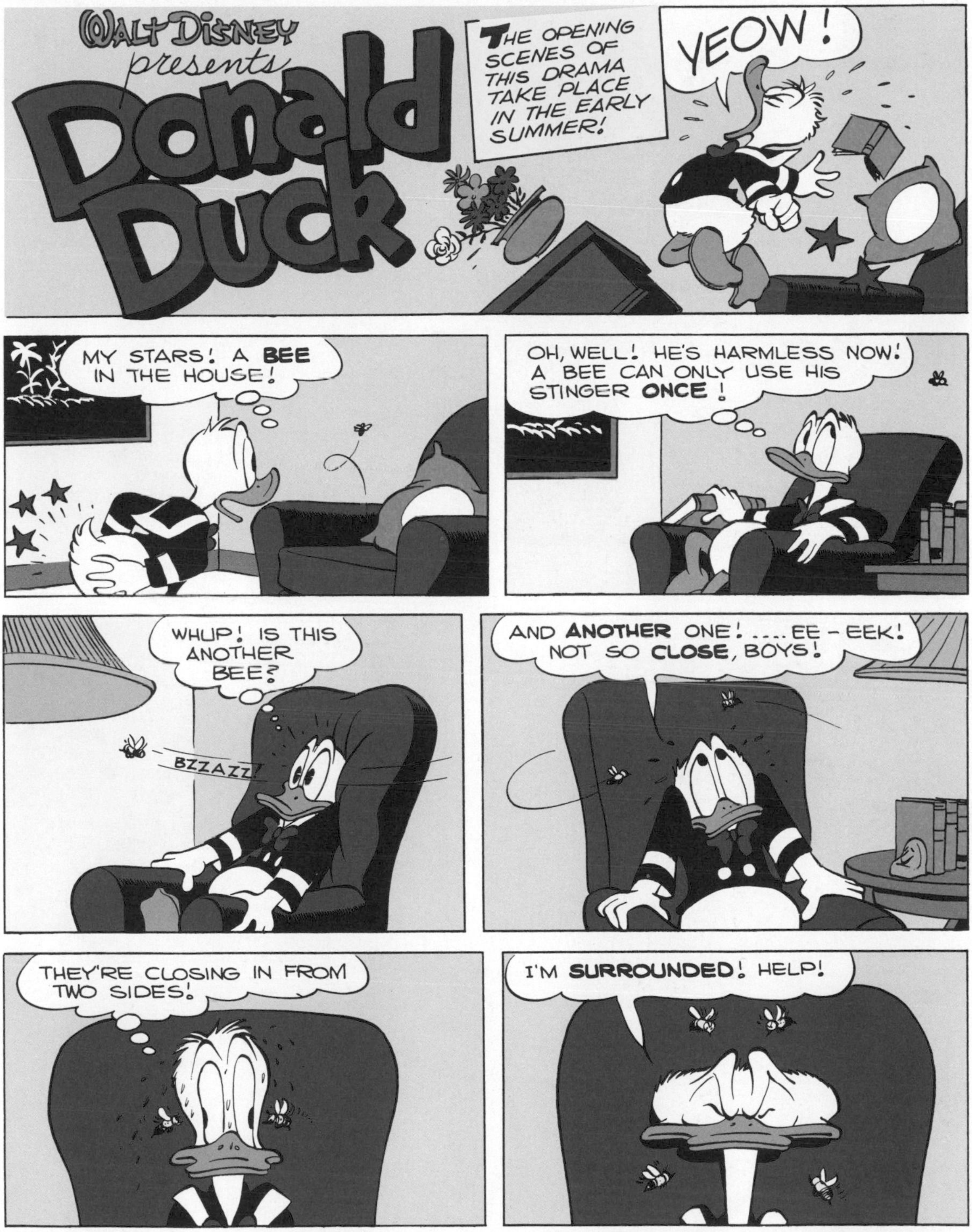
WALT DISNEY
presents
Donald Duck
THE OPENING SCENES OF THIS DRAMA TAKE PLACE IN THE EARLY SUMMER!
YEOW!
MY STARS! A BEE IN THE HOUSE!
OH, WELL! HE'S HARMLESS NOW! A BEE CAN ONLY USE HIS STINGER ONCE!
WHUP! IS THIS ANOTHER BEE?
BZZAZZ!
AND ANOTHER ONE! ....EE-EEK! NOT SO CLOSE, BOYS!
THEY'RE CLOSING IN FROM TWO SIDES!
I'M SURROUNDED! HELP!

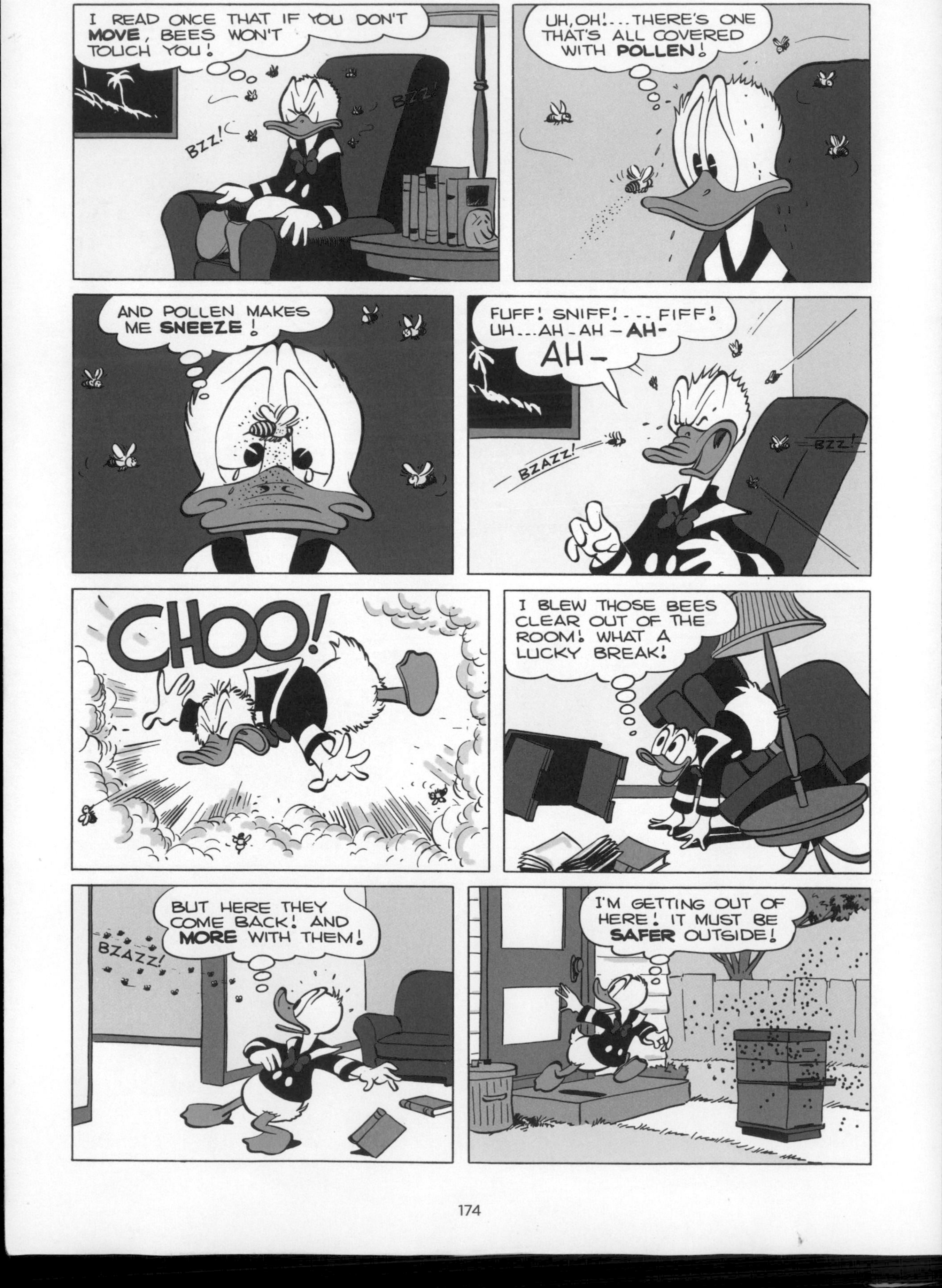
I READ ONCE THAT IF YOU DON'T MOVE, BEES WON'T TOUCH YOU!
BZZ!
BZZ!
UH, OH!... THERE'S ONE THAT'S ALL COVERED WITH POLLEN!
AND POLLEN MAKES ME SNEEZE!
FUFF! SNIFF! ... FIFF! UH...AH-AH-AH- AH-
BZAZZ!
BZZ!
CHOO!
I BLEW THOSE BEES CLEAR OUT OF THE ROOM! WHAT A LUCKY BREAK!
BUT HERE THEY COME BACK! AND MORE WITH THEM!
BZAZZ!
I'M GETTING OUT OF HERE! IT MUST BE SAFER OUTSIDE!

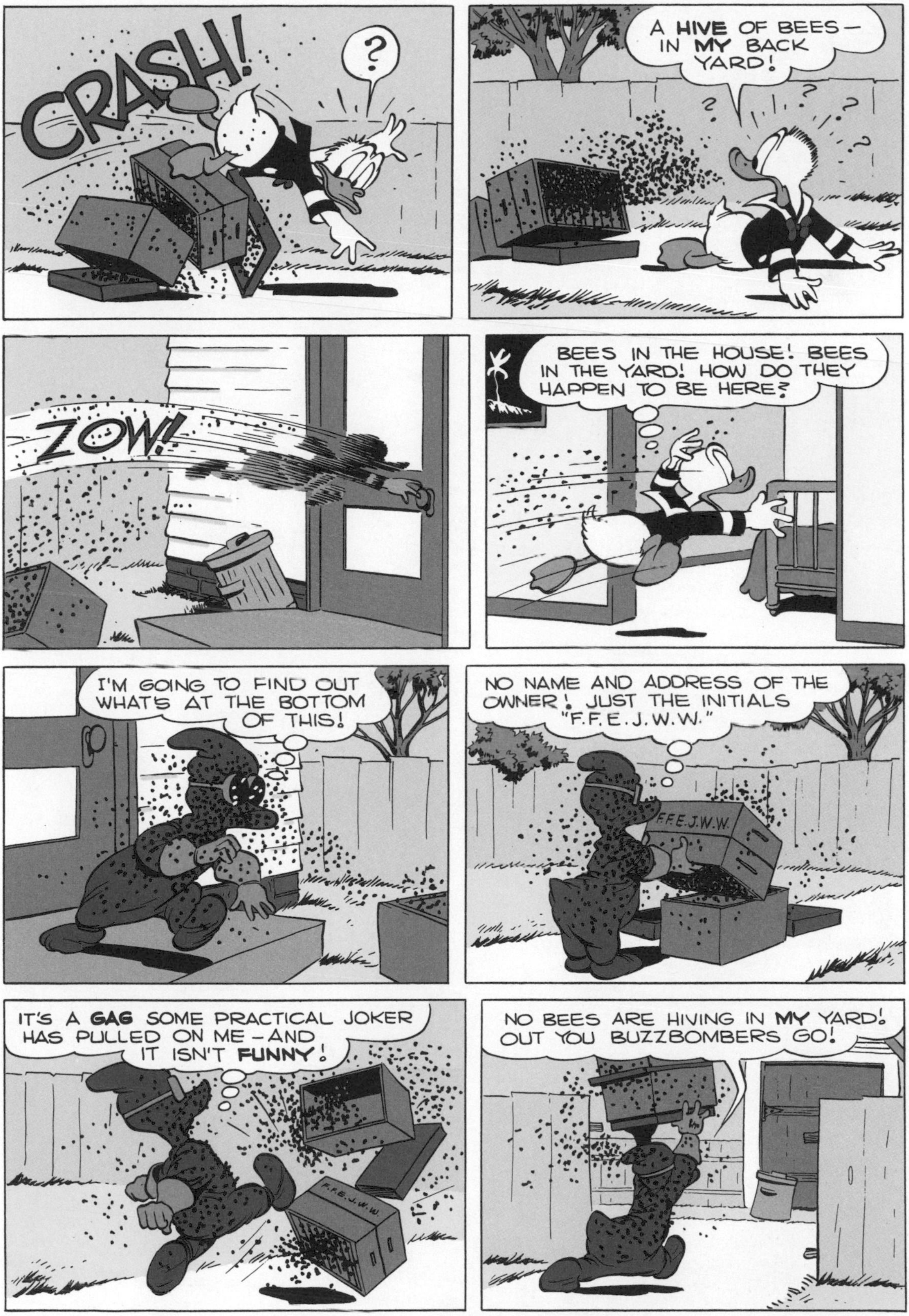
CRASH!
?
A HIVE OF BEES— IN MY BACK YARD!
? ? ? ?
ZOW!
BEES IN THE HOUSE! BEES IN THE YARD! HOW DO THEY HAPPEN TO BE HERE?
I'M GOING TO FIND OUT WHAT'S AT THE BOTTOM OF THIS!
NO NAME AND ADDRESS OF THE OWNER! JUST THE INITIALS "F.F.E.J.W.W."
F.F.E.J.W.W.
IT'S A GAG SOME PRACTICAL JOKER HAS PULLED ON ME—AND IT ISN'T FUNNY!
F.F.E.J.W.W.
NO BEES ARE HIVING IN MY YARD! OUT YOU BUZZBOMBERS GO!

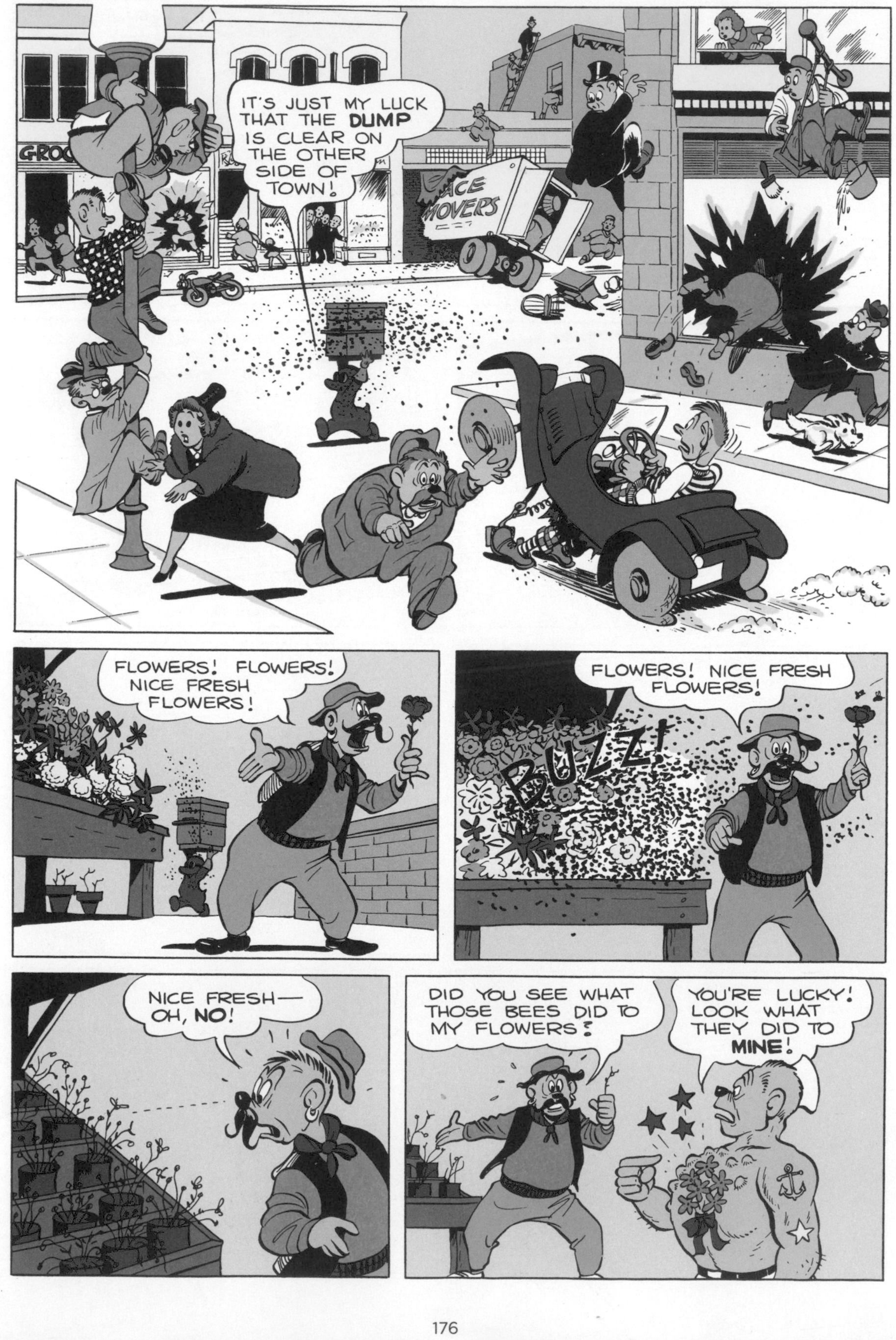
IT'S JUST MY LUCK THAT THE **DUMP** IS CLEAR ON THE OTHER SIDE OF TOWN!
ACE MOVERS
FLOWERS! FLOWERS! NICE FRESH FLOWERS!
FLOWERS! NICE FRESH FLOWERS!
BUZZ!
NICE FRESH— OH, **NO**!
DID YOU SEE WHAT THOSE BEES DID TO MY FLOWERS?
YOU'RE LUCKY! LOOK WHAT THEY DID TO **MINE**!

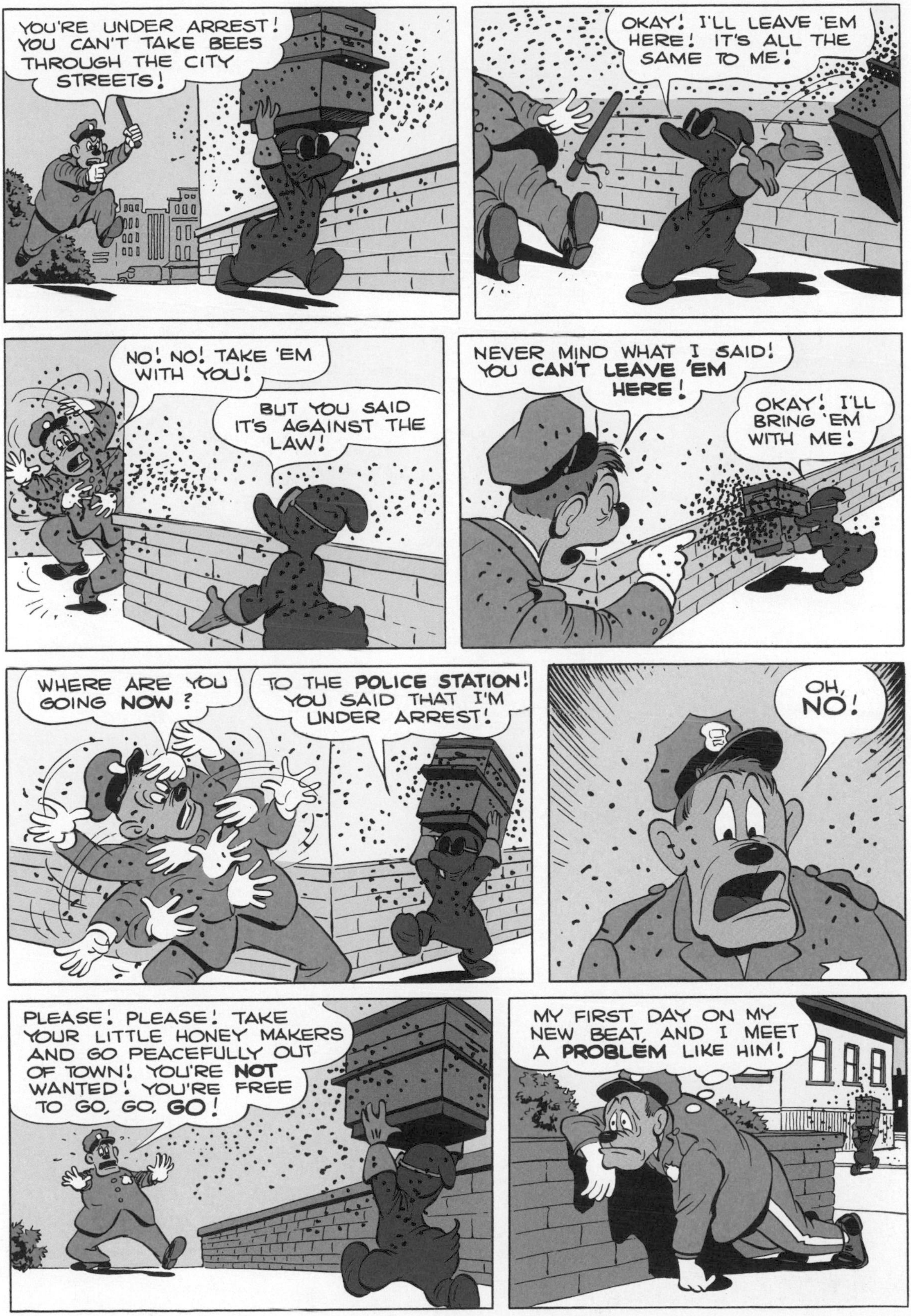
YOU'RE UNDER ARREST! YOU CAN'T TAKE BEES THROUGH THE CITY STREETS!
OKAY! I'LL LEAVE 'EM HERE! IT'S ALL THE SAME TO ME!
NO! NO! TAKE 'EM WITH YOU!
BUT YOU SAID IT'S AGAINST THE LAW!
NEVER MIND WHAT I SAID! YOU CAN'T LEAVE 'EM HERE!
OKAY! I'LL BRING 'EM WITH ME!
WHERE ARE YOU GOING NOW?
TO THE POLICE STATION! YOU SAID THAT I'M UNDER ARREST!
OH, NO!
PLEASE! PLEASE! TAKE YOUR LITTLE HONEY MAKERS AND GO PEACEFULLY OUT OF TOWN! YOU'RE NOT WANTED! YOU'RE FREE TO GO, GO, GO!
MY FIRST DAY ON MY NEW BEAT, AND I MEET A PROBLEM LIKE HIM!

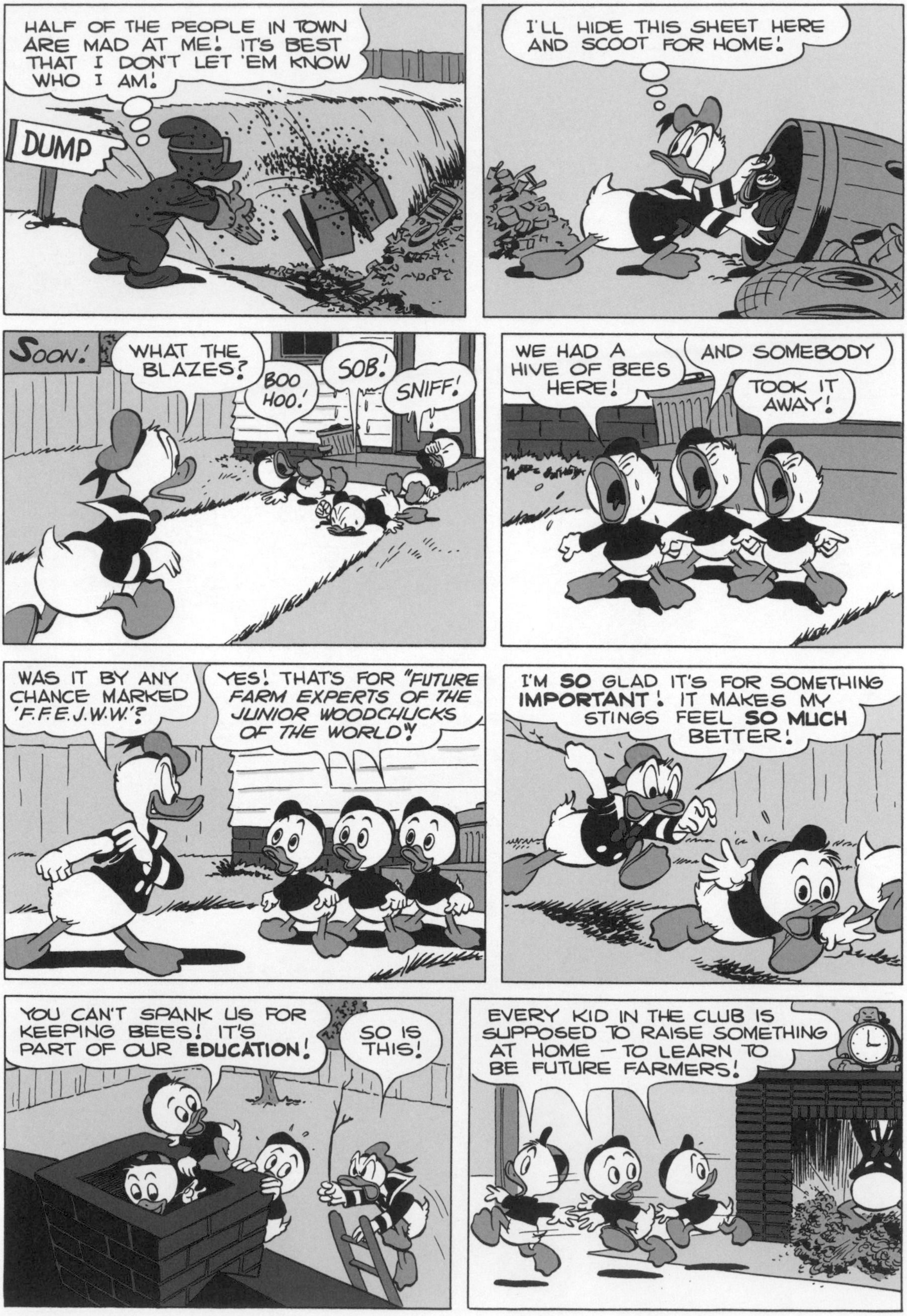
HALF OF THE PEOPLE IN TOWN ARE MAD AT ME! IT'S BEST THAT I DON'T LET 'EM KNOW WHO I AM!
DUMP
I'LL HIDE THIS SHEET HERE AND SCOOT FOR HOME!
SOON!
WHAT THE BLAZES?
BOO HOO!
SOB!
SNIFF!
WE HAD A HIVE OF BEES HERE!
AND SOMEBODY
TOOK IT AWAY!
WAS IT BY ANY CHANCE MARKED 'F.F.E.J.W.W.'?
YES! THAT'S FOR "FUTURE FARM EXPERTS OF THE JUNIOR WOODCHUCKS OF THE WORLD"!
I'M SO GLAD IT'S FOR SOMETHING IMPORTANT! IT MAKES MY STINGS FEEL SO MUCH BETTER!
YOU CAN'T SPANK US FOR KEEPING BEES! IT'S PART OF OUR EDUCATION!
SO IS THIS!
EVERY KID IN THE CLUB IS SUPPOSED TO RAISE SOMETHING AT HOME — TO LEARN TO BE FUTURE FARMERS!

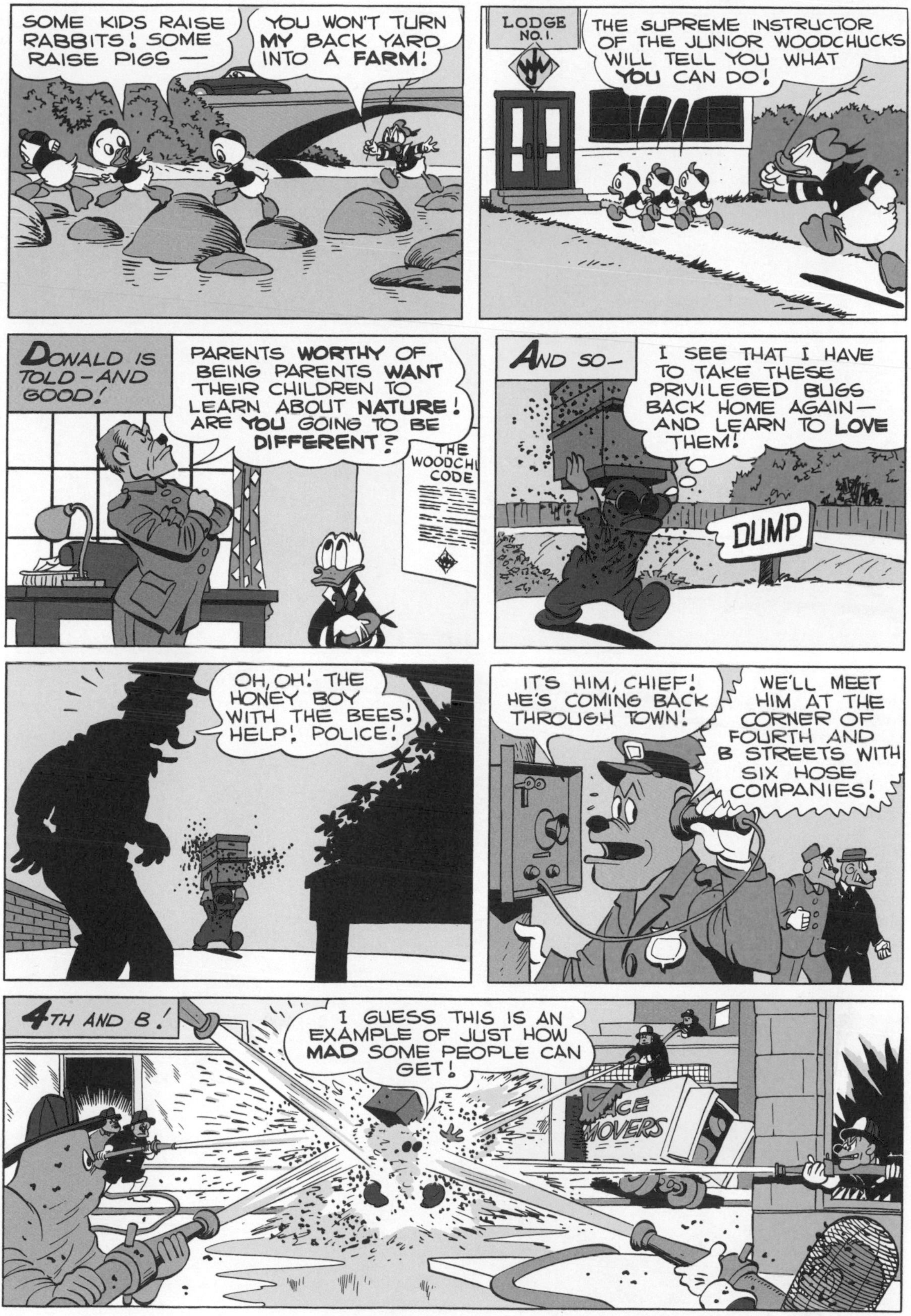
SOME KIDS RAISE RABBITS! SOME RAISE PIGS —
YOU WON'T TURN MY BACK YARD INTO A FARM!
LODGE NO. 1.
THE SUPREME INSTRUCTOR OF THE JUNIOR WOODCHUCKS WILL TELL YOU WHAT YOU CAN DO!
DONALD IS TOLD—AND GOOD!
PARENTS WORTHY OF BEING PARENTS WANT THEIR CHILDREN TO LEARN ABOUT NATURE! ARE YOU GOING TO BE DIFFERENT?
THE WOODCHU CODE
AND SO—
I SEE THAT I HAVE TO TAKE THESE PRIVILEGED BUGS BACK HOME AGAIN— AND LEARN TO LOVE THEM!
DUMP
OH, OH! THE HONEY BOY WITH THE BEES! HELP! POLICE!
IT'S HIM, CHIEF! HE'S COMING BACK THROUGH TOWN!
WE'LL MEET HIM AT THE CORNER OF FOURTH AND B STREETS WITH SIX HOSE COMPANIES!
4TH AND B!
I GUESS THIS IS AN EXAMPLE OF JUST HOW MAD SOME PEOPLE CAN GET!
ACE MOVERS

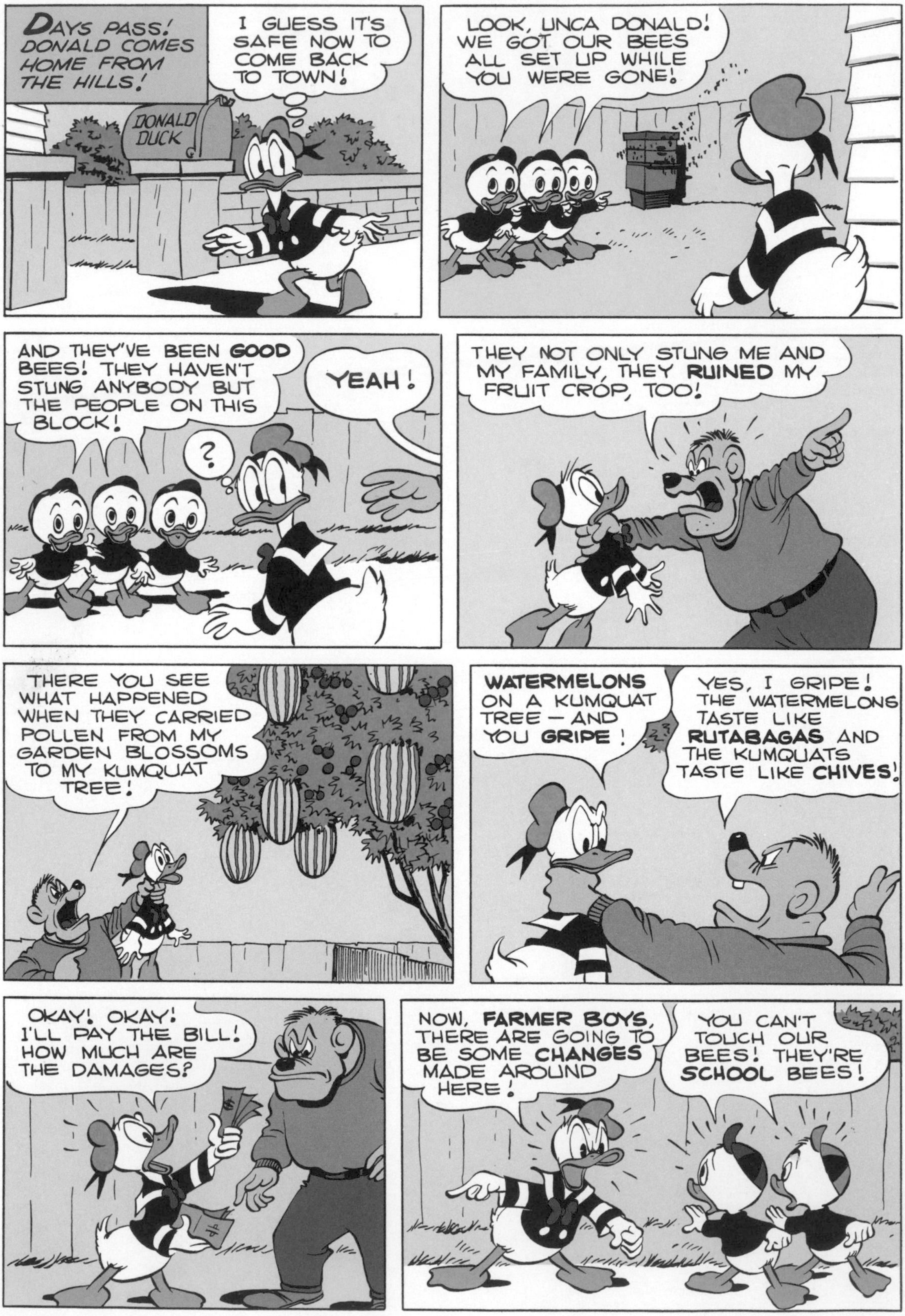

DAYS PASS! DONALD COMES HOME FROM THE HILLS!
I GUESS IT'S SAFE NOW TO COME BACK TO TOWN!
DONALD DUCK
LOOK, UNCA DONALD! WE GOT OUR BEES ALL SET UP WHILE YOU WERE GONE!
AND THEY'VE BEEN GOOD BEES! THEY HAVEN'T STUNG ANYBODY BUT THE PEOPLE ON THIS BLOCK!
YEAH!
?
THEY NOT ONLY STUNG ME AND MY FAMILY, THEY RUINED MY FRUIT CROP, TOO!
THERE YOU SEE WHAT HAPPENED WHEN THEY CARRIED POLLEN FROM MY GARDEN BLOSSOMS TO MY KUMQUAT TREE!
WATERMELONS ON A KUMQUAT TREE — AND YOU GRIPE!
YES, I GRIPE! THE WATERMELONS TASTE LIKE RUTABAGAS AND THE KUMQUATS TASTE LIKE CHIVES!
OKAY! OKAY! I'LL PAY THE BILL! HOW MUCH ARE THE DAMAGES?
NOW, FARMER BOYS, THERE ARE GOING TO BE SOME CHANGES MADE AROUND HERE!
YOU CAN'T TOUCH OUR BEES! THEY'RE SCHOOL BEES!

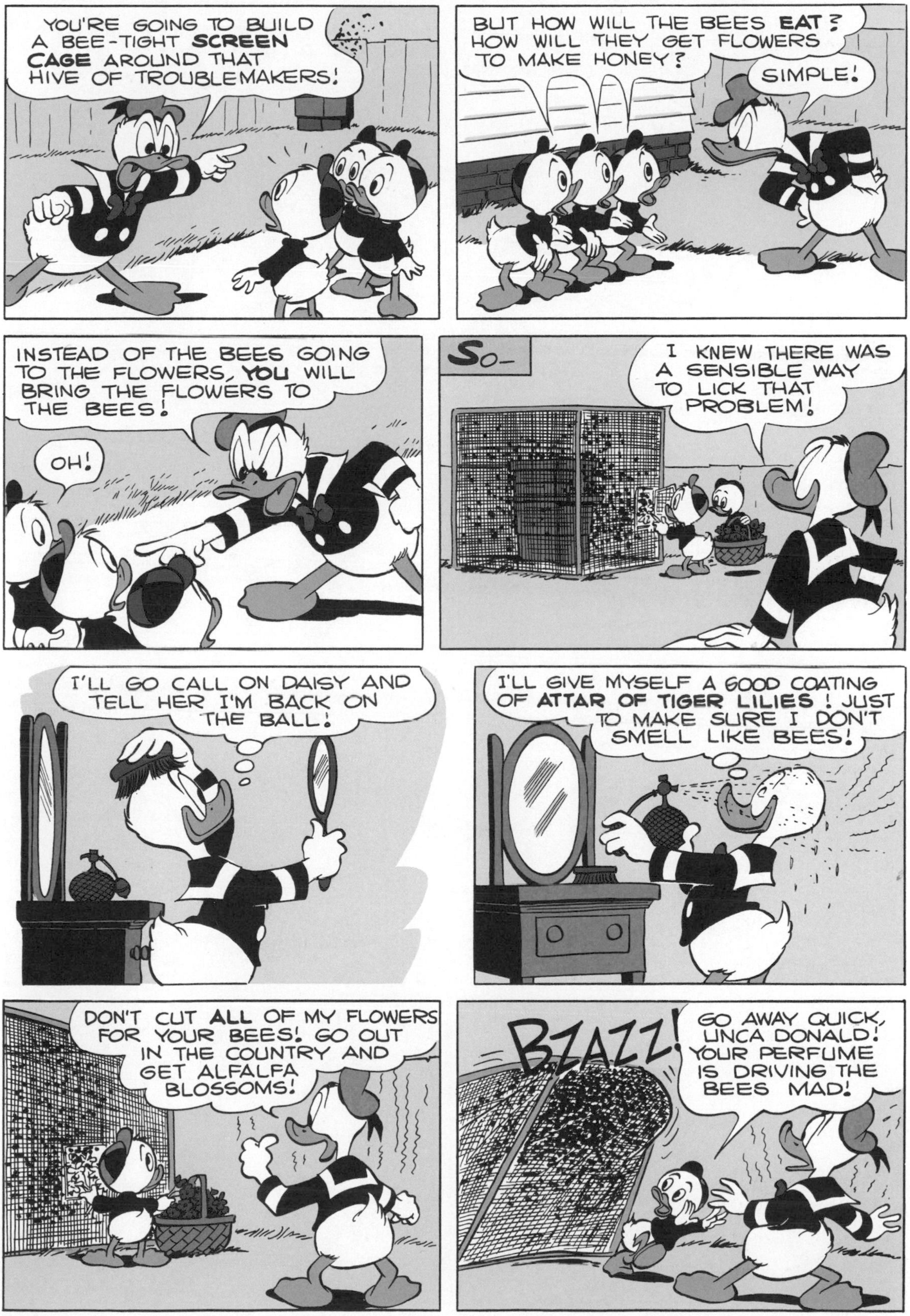

YOU'RE GOING TO BUILD A BEE-TIGHT SCREEN CAGE AROUND THAT HIVE OF TROUBLEMAKERS!
BUT HOW WILL THE BEES EAT? HOW WILL THEY GET FLOWERS TO MAKE HONEY?
SIMPLE!
INSTEAD OF THE BEES GOING TO THE FLOWERS, YOU WILL BRING THE FLOWERS TO THE BEES!
OH!
SO—
I KNEW THERE WAS A SENSIBLE WAY TO LICK THAT PROBLEM!
I'LL GO CALL ON DAISY AND TELL HER I'M BACK ON THE BALL!
I'LL GIVE MYSELF A GOOD COATING OF ATTAR OF TIGER LILIES! JUST TO MAKE SURE I DON'T SMELL LIKE BEES!
DON'T CUT ALL OF MY FLOWERS FOR YOUR BEES! GO OUT IN THE COUNTRY AND GET ALFALFA BLOSSOMS!
BZAZZ!
GO AWAY QUICK, UNCA DONALD! YOUR PERFUME IS DRIVING THE BEES MAD!

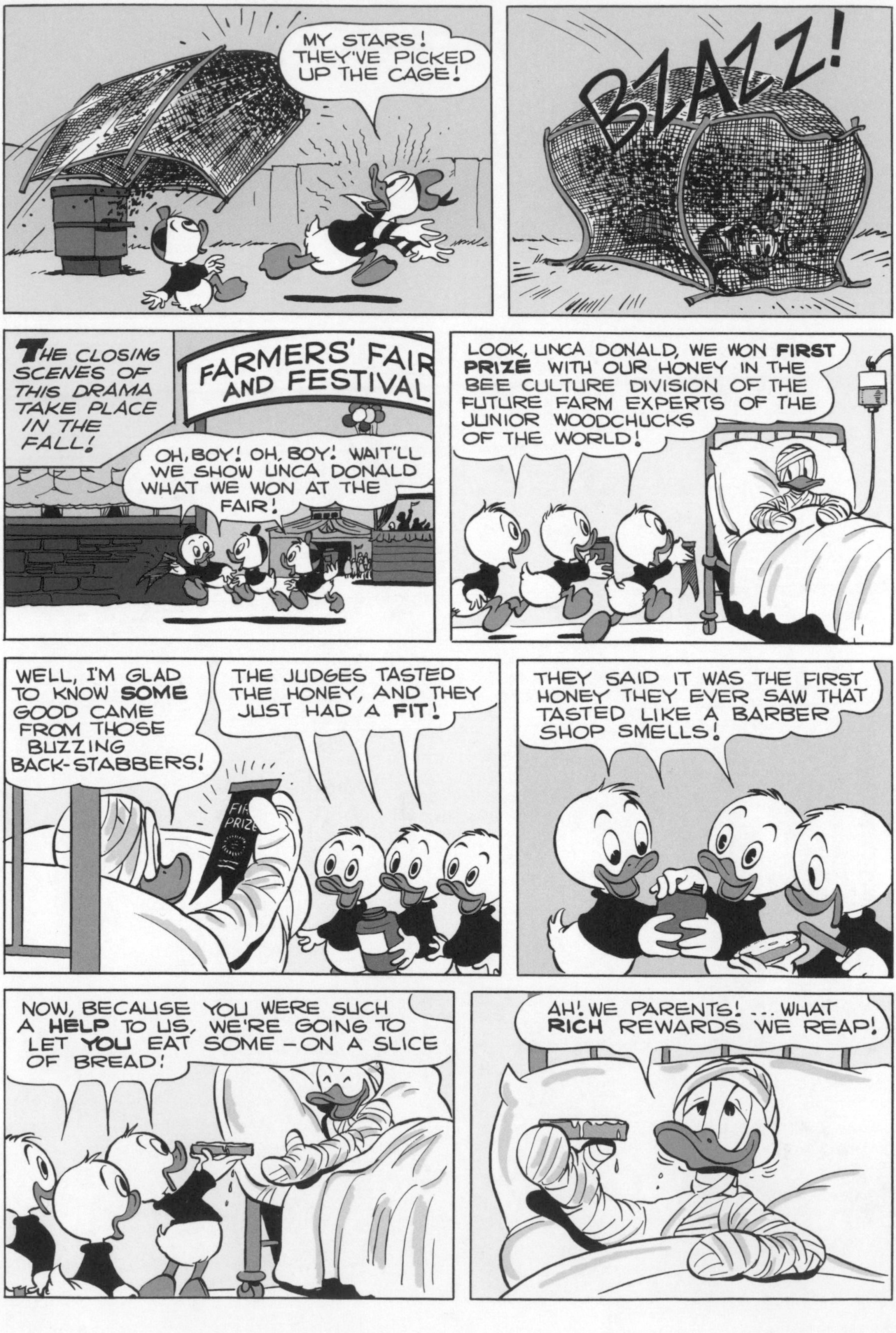
MY STARS! THEY'VE PICKED UP THE CAGE!
BZAZZ!
THE CLOSING SCENES OF THIS DRAMA TAKE PLACE IN THE FALL!
FARMERS' FAIR AND FESTIVAL
OH, BOY! OH, BOY! WAIT'LL WE SHOW UNCA DONALD WHAT WE WON AT THE FAIR!
LOOK, UNCA DONALD, WE WON FIRST PRIZE WITH OUR HONEY IN THE BEE CULTURE DIVISION OF THE FUTURE FARM EXPERTS OF THE JUNIOR WOODCHUCKS OF THE WORLD!
WELL, I'M GLAD TO KNOW SOME GOOD CAME FROM THOSE BUZZING BACK-STABBERS!
THE JUDGES TASTED THE HONEY, AND THEY JUST HAD A FIT!
THEY SAID IT WAS THE FIRST HONEY THEY EVER SAW THAT TASTED LIKE A BARBER SHOP SMELLS!
NOW, BECAUSE YOU WERE SUCH A HELP TO US, WE'RE GOING TO LET YOU EAT SOME — ON A SLICE OF BREAD!
AH! WE PARENTS! ... WHAT RICH REWARDS WE REAP!

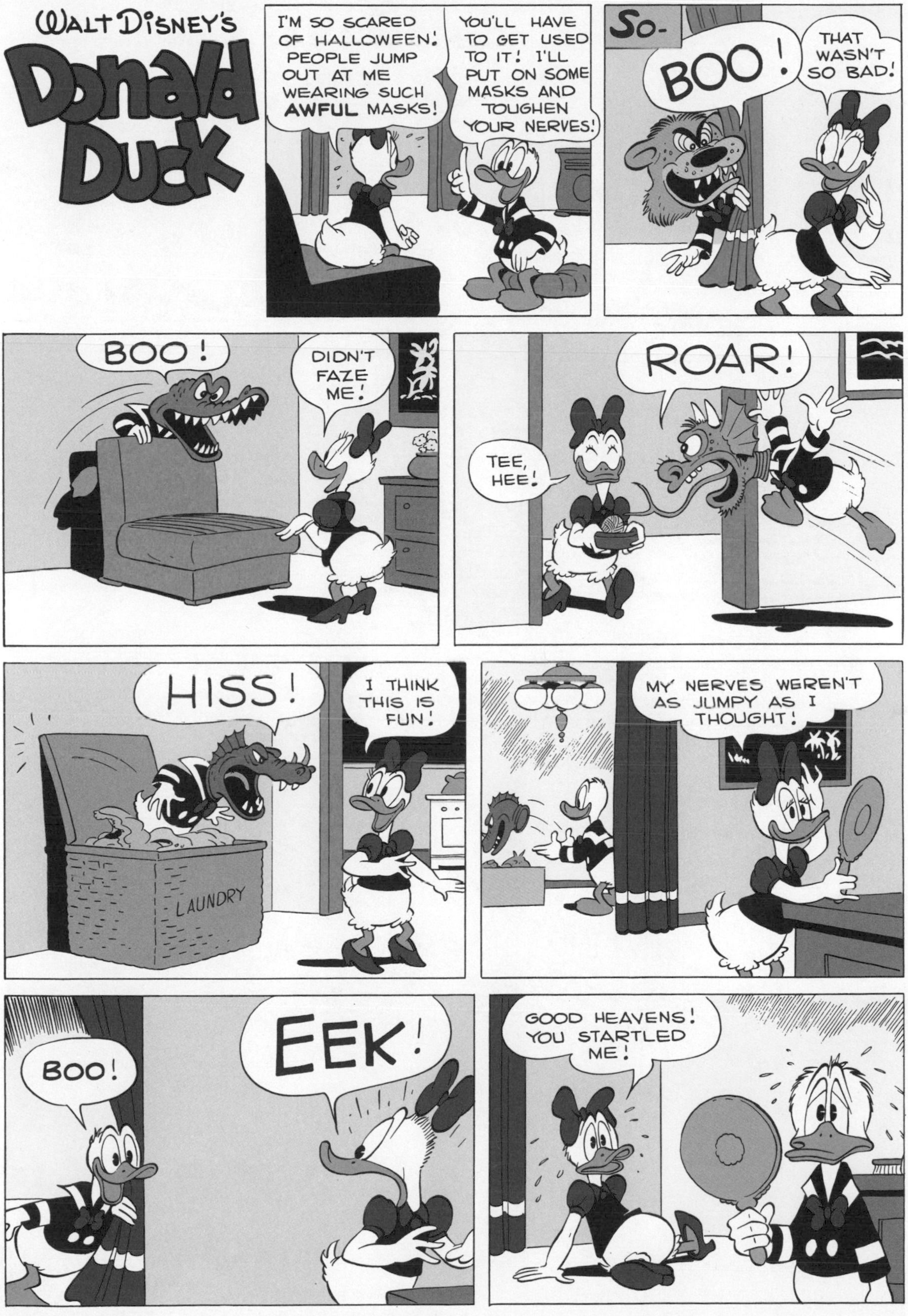
WALT DISNEY'S
Donald Duck
I'M SO SCARED OF HALLOWEEN! PEOPLE JUMP OUT AT ME WEARING SUCH AWFUL MASKS!
YOU'LL HAVE TO GET USED TO IT! I'LL PUT ON SOME MASKS AND TOUGHEN YOUR NERVES!
SO-
BOO!
THAT WASN'T SO BAD!
BOO!
DIDN'T FAZE ME!
ROAR!
TEE, HEE!
HISS!
I THINK THIS IS FUN!
LAUNDRY
MY NERVES WEREN'T AS JUMPY AS I THOUGHT!
BOO!
EEK!
GOOD HEAVENS! YOU STARTLED ME!

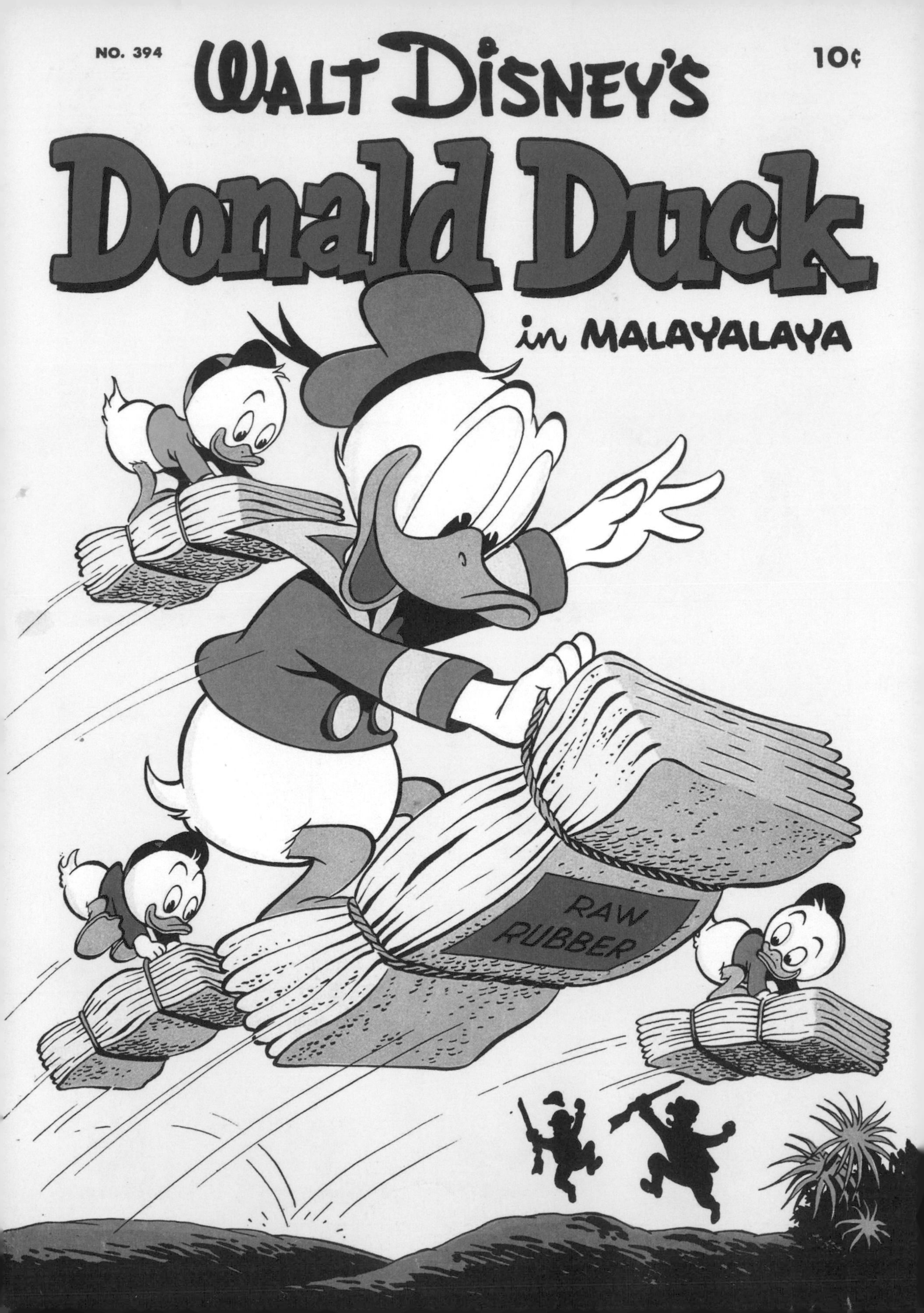
NO. 394
WALT DISNEY'S
10¢
Donald Duck
in MALAYALAYA
RAW RUBBER

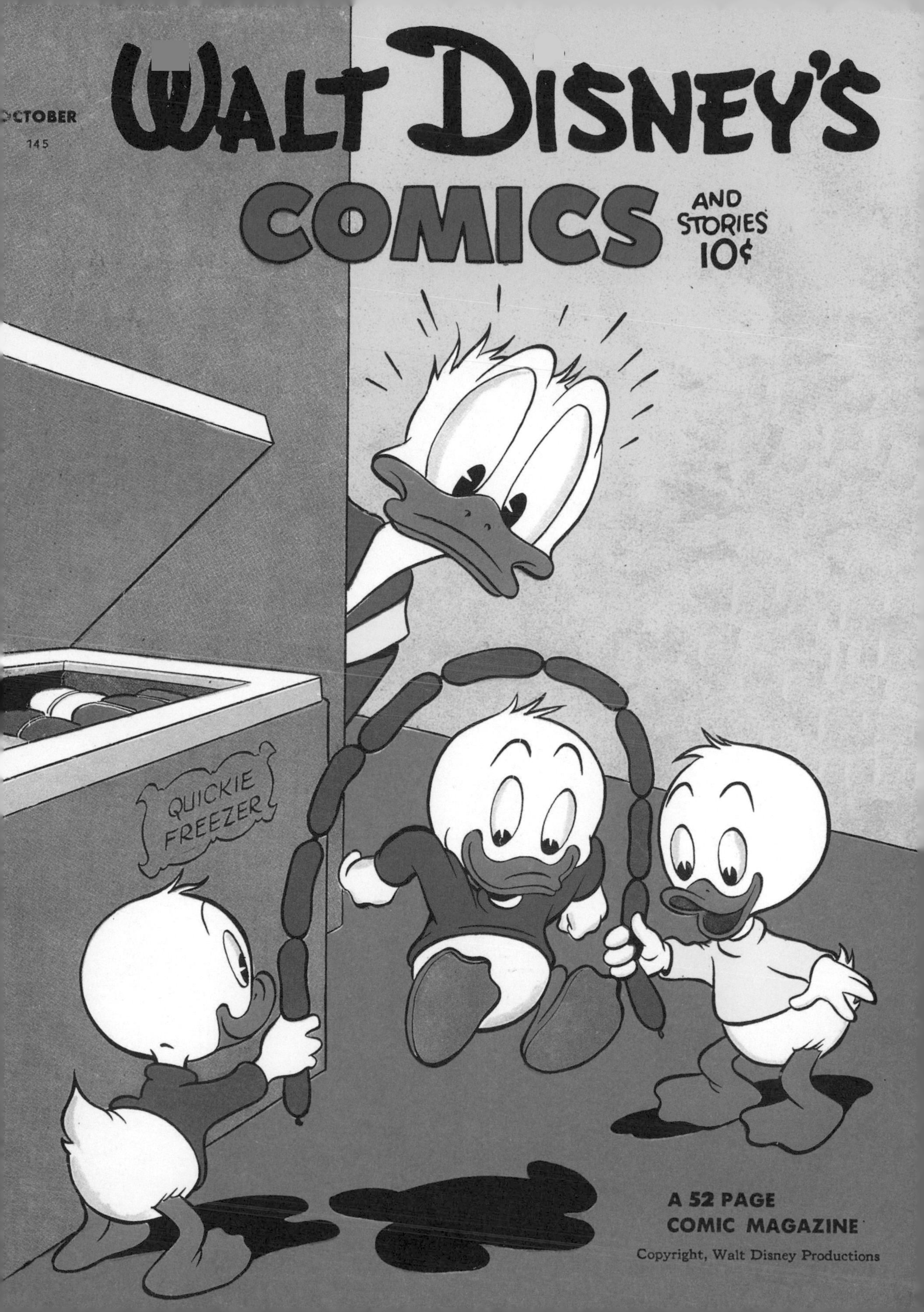

CTOBER
145
WALT DISNEY'S
COMICS
AND STORIES
10¢
QUICKIE FREEZER
A 52 PAGE
COMIC MAGAZINE
Copyright, Walt Disney Productions

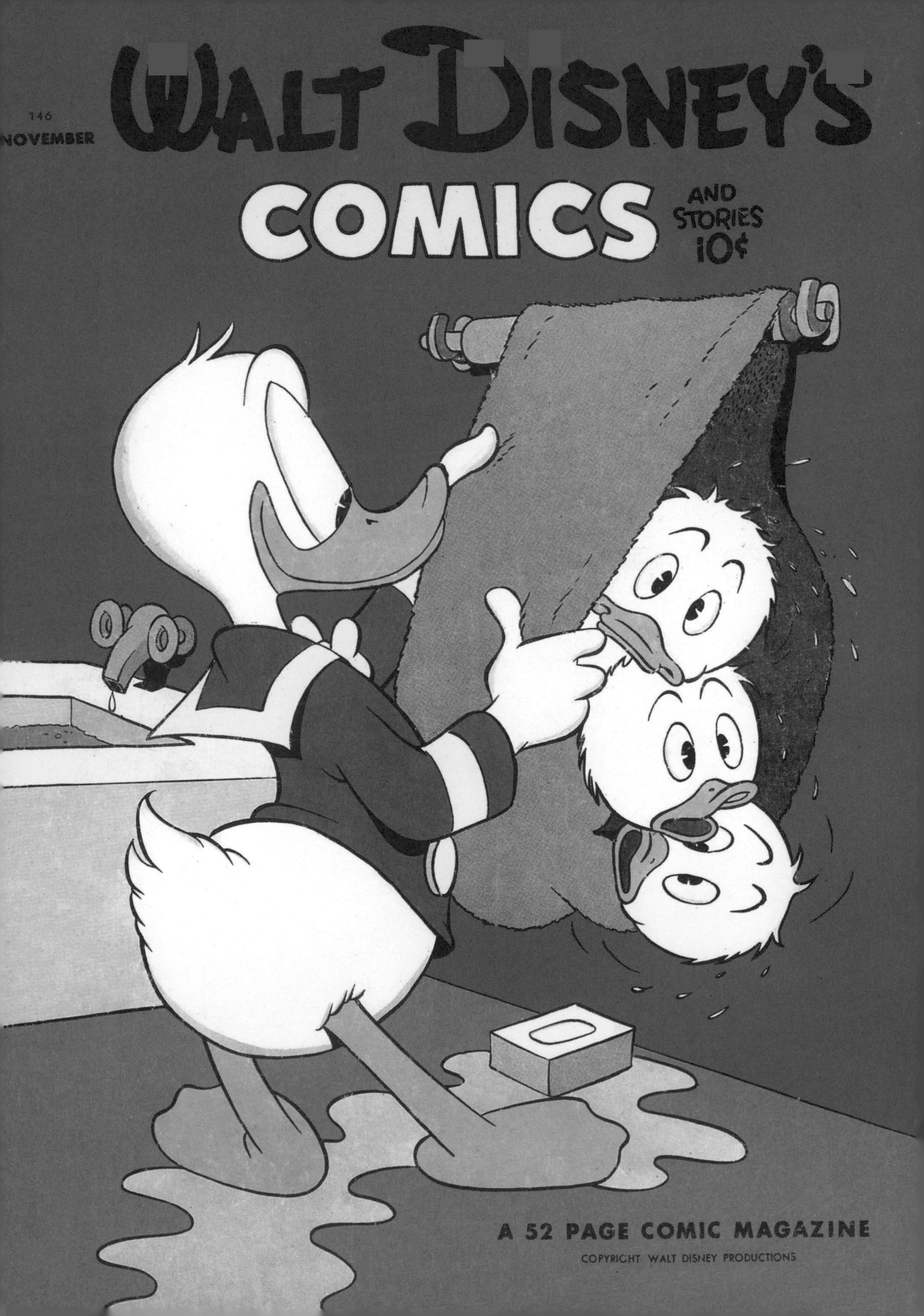
146
NOVEMBER
WALT DISNEY'S
COMICS
AND STORIES
10¢
A 52 PAGE COMIC MAGAZINE
COPYRIGHT WALT DISNEY PRODUCTIONS

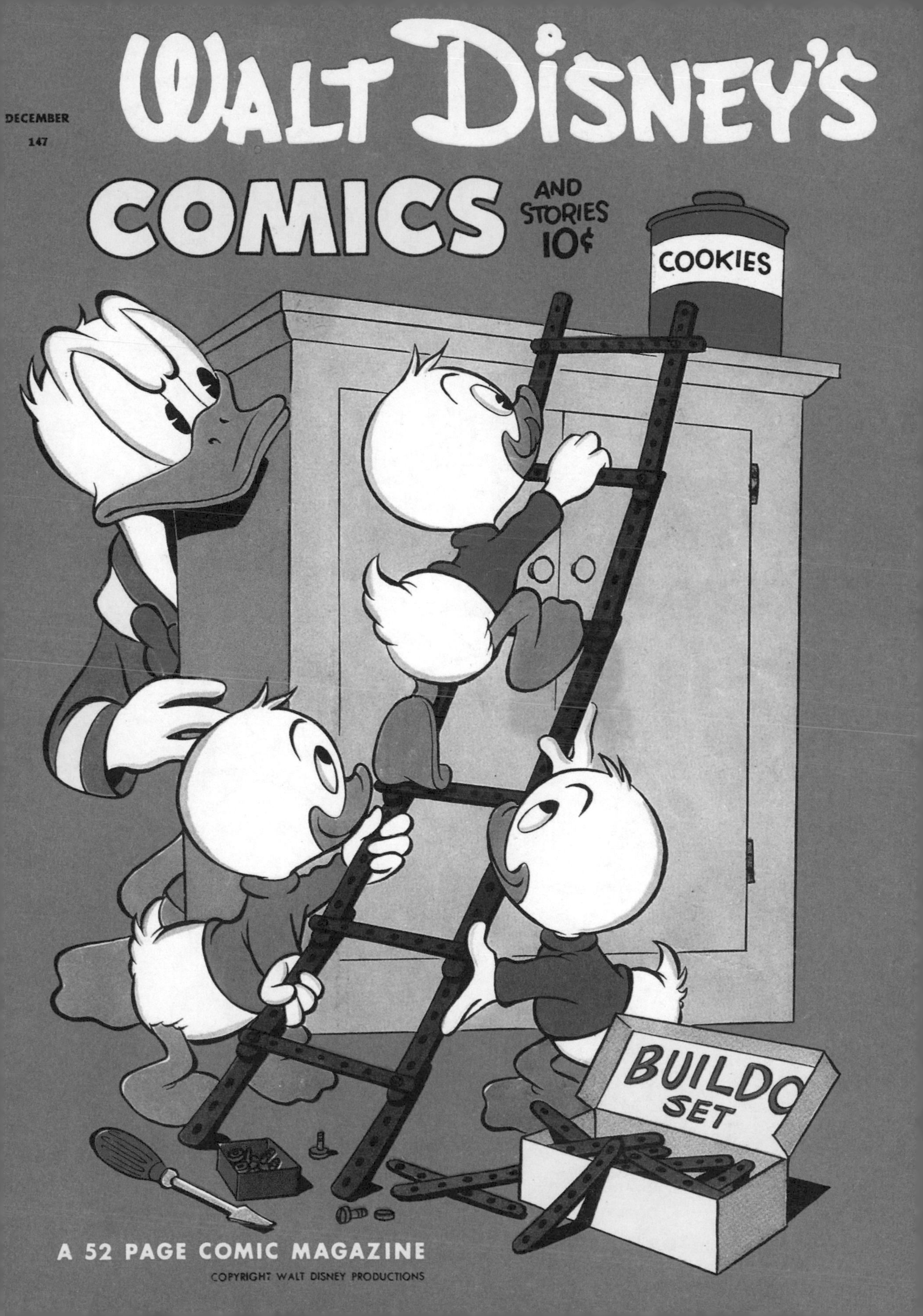
DECEMBER
147
WALT DISNEY'S
COMICS
AND STORIES
10¢
COOKIES
BUILDO SET
A 52 PAGE COMIC MAGAZINE
COPYRIGHT WALT DISNEY PRODUCTIONS

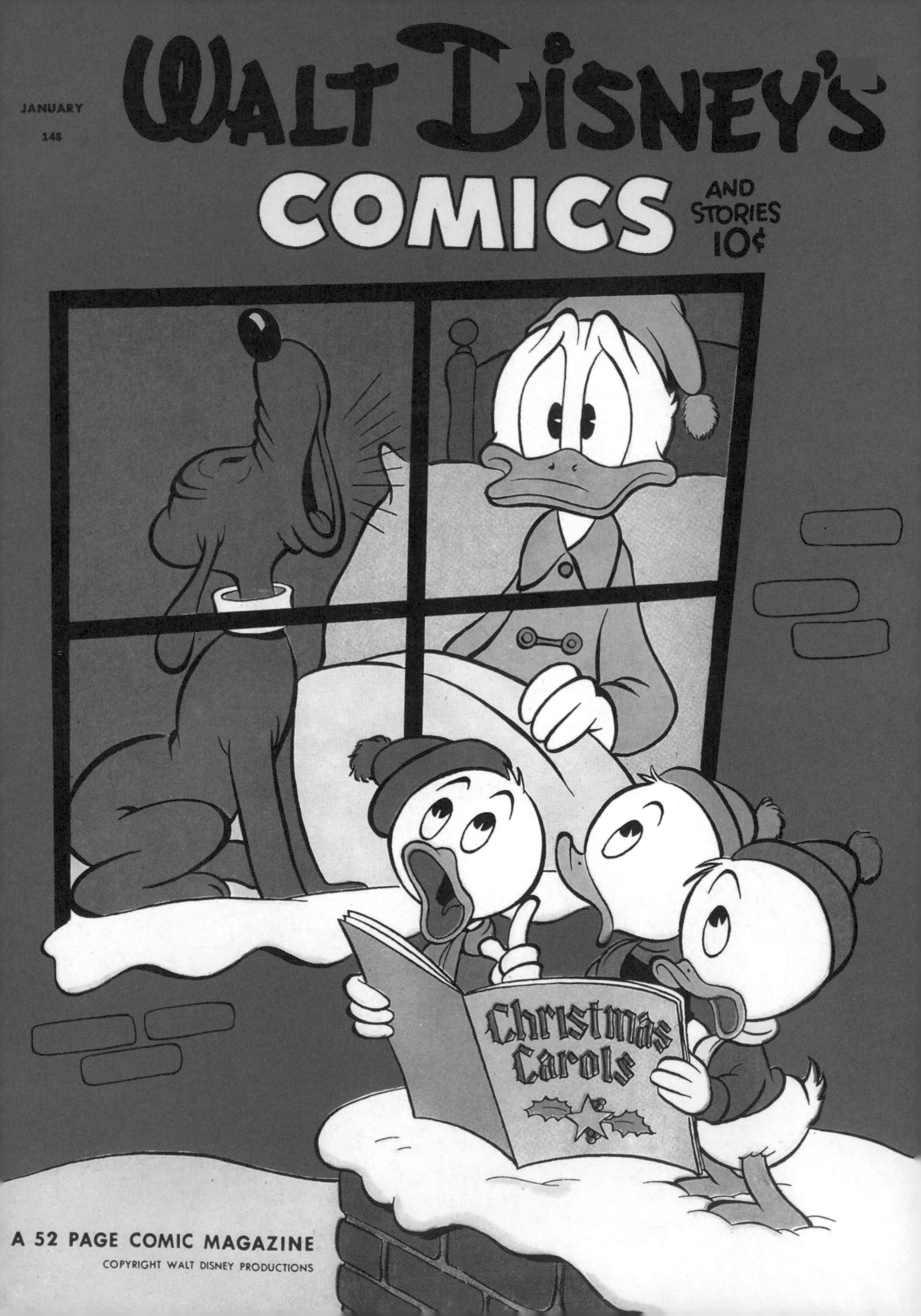
JANUARY
148
WALT DISNEY'S
COMICS
AND STORIES
10¢
Christmas Carols
A 52 PAGE COMIC MAGAZINE
COPYRIGHT WALT DISNEY PRODUCTIONS

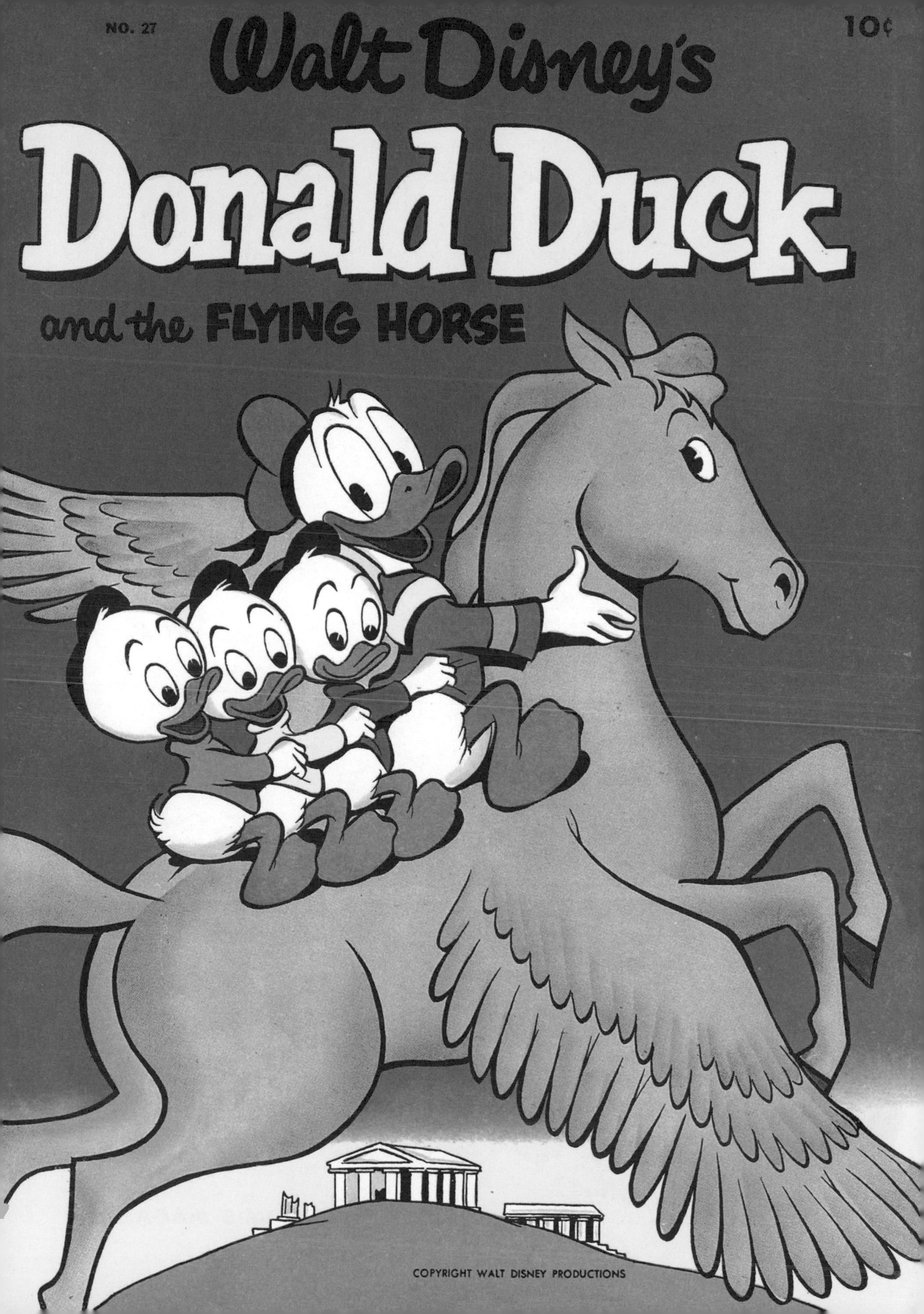

NO. 27
10¢
Walt Disney's
Donald Duck
and the FLYING HORSE
COPYRIGHT WALT DISNEY PRODUCTIONS

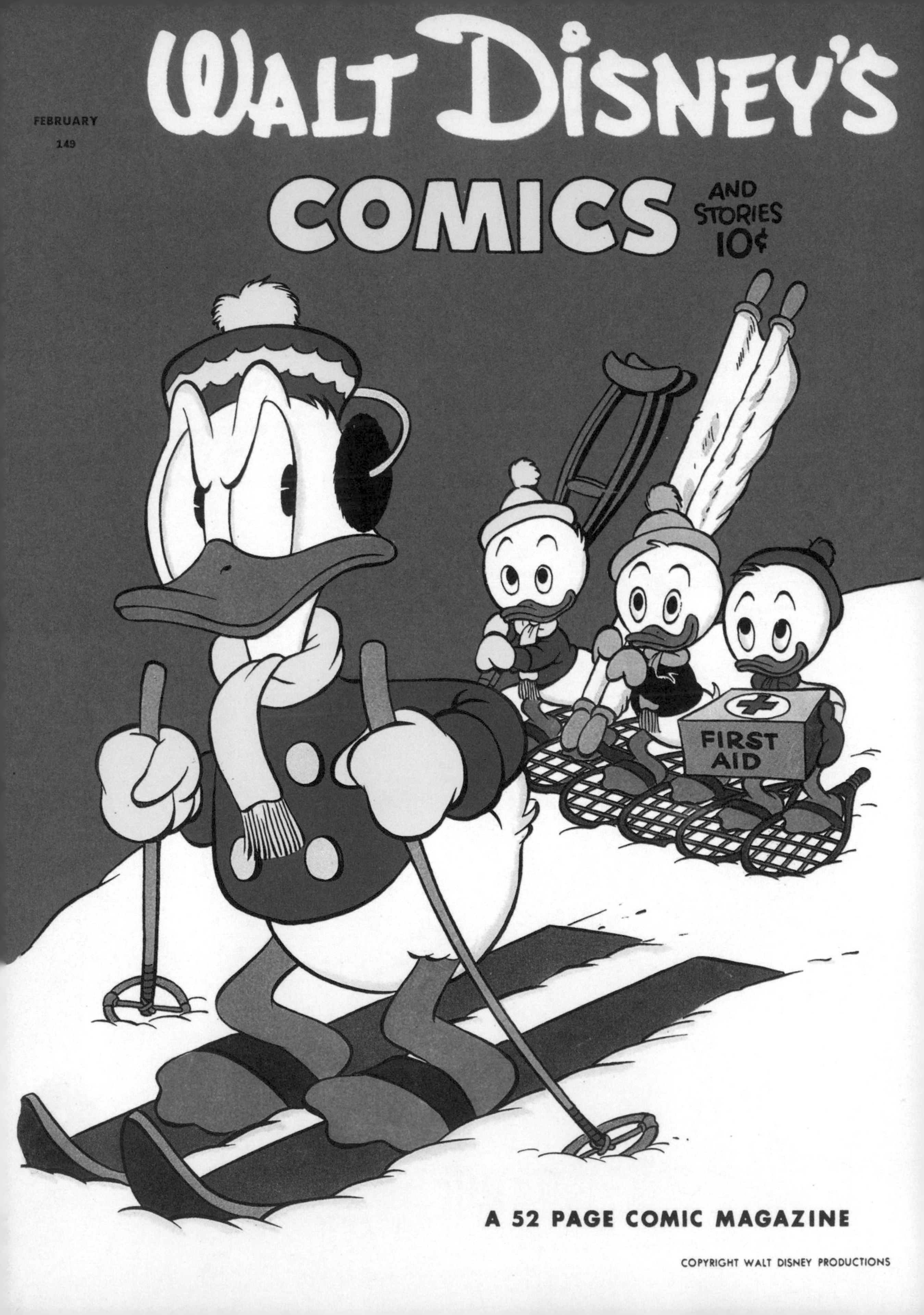
WALT DISNEY'S
FEBRUARY
149
COMICS
AND STORIES
10¢
FIRST AID
A 52 PAGE COMIC MAGAZINE
COPYRIGHT WALT DISNEY PRODUCTIONS

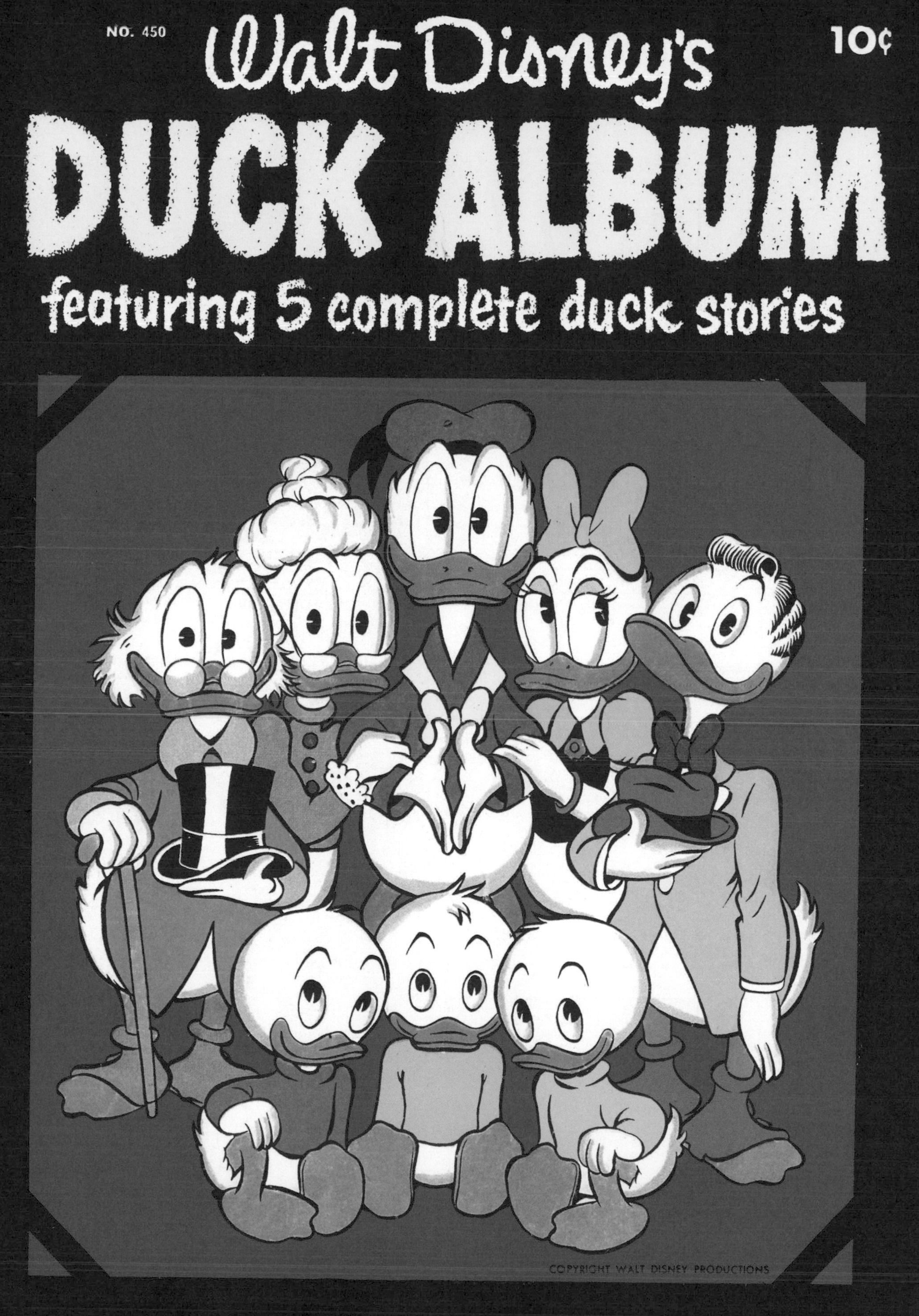
NO. 450
Walt Disney's
10¢
DUCK ALBUM
featuring 5 complete duck stories
COPYRIGHT WALT DISNEY PRODUCTIONS

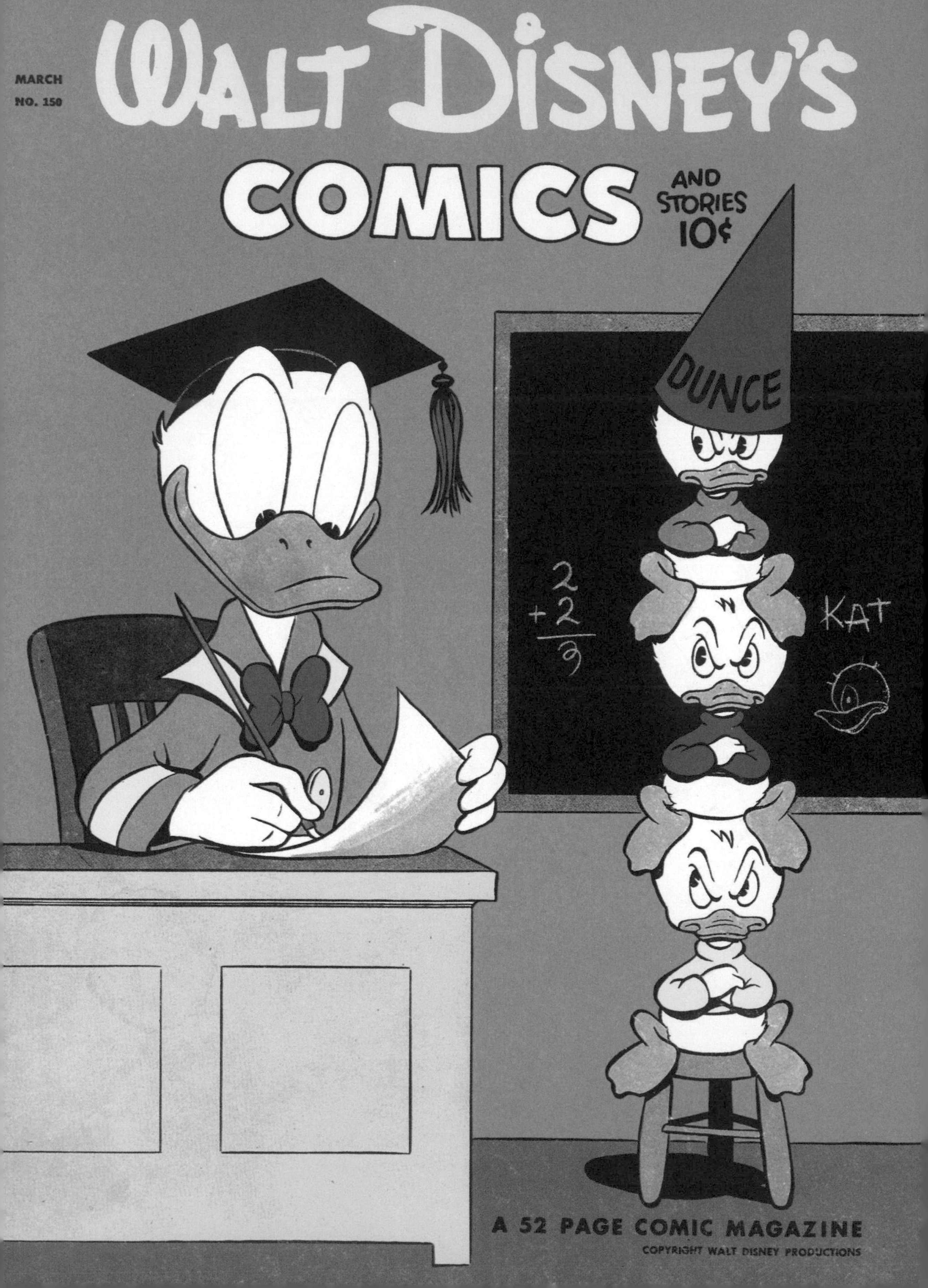
MARCH
NO. 150
WALT DISNEY'S
COMICS
AND STORIES
10¢
DUNCE
2
+2
3
KAT
A 52 PAGE COMIC MAGAZINE
COPYRIGHT WALT DISNEY PRODUCTIONS

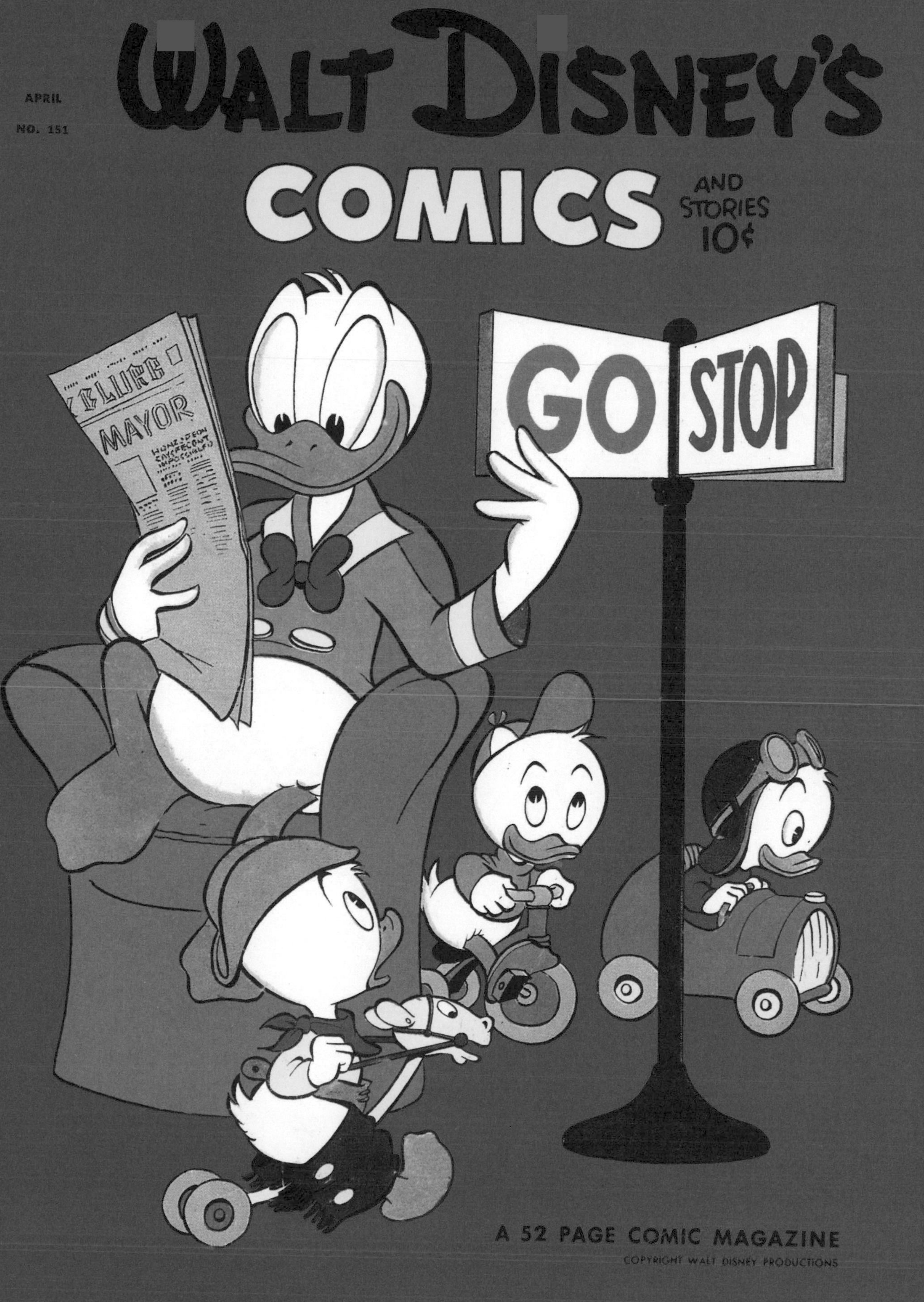

WALT DISNEY'S
APRIL
NO. 151
COMICS
AND STORIES
10¢
MAYOR
GO
STOP
A 52 PAGE COMIC MAGAZINE
COPYRIGHT WALT DISNEY PRODUCTIONS

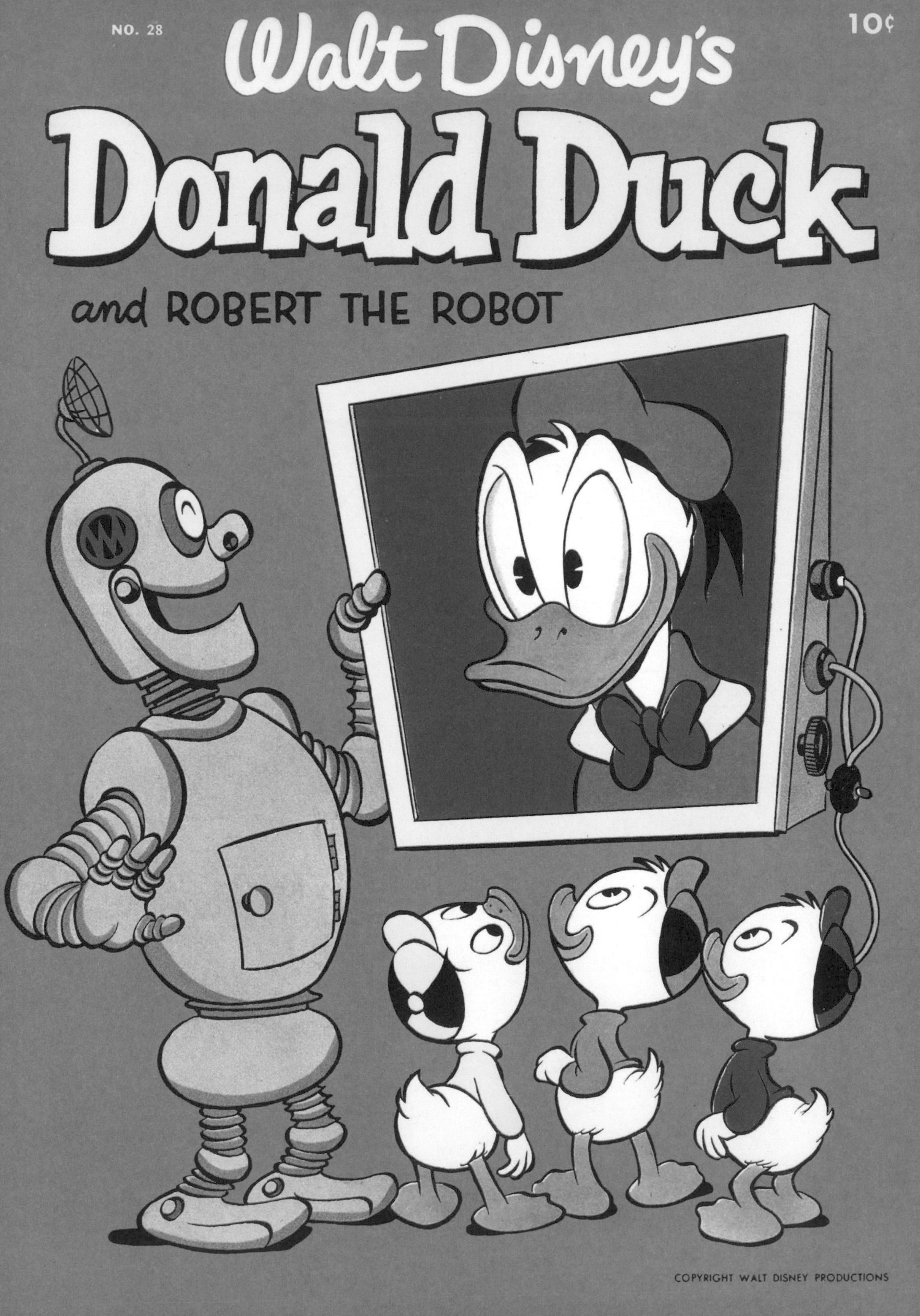
NO. 28
Walt Disney's
10¢
Donald Duck
and ROBERT THE ROBOT
COPYRIGHT WALT DISNEY PRODUCTIONS

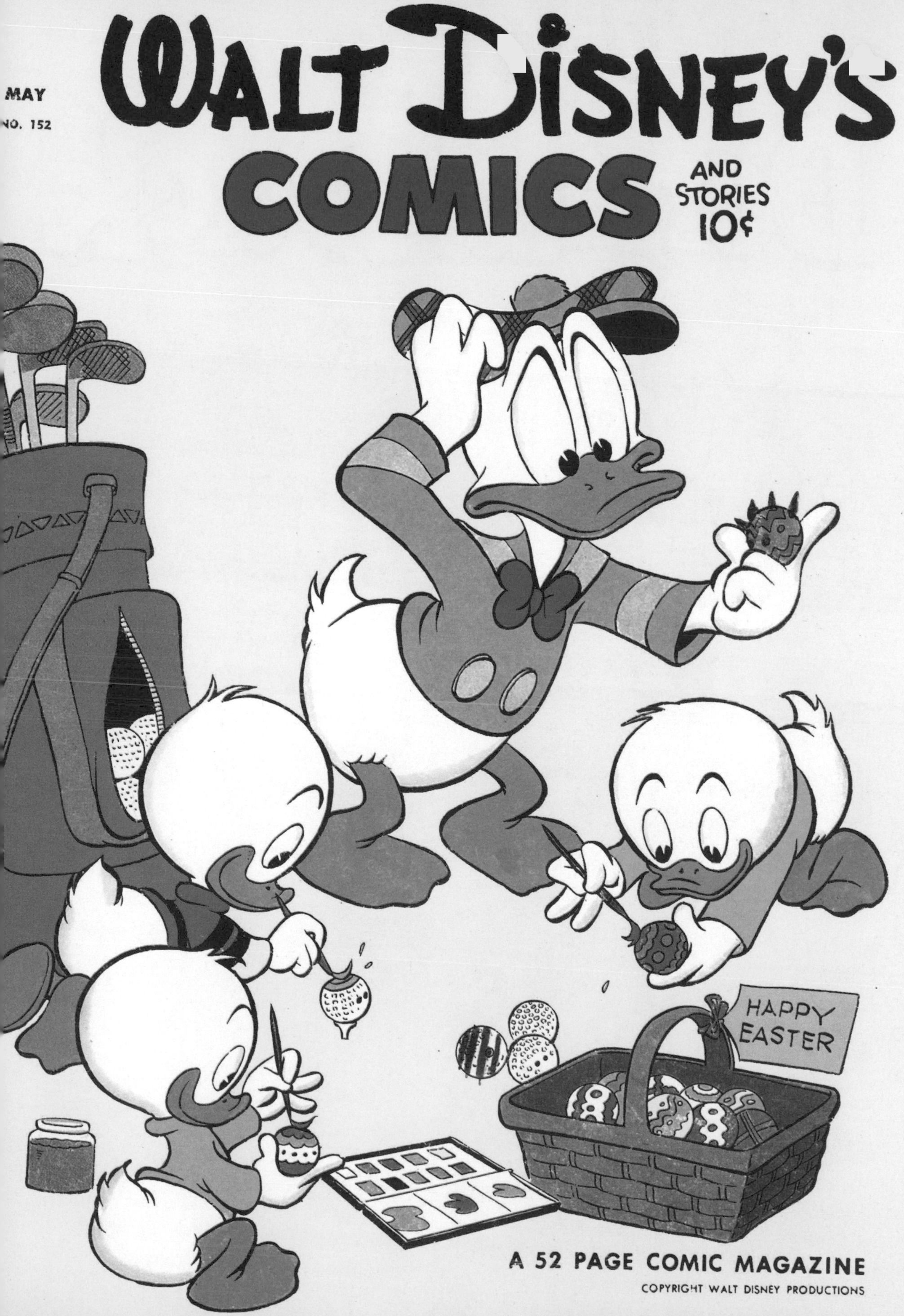
MAY
NO. 152
WALT DISNEY'S
COMICS
AND STORIES
10¢
HAPPY EASTER
A 52 PAGE COMIC MAGAZINE
COPYRIGHT WALT DISNEY PRODUCTIONS

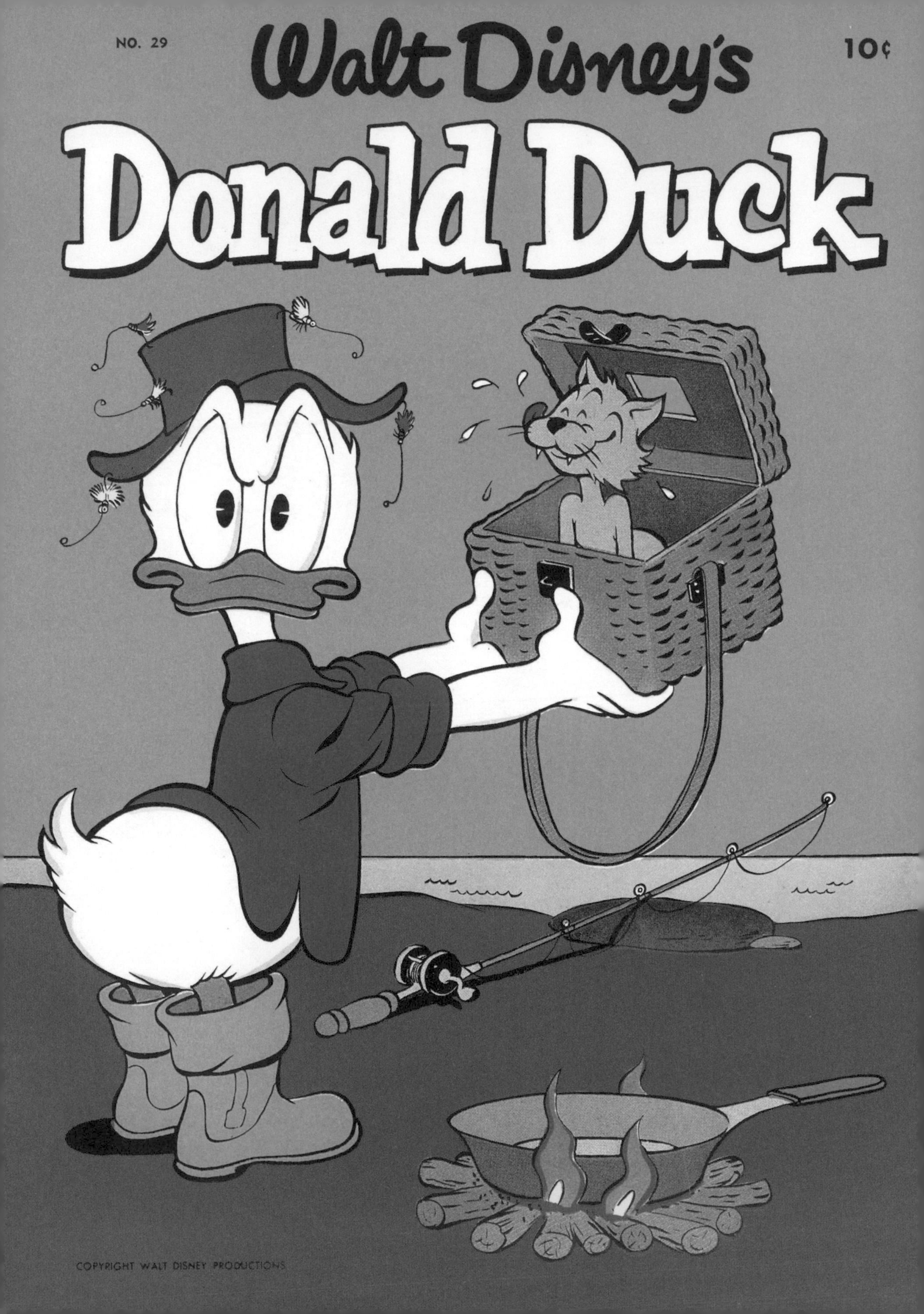
NO. 29
Walt Disney's
10¢
Donald Duck
COPYRIGHT WALT DISNEY PRODUCTIONS

WALT DISNEY'S COMICS AND STORIES

JUNE
NO. 153

10¢

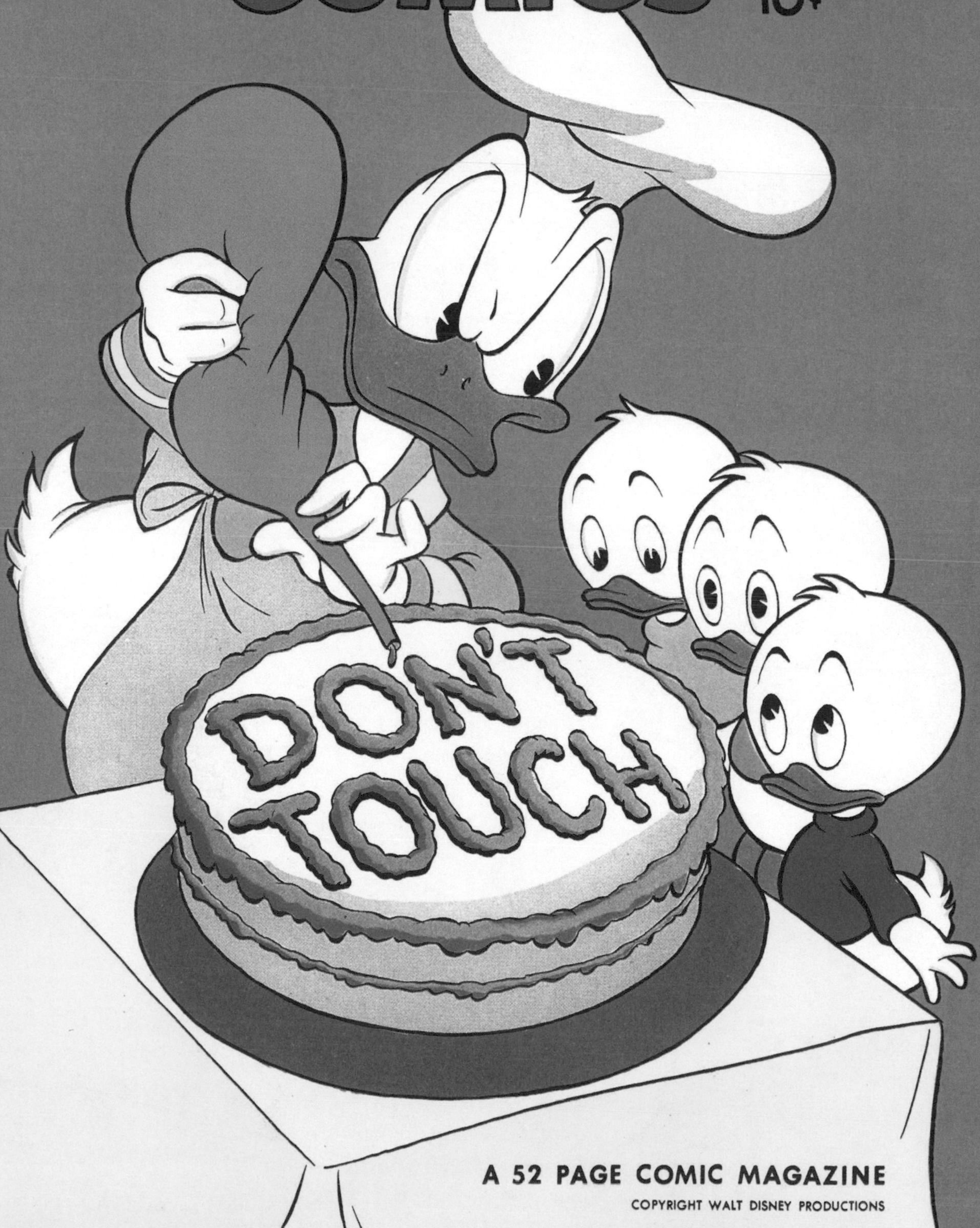
DON'T TOUCH

A 52 PAGE COMIC MAGAZINE

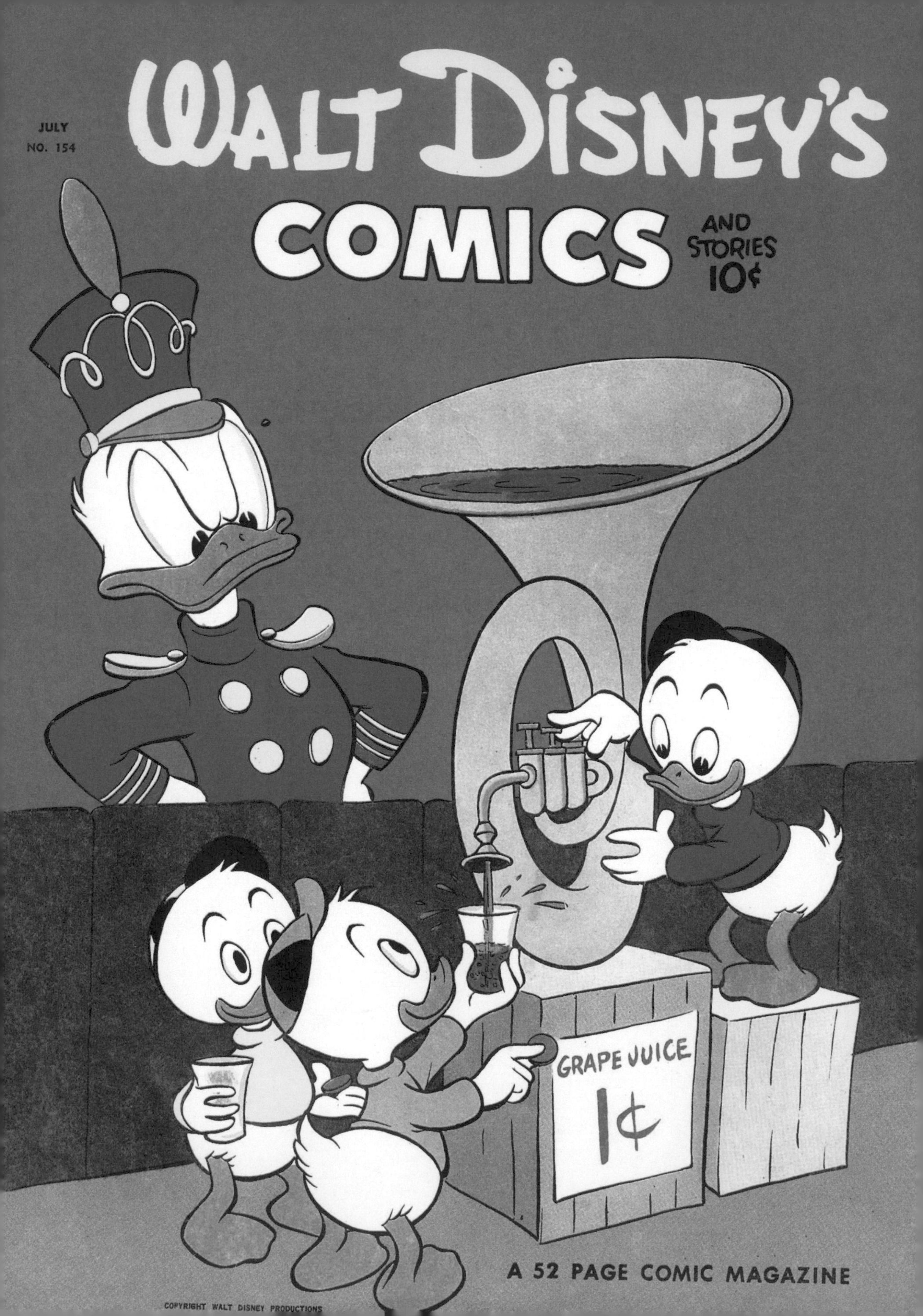

WALT DISNEY'S
JULY
NO. 154
COMICS
AND STORIES
10¢
GRAPE JUICE
1¢
A 52 PAGE COMIC MAGAZINE
COPYRIGHT WALT DISNEY PRODUCTIONS

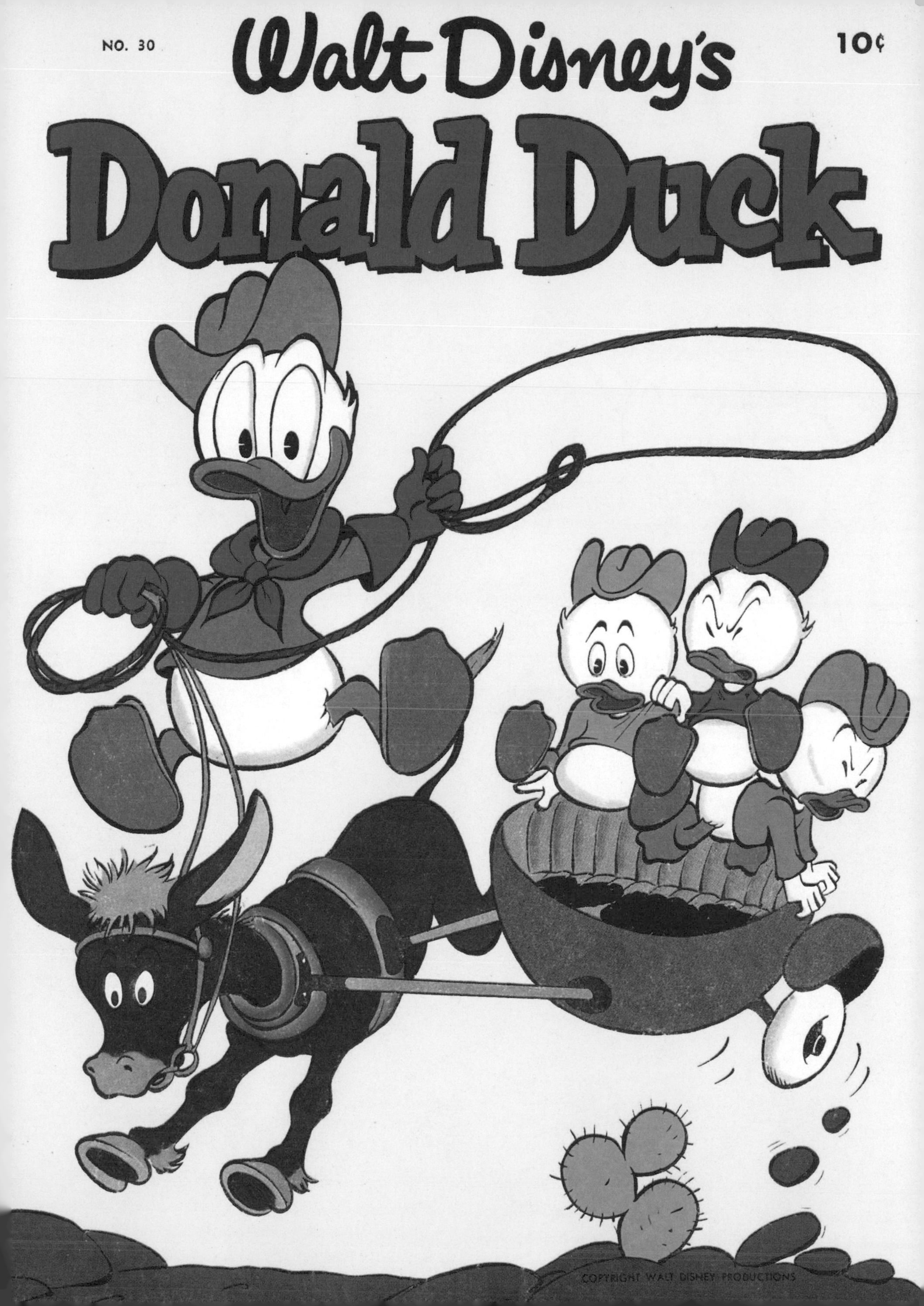

NO. 30
Walt Disney's
10¢
Donald Duck
COPYRIGHT WALT DISNEY PRODUCTIONS

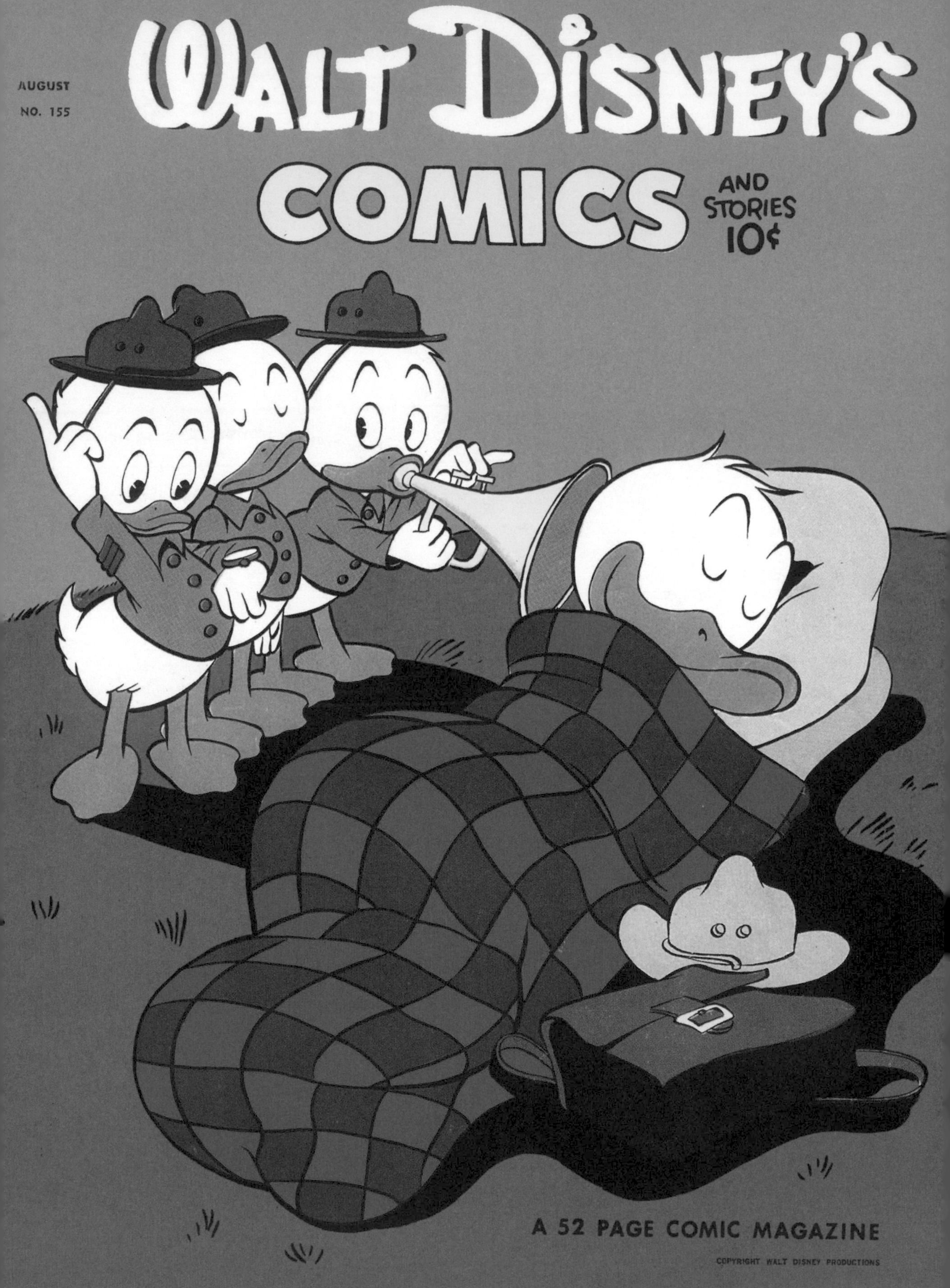
AUGUST
NO. 155
WALT DISNEY'S
COMICS
AND STORIES
10¢
A 52 PAGE COMIC MAGAZINE
COPYRIGHT WALT DISNEY PRODUCTIONS

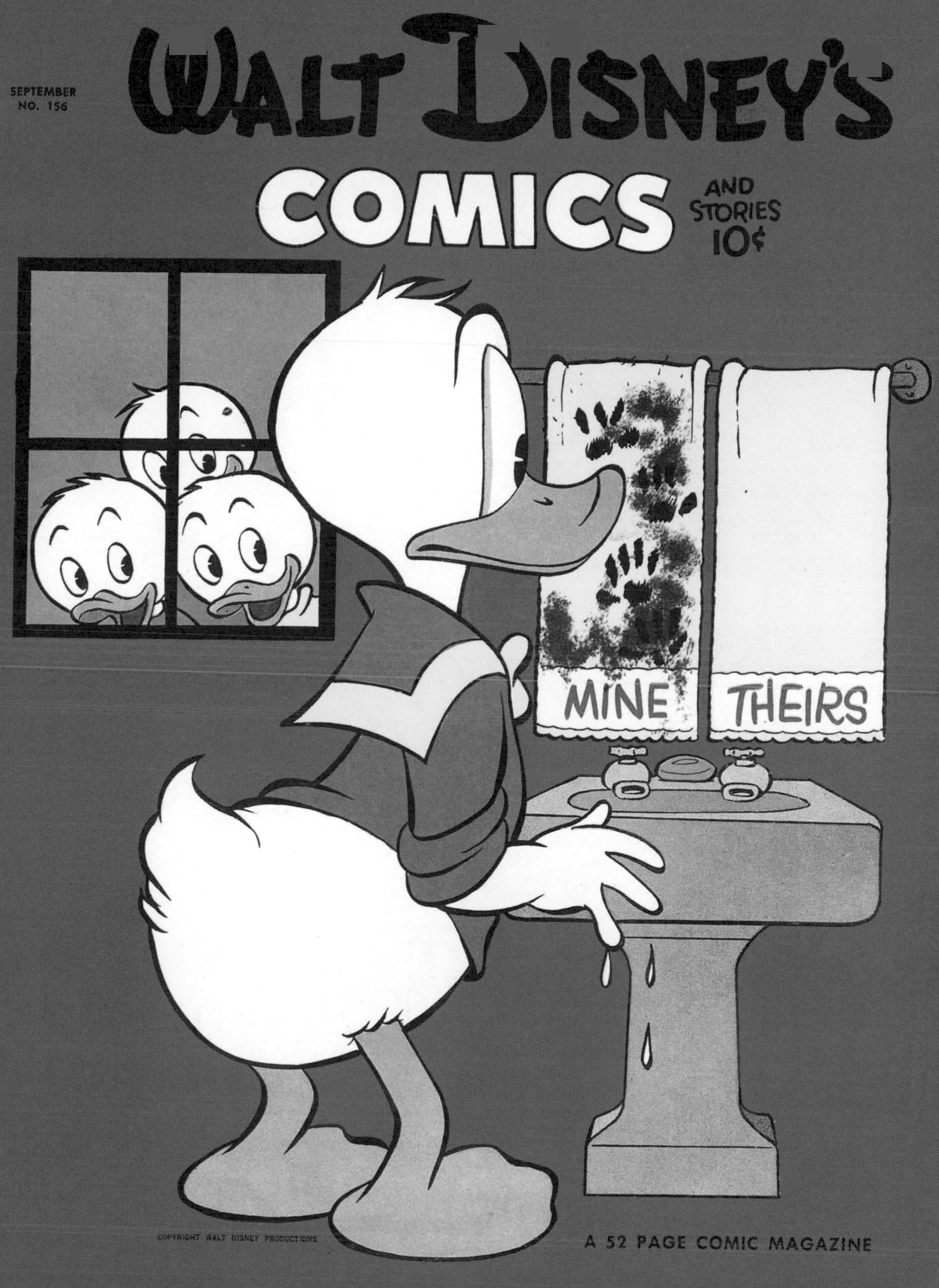
SEPTEMBER
NO. 156
WALT DISNEY'S
COMICS
AND STORIES
10¢
MINE
THEIRS
COPYRIGHT WALT DISNEY PRODUCTIONS
A 52 PAGE COMIC MAGAZINE

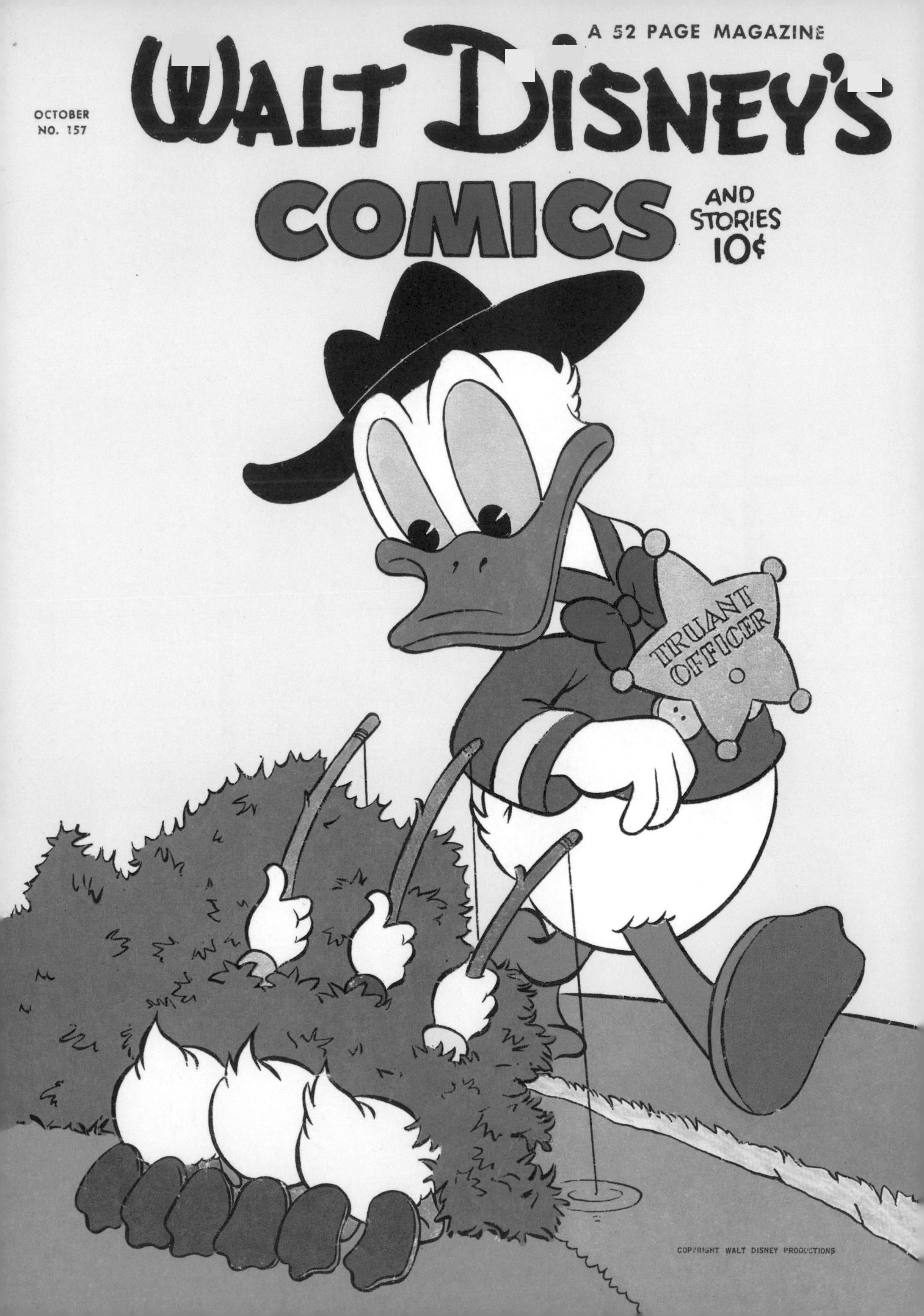
A 52 PAGE MAGAZINE
OCTOBER
NO. 157
WALT DISNEY'S
COMICS
AND STORIES
10¢
TRUANT OFFICER
COPYRIGHT WALT DISNEY PRODUCTIONS

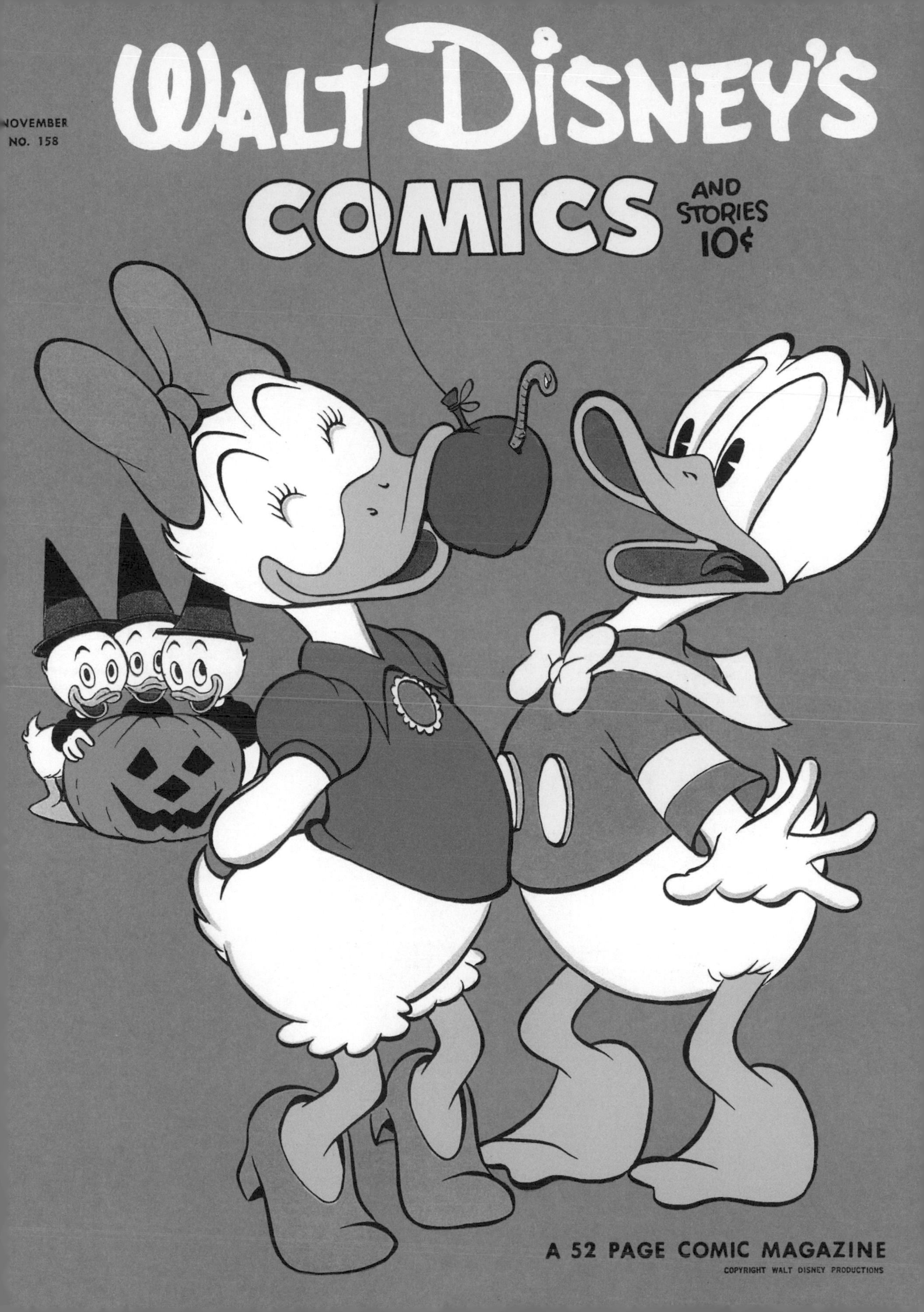

WALT DISNEY'S
NOVEMBER
NO. 158
COMICS
AND STORIES
10¢
A 52 PAGE COMIC MAGAZINE
COPYRIGHT WALT DISNEY PRODUCTIONS

NO. 26
WALT DISNEY'S
10¢
Donald Duck
in TRICK or TREAT
COPYRIGHT WALT DISNEY PRODUCTIONS

Story Notes

TRICK OR TREAT *p. 1*

By the time of "Trick or Treat," Carl Barks had been writing and drawing Donald Duck comic book adventures for ten years. Not only had he developed a storyworld and a set of supporting characters specifically for the comics, but, more importantly, he had also developed Donald's character in a way that was unique to, and better suited for, the printed page.

The unusual assignment to create a 32-page adaptation of a new Walt Disney animated cartoon short served as a striking reminder of just how far beyond his animated origins Barks's Donald had grown. The Donald of the animated *Trick or Treat* is an unrepentant jerk who doesn't think twice about pulling the nose of a visitor so hard she tumbles off his stoop or giving his nephews firecrackers with lit fuses instead of candy. The animated Donald speaks primarily in groans of frustration and cackles of victory. He is essentially a cardboard character and a foil for Hazel the Witch, who has arrived to aid the nephews in their time of need.

Of all the differences between animation and comic books, however, the most pressing with this assignment was the fact that a script for an eight-minute musical holiday cartoon did not provide nearly enough narrative material to fill a 32-page comic book feature. Saddled with a fairly bland physical comedy,

The opening to the "Trick or Treat" animated cartoon. Barks based his splash panel on this scene but his editor thought Barks's version might be too scary. His original panel has now been restored. See page 1.

Barks seized the opportunity to use the additional pages he needed to compose to add a dash of creativity and wit. The first of these, Dewey's heroic sacrifice to secure the billy goat whiskers needed for Witch Hazel's potion, was deemed acceptable by Barks's editor at Western Publishing, Alice Cobb. (Western Publishing supplied all the editorial material for Dell Comics at that time.)

Barks's second and third major additions, however, received a much cooler reception. The sequence beginning on page 16 in which Hazel disguises herself as a sexy duck in another attempt to "get candy from a skunk" (an attempt that would have been successful if not for Hazel's last-moment gloating over Donald's gullibility) was not deemed acceptable. Barks's third addition was the invention of one of his wildest and

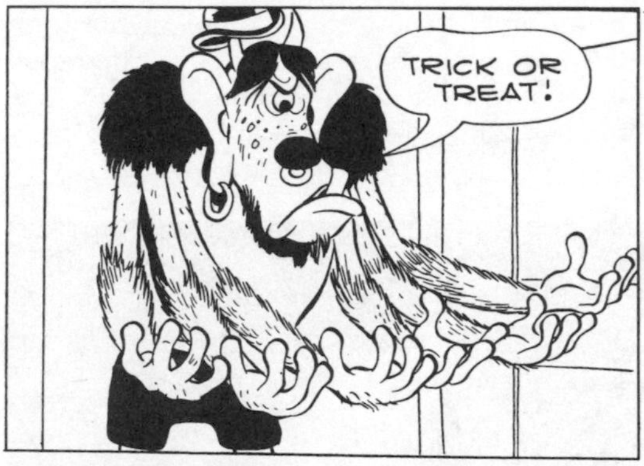
TRICK OR TREAT!

most colorful creations, Smorgasbord, a surly, psychedelic six-armed ogre, who successfully wrangles plenty of candy from Donald but succumbs to the lure of just one more piece — a stick of dynamite in disguise. Also not acceptable.

As Barks remembered, "Alice Cobb deleted the extra business and *didn't pay me* for the unwanted pages. She was that mad."

Despite the considerable success he'd had when he'd worked at Walt Disney Studios, Barks was never immune to censorship and second-guessing by his comic book editors (who, presumably, had their own ideas of what would simultaneously satisfy the Disney organization, entertain the kids, and win the approval of parents), but it is clear that Cobb's displeasure was exceptional in this case. While the removal of the sexy duck sequence can be understood in terms of good old-fashioned prudery (Barks always had much more faith in the maturity of his readers than did his bosses), the removal of Smorgasbord is harder to fathom.

Indeed, it only makes sense when put into the context of the very first cut made to Barks's story: the removal of the opening half-page splash with its ominous graveyard looming in the foreground. In Barks's original version, restored here, that panel serves as a visual mirror to the half-page panel that concludes the story and in which the spooky landscape is transformed into a festive holiday scene thanks to the interventions of Witch Hazel.

Despite its close resemblance to the opening shot in the cartoon, the splash panel that Barks initially drew was evidently too gothic, too creepy — in other words, too close to the horror comics that were then bringing increasingly negative attention to the comic book industry. Although the Comics Code, which would essentially ban horror comics for a generation was still two years away, Dell/Western were already trying to put as much distance as possible between themselves and the purveyors of such fare. (Barks swapped out that single half-page opening panel for a one-and-a-half-page sequence that moved the bottom half of the original page 1 to the bottom half of page 2. See page 417 for details.)

Happily, here we have "Trick or Treat" restored as Barks intended, Smorgie the Bad included. And the comic book and animated versions of the story allow us to see clearly, as Barks himself understood in 1952, the growing differences between his Donald and the mercurial onscreen cartoon star. As it would happen, this was to be Barks's last feature-length story for *Donald Duck*. He shifted his focus to Uncle Scrooge — a character he had created and over which he rightly imagined he might exercise more control.

— JARED GARDNER

Notes on the restoration: When this story was originally restored in November 1986 as part of Another Rainbow's Carl Barks Library project, it was the culmination of years of research to locate the missing pages and re-assemble the story. In the end, only one panel could not be found (the last panel on page 27), so the restorers re-created it by using Barks figures from elsewhere in the story. We have elected to follow their lead in this volume, still hopeful that the missing panel may yet turn up one day. Additionally, Marie Severin was given the assignment to color the restored version of the story and we have likewise been guided by her work in coloring "Trick or Treat" for this volume.

HOBBLIN' GOBLINS *p. 33*

Maybe there was a goblin at Western's California office in 1952, for it was not a good year for Carl Barks. He had long enjoyed creative freedom with the Ducks, but now, in the span of just a few months, he faced the heaviest editorial scrutiny of his career. The infamous "golden apples" 10-pager was shelved, five pages were censored from "Back to the Klondike" for violence and innuendo (*Walt Disney's Uncle Scrooge: "Only a Poor Old Man,"* volume 12 in this series), and a whopping nine pages were cut from "Trick or Treat" to make it a strict adaptation of the animated cartoon.

To add insult to injury, Barks had to come up with replacement stories ("Somethin' Fishy Here" and "Hobblin' Goblins") to fill out the affected issues, and was left unpaid for

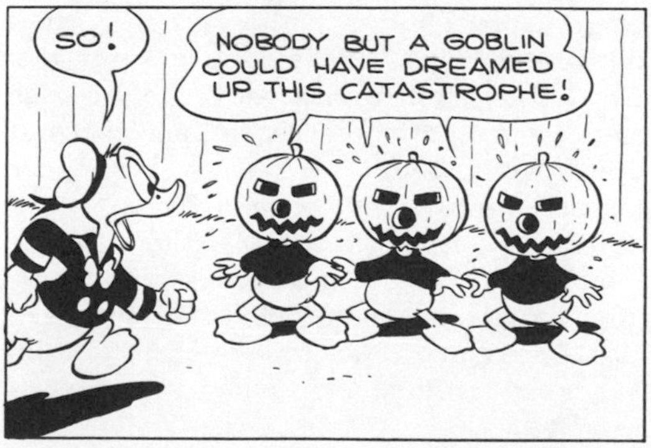
SO!
NOBODY BUT A GOBLIN COULD HAVE DREAMED UP THIS CATASTROPHE!

14 pages. "Nobody but a goblin could have dreamed up this catastrophe!"

Barks took fewer chances as a result, and the evidence shows up as early as "Hobblin' Goblins." It reads just like one of Barks's standard, crisp 10-pagers, and thus, the implausibility of Gyro Gearloose's Goblin Foiler foiling Huey, Dewey, and Louie at every turn becomes entirely plausible. Yet the nephews' star billing is an omen of things to come.

In the following years, the kids' increasing presence would keep Donald (and Barks) on a leash of sorts for fear of stirring the Western brass's ire with "inappropriate" content. It's almost as if Barks did it to have the excuse, "Be on your best behavior, kids are here!" Rowdiness would be toned down and juvenility amped up, but they're in equal measure here and the balance works.

Certainly the idea of dancing for two hours with a gaggle of girls is far more nightmarish to a little boy than an outing with Smorgie the Bad!

— THAD KOMOROWSKI

THE HYPNO-GUN *p. 43*

When he finds Huey, Dewey, and Louie playing with a toy gun that spins a hypnosis spiral (an actual novelty item of the early 1900s, devised to facilitate putting people into hypnotic trances), Donald doesn't realize the kids are only pretending to be hypnotized. He admonishes his nephews, claiming hypnosis is dangerous and someone with a gullible mind would never recover.

Muttering about factories that make such toys, Donald is about to toss the device into the river when he decides to try it out for himself. He sets out to hypnotize his Uncle Scrooge into giving him money. Going along with the gag, Scrooge hands his nephew a sack of cash. Then, pretending to be "unhypnotized," he borrows the toy and (*Bing!*) actually hypnotizes Donald.

Scrooge proceeds to hypnotize his nephew into believing himself to be the toughest bill collector that ever lived. Armed with the toy hypno-gun, the world's toughest bill collector encounters the world's toughest deadbeat, who grabs the hypno-gun and (*Bing!*) makes Donald believe he's a tiny harmless gopher.

But then the deadbeat decides to make a monkey out of Donald by (*Bing!*) turning him into a bill-collecting gorilla. That's when Donald gets his revenge, gives the deadbeat a sound thrashing, and collects the outstanding one dollar for Uncle Scrooge.

Back at the money bin, and still thinking he's a gorilla, Donald gives Scrooge the dollar. Donald appears dangerous, so (*Bing!*) Scrooge unhypnotizes the toughest bill collector that ever lived.

Later, the kids meet up with Donald, who is carrying the bag of money Scrooge gave him for collecting the dollar from the world's toughest deadbeat.

"Which just goes to show," Donald warns his nephews, what a toy like this hypno-gun "will do to someone with a *gullible mind!*"

And he tosses the hypno-gun into the drink.

— JOSEPH COWLES

OMELET *p. 53*

Donald, Daisy, Huey, Dewey, and Louie are enjoying a peaceful drive through the countryside when they come to the small settlement of Omelet. The kids become alarmed that their uncle plans to drive through the town; he tells them there's no way around but not to worry as he brought disguises so they won't be recognized. Nevertheless, the boys remain nervous.

Daisy is puzzled, wanting to know what is going on and why a town of all-new buildings in such a lovely sunny spot has such an odd name. Donald proceeds to narrate the sad details of how sleepy little Pleasant Valley came to be named "Omelet." It's a tragic tale packed with gag upon gag of misfortunes that uproariously escalate, escalate, and escalate before ending in a scrambled disaster.

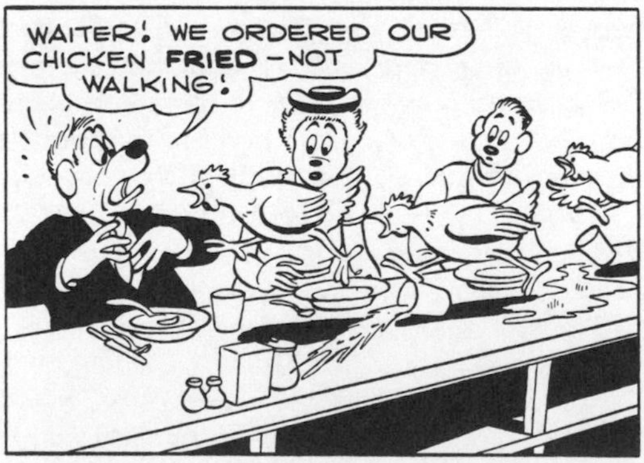
WAITER! WE ORDERED OUR CHICKEN FRIED—NOT WALKING!

A few years before concocting this wild tale of feathers, eggs, chickens, and chaos, Carl Barks and his wife had acquired several acres of ranch land in California's peaceful San Jacinto Valley. Soon thereafter, Barks resigned his position in the story department of Walt Disney Studios to retire from the frenetic world of movie-making, hoping to enjoy life as a gentleman chicken rancher, planning to support himself by wholesaling fresh eggs and chickens to local markets and selling feathers to bedding manufacturers.

Barks's personal chicken ranching adventures did not fare well, but his experiences (slightly exaggerated) led to this utterly nonsensical, yet totally believable, impossibly outrageous mirthful tale of a family of ducks raising ten thousand chickens, and how their mismanagement brings delightful mayhem and disaster to a quiet little community (which is strikingly similar to old San Jacinto).

— JOSEPH COWLES

A CHARITABLE CHORE *p. 63*

No good deed goes unpunished. Donald should know this old saying (ascribed to Oscar Wilde), when he joins Daisy's initiative to provide a free Thanksgiving dinner for a needy person whose name is drawn at random from a box. Donald picks the name of his cousin Gladstone, who qualifies for the program because he is permanently unemployed (but is certainly not hurting because his inexhaustible good luck provides him with everything he needs). Donald tries to skip out on offering Gladstone a meal, but Gladstone threatens to tell the press that Donald refuses to feed a starving man.

Donald, having made plans to travel to Florida with his nephews to get out of his commitment, winds up being forced to take Gladstone along. Gladstone chooses a room in a luxurious hotel and "generously" spends Donald's money. The Ducks can't stand him any more, and they strand their tormentor on a tiny island in the middle of a swamp. Gladstone escapes, returns to the hotel, and stuffs himself with so much turkey that he has to be hospitalized.

Donald, financially ruined by paying for Gladstone's medical care (in addition to the hotel bill), tells Daisy to put his own name on the list of needy people.

Barks's stories, like all classics, are timeless, and "A Charitable Chore," with its satirical wit, is more contemporary now than it was in 1952 when it was first published. In the Western World (especially in Europe), it is a common trope that undeserving people benefit from welfare at the expense of the really needy. The fear is that, in an age of economic crisis, the high demand for welfare assistance can impoverish middle-class citizens like Donald.

Donald should know he can't win with Gladstone (at least in a 10-pager like this; in longer stories, he sometimes gets even with his cousin, one of Barks's most despised creations), but he keeps on trying. Had he just provided the Thanksgiving dinner he promised, he would have saved a lot of money (but there would have been no story).

In the end, Donald actually deserves his comeuppance, not just for his ridiculous schemes to get out of his promise, but for his hypocrisy, too: it's quite clear he decides to offer a meal only to impress Daisy, who is in charge of the charity (a fact that Gladstone also knows, which is why his threat to embarrass Donald in the media is so effective). As is evident in other Barks stories, charity is, after all, a public relations affair.

— STEFANO PRIARONE

TURKEY WITH ALL THE SCHEMINGS *p. 73*

This bit of Christmas cheer is Carl Barks at his most characteristic and uncharacteristic. The sublime opening with Donald running his annual marathon of Christmas obligations is the epitome of cynical Barks. No hint of yuletide warmth here, or elsewhere in the story — just bills to pay and material possessions to dole out.

Now "flat-busted broke" and left with only a can of beans for himself, Donald schemes to have Scrooge pay for his Christmas repast by posing as a tycoon who'll only talk business over sumptuous meals. In other stories, Donald routinely tries to get Scrooge to foot a bill, and there is always a gleam in Scrooge's eye that says he knows exactly what's going on. In "Turkey With All the Schemings," Scrooge is genuinely bamboozled by Donald's disguise — even when Donald eats his phony mustache! The unusual dynamic unavoidably recalls other chiseling funny animals, The Fox and the Crow being the most obvious example. (One almost expects Donald to shout "Foxie!" across the table ...)

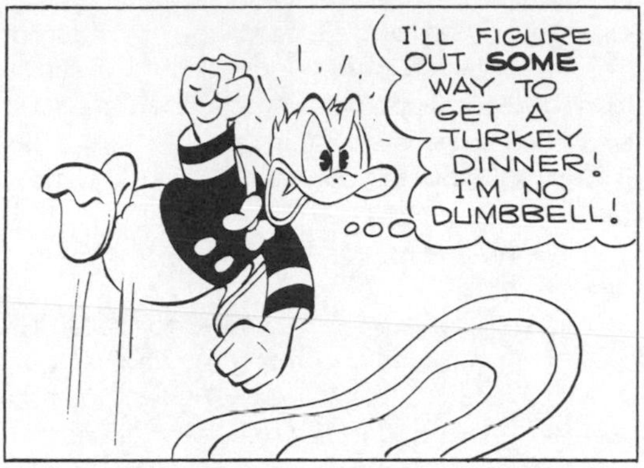
I'LL FIGURE OUT **SOME** WAY TO GET A TURKEY DINNER! I'M NO DUMBBELL!

This unlikely conflict would've fallen flat in a lesser writer's hands. Here, in Carl Barks's Golden Age, it's one of the funniest Donald/Scrooge encounters and completely in character. In his hunger, it never occurs to Donald that Scrooge might — just might — be too cheap to pay his dinner guest's bill, regardless of whatever big business deal is at stake.

When Donald is exposed, Scrooge is riled enough to use his money as a weapon. He plops down a million bucks to buy the Ritz simply so he can force "Señor Petrolio de Balonio de Donald Ducko" to wash dishes in his kitchen straight through New Year's as punishment for his scam. A standard Barks plotline may have taken a holiday, but Barks's Ducks are Barks's Ducks year-round.

— THAD KOMOROWSKI

FLIP DECISION *p. 83*

On the first page of "Flip Decision" Donald is converted to the philosophy of Flipism when he hears an old-fashioned medicine-show spiel in a Duckburg tent and buys a one-dollar Flipism manual from the fast-talking Professor Batty. On page 2, Donald starts to speak in charming and unexpected rhymes — which stop abruptly at the bottom of page 3 — while the ducks travel far from Duckburg using the principles of Flipism as their only guide. After an encounter with a non-flipping unflappable house mover, the ducks are forced to drive through a mudhole they had avoided earlier. They end up cold, wet, and confronted by a tangle of lanes, ramps, and impossible-to-follow road signs, part of the rapidly expanding California State Highway System (familiar even to people outside of California from Jack Benny's freeway jokes on his radio and TV shows every Sunday evening). This is Barksian social commentary at its most barbed and topical.

Donald is hauled before an irascible wise-old-owl judge who fines him fifty dollars — a formidable amount in 1953 — "for letting a dime do your thinking for you!" and sets off in a foul mood to track down Professor Batty. Instead, he encounters Daisy, who is visiting her sister and about to take her three nieces to see *Gore in the Gully*, the very film Donald's nephews wanted to see at the beginning of "Flip Decision."

Everything ends with balance and precision. Daisy gets dressed up in her fur-collared coat, fur muff, and flower-trimmed hat. April, May, and June — perfect little ladies in their debut comics appearance — accompany the delighted Huey, Dewey, and Louie. Only Donald, who has just been given a royal dressing-down, looks a bit overwhelmed as he and Daisy head up the procession.

Meanwhile, Professor Batty is hiding out across the street, ready to skip town and thinking nervously about the mayhem he saw in Donald's eyes.

— BILL MASON

MY LUCKY VALENTINE *p. 93*

Carl Barks never forgot that his primary professional obligation was to entertain children. But that requirement scarcely prevented him from additionally broaching adult concerns and addressing mature sensibilities. Case in point: "My Lucky Valentine."

After establishing the two separate challenges for the nephews and Donald, Barks follows the latter and not just because he's the titular character. Although children might more readily identify and empathize with the nephews and their pursuits, Donald's conflicts remain the potentially richer and more resonant, dealing as they do with responsibility, principle, and confounding jealousy.

Donald's struggles with the elements and his own shortcomings shift from morality play to farce through consummate comedic rendering, impeccable timing, and dynamic choreography. Early and late we also have the jokiness of the Woodchuck titles. Young readers may get a laugh out of terms like "commandants" and "chevaliers," words as mysterious as they are funny sounding. "Rear admirals" — ha-ha! Adults of that time might have been amused by the scouts' initial status of ten-star generals, making each twice the rank achieved by then-President Eisenhower during the not-so-distant World War II.

It's also this profusion of awards that Donald blames for his concluding blow-up. A literal-minded child might accept that explanation, especially primed by the last

QUIET! WHO KNOWS BUT WHAT FLIPISM MAY LEAD US TO GREAT ADVENTURE, RICHES, OR EVEN FAME!
LOOKS LIKE IT'S LED US INTO A MUDHOLE!
KEEP YOUR CHIN UP!

page's heaping up of convoluted honoraria. But the adult will recognize it as merely a convenient dodge, a sop that is bandaging a different wound entirely. After his physical ordeal and ethical quandary, Donald must yet endure the praise Daisy lavishes on Gladstone for the gander's relatively trifling exertion. Donald can only seethe, mutter, and flee in the face of this stinging demonstration of an indifferent world's utter lack of fairness.

True cause and effect remain more acutely pitched to experienced grown-ups than undaunted children. Donald does not disclose to the ducklings — their hat tails freshly repositioned to signify their recent successes — the real reason for his discontent. It wouldn't be funny.

— RICH KREINER

THE EASTER ELECTION *p. 103*

For the guy who always "gets all the breaks," Gladstone Gander exhibits contempt more than dumb luck in "Easter Election." The Gladstone Luck is quite inactive here, bringing to mind those earlier stories in which Barks hadn't established the luck angle and Gladstone was simply a smarmy foil for Donald. For once, the pest doesn't mind working (he actually expends the effort to dye five dozen eggs and hand-letter personal insults on them), so long as it puts him ahead of Donald in the race to become Grand Marshal in the Duckburg Easter Parade.

Save for one moment where Donald attempts to give Gladstone his comeuppance for a dirty trick, our hero is positively passive compared to Gladstone's vindictiveness throughout the story. In light of other stories in which the cousins' personalities are in constant conflict, like "Gladstone's Usual Good Year" and "Gladstone's Terrible Secret," (both in *Walt Disney's Donald Duck: "A Christmas for Shacktown,"* volume 11 in this series) the uneven brawling in "Easter Election" can't help but look like a step down.

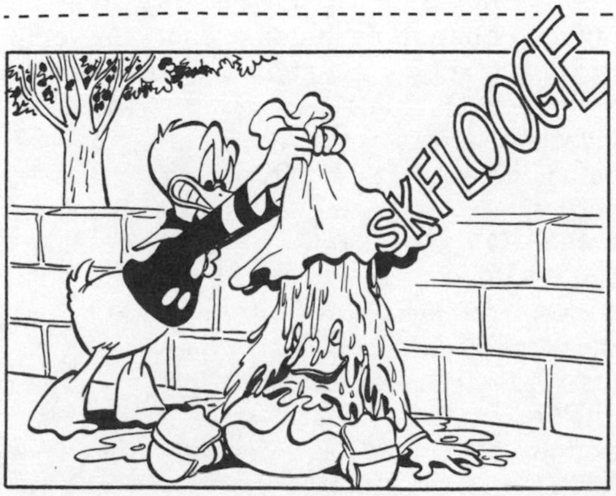
SKFLOOGE

Still, bright moments come in the form of sight gags and staging. Barks's delightful drawings of the kid constituents' nasty faces when they realize that Donald's treats are soaked with kerosene and covered with insulting messages, are juvenile outrage personified. The onstage applause contest between Donald and Gladstone couldn't have been framed any simpler or funnier. Barks shows off his narrative prowess, and never-ending cynicism, by saving any real use of Gladstone's luck for when he loses the esteemed title of Grand Marshal to Donald. Once again, you just can't beat that Gladstone Luck — even when you do beat it.

— THAD KOMOROWSKI

THE TALKING DOG *p. 113*

"Times are tough, huh, bud?" You can't help but have a tough time when everyone and everything is encased in the heavy bile found in "The Talking Dog." Donald doesn't want to hear about his nephews' talking dog fantasy, the nephews want no part of Donald's attempts at TV fame and fortune (because he won't buy them a talking dog), and Gyro Gearloose refuses any inventor's fee for his "talking" dog just to prove Donald wrong out of spite! And that's just the regular characters covered, never mind the incidentals gibing Donald at every turn.

Barks had had Donald seek fame and fortune by way of Easy Street before, but something about television really triggered the cartoonist's cynicism for this story. The general phoniness of TV quiz shows in 1953 was well-known through the likes of *You Bet Your Life* and *What's My Line*, even without the taint of *The $64,000 Question's* scandal later in the decade. The concept of "answering a question that answers itself" for big money drives Barks to have phoniness underlie every nook and cranny of "The Talking Dog."

Donald never attempts anything truly original or unusual to get a spot on the TV show. The titular dog uses Gyro's electronic voice box to utter a single phrase. The TV manager is predictably insincere in his promise to put Donald on the air and immediately casts Donald's canine "discovery" aside to bring Huey, Dewey, and Louie's "singing" cat on the show instead.

If Carl Barks had his way, anyone this artificial would never receive riches and stardom, a fact made clear by the story's satisfying and sardonic conclusion. Yet as the preceding pages remind us, Barks's ideal is not the world Donald Duck lives in. "You're not kiddin'!"

— THAD KOMOROWSKI

WORM WEARY *p. 123*

At first, "Worm Weary" seems like a slight tale that brings a high concept (worms bred to entice fish onto fishermen's hooks) to a familiar Barks plot: Donald Duck finds a shortcut to a goal, but something goes wrong, and Donald eventually learns (at least until the next story) that shortcuts are more trouble than hard work and determination.

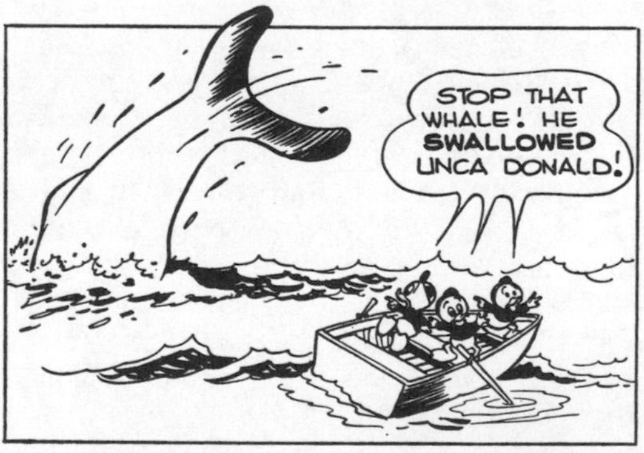
STOP THAT WHALE! HE SWALLOWED UNCA DONALD!

In reading the first six pages of the story, then, the pleasures are incidental and allusive: the name "Old Bombastro" for a massive fish, for instance, and how Barks accidentally predicted our 21st century bespoke world, where even survival staples like water and salt (and probably worms, somewhere) come in thousands of artisanal varieties. Capital thrives both by creating new products and by manufacturing a need for already extant goods, and Donald just has to have Gladstone's new type of worm.

The last four pages of "Worm Weary," however, enter into dark territory. As the worms relentlessly drag fish out of the pond, Barks gives us panels like the second and third ones on page 131, where fishermen bewail that the worms will "multiply into billions" and "spread out to catch every fish on Earth," with the result that "humanity will perish!" Hilarious, until we realize that some scientists are warning that our current reckless overfishing from and pollution of the oceans has begun a collapse of marine biodiversity that will leave us with nothing left to harvest from the seas by 2050. And in the face of the impending worm-caused ecological catastrophe, the fishermen act in a depressingly familiar way, ready to scapegoat Donald (complete with tar and — redundant for a duck! — feathers) rather than solve the problem.

After the disturbing, inadvertent prescience of most of "Worm Weary," Gladstone's *deus ex machina* pronouncement that his worms are programmed to die off feels forced and unconvincing. The worms "expire" and we cheer for a different extinction. Donald avoids tar-and-feathering, but the fishermen (and Donald) attack Gladstone with sticks and rocks. Nobody learns anything.

— CRAIG FISCHER

MUCH ADO ABOUT QUACKLY HALL *p. 133*

An artist who produces as much as Carl Barks did and for as long as he did is doomed to days when inspiration fails. On such a day was hatched the tale now known as "Much Ado About Quackly Hall." The story depends entirely on a twist ending that can only be preserved by cheating — by artificially concealing Mr. Winterbeard's intention to turn Quackly Hall into a children's paradise. Worse, when reread in light of the reveal, Donald and Mr. Winterbeard's actions don't appear natural but are merely clumsy camouflage. Why, for example, would there be so little concern for safety on a playground? Nor is the story rescued by the sight gags, which are little more than a series of pro-forma pratfalls.

So how would Barks have handled the premise on a good day? First, he would have realized that the cheat is unnecessary because a reader who knew that the nephews were shooting themselves in their webbed feet would enjoy the story all the more. Second, he would have Donald act like Donald. Why would the fanatic competitor we've seen time and time again be so listlessly passive when the one sucker for his unsalable property was slipping away? The gags would escalate as each booby trap becomes more ingenious. Mr. Winterbeard's reactions would be more ambiguous, to build the suspense.

About halfway through, the nephews would learn of Winterbeard's true intentions, and try to defuse the traps, only to make them blow off more explosively. It would be only on the last page that Winterbeard would reveal his perverse reasons for wanting the death trap after all, delivering the happy ending while giving the reader the minimum amount of time to think about it. It would end with a perfectly satisfying punch line whose nature I can't guess. Who do you think I am, Carl Barks?

— R. FIORE

SOME HEIR OVER THE RAINBOW *p. 143*

Only the genius of Barks could come up with those delightful "centrifugalillion dollars" to quantify the considerable capital amassed by Uncle Scrooge. Here Scrooge worries about which of his relatives will be capable of managing such wealth responsibly after he's gone. In this modern rendering of the "parable of the talents," the great tycoon covertly endows each of his three closest relatives (with Huey, Dewey, and Louie considered, even by Scrooge himself, as a single atomic character) with a symbolic and literal "pot of gold" to witness what they will do with it.

Barks never used his stories to preach about religious issues: his biblical reference is only implicit, as a theme that is an integral part of Western culture. His repeated use of the term "faith," a core topic of this story, has nothing to do with the Christian faith: it's about passionately believing in what you do. The nephews recognize the value of faith and its beneficial effects; and, although it is never explicitly shown, this is the trait that most closely links them to Uncle Scrooge, who built his empire from his first dime through unwavering faith in his ability to overcome any difficulties

Scrooge, like the reader, despises Gladstone, a parasite of society whose fortunes depend on luck rather than hard work. Morally, it is the nephews who are the true heirs of the pioneering spirit of Scrooge,

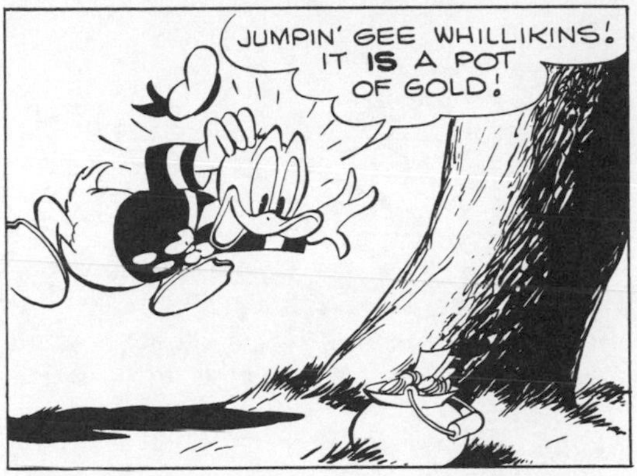
JUMPIN' GEE WHILLIKINS! IT IS A POT OF GOLD!

with their resourcefulness, their insight, their determination, and their unstoppable intellectual curiosity, and it is only fitting that the outcome of the competition should confirm that. When you persist with the faith that the nephews initially mentioned, sooner or later you are rewarded with success.

— LEONARDO GORI and FRANCESCO STAJANO

THE MASTER RAINMAKER *p. 153*

Aficionados have long noticed a commonality among several of Carl Barks's Donald Duck ten-pagers. In plot, structure, and theme they play out what one author called "the brittle mastery of Donald Duck." Each begins with Donald demonstrating an astonishing skill in a given field or occupation, be it barber, demolitions expert, or, here, rainmaker. Initial feats of superhuman ability inevitably give way to calamitous comeuppance, thanks to an all-too-human character flaw.

Toppling from lofty pedestals has been the stuff of high tragedy since the ancient Greeks, where the skids were classically greased by excessive pride, ambition, or overconfidence. Here, Donald is largely free of those traditional vices; he has a honed and accurate assessment of his talent and conducts his business honorably. Yet the dictates of

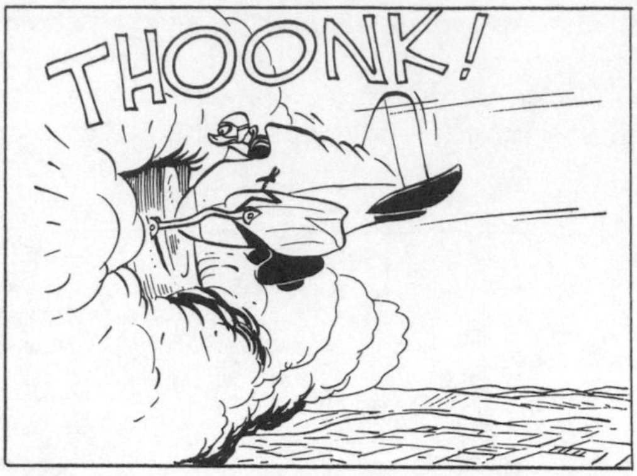
THOONK!

high comedy prove just as demanding and merciless: instead of succumbing to hubris, Donald yields to a less eminent "weak spot" — the green-eyed monster of jealousy so vividly personified on page 158.

But until his crash to Earth, Donald hits heights so great that he can blithely ignore the laws of the natural world. His plane flies despite the "dozer blade" positioned directly in front of its propeller; raindrops strike the ground according to his very exacting designs; his plane has a reverse gear! And surely more than one child has had early notions about the composition and malleability of clouds akin to those sculpted by Donald's manipulations: plowing into them as if they were banks of snow, shaving them at right angles, parking a perfectly formed cylinder for later use ...

Of course, Donald hardly needs mastery, brittle or otherwise, to invite catastrophe. This very volume also presents "Omelet" (one of Barks's personal favorites) where no special expertise is required for him to make an absolute botch of things.

— RICH KREINER

THE MONEY STAIRS *p. 163*

Among Barks's Donald Duck 10-pagers, "The Money Stairs" looks peculiar. It opens with a challenge by Donald to Uncle Scrooge and by the third page, it's starting to look a bit strange as an unusually free-spending Scrooge takes a swallow of a pep tonic and an elixir of youth which cost "$10.00 a drop" and "$1,000.00 an ounce," respectively. OK, he does that for a reason. He has to try climbing the towering pointed peak known as Old Demon Tooth, previously shown by Barks (as Demontooth Mountain) in "The Golden Christmas Tree" (*Walt Disney's Donald Duck: "Lost in the Andes,"* volume 7 in this series).

Most of "The Money Stairs," in fact, concerns Donald's and Scrooge's efforts to beat the other to the mountaintop, and Barks's intensive use of panels with slanted borders beautifully complements his depiction of the steep mountainside. The last four panels also have irregular margins, which might have to do with the story's dream ending.

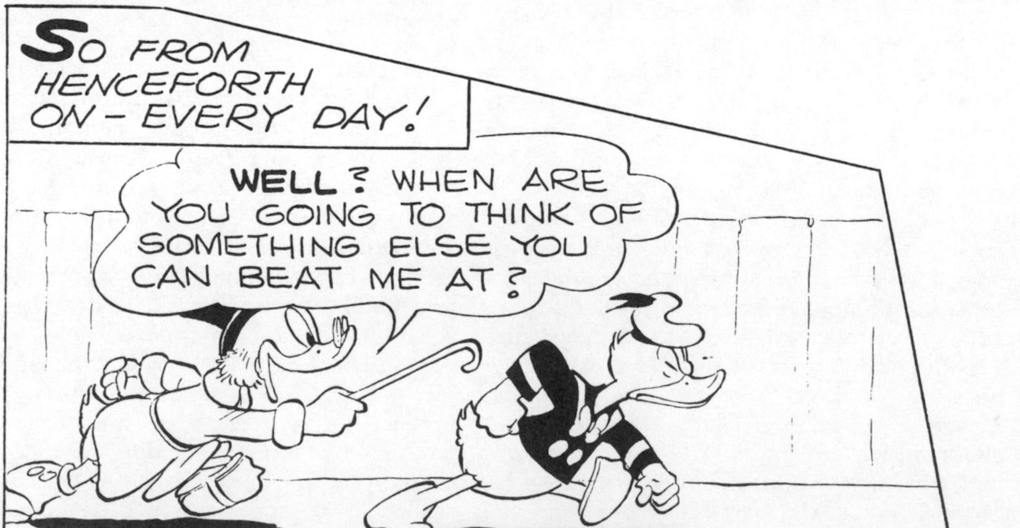
SO FROM HENCEFORTH ON – EVERY DAY!
WELL? WHEN ARE YOU GOING TO THINK OF SOMETHING ELSE YOU CAN BEAT ME AT?

After Carl Barks completed "The Money Stairs," he decided he didn't like the ending, so he cut this panel and changed the ending to the one you see on page 172.

In fact, an unused panel that fits in place of panel 7 on page 172 has the caption "So from henceforth on — every day!" and shows a gloating Scrooge walking after an irate Donald saying, "Well? When are you going to think of something else you can beat me at?" In the original ending, then, Donald did not wake up from a dream.

Barks himself confirmed that in an October 3, 1973 letter to Kim Weston: "[This] was quite likely changed to a dream ending by me. I believe I recall looking at the panel of Uncle Scrooge's money ramp and deciding it looked too impossible to be real."

— ALBERTO BECATTINI

BEE BUMBLES *p. 173*

The comedic devices, techniques, and sources that Carl Barks routinely incorporated into his work defy ready cataloging. Consider just a transitional page, the eighth, of "Bee Bumbles" (p. 180). From Donald tiptoeing (tipwebbing?) home in the first panel through the two nephews gesticulating emphatically in synchronized motion ("They're school bees!") in the final panel, there are no generic poses. That memorable tree with its hanging fruit is a singular vision. Verbally, dry wit has the virtuous bees stinging only people on their block while imagination runs riot in the surreal mash-ups of watermelons and rutabaga, kumquats and chives.

The time Barks spent working on Duck cartoons at the Disney animation studio consistently informed his comics. Exhibit A is the opening sequence here, as bees incrementally infiltrate Donald's personal space. Certainly the distortion of Donald's head at the bottom of page 173 was a reliable staple of cartoon clowning. During his career, Barks also worked as a gag cartoonist, composing single drawings for humor magazines. And they hardly come any more composed and antic than the oversized panel of Donald marching the beehives through town. The panic he induces is markedly unvoiced, so the scene additionally reminds of the chaos cultivated in silent film comedies, a kind of Keystone Kops come to Duckburg. Note, too, the fleeing society matron, the climbing tycoon, and the laborers, all stereotypical figures in those early movies.

In another possible nod to period entertainments, a fully compliant Donald gets the better of the officer on page 177, much as a pair of radio comedians might have the underdog outmaneuver an authoritative straight man during a broadcast skit. Yet some effects seem to have no antecedents, Barks creating them on the spot. The exposition that runs from page 178 to 179, delivered during headlong pursuit, is a continuous dialogue divvied up among successive, separated backdrops. It's a fluid unification of place, motion, and moment that Barks conveys with a novel liveliness.

— RICH KREINER

THE DONALD DUCK ONE-PAGERS

Both of the one-page story gags in this volume revolve around Halloween tricks. Once upon a time, pranksters would dismantle vehicles in the dark of night, hoist the parts atop a barn, and reassemble them. In "A Prank Above" (p. 42), Donald and the nephews are trick-or-treating when a man suggests putting a buggy on a roof. It's a swell Halloween prank and they labor long and hard through the night doing just that. The next morning, the ducks rush back to see just how upset the buggy owner is. But the trick is on them, as the barn owner has just saved himself plenty of money by getting them to put the wagon on his roof as a promotional gimmick for his antique shop.

Then, in "Frightful Face" (p. 203), Daisy tells Donald she doesn't enjoy Halloween because people jump out wearing terrible masks. Donald volunteers to put on masks and "toughen her nerves." The lion mask (*Boo!*) isn't so bad, the crocodile (*Boo!*) doesn't faze her, the devil mask (*Roar!*) elicits only a "Tee Hee," and she thinks his leaping from the laundry basket as a dragon (*Hiss!*) is fun. In fact, Daisy's nerves aren't as delicate as she thought — until Donald, without a mask, peeks around the corner (*Boo!*) and startles her.

— JOSEPH COWLES

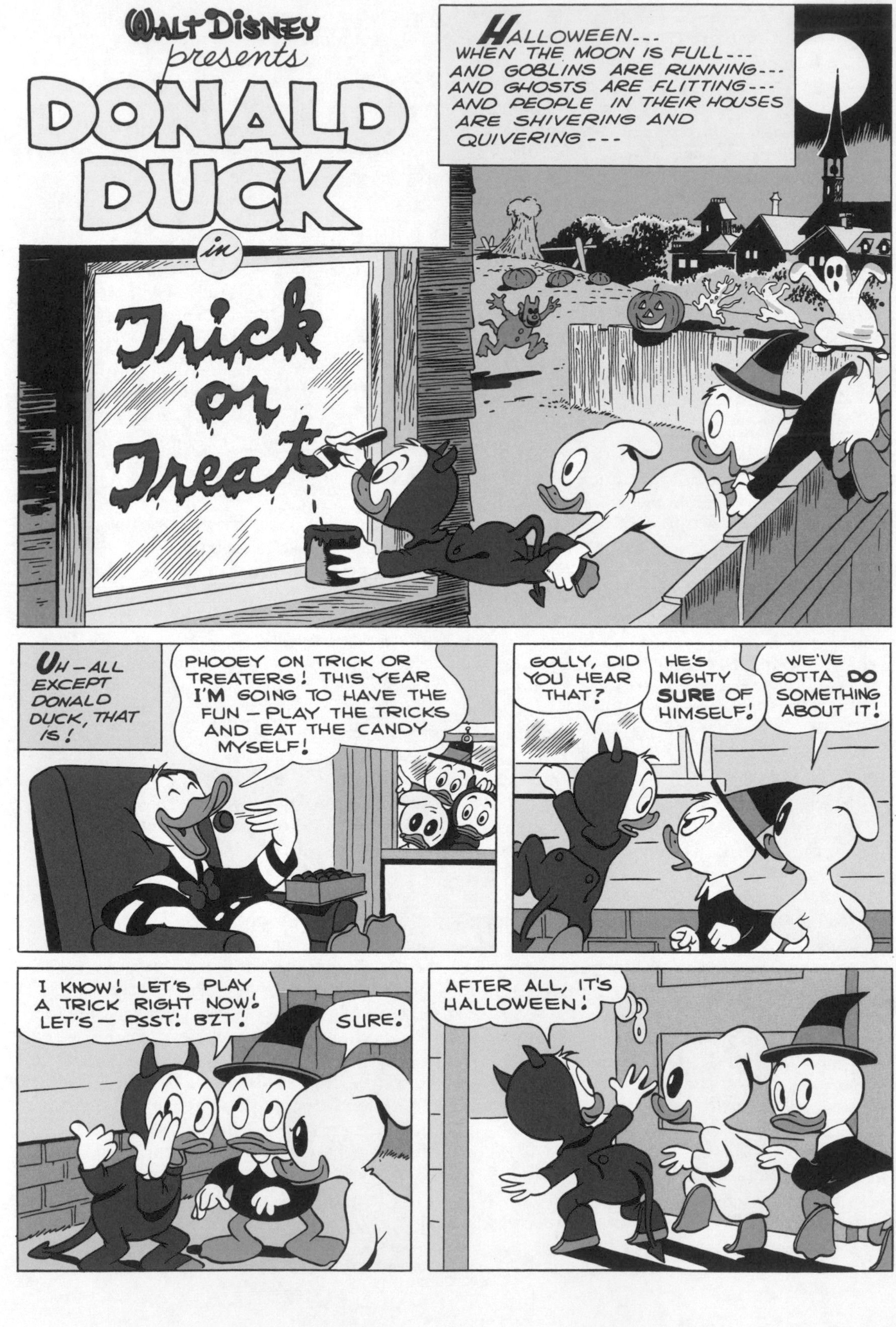
WALT DISNEY
presents
DONALD DUCK
in
Trick or Treat
HALLOWEEN--- WHEN THE MOON IS FULL--- AND GOBLINS ARE RUNNING--- AND GHOSTS ARE FLITTING--- AND PEOPLE IN THEIR HOUSES ARE SHIVERING AND QUIVERING---
UH-ALL EXCEPT DONALD DUCK, THAT IS!
PHOOEY ON TRICK OR TREATERS! THIS YEAR I'M GOING TO HAVE THE FUN-PLAY THE TRICKS AND EAT THE CANDY MYSELF!
GOLLY, DID YOU HEAR THAT?
HE'S MIGHTY SURE OF HIMSELF!
WE'VE GOTTA DO SOMETHING ABOUT IT!
I KNOW! LET'S PLAY A TRICK RIGHT NOW! LET'S-PSST! BZT!
SURE!
AFTER ALL, IT'S HALLOWEEN!

SO! .... MAYBE I'D BETTER LOCK MY CANDY IN A **SAFE** PLACE!
HEH! HEH! TRICK OR TREAT, UNCA DONALD!
CANDY
CHOCOLATES
COOKIES
WELL, HERE'S THE **TRICK**!
CANDY
CHOCOLATES
JUST FOR THAT, THE WITCHES WILL GET YOU!
HA! WITCHES! YOU CAN'T SCARE ME— THERE'S NO SUCH THING!
OH, YEAH? SUPPOSE WE LOOK IN ON A **REAL** HALLOWEEN WITCH! HER NAME IS HAZEL AND HER BROOM IS BEELZEBUB!

The Cutting Room Floor

The version of "Trick or Treat" that leads off this volume is fully restored to what Carl Barks intended his readers to see when he adapted Walt Disney's animated cartoon of the same name. It is not the truncated version that greeted readers of *Donald Duck* #26 in 1952. Nine pages of Barks's work were chopped out in that printing. (See the "Trick or Treat" and "Hobblin' Goblins" entries in the Story Notes section.)

Faced with an editorial directive to get rid of his original splash panel — which took up the top half of page 1 — Barks decided to start off the story a different way. That resulted in the sequence you see on these two pages.

When the story was restored to its new official version, this second, alternate opening no longer fit. We present it here for you as an "extra" — newly colored by Rich Tommaso to match the color palette for the restored version. You will also notice that the caption that introduces Hazel and her broom in the new complete version has been shortened to make the narrative flow smoothly.

If you want to read the opening the way it was presented initially, read this page-and-a-half sequence first, then turn to page 1, skip the first panel, keep in mind the altered caption, and continue reading with panel 2.

— MICHAEL CATRON

Carl Barks

LIFE AMONG THE DUCKS

by DONALD AULT

ABOVE: *Carl Barks at the 1982 San Diego Comic-Con. Photo by Alan Light.*

"I was a real misfit," Carl Barks said, thinking back over an early life of hard labor — as a farmer, a logger, a mule-skinner, a rivet heater, and a printing press feeder — before he was hired as a full-time cartoonist for an obscure risqué magazine in 1931.

Barks was born in 1901 and (mostly) raised in Merrill, Oregon. He had always wanted to be a cartoonist, but everything that happened to him in his early years seemed to stand in his way. He suffered a significant hearing loss after a bout with the measles. His mother died. He had to leave school after the eighth grade. His

father suffered a mental breakdown. His older brother was whisked off to World War I.

His first marriage, in 1921, was to a woman who was unsympathetic to his dreams and who ultimately bore two children "by accident," as Barks phrased it. The two divorced in 1930.

In 1931, he pulled up stakes from Merrill and headed to Minnesota, leaving his mother-in-law, whom he trusted more than his wife, in charge of his children.

Arriving in Minneapolis, he went to work for the *Calgary Eye-Opener*, that risqué magazine. He thought he would finally be drawing cartoons full time, but the editor and most of the staff were alcoholics, so Barks ended up running the whole show.

In 1935 he took "a great gamble" and, on the strength of some cartoons he'd submitted in response to an advertisement from the Disney Studio, he moved to California and entered an animation trial period. He was soon promoted to "story man" in Disney's Donald Duck animation unit, where he made significant contributions to 36 Donald cartoon shorts between 1936 and 1942, including helping to create Huey, Dewey, and Louie for "Donald's Nephews" in 1938. Ultimately, though, he grew dissatisfied. The production of animated cartoons "by committee," as he described it, stifled his imagination.

For that and other reasons, in 1942 he left Disney to run a chicken farm. But when he was offered a chance by Western Publishing to write and illustrate a new series of Donald Duck comic book stories, he jumped at it. The comic book format suited him, and the quality of his work persuaded the editors to grant him a freedom and autonomy he'd never known and that few others were ever granted. He would go on to write and draw more than 6,000 pages in over 500 stories and uncounted hundreds of covers between 1942 and 1966 for Western's Dell and Gold Key imprints.

Barks had almost no formal art training. He had taught himself how to draw by imitating his early favorite artists — Winsor McCay (*Little Nemo*), Frederick Opper (*Happy Hooligan*), Elzie Segar (*Popeye*), and Floyd Gottfredson (*Mickey Mouse*).

He taught himself how to write well by going back to the grammar books he had shunned in school, making up jingles and rhymes, and inventing other linguistic exercises to get a natural feel for the rhythm and dialogue of sequential narrative.

Barks married again in 1938, but that union ended disastrously in divorce in 1951. In 1954, Barks married Margaret Wynnfred Williams, known as Garé, who soon began assisting him by lettering and inking backgrounds on his comic book work. They remained happily together until her death in 1993.

He did his work in the California desert and often mailed his stories into the office. He worked his stories over and over "backward and forward." Barks was not a vain man but he had confidence in his talent. He knew what hard work was, and he knew that he'd put his best efforts into every story he produced.

On those occasions when he did go into Western's offices he would "just dare anybody to see if they could improve on it." His confidence was justified. His work was largely responsible for some of the best-selling comic books in the world — *Walt Disney's Comics and Stories* and *Uncle Scrooge*.

Because Western's policy was to keep their writers and artists anonymous, readers never knew the name of the "good duck artist" — but they could spot the superiority of his work. When fans determined to solve the mystery of his anonymity finally tracked him down (not unlike an adventure Huey, Dewey, and Louie might embark upon), Barks was quite happy to correspond and otherwise communicate with his legion of aficionados.

Given all the obstacles of his early years and the dark days that haunted him off and on for the rest of his life, it's remarkable that he laughed so easily and loved to make others laugh.

In the process of expanding Donald Duck's character far beyond the hot-tempered Donald of animation, Barks created a moveable locale (Duckburg) and a cast of dynamic characters: Scrooge McDuck, the Beagle Boys, Gladstone Gander, Gyro Gearloose, the Junior Woodchucks. And there were hundreds of others who made only one memorable appearance in the engaging, imaginative, and unpredictable comedy-adventures that he wrote and drew from scratch for nearly a quarter of a century.

Among many other honors, Carl Barks was one of the three initial inductees into the Will Eisner Comic Book Hall of Fame for comic book creators in 1987. (The other two were Jack Kirby and Will Eisner.) In 1991, Barks became the only Disney comic book artist to be recognized as a "Disney Legend," a special award created by Disney "to acknowledge and honor the many individuals whose imagination, talents, and dreams have created the Disney magic."

As Roy Disney said on Barks's passing in 2000 at age 99, "He challenged our imaginations and took us on some of the greatest adventures we have ever known. His prolific comic book creations entertained many generations of devoted fans and influenced countless artists over the years.... His timeless tales will stand as a legacy to his originality and brilliant artistic vision."

Contributors

Donald Ault is Professor of English at the University of Florida, founder and editor of *ImageTexT: Interdisciplinary Comics Studies*, author of two books on William Blake (*Visionary Physics* and *Narrative Unbound*), editor of *Carl Barks: Conversations,* and executive producer of the video *The Duck Man: An Interview with Carl Barks*.

Alberto Becattini was born in Florence, Italy. He has taught high school English since 1983. Since 1978, he has written essays for Italian and U.S. publications about comics, specializing in Disney characters and American comics generally. Since 1992 he has been a freelance writer and consultant for The Walt Disney Company-Italy, contributing to such series as *Zio Paperone, Maestri Disney, Tesori Disney, Disney Anni d'Oro, La Grande Dinastia dei Paperi*, and *Gli Anni d'Oro di Topolino*.

Joseph Robert Cowles is a lifelong Donald Duck fan who became friends with Carl and Garé Barks while a teenager working at Disneyland in the 1950s. He writes for the quarterly newsletter of the Carl Barks Fan Club, contributed materials and commentary to Egmont's *Carl Barks Collection,* and is the author of *Recalling Carl,* a pictorial dissertation contending that Disney should be making feature films of Barks's stories. His Carl Barks website is TheGoodArtist.com.

R. Fiore, he explains, makes his way in life working Square John jobs, when they let him, not far from Historic Duckburg. This marginal existence has even from time to time led onto the grounds of the Walt Disney Company, which is an interesting place. In his spare time he's been writing about comic strips and animation longer than you've been alive, my child.

Craig Fischer is Professor of English at Appalachian State University. His Monsters Eat Critics column, about comics' multifarious genres, runs at *The Comics Journal* website (tcj.com).

Jared Gardner studies and teaches comics at the Ohio State University, home of the Billy Ireland Cartoon Library & Museum. He is the author of three books, including *Projections: Comics and the History of 21st-Century Storytelling* (Stanford University Press, 2011). He is a contributing writer to *The Comics Journal*.

Leonardo Gori is a comics scholar and collector, especially of syndicated newspaper strips of the '30s and Italian Disney authors. He wrote, with Frank Stajano and others, many books on Italian "fumetti" and American comics in Italy. He has also written thrillers, which have been translated into Spanish, Portuguese, and Korean.

Thad Komorowski is an animation historian with a longstanding professional relationship with Disney comics. He currently translates stories for IDW's Disney comic books and is a regular contributor to Fantagraphics's Carl Barks and Floyd Gottfredson archival collections. He is the author of *Sick Little Monkeys: The Unauthorized Ren & Stimpy Story* and co-author of a forthcoming history on New York studio animation.

Rich Kreiner is a longtime writer for *The Comics Journal* and a longtime reader of Carl Barks. He lives with wife and cat in Maine.

Bill Mason has been a teacher in the Humanities Department at Dawson College, Montreal, Canada, since 1971. The first Carl Barks story he remembers reading is "The Old Castle's Secret," which was originally published when he was in the second grade.

Stefano Priarone was born in Northwestern Italy about the time when a retired Carl Barks was storyboarding his last Junior Woodchucks stories. He writes about popular culture in many Italian newspapers and magazines, was a contributor to the Italian complete Carl Barks collection, and wrote his thesis in economics about Uncle Scrooge as an entrepreneur (for which he blames his aunt, who read him Barks Scrooge stories when he was 3 years old).

Francesco ("Frank") Stajano began reading Disney comics in preschool and never grew out of it — the walls of his house are covered in bookshelves and many of them hold comics. He has written on Disney comics, particularly with Leonardo Gori, and had the privilege of visiting Carl Barks at his home in Oregon in 1998. In real life he is an associate professor at the University of Cambridge in England.

Where did these Duck stories first appear?

The Complete Carl Barks Disney Library collects Donald Duck and Uncle Scrooge stories by Carl Barks that were originally published in the traditional American four-color comic book format. Barks's first Duck story appeared in October 1942. The volumes in this project are numbered chronologically but are being released in a different order. This is Volume 13.

Stories within a volume may or may not follow the publication sequence of the original comic books. We may take the liberty of rearranging the sequence of the stories within a volume for editorial or presentation purposes.

The original comic books were published under the Dell logo and some appeared in the so-called *Four Color* series — a name that appeared nowhere inside the comic book itself, but is generally agreed upon by historians to refer to the series of "one-shot"

comic books published by Dell that have sequential numbering. The *Four Color* issues are also sometimes referred to as "One Shots."

Most of the stories in this volume were originally published without a title. Some stories were retroactively assigned a title when they were reprinted in later years. Some stories were given titles by Barks in correspondence or interviews. (Sometimes Barks referred to the same story with different titles.) Some stories were never given an official title but have been informally assigned one by fans and indexers. For the untitled stories in this volume, we have used the title that seems most appropriate. The unofficial titles appear below with an asterisk enclosed in parentheses (*).

Some of the issues listed below had covers by Barks but contained no interior work by him. The following is the order in which the stories in this volume were originally published.

Four Color #394 (May 1952)
Cover only

Walt Disney's Comics and Stories #145 (October 1952)
Cover • The Hypno-Gun (*)

Donald Duck #26 (November 1952)
Cover • A Prank Above (*)
Trick or Treat
Hobblin' Goblins
Frightful Face (*)

Walt Disney's Comics and Stories #146 (November 1952)
Cover • Omelet (*)

Walt Disney's Comics and Stories #147 (December 1952)
Cover • A Charitable Chore (*)

Walt Disney's Comics and Stories #148 (January 1953)
Cover • Turkey with All the Schemings (*)

Donald Duck #27 (January 1953)
Cover only

Walt Disney's Comics and Stories #149 (February 1953)
Cover • Flip Decision (*)

Four Color #450 (February 1953)
Cover only

Walt Disney's Comics and Stories #150 (March 1953)
Cover • My Lucky Valentine (*)

Donald Duck #28 (March–April 1953)
Cover only

Walt Disney's Comics and Stories #151 (April 1953)
Cover • The Easter Election (*)

Walt Disney's Comics and Stories #152 (May 1953)
Cover • The Talking Dog (*)

Donald Duck #29 (May 1953)
Cover only

Walt Disney's Comics and Stories #153 (June 1953)
Cover • Worm Weary (*)

Walt Disney's Comics and Stories #154 (July 1953)
Cover • Much Ado About Quackly Hall (*)

Donald Duck #30 (July 1953)
Cover only

Walt Disney's Comics and Stories #155 (August 1953)
Cover • Some Heir Over the Rainbow (*)

Walt Disney's Comics and Stories #156 (September 1953)
Cover • The Master Rainmaker (*)

Walt Disney's Comics and Stories #157 (October 1953)
Cover • The Money Stairs (*)

Walt Disney's Comics and Stories #158 (November 1953)
Cover • Bee Bumbles (*)

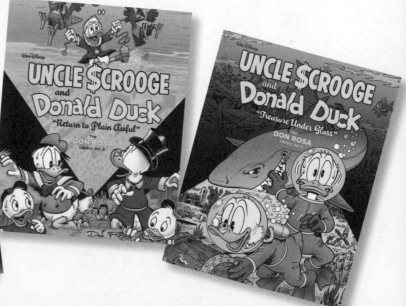